THE PRINCIPLES OF MORAL
AND CHRISTIAN PHILOSOPHY

VOLUME 2
Christian Philosophy

NATURAL LAW AND
ENLIGHTENMENT CLASSICS

Knud Haakonssen
General Editor

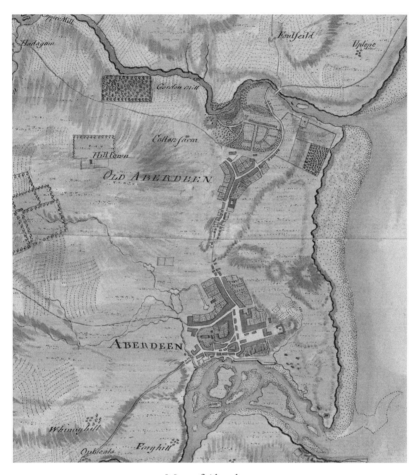

Map of Aberdeen

NATURAL LAW AND
ENLIGHTENMENT CLASSICS

The Principles of Moral and Christian Philosophy

VOLUME 2

Christian Philosophy

George Turnbull

Edited and with an Introduction by
Alexander Broadie

*Philosophical Works and Correspondence
of George Turnbull*

LIBERTY FUND
Indianapolis

This book is published by Liberty Fund, Inc., a foundation established to encourage study of the ideal of a society of free and responsible individuals.

The cuneiform inscription that serves as our logo and as the design motif for our endpapers is the earliest-known written appearance of the word "freedom" (*amagi*), or "liberty." It is taken from a clay document written about 2300 B.C. in the Sumerian city-state of Lagash.

09 08 07 06 05 C 5 4 3 2 1
09 08 07 06 05 P 5 4 3 2 1

Cover art and frontispiece are the Aberdeen detail of the William Roy Map, created from 1747 to 1755, and are used by permission of the British Library (Shelfmark Maps C.9.b.21 sheet ½).

Library of Congress Cataloging-in-Publication Data
Turnbull, George, 1698–1748.
The principles of moral and Christian philosophy:
philosophical works and correspondence of George Turnbull
edited and with an introduction by Alexander Broadie.
p.   cm.—(Natural law and enlightenment classics)
Includes bibliographical references.
Contents: v. 1. The principles of moral philosophy.
ISBN 0-86597-455-1 (alk. paper)   ISBN 0-86597-458-6 (pbk.: alk. paper)
ISBN 0-86597-454-3 (set: alk. paper)   ISBN 0-86597-457-8 (set: pbk.: alk. paper)
1. Ethics—Early works to 1800.
2. Christian ethics—Anglican authors—Early works to 1800.
3. Natural law—Religious aspects—Church of England—Early works to 1800.
4. Christianity—Philosophy—Early works to 1800.
I. Broadie, Alexander.   II. Title.   III. Series.
BJ1012.T82   2005
241'.043—dc22   2004057633
ISBN 0-86597-456-X (v. 2: hc)   ISBN 0-86597-459-4 (v. 2: sc)

LIBERTY FUND, INC.
8335 Allison Pointe Trail, Suite 300
Indianapolis, Indiana 46250-1684

CONTENTS

INTRODUCTION

George Turnbull's *Christian Philosophy,* volume 2 of his *Principles of Moral and Christian Philosophy,* was undoubtedly written by a devout Christian, though whether Turnbull throughout his life endorsed the kind of Christianity to be found in volume 2 is doubtful.

It is reasonable to suppose that he did at least begin as a Calvinist, for that was the kind of religion he would have learned from his father, the Church of Scotland minister George Turnbull senior, who was ministering to the Church of Scotland parish of Alloa in the Scottish county of Clackmannanshire when George junior was born.[1] We do not know what sort of Calvinist George Turnbull senior was (for Scottish Calvinism covers a broad spectrum of belief), but if George Turnbull the younger began as a Calvinist of the more robust sort, he must have started to move away from this position when still quite young. For in Edinburgh in his later teens, after completing his studies for the arts degree (M.A.), he joined the newly founded Rankenian Club, whose ideological bias toward Lord Shaftesbury did not sit comfortably with Calvinism (though it could be made to sit more or less uncomfortably with it). In 1718 Turnbull tried (under the assumed name Philocles) to start a correspondence with the Irish freethinker John Toland (1670–1722), whose espousal of a form of Spinozistic pantheism[2] (or atheism, as many judged it to be) made any hint of agreement with Toland a potentially risky enterprise for a youth wanting to make his way in the

---

1. He moved to take charge of the parish of Tyninghame in East Lothian one year later.

2. See Jonathan I. Israel, *Radical Enlightenment: Philosophy and the Making of Modernity 1650–1750* (Oxford: Oxford University Press, 2001), 609–14.

world. At about the same time Turnbull wrote a short work on religious toleration which, as he later claimed, was rejected by publishers because, in an age when religious free thought carried with it sanctions of one form or another, the publishers whom Turnbull approached were not prepared to take responsibility for marketing a tract advocating such thinking. Indication of Turnbull's strength of opinion in the matter is found in a letter he wrote at about this time to the Irish peer Lord Molesworth. In a manner characteristic of Molesworth, Turnbull affirms that "our Colleges are under the Inspection of proud domineering pedantic Priests whose interest it is to train up the youth in a profound veneration of their Senseless metaphysical Creeds & Catechisms, which for this purpose they are daily inured to defend against all Doubters & Enquirers with the greatest bitterness and contempt, in a stiff formal bewildering manner admirably fitted indeed to Enslave young understandings betimes and to beget an early antipathy against all Free thought."[3]

It is hard to believe that the Marischal faculty knew about Turnbull's vigorous advocacy of religious free thought or his broadly sympathetic attitude to Toland. But, in any case, after becoming regent at Marischal College in 1721, Turnbull moved toward a more orthodox position; though not immediately, as witness the fact that the aforementioned letter to Molesworth was sent a full year after Turnbull had taken up his appointment at the college. The softer position he adopted in his teaching involved emphasis on the central role of revelation in religion, though he did believe, and say, that, to speak generally, the Christian revelation could hold its own under cross-examination before the tribunal of reason since it satisfied criteria of rationality, such as consistency with itself and also with experience.

The Principles of Moral and Christian Philosophy probably represents

---

3. Letter dated 3 August 1722. The letter is quoted in M. A. Stewart, "George Turnbull and educational reform," in J. J. Carter and Joan M. Pittock, eds., *Aberdeen and the Enlightenment* (Aberdeen: Aberdeen University Press, 1987), 95–103; see 96. For much of the biographical information in this introduction (as for the introduction to volume 1) I have relied on this article by Stewart and also on Paul Wood, "George Turnbull (1698–1748)," *Oxford Dictionary of National Biography* (Oxford: Oxford University Press, 2004).

rather closely the belief system that Turnbull espoused both at Marischal and in the years thereafter until publication of the work. The period included a dramatic shift in Turnbull's institutional religious allegiance. His matriculation at Exeter College, Oxford, with the aim of securing the degree of bachelor of civil law (duly granted in 1733) was probably due to his decision to seek a position in the Church of England. He was unable to take the matter any further in the short term because of his financial situation. Instead he spent time in Italy as private tutor to Lord Rockingham's son. But finally in 1739, through the good offices of Thomas Birch[4] and the Latitudinarian thinker Arthur Ashley Sykes,[5] Turnbull was ordained into the Church of England by Benjamin Hoadly (1676–1761),[6] bishop of Winchester. In 1741 Turnbull was appointed a chaplain to the Prince of Wales, and in 1742 Thomas Rundle (ca. 1688–1743), bishop of Derry, appointed Turnbull rector of the parish of Drumachose, County Derry. However, he spent no more than two years, and perhaps less than that, in his new charge, for by 1744 he was touring Italy as a private tutor to Horatio Walpole, and he never returned to Britain.[7] That his death in 1748 was in The Hague was fitting for a man who seemed forever on the move. He was also restless in the spiritual sense, though consideration of the ecclesiastical circles within which he moved, and consideration of the individuals whom he cultivated, such

4. Birch was treasurer of the Society for the Encouragement of Learning, which Turnbull had joined soon after its inception in 1735. Turnbull had had hopes at one point of being appointed its treasurer and, also, of receiving the society's support for the publication of his *Treatise on Ancient Painting* (which was eventually published, without the society's help, in 1740). Birch, a Fellow of the Royal Society, and secretary of the society from 1752 to 1765, was one of many English divines, most of them at Oxford, assiduously cultivated by Turnbull.

5. A strong advocate of rationalist Protestantism, whose stance at times bears a passing resemblance to that of David Hume. See Sykes's discussion of miracles in his *The Principles and Connexion of Natural and Revealed Religion* (London, 1740).

6. Hoadly led the extreme Latitudinarian party in the church. He had no time for the mysteries of the faith, insisting instead that religious beliefs should be able to withstand cross-examination by reason.

7. If, as I conjecture in the introduction to volume 1, Turnbull had contracted tuberculosis or bronchitis, then he may well have thought that a lengthy stay in Italy would be of benefit to his health.

as Sykes and Hoadly, suggest that he was on the liberal wing of the church—light on dogma and insistent on the importance of religious belief satisfying suitable criteria of rationality.

Within this position he was sufficiently discriminating to be strongly hostile to others who might also be thought to belong more or less loosely to the liberal, rationalist side of the Church. The evidence for this is a series of works written in the 1730s, some of which have as their targets Matthew Tindal (ca. 1657–1733) and Anthony Collins (1676–1729). Tindal had begun as an Anglican and had then converted to Catholicism in the hope of gaining the wardenship of All Souls College, Oxford, under James II. He subsequently reconverted to Anglicanism, became a Latitudinarian, then a deist, and is even reported to have said that there is no such thing as revelation. His books, such as *Rights of the Christian Church Asserted* (1706) and *Christianity as Old as Creation* (1730) were excoriated by many, and Turnbull joined in the excoriation. Anthony Collins was judged by numerous commentators, including Turnbull, to have denied divine providence, revelation, miracles, and the immortality of the soul, a judgment based particularly on his *A Discourse on Free-thinking* (1713). A further work by Turnbull, *A Philosophical Enquiry Concerning the Connexion Betwixt the Doctrines and Miracles of Jesus Christ,* should be mentioned here. In this short book, which he wrote in 1726 and published five years later, he argued, in line with lectures he had delivered to his students at Marischal College, that just as scientific propositions are demonstrated by experiments, so also Christian teaching regarding the afterlife is demonstrated by the miracles performed by Christ. The chief targets of this work were Tindal and Collins.

The following year (1732), in *Christianity Neither False nor Useless, Tho' Not as Old as the Creation,* Turnbull again had Tindal in his sights, as is indicated by the title's reference to Tindal's *Christianity as Old as Creation.* In this attack Turnbull takes up cudgels on behalf of Samuel Clarke, who had argued: "[I]f by the *Course of Nature,* be meant only (as it truly signifies) the *constant and uniform manner* of Gods acting either immediately or mediately in preserving and continuing the Order of the World; then, in that Sense, indeed a Miracle may be rightly defined to be an effect produced contrary to the usual Course or Order of

Nature, by the unusual Interposition of some Intelligent Being Superiour to Men."[8] On the basis of this and of closely related arguments of Clarke's, Turnbull examines the nature and attested occurrence of miracles in the course of defending Clarke on the relation between revelation and natural religion.

The revelation at issue is of course the Christian one, and Turnbull's commitment to it is nowhere more clearly in evidence than in his *An Impartial Enquiry into the Moral Character of Jesus Christ* (1740), in which he seeks to argue that the works of Jesus bear testimony to the truth of his teachings on moral matters, and that he is shown by those teachings to be the greatest among moral philosophers.

The overarching concept in Turnbull's *Christian Philosophy* is that of God's moral government of the world, a government that is particularly at work in the allotment of recompense for our good and evil deeds. And the Biblical text that runs as a leitmotif through Turnbull's discussion is: "Be not deceived; God is not mocked: for whatsoever a man soweth that shall he also reap" (Galatians 6:7–8). Turnbull attends to the relationship between this life and the next, and argues that our future state will correspond exactly to our present one by a divine dispensation that is universal in the sense that God does not, so to say, need to make a separate decision in respect of each person, for he has established a rule or law that governs the outcome for each and every individual on the basis of how each has lived. Turnbull stresses that the situation is exactly as in the natural world. It is by a law established by God that fire heats things and ice cools them—and by a law likewise that people are recompensed in due season for their deeds. That, in short, is how the system works, and divine providence is to be understood in these terms.

Turnbull is engaged in an exercise of rational (or natural), not of revealed, theology; and since he is placing great weight on a proof text in the New Testament, he begins by demonstrating the existence of a morally and intellectually perfect being, God, and then argues that the con-

8. Samuel Clarke, *A Discourse Concerning the Unchangeable Obligations of Natural Religion and the Truth and Certainty of the Christian Revelation,* Boyle Lecture 1705 (London, 1706), 356–57.

tent of the Christian revelation, at least in respect of its moral dimension, can withstand cross-examination. It is with this in mind that Turnbull argues that if a messenger from God has to address a people who do not know God, the messenger must first persuade the people, by rational means alone, that God exists and that he is good and wise. Turnbull spells out the argument by which persuasion can be effected. It is based on a concept of power that has since become particularly associated with Thomas Reid. Reid follows Turnbull very precisely in denying that no purely material thing has power, and that power resides only in a being with intellect and will. The underlying consideration, stressed by both Turnbull and Reid, is that any purely material thing, far from being powerful, is entirely powerless to respond otherwise than the way in which it does to forces operating upon it. The sun does not exercise power in heating this planet, for it cannot *not* heat it—it is powerless not to.[9] Turnbull was not the first to offer this account of power, but the probability is that it was from Turnbull that Thomas Reid, then in his midteens at Marischal, first learned it.

Turnbull proceeds to deal with the fact that the existence of God renders problematic the existence of evil, and he responds to this challenge in a traditional way by admitting that there are evils but that they do not characterize creation as a whole, for they are permitted to exist not for their own sake or because God takes pleasure in them, but because they are the outcome of laws that are designed to produce the best possible world overall. Things that seem evil are seen by us from an overly narrow perspective, and if we had "one united view," the apparent evils would be judged to play a necessary role in the unfolding of a perfect universe.

Among apparent evils are those that befall the virtuous, evils that therefore cannot be seen as a punishment for wrongdoing. But Turnbull has a more ample perspective. For this life is, as he reminds his readers, a time of probation, and the apparent evils that befall us enable us to

9. Thomas Reid, *Essays on the Active Powers of the Human Mind,* Essay I, in *The Works of Thomas Reid, D.D.,* ed. Sir William Hamilton, 6th ed., 2 vols. (1863; reprint, Bristol: Thoemmes, 1999).

grow in spiritual and moral strength by the exercise of self-discipline in adversity. They can therefore even be seen as goods graciously bestowed on us by God, goods that create a space for us within which we can grow toward our perfection. In fact, Turnbull insists that we can grow by our response to apparent goods as well as to apparent evils. No less than poverty, prosperity presents us with the opportunity to enhance our moral substance and to demonstrate our self-discipline. This might seem an unexpected line, but Turnbull's focus on prosperity as a "means of trial" fits the traditional suspicion of luxury as a potential cause of moral and spiritual corruption. In that sense, every circumstance or state in which we find ourselves is good, at least to this extent, in that it constitutes an opportunity for us to do good and to become better.

Whether or not we then do good is in our power, which, as Turnbull reiterates, is very extensive, and always extensible if only we make the effort to gain more knowledge of the natural world. Such knowledge of the laws by which God governs the world empowers us to use nature's divine laws to secure our own purposes and make our lives more fully embody our own values. God's governance of nature by means of general laws is crucial to Turnbull since otherwise we should have absolutely no means of knowing how to use it purposefully. We would be forever in a state of infancy similar to the one—stressed in volume 1—that would arise if the law of habits did not inform our nature.

The law of habits is also put to work in volume 2, this time in connection with the thought that recompense in the next life must be appropriate to our virtue or vice in this life, for the law of habits underlies our moral liberty. Such liberty implies not only knowledge of our circumstances and of natural law, but also a faculty of reason that exerts authority in us according to the dictates of right judgment. Just as repetition makes bad habits a ruling power in our souls, so also it is by repetition that reason acquires its "rightful power and authority of governing": "This is the consequence of the law of habits, which renders us capable of improvement to perfection" (p. 669). On this crucial matter Turnbull deploys the first volume's doctrine that moral liberty consists in the habit of deliberating prior to acting, thereby preventing our appetites from hurrying us into action.

The disposition to give reason its head as against appetite is in accordance with "the order and perfection in our constitution," or "our natural make and constitution." Turnbull concludes that a person so disposed is a "law to himself," in the sense that he has within himself a principle whose office is to give law to his appetites and affections. This is life according to our natural frame and, hence, according to God's intention for us. Our constitution is therefore a "law to itself" in the strict sense, for it was enacted by God as lawgiver when he created our constitution, particularly the mental part anatomized in volume 1 of the *Principles*. Moving in these deep theological waters, Turnbull always sees himself as guided by the light of reason. He only ever argues on the basis of revelation when the revelation has itself been subjected to critical scrutiny and shown to be at least consonant with reason and, in many cases, to be an irresistible conclusion from reasonable premises.

The main title of volume 2, *Christian Philosophy*, would on its own raise expectations that central Christian doctrines, such as the Trinity, would be discussed. The work is in fact an exercise in natural, not revealed, theology, and this is clearly indicated by its lengthy subtitle: *The Christian doctrine concerning God, providence, virtue, and a future state, proved to be agreeable to true philosophy, and to be attended with a truly philosophical evidence.* The subtitle tells us what the book really is about, and Turnbull argues that while he assuredly needs the doctrines of volume 1, he does not need to discuss such concepts as that of the Trinity in order to establish his main thesis, namely, that it is possible to demonstrate the truth of St. Paul's declaration: "Whatsoever a man soweth that shall he reap."

Turnbull presents an array of insights that bear a strong resemblance to ones found in the writings of his pupil Thomas Reid. How far Reid was directly influenced by Turnbull's lectures, delivered to the class of 1723 at Marischal, is a matter of speculation. But it is difficult to resist the suspicion that Turnbull, a restless, energetic person who was intellectually and morally strong, must have made a considerable impact on Reid and indeed on all the boys in his charge.

CHRISTIAN PHILOSOPHY

THE

PRINCIPLES

OF

MORAL

AND

CHRISTIAN

PHILOSOPHY.

IN TWO VOLUMES.

By George Turnbull, LL. D.

VOL. II.

CONTAINING,

Christian Philosophy: or the Christian Doctrine concerning God, Providence, Virtue, and a Future State, proved to be agreeable to True Philosophy, and to be attended with a Truly Philosophical Evidence.

LONDON:

Printed for J. Noon, at the *White Hart,* near *Mercer's Chapel* in *Cheapside.* MDCCXL. <v>

CHRISTIAN PHILOSOPHY:

OR, THE

CHRISTIAN DOCTRINE

CONCERNING

GOD, PROVIDENCE, VIRTUE,

AND A

FUTURE STATE,

Proved to be

Agreeable to TRUE PHILOSOPHY,

And to be attended with

A TRULY PHILOSOPHICAL EVIDENCE.

By George Turnbull, LL. D.

Be not deceived, God is not mocked, whatsoever a man soweth that shall he also reap. Gal. vi. 7.

Factus a Deo mundus ut homines nascerentur; nascuntur autem homines ut Deum patrem agnoscant, ut colant, in quo justitia est: colunt ut mercedem immortalitatis accipiant: accipiunt immortalitatem, ut in aeternum Deo serviant. Videsne, quemadmodum sibi connexa sint & prima cum mediis, & media cum extremis? Inspiciantur singula: & videamus utrumne illis ratio quoque subsistat.
Lactantius, Divin. Inst. cap. 10.[1]

LONDON:

Printed for J. Noon, at the *White Hart,* near *Mercer's Chapel* in *Cheapside.* MDCCXL. <vi>

---

1. Lactantius, *Divine Institutes,* bk. 7, ch. 6: "The world was made by God so that human beings should be born. Human beings are born so that they should know God the father and should worship him, wherein lies justice. They worship him so that they may gain the reward of immortality, and so may serve God in eternity. Do you not see how these are connected, the first with the intermediate, and the intermediate with the last? Let us look at each of them and let us see whether there is a reason for them being as they are." The first three sentences closely resemble a passage in the critical edition of *Divinarum institutionum,* bk. 7, ch. 6. The remaining two sentences are comment on the first three.

PREFACE

The design of The Principles of MORAL PHILOSOPHY, *&c. is, to reduce appearances or facts in the moral world to general laws, in the same manner that appearances in the natural world are reduced into general laws by natural philosophers; and by pointing out several wise and good final causes of those general laws, to vindicate the ways of God to man, and prove that order is kept in the moral as well as in the natural world. Now, to compleat the scheme of moral philosophy there delineated, two things chiefly appear to be wanting.*

I. *To trace several great revolutions recorded in history to certain principles or general laws arising from, founded in, or well adapted to the general powers and affections of human nature and their laws, which are described and justified in that enquiry.*

Order made it necessary to begin with an explication of those powers and affections belonging to man and their laws, which are, if one may so speak, the radical or elementary principles of human nature; the foundation or ground-work of the whole complex fabrick, which may be called the human system. *And having done my best to accomplish that first and essential part, let me only suggest here, "That the ingenious* Harrington, *though it was not his immediate or direct design to illustrate the wisdom and goodness of providence in the government of moral affairs, has, how-<vii>ever, given an analysis of the more remarkable changes in the* Spartan, *the* Athenian, *the* Roman, *and other states, which clearly unfolds to us several springs or causes of moral events, which will quickly be perceived by every intelligent, attentive considerer, to be necessary consequences of that general constitution of mankind we have endeavoured to illustrate and defend: springs or causes of moral events, which are either absolutely unchangeable in the nature of things; or so admirably adjusted to the very end of the present state of man-*

kind, that no change can be imagined with respect to them which would not thwart or obstruct that end, nay, destroy the whole building." [2]

He justly observes, "That to make principles or fundamentals, belongs not to men, to nations, nor to human laws. To build upon such principles or fundamentals as are apparently laid by God, in the inevitable necessity or law of nature, is that which truly appertains to men, to nations, and to human laws. To make any other fundamentals, and then build upon them, is to build castles in the air." [3] *And accordingly, all his reasonings about human societies, and their mutations and vicissitudes, are fetched from nature, from principles or causes founded in constitutions belonging to human nature. In the same manner that the chief phenomena in the mundan system are reduced, by natural philosophers, into the laws of centripetal and centrifugal forces, hath this Author reduced several great phenomena in the moral world into a few very simple moral laws or principles, which are as steady and regular in their operation as any laws in the material world; and as necessary to order and general good in the moral world, as those are in the natural system. He hath not indeed said that he has done so, i.e. he hath not made this comparison. Natural philosophy hath been much improved since his time. But he hath in fact done it. The same analysis from which he reasons about government, and deduces his maxims or laws of politics, serves to shew, that various revolutions in human societies, which to common readers appear no less anomalous and uncouth than comets may yet seem to one unacquainted with the* Newtonian *philosophy,* <viii> *are in reality the results of moral laws or principles, which are as uniform in their effects as the law of gravity, for instance, in the material system, and as conducive, as requisite to general order, harmony and good in the moral world, as gravity is in its sphere. This, however, it is sufficient for me to have but just suggested here. And several things in this enquiry into the doctrine of reason and revelation,*

---

2. James Harrington (1611–77). The analysis to which Turnbull refers is ubiquitous in Harrington's writings, but see especially *The Commonwealth of Oceania,* in *The Political Works of James Harrington,* ed. J. G. A. Pocock (Cambridge: Cambridge University Press, 1977).

3. Harrington, *Aphorisms Political* no. 85, in *Political Works,* ed. Pocock, 773.

concerning providence, virtue, and a future state, will make my meaning better understood, if it be not already sufficiently plain.

II. *The other thing which appeared to me to be wanting to render the scheme of moral philosophy delineated in* The Principles, *& c. more compleat, is attempted in this essay; which is to shew, that the scripture doctrine concerning God, providence, human nature, virtue or human perfection, and a future state, is so far from being inconsistent with reason, that it is capable of clear proof from principles of reason. The scripture doctrine upon these momentous articles is here compared with what experience and reason teach, in order to render justice, at one and the same time, both to reason and to revelation. Some think the law of reason, or the light of nature, as it is commonly called, does not extend so far as it really does; and seem to imagine they magnify revelation, in proportion as they depress and vilify human understanding. Others misrepresent christianity as giving a very imperfect account of God, providence, human nature, human duties, and a future state. But the truth of the matter seems to be, that revelation gives us a very clear, consistent and comfortable view of these important matters; and that reason does not leave us in the dark about them, so much at least as some have asserted. It is certainly of importance to prove both these points. And therefore, whatever may be thought of the execution, the attempt will be approved by every lover of truth. The government of God by general laws: the consistency of the evils, natural and moral, which prevail in the world, with wise and good; with perfect administration: the relation of <ix> our present life to a future immortal one, as a probationary state, &c.—all the truths, in one word, which are explained in the* Principles of Moral Philosophy, *are here reviewed, in order to shew them to be either direct doctrines of revelation, or to be deducible from such by necessary consequence: for that effect, without repeating any of the reasonings in that treatise, they are here set in various new lights. And I shall not make any apology for endeavouring to do so. If any truths be of consequence, they are. And the variety of men's understandings makes it necessary to set what is of moment for all men to understand and be convinced of, in various points of view. All I have said might easily have been compressed into much narrower and conciser bounds. But I did not write for philosophers merely, but in order to be as generally useful as I could. There are a few things, perhaps, in the second section, which* *may be thought by some too abstruse, too metaphysical. But the first, third, and fourth sections make a compleat body of Christian Ethics without it; and therefore that section may be passed by, if any one finds it too much upon the abstract way of reasoning for his taste or capacity, tho' it would have been very improper to have overlooked the things there mentioned, in an essay of this nature. What is there said with relation to certain arguments offered by some to prove* necessity, *is merely designed to shew, that such reasonings are but verbal labyrinths. The question is a question of fact. And every one who is acquainted with the philosophers (if they may be called such) who have taken delight in perplexing and inveigling, knows what wordy mazes have been contrived by them to confound the plainest facts (such as the reality of motion, for example) and to bewilder the understanding in sophistical intricacies, out of which it is not easy for one to extricate himself, however sure he may be of the truth that is thus beset and puzled with studied subtleties. Moral as well as natural philosophy, is an enquiry into fact: let us therefore keep in the former, as natural philosophers now at last do in the latter, to experiment and fact; and after <x> their example, shake our selves loose of, and despise all verbal wranglings. No law of matter and motion, no connexion in the natural world is more certain than this fact in the moral world, "That by the laws of our nature some things are dependent upon our will as to their existence or non-existence: and with regard to all such, man is free."*

I have called this treatise, CHRISTIAN PHILOSOPHY, *because I have intirely confined myself in it to certain truths, which make up the whole of natural religion, and which for that reason must be essential, fundamental, in a divine revelation. Let me only add; That to misrepresent the Christian institution must certainly be as unfair as to misrepresent any other writings; which is allowed to be inconsistent with candour, with all pretensions to common justice and equity. To depreciate reason in order to exalt revelation, is no less absurd than it would be to talk of putting out our eyes in order to see better with glasses. But as for those, who imagine that the utility of a revelation cannot be acknowledged without vilifying human reason, the noblest gift of God, let them consider, That revelation, which can only address itself to reason, cannot encroach upon the reach or province, far less supersede the use of that faculty. It may add to reason, add to its compass, by giving it a proper evidence for certain very important facts not discoverable by ordi-*

nary experience, or without extraordinary instruction; but it cannot take from it, or render it less extensive: The evidence it carries with it of its truth, is offered to reason to be judged of by it. And surely, nothing that tends to enlarge our prospect of the government of the world, can weaken or degrade human understanding. To relinquish reason, to give up with it, or refuse to trust to it, must be a remediless error. But without abandoning reason, a fair hearing cannot be refused to testimony, attended with a specious evidence of truth. And as to admit testimony without sufficient evidence of its credibility, is unreasonable; so certainly it is contrary to reason to reject testimony on any account but the want of proper and full evidence. Now, in the conclusion to this treatise, I have endeavoured to prove, that the testimony of Jesus Christ con-<xi>cerning the truth of the doctrines he taught, is accompanied with a proper, a full, a truly philosophical evidence. To be set right where I am mistaken, will ever be to me a most obliging favour and service.

The authors from whom any thing is borrowed are mentioned in the margin. The paraphrases on texts of scripture are chiefly taken from Dr. Samuel Clarke'*s excellent Sermons.*[4]

---

4. In these early pages Turnbull is focused on Clarke's Sermon 119, in *The Works of Samuel Clarke, D.D.,* 4 vols. (London, 1738), vol. 2.

THE CONTENTS*

*The pagination in the Contents is that of the 1740 edition. Within the text, the 1740 pagination is indicated by angle brackets.

475

and are able to try and judge it by some certain rule.—But he may reason with them in this manner, The works I do, shew my extensive knowledge of nature; and you have no reason to doubt of my candor and benevolence; you have therefore reason to believe me when I assure you, that the universe is made, preserved, and governed by an infinitely wise, powerful, and good being; and that the more you search into nature, and the larger views you become capable of taking of it by the sedulous exercise of your reason, the more and clearer proofs you shall find of this truth.—This reasoning is truly philosophical.— We reason in this manner every day in many instances; and such a testimony is in itself of a very satisfactory kind.   p. 19

Our Saviour and his apostles suppose the divine perfections to be known from the consideration of God's Works of creation and providence.—They appeal to God's works as sufficient proofs of his power, wisdom, and goodness.—They suppose the principles of natural religion to be known in that way.—They reason about them as truths easily discoverable by reason

p. 20, 21

Proposition II.

The existence of one infinitely powerful, wise and good mind, the Creator, Upholder, and Governor of all things, is a truth that lies plain and obvious to all who will but think.

There must be in nature actually existing some being, who is the original fountain of all derived power, and whose power is underived; or all power is derived from nothing. This argument is illustrated by considering our idea of power.—What it is.—And whence we have it   p. 22, 23

There is, there can be but one author of that immense system of which mankind are a part.—There can be but one independent mind

p. 24, 25, 26

An original, independent mind cannot be malicious.—Such a mind must be perfectly benevolent.—And the author of our system is perfectly benevolent, otherwise the order which prevails in nature, and our capacity of perceiving order and general good, and our disposition to delight in it, are either blindly or maliciously produced.—This argument illustrated

p. 27, 28, 29

We find several reasonings to that effect in the sacred writings

p. 30, 31, 32, 33

The absurdity of saying that goodness in God is not the same as goodness in men, but something of quite another kind, and which we understand not   p. 34

Proposition III.

If the Author and Governor of all things be infinitely perfect, then, Whatever is, is right: *of all possible systems he hath chosen the best, and consequently there is no absolute evil in the universe.*

The creation of an all-perfect mind must be the image of its creator.—It must therefore be perfect.—It is absurd to suppose the author of the universe, our creator, not to act with intelligence and freedom, since we are intelligent agents.—And a perfectly wise and benevolent mind must have chosen the best of all possible systems.—The system in which there is the greatest quantity of perfection and happiness which can possibly take place   p. 35, 36

Whence then comes evil? There is no evil in an absolute sense.—No evil with regard to the whole.—Because all the evils which take place are the result of powers and general laws of powers, the uniform operation of which produces the greatest perfection and good in the whole   p. 37

A distinction of *Leibnitz* between the antecedent and the consequential will of God recognized   p. 38

His error in ascribing an energy or productive operativeness to motives which cannot possibly belong to them   p. 38, 39

In a state or system where there are free-agents, or where there is place for prudence and virtue, different methods of acting must have different effects.—And as it is fit there should be a great variety of beings capable of happiness, so it is fit there should be general methods by which all the different orders of beings in the same system may have pleasure.—But beings, whether of different bodily organizations, or of different mental structures, cannot receive pleasure in the same way, or according to the same order   p. 39, 40

If we take an united view of several things in our system relative to moral and natural evils, we shall quickly perceive that when we complain of the government of the world, on account of the evils prevailing in it, we foolishly demand some absurdity, or some change to the worse   p. 40, 41

The scripture account of the government of the world and of the sources of evils natural and moral considered. God, after he had created the world, and established the general laws constituting its course and order, pronounced the whole good   p. 41

There are many beautiful hymns in scripture to the praise of the creation and its creator and governor   p. 42

Yet God is said to be the author of evil; to create it.—The meaning is, God intends and pursues the universal good of his creation, and the evils which happen in it, are permitted to happen, not that there may be evils in it, but

PROPOSITION IV.

If God hath chosen and established all things, as may best conduce to the greater good of the whole system; then excellent, full care is taken of moral beings in that system; or of that part in which virtue is concerned.

PROPOSITION V.

If this be the universal rule with respect to all moral beings, "That whatsoever one soweth, that shall he reap." Then is every moral system well governed; then are moral beings perfectly well taken care of.

If the administration of moral beings be just, faithful, and good, that rule must obtain.—And alternately if that rule obtain, the administration is righteous; it is faithful and good   p. 60

This argument explained.—The rule supposes moral beings furnished with powers capable of moral improvements and of proportionable degrees of happiness   p. 61

It supposes moral beings placed in circumstances requisite to, or proper for the exercises of their moral powers.—Powers otherwise placed are created in vain.—There is no symptom of such useless profusion of powers, or vain creation in nature   p. 61, 62

The rule supposes or implies in it the dependence of the improvement of moral powers, and of the happiness resulting therefrom upon the moral being itself.—It supposes the improvement of moral powers to be a progressive work.—And it supposes the progressive improvements of moral powers to depend upon the disposition and will of the moral being to set itself to make improvements.—It likewise supposes certain fixed general laws ascertainable by moral beings, determining their spheres of activity, and the consequences of their different methods of acting   p. 62, 63

It supposes moral beings so framed as to have a particular satisfaction in their own acquisitions or improvements.—And finally, it supposes, that upon the whole, or in the sum of things, happiness is proportioned to moral improvement, virtue, or good desert   p. 64

Such administration is just, righteous, faithful, perfectly good   p. 65

PROPOSITION VI.

If the rule defined be really observed with respect to mankind in their present state, we have ground to conclude, that it is an universal law in God's moral government.

It hath been inferred to be a rule necessary to good administration from the very nature of good moral administration; and not from any thing particular in man's frame.—It hath therefore been deduced from such principles as prove it to be an universal law.—The apostle infers it from such universal principles.—From the moral perfections of God   p. 67

But if it can be once proved from experience to be a rule that takes place with respect to mankind here in their present state, as shall be proved; it may from hence be inferred to be an universal law in all moral systems.—Provided analogy be a good foundation to reason upon in any case.—If we cannot reason so, we cannot prove gravitation to be an universal law in our mundan system, because it gives a simple, harmonious account of it.—Which is more, if it be not an universal law, then are not all moral beings governed by a law suited to the powers in which they are analogous one to another.—which cannot be supposed   p. 68, 69

Proposition VII.

Experience proves this to be the law with respect to mankind in their present state. "That whatsoever a man soweth, that shall he also reap."

The scripture asserts it to be the law with regard to our future state and the final issue of things.—And we may justly conclude, that what is the law in the divine government of mankind with respect to a succeeding life, is the present law, as far as the nature of a preparative state to a future one admits.— But let us enquire into fact   p. 70

Only let us first consider how philosophers reason from experiments about natural appearances and their general laws, for we may reason in the same manner about moral appearances and their general laws   p. 71

Let it likewise be premised that from the care of providence about the brute creation, in providing them with instincts suited to their various kinds and respective oeconomies we have reason to presume similar care about moral beings—about mankind   p. 72

When we consider the state of mankind, we find it is the general law that one reaps as he sows.—Almost all our pleasures and pains are put in our own power, or depend upon our conduct.—Our sphere of power is very extensive.—We ought to study to know what is and what is not in our power: our τα εφ ημιν and our τα ουκ εφ ημιν—That is not the only thing we ought to study; but it is one principal thing   p. 73, 74

To have a clearer view of this matter, let us consider our power with respect, 1. to externals; and, 2. with respect to internals.—Our power in general is got by getting knowledge: it augments with our knowledge,—And we are fitted for extending our knowledge of nature, and by consequence our dominion in nature, to a very great degree   p. 75–79

Why then has natural knowledge made such slow and small advances?
                                                                      p. 80

This takes its rise from various causes; all of which are originally founded in very useful affections or dispositions in our make   p. 81

Many, very many take their rise from our social dependence; or our being
made for society, and for arriving to our greatest perfection and happiness in
a social way, by mutual assistance, and by combining ourselves into proper
governments adapted to promote the best general interest   p. 103

This consideration illustrated   p. 104, 105

But what, after all, do these limitations upon the law of industry, which
have been mentioned, and traced to their sources, amount to? There must be
differences among mankind—there must be a *natural aristocracy among mankind* (to use the words of a great author) to be the foundation of society and
government. And these differences give occasion to the exercises of many noble virtues.—A reasoning of St. *Paul's* about variety of gifts in the church
applied to society in general   p. 106–113

The laws or causes whence the limitations upon the general law of industry
proceed, are necessary to the greater good—and great advantages may be deduced by prudence and virtue from the evils redounding from such limitations—from all the evils that prevail in the world in general   p. 114

All things considered, *i.e.* the general law of industry and its limitations
being duly weighed, all men are upon the most equal footing consistent with
the greater good of the kind, with respect to external and internal advantages.—Tho' some may be in more advantageous circumstances than others
for acquiring knowledge; yet virtue, *i.e.* self-command, is acquirable in every
state.—And a virtuous mind may soon acquire knowledge with the assistance
of others in a future state   p. 114

And tho' some have not in this life occasion to exert several virtues; yet all
who have attained to the love of virtue, and to self-dominion, have *the root
of the matter* in them; the never dying root of moral happiness   p. 115

Let us add to this, that the various vicissitudes in human life render our
present state a noble school for improving us in moral knowledge.—And if
we remember, that as there must be different abilities, turns, and situations
in every social state; so this being our probationary state, all the differences
which now obtain must be considered as differences belonging to a probationary state.—The only question therefore with regard to them must be,
"whether they are improper or unsuitable to such a state, as such"

p. 116, 117

Corolary I.

If we may reason from analogy we may conclude, that the law which hath
been found to take place in our present state shall likewise take place in our
future state, if there be a future state, without any limitations, but such as are

necessary to the greater good.—The apostle asserts, it is the law with regard to our future state, "That every one shall reap there as he hath sown here." And as we may from hence presume, that it is the law here as far as the design of our present state of discipline allows it to prevail; so, having found it to be the law here, without any other exceptions or limitations but what are requisite to general good, or to our probationary state as such, we can have no reason to doubt, that in the final issue of things, or in a future state, every one shall reap as he hath sown   p. 117, 118

Corolary II.

From the present state of things we must infer, that there is a future state in which virtuous improvements shall have their full effect, their full reward; all the happiness they are naturally capable of, in consequence of their being placed in circumstances suited to them. If there be not, then is not the administration perfect—but if there be, then is it perfect—and we have good reason, from the consideration of all things, to think it is as perfect as the scripture asserts it to be.—If this be our probationary state for a future one, in which every one shall reap as he sows, it is a perfect state; the government is good.—Now the scripture asserts it to be such; and it plainly appears to be such   p. 119–121

SECTION II.
The scripture doctrine concerning providence
more fully explained, &c.

A Preliminary OBSERVATION upon REASON.

The scripture does not command us to relinquish, to distrust our reason, but on the contrary to exercise it diligently and impartially; without fear, but with caution; boldly, but with a due sense of the needfulness of accurate attention.—Reason is our glory—our guide—our distinguishing excellence.—The chief business of reason is to direct our conduct—to enquire for that end into the frame and constitution of things—our make, the end of our creation, the will of our maker, the moral excellencies manifested by his works.—Things may be dark to us who see not the whole.—We must judge by parts or samples.—We are made to judge so of the whole, and of its author.—Whereever we perceive agreement or disagreement of ideas clearly, we have certainty.—Where we perceive likelihood in a certain degree, we have probability to that degree.—We may be certain of a truth, and yet not be able to answer several questions nearly relating to it.—There can, however, be no objections against a truth, which are arguments *ab absurdo* against that truth.—Truth cannot lead to absurdity   p. 123–130

PROPOSITION I.

The government of the Author of the universe is universal and irresistible.

Such it must be in the nature of things—such the scripture asserts it to be.—The only difficulty here is about God's foreknowledge of events, depending upon the free actions or determinations of moral agents.—Predictions in scripture prove there is such foreknowledge.—But if it be not impossible; or if it can take place in particular cases, it must be universal.—The scriptures assert it is universal—and it must be such, in order to God's being a moral governor—in order to his punishing and rewarding in a future life

p. 130–132

Predetermination by God that such and such things shall happen, is allowed to be repugnant to freedom of agency—To say all things which happen in a system are predetermined by the author of the system to happen, is to say, there are no created agents endued with power and choice, or invested with certain spheres of activity in that system.—Foreknowledge founded upon such predetermination is therefore granted to be inconsistent with liberty, agency, or a sphere of activity.—But may there not be foreknowledge where there is no predetermination; or foreknowledge of the choices and actions of free agents?   p. 133

Some have thought not; and that knowledge of the powers given, and all their possible determinations or exertions, together with the exact knowledge of all the laws relating to the powers given, is sufficient for the right government of moral beings.—But others think fore-knowledge of every particular choice, resolution, or action of every created agent is not inconsistent with free agency   p. 134

And to illustrate this, several considerations are offered and enlarged upon   p. 135–138

But having little new to add upon this obscure subject, it remains to consider, what is the meaning of a kingdom of the Devil in scripture.—Now, by considering the genius of the *Jewish* language, it appears, that it means a kingdom of unrighteousness or vice.—Not a power of acting in opposition to divine providence in a literal sense. All modern languages have a good deal of the same kind of phraseology in them: or have adopted them from the scripture language   p. 139–141

PROPOSITION II.
The divine providence is clearly and expressly asserted in scripture to be infinitely wise and good, &c.

by samples with complacency and assurance proportioned to the degrees of likelihood.—This is fact.—And it is an argument of the wisdom and goodness of our author in adjusting the temperature of our minds to our situation   p. 153–155

Further, we cannot conceive a system in which there are free-agents where certain actions must not be attended with hurtful consequences, and others with good ones   p. 156, 157

Hence we may conclude, that all is good.—That is the more probable opinion.—The mind by these considerations is naturally disposed to presume all is good.—And the reason of this is, that we are so made   p. 158, 159

2. Another observation is this, *viz.* That the faithfulness, veracity, and other attributes ascribed to God in scripture, are perhaps comprehended in the idea of perfect goodness, or they may be deduced from it.—But we may infer, that they belong to God from our being made to approve veracity, candour, equality, uniformity, simplicity, and consistency in themselves, without taking their tendency to promote the greater good into the consideration.—These qualities are approved by our mind as immediately as benevolence, and on their own account.—We can see why we are so made, upon supposition that our strict adherence to truth be necessary to promote the greater good of society, since we are not in all cases capable of judging immediately what that greater good requires.—Nay, tho' we could, we may see a good reason for so constituting us, that we might immediately approve truth and veracity, *&c.* for such a determination is a corroborative, an assistant to benevolence, and a guide to it.—And being so made, the presumption lies, that to God himself these qualities appear amiable in themselves.—And that the observance of them by him is necessary to the greater good of his creation.—The presumption lies so, independently of all other considerations   p. 160–163

But in every case we can put or imagine, God's departing from veracity would be exceedingly hurtful.—And therefore we may justly conclude, that the universal observance of veracity, faithfulness, and uniformity is necessary to the greater good of moral beings, the chief end of God's creation and government   p. 164

One thing is certain. They are rules of action with regard to us, which we have no right to depart from.—They are intended to be rules for our conduct in pursuing the universal good of our kind   p. 165

But this leads me to consider, what it is which the holy scripture calls the mercy, the compassion, the forgiving disposition of God   p. 165, 166

The scripture ascribes these attributes to God.—And the conduct of providence shews they belong to God.—It was observed by a wise heathen,

That this world is our state of probation; and the next our state of rewards and punishments.—That many wicked men being mercifully spared, are led at last to repentance.—That many wicked men are fathers of good children.—That by the bad the virtuous are exercised and tried.—That the wicked far from being happy in the most prosperous circumstances, are really very miserable.—That by the general laws providence observes, the ruin of states, and of particular persons, is brought about in a more instructive way than it could be by partial, immediate, extraordinary punishments.— That no wicked man can be destroyed without involving others not so bad, perhaps good, in his perdition.—That men are fitted to study the conduct of providence; and ought to imitate it.—Now this conduct of sparing sinners, or forbearing them, is designed to lead us to a merciful, forgiving temper.—Every man falls short of his duty, and stands in need of compassion and forbearance from God.—But who can have confidence to ask or hope for it, unless he have a forgiving compassionate temper towards his fellow creatures?   p. 167, 168

PROPOSITION III.

The divine, infinitely wise, just, faithful, good providence governs the whole universe by general laws; nor is what is said in scripture of special, miraculous interpositions of providence inconsistent with such government.

PROPOSITION IV.
The providence of God works agreeably to, or consistently with the liberty of moral agents.

of activity, we are not, so far as it reaches, accountable agents, capable of praise and blame, virtue and demerit.—We are naturally determined to think we are such.—We are treated as if we were such in the conduct of providence.—And the scripture considers us as such   p. 206, 207

COROLARY I.

Hence we may see in what sense the world is a perfect scheme: not that there are not corruptions and consequences of corruptions in it, without which it would be better: but because those corruptions and their consequences which take place in it, take place according to, and in consequence of powers and laws of powers requisite to general good.   p. 208

Not that the scheme is at every instant, or in the present course of things already perfect or finished, but because it is a scheme which is advanced or carried on according to the best general laws for the greater good.—Did the scheme of providence with regard to mankind end here in this life, it would be a very imperfect scheme.—But considered as not ending here, but tending towards another life, it is perfect.—It is therefore such a scheme.—The scripture asserts it to be such.—It must be such, if the Creator and Administrator be infinitely wise, perfect, and good.—And analogy leads us to conceive of our present life, as a probationary state, to be succeeded by a future life, which is to be its harvest.—So the apostle speaks.—And such does the constitution and course of things appear to be   p. 209, 210

COROLARY II.

If God be infinitely good, and his government be infinitely perfect, as the scripture assures us it is, and as reason and analogy plainly prove it to be, then is all praise and adoration due to God.—It is a reasonable exercise.—It is a pleasant one.—It has an excellent effect on the temper and disposition of the mind—it promotes benevolence   p. 211, 212

The pattern of worship, commonly called *the Lord's-prayer,* shews us, that the design of prayer or worship is to praise God with serious, warm affection.—To resign ourselves with complacency and delight to the all-governing will.—To ask virtue, and to ask it is to have it.—And to indulge ourselves in acts of benevolence towards all men,—In acts of forgiveness towards our enemies,—And in a sense of our own obligations to the compassion and forbearance of God, designed to lead us to repentance, that becoming virtuous we may be capacitated for rational or virtuous happiness in the life to come,

SECTION III.

PROPOSITION I.
The moral perfection we are called by revelation to pursue, may be reduced to those two generals. The perfection of our understanding, and the perfection of our will or temper.

All men, in all ages, have acknowledged its worth and excellence. Every man perceives it to be his duty, his dignity, his happiness   p. 250, 251

Its connexion with our interest, in all respects, is obvious.—It does not require a nice or difficult computation to discover it.—There are and always have been very significant proverbs in all countries, expressing the wisdom of virtuous and the folly of vitious conduct,—or strongly declaring, as *Homer* expresses it, *"That never, never wicked man was wise."* Some proverbs in *Solomon* to this purpose commented upon   p. 252–257

But it is proper to consider some other views christianity gives us of our duty, dignity and interest   p. 258

PROPOSITION II.

According to revelation, we are made and placed in our present state chiefly to endeavour to attain to the love of the pleasures arising from rational, virtuous exercises; and to the contempt of mere sensual pleasure, in comparison of them: And this reason itself plainly proves to be the chief end of our being, from the very nature of our frame, and from our present situation, which are admirably well adapted one to another.

The Christian revelation plainly represents our duty in this manner
p. 258, 259

Let us therefore look into our frame and constitution, that we may see what may be inferred from hence   p. 260

If we consider our whole frame, as we are compounded of affections, appetites and passions to be governed, and reason to govern, it appears to be the end of our creation, that reason should be established by us in our minds, as the ruling principle; as our judge and law-giver   p. 261

If we may reason at all about final causes that conclusion must hold good   p. 262

The natural happiness of a being must be similar to, of a kind with, and result from its frame and composition.—We are therefore made for rational exercises, and virtuous happiness   p. 263

Our chief happiness cannot result from the exercises of those affections which have, with respect to others in our frame, the most distant relation to our guiding principle.—It must arise from the exercise of our reason, as our governing principle over the affections in our frame, naturally subjected to it, and intended to be governed by it   p. 264, 265

If our end may be inferred from our frame, the will and intention of our Author may be inferred from our frame.—These two must coincide, or mean the same thing.—Wherefore it must be the will and intention of our author, that reason act in us as a ruling principle   p. 266

The constitution of man, which, considered by itself, is itself *a law* to man, is, considered as pointing out to us the will of our Author with relation to our conduct, a law in the strict sense of the word, *the law of our Maker*

p. 267

But this conclusion being fixed, to endeavour after moral perfection is our *duty;* or we are *obliged* to it in every sense of the words *duty* and *obligation*

p. 267

Now, this principle being established, it follows; that it must be our interest on the whole to endeavour to attain to moral perfection.—Even tho' our acting so should at present be sometimes attended with an over-ballance of pain; because that cannot possibly be the case for ever, or upon the whole, under good administration.—But all things around us shew we are under the administration of an infinitely wise and good being.—Our own frame proves it   p. 268

And, in fact, acting agreeably to reason is always our best interests, or greatest happiness, the extraordinary case of persecution excepted.—In which case there is a satisfaction attending the strength of mind, in adhering to virtue, which is an unspeakable feast to those who seem to suffer, and to them presages a future glorious recompence.—This is the language of reason, as well as of revelation, That virtue by its sufferings shall be fitted for a peculiarly glorious share of after-happiness.—It must be so under that good administration of which every thing we see bears evident marks.—And whence else is it, that virtue is so delightful, so pleasant in its exercises, even while it suffers, but because the author of nature hath so constituted moral beings, that virtue, in proportion to its advances, fills the mind with proportionably great joy.— Hath such a constitution the appearance of a malignant, vitious author?

p. 269

If we attend to our constitution, we shall find that the gratification any sensible object gives us, is naturally in proportion to the violence of the craving nature excites in us when such gratification is necessary to the sustenance of our bodies.—Abstract from the pleasures accompanying sensible gratifications those which belong to the social part of our frame, and nothing remains but what is mere relief from painful appetite.—And excesses create pain and uneasiness.—We are not made therefore for luxury or debauchery

p. 270

On the other hand, how pure, how uncloying are all the exercises of our understanding in the contemplation of order, harmony, and general good.—

COROLARY I.

COROLARY II.

COROLARY III.

Proposition IV.

The scripture represents the future state of the virtuous as a state in which they are separated from the vitious.

This is a mixed state;—and consequently the natural effects of virtue must be mixed with those of vice.—But a separation being made, virtue will have its natural tendency unobstructed.—The tares, according to our Saviour's similitude, must grow up with the wheat till the harvest come.—Then is the time for separation;—and this separation must have very happy effects.—This illustrated by some considerations   p. 433–435

Proposition V.

The scripture represents the future state of the virtuous as a state free from all pains and uneasinesses; and the state of the vitious, as one in which none of their sensual appetites and passions can have any gratifications.

It must be free from all those occasioned by vice.—It must likewise be free from all sensitive pains,—not only during our separation from bodies,—but

Proposition VI.

The scripture represents virtue or holiness, not only as the condition of, and the qualification for the happiness of a future state; but it represents the happiness of a future state, as consisting in and resulting from virtuous exercises and enjoyments; and it represents it as immortal, or enduring for ever.

But it is not represented as arising from contemplation, admiration, and devotion only,—but from action, virtuous employment.—Nothing here leads us to conceive of a future state as a disunited unactive state,—but contrariwise, as a social, united, active one   p. 449

And revelation represents it as such.—The scripture no where represents to us any state of inactive happiness.—The happiness of God consists in the continual communication of his goodness.—The happiness of all celestial beings, in being ministring spirits to God,—in instrumentality in promoting the great ends of the divine government.—*Jesus Christ* is represented as delighting in executing a commission from God.—This illustrated   p. 450

Hence several things of importance may be inferr'd;—particularly, that beings of the highest orders, in their most happy state, may have occasion for patience, resignation to the divine will, magnanimity, &c.—*Christ* is set before us as a pattern and motive to the sedulous study of those virtues.—We have therefore no ground from reason or scripture to apprehend that a future state is an inactive one   p. 452, 453

And what an immense variety of happy employments may we imagine to ourselves in a future state, in consequence of perfect union and harmony,— perfect government?—In order to have some faint idea of it, let us consider how happy the good government human nature is capable of would make men even in this state, in consequence of its excellent orders and constitutions
                                                                   p. 453–455

It must be a social state;—a state in which the law of industry, or of acquisition by exercise and diligence, takes place,—otherwise it would not be a state of virtue and merit.—It must be a state in which the sphere of activity or dominion is large, and ever enlarging,—in which there is a best interest to be pursued, which is continually advancing, being continually promoted to greater and greater perfection.—This illustrated.—It is the idea revelation gives us of a future state;—and it is the idea, experience, and analogy, or reason, leads us to conceive of it.—It is the idea all philosophers, in all ages, have had of it   p. 456–458

According to the scripture doctrine, it is an unchangeable state.—The security of the virtuous cannot arise from any impossibility of falling away,— whence then does it arise?—from the strength of habits formed in a state of discipline,—from large views of the moral rectitude of God's government,— from experience of the advantages and rewards of virtuous acquisitions,— from the noble emulation excited by examples,—and perhaps, in a great measure, from the perfection of government in that city of God   p. 459–463

All that hath been said concerning God, providence, virtue, and a future state, is included in that emphatical saying of St. *Paul;* "Be not deceived: God is not mocked; for whatsoever a man soweth, that shall he also reap"; and the language of it is, "Let us not therefore be weary in well-doing, for in due season we shall reap, if we faint not"   p. 464

CONCLUSION.

An argument to prove that the teaching of *Christ* was attended with a proper, a full, a truly philosophical evidence.—The works he did, and gave his apostles power to do, were samples analogous in kind, and proportioned in quantity or moment to his claim as our instructor in certain truths. The absurdity of saying, that works cannot prove the truth of doctrines.—All doctrines are facts, and all facts are doctrines:—It is therefore to say, that facts and facts have, can have no relation.—In philosophy, natural and moral truths are inferred from facts, from works.—The relation of *Christ's* works to his claim to a well-qualified instructor consider'd.—The relation of *Christ's* works to the particular doctrines he taught, considered.—The relation of *Christ's* works to his pretension to a commission from God to teach, considered.— Revelation does not, cannot encroach upon reason.—The absurdity of asserting the inutility of revelation, even supposing nothing revealed but what reason may easily discover.—The absurdity of asserting it to be inconsistent with divine wisdom and goodness to give mankind at any time supernatural instruction in important truths,—or an extraordinary call to virtue and piety. The reasonings of *Christ* to prove his qualifications to instruct, and the credibility of his testimony, considered.—Christianity is a reasonable doctrine, and is attended with a truly philosophical evidence.   p. 469–490

FINIS.

INTRODUCTION

An EXPLICATION of the TEXT.
GAL. vi. 7.

Be not deceived; God is not mocked: for whatsoever a man soweth that shall he also reap. For he that soweth to his flesh, shall of the flesh reap corruption: but he that soweth to the spirit, shall of the spirit reap life everlasting.[5]

In these words, we may observe, 1. A rule in the divine moral government, which is indeed the foundation of true religion, asserted in the strongest terms. Be not deceived, let no false teacher deceive you; and take care you do not deceive yourselves, because sin, or the love of vicious pleasure, is deceitful above all things; for whatever you may vainly imagine, whatever you may be inclined or seduced to believe, this is an immutable law in the divine government, "That as one soweth so shall he also reap." This is the law in all moral systems; and the law with regard to man as he is a rational agent, which GOD hath, in justice, righteousness and benevolence, established; GOD, whose counsels cannot be mocked, <2> frustrated or eluded: the law with regard to this our present state, as far as the ends of it require or permit; and the law according to which our fate will be determined in the life to come, to which this is but a prelude; to which this bears the same relation and proportion in the moral world, as seed-time does to harvest in the natural. When GOD's scheme of government is so far advanced with respect to every man in particular, and to mankind in general, then shall this most equitable rule be more plainly perceived to have been the measure of the divine

---

5. Gal. 6.7–8.

conduct with regard to all men, than it can be at present, while we see but so small a part of the system which providence is carrying on to perfection.

Be not deceived, (GOD is not mocked.) The word *mock,* (as the learned and worthy Dr. *Samuel Clark* observes in his excellent sermon on this text)[6] which in the *new Testament* is in the original expressed by two or three synonimous terms, in its literal and most proper sense, signifies *deceiving* any person, *deluding* him, or *disappointing* his expectation. Thus,[a] when *Herod* had ordered the wise men to bring him word where JESUS was; and by their returning privately into their own country another way, found himself disappointed of his expectation; the text expresses it, that he saw *he was mocked of the wise men.* At other times, it signifies *affronting or abusing* any person by *open violence;*[b] and they shall deliver him to the *Gentiles* to *mock,* and to scourge, and to crucify him. And sometimes it signifies pretending *obedience and respect by way of derision, in a scornful insulting and despiteful manner.* Thus,[c] when they had platted a crown of thorns, they put it upon his head, and a reed in his right hand for a sceptre, and they bowed the knee before him, and *mocked him.*

In the literal and proper sense (continueth this admirable interpreter) of the phrase, it is impossible in <3> the nature of things, that GOD should in any of these ways be *mocked.* But figuratively, consequentially, and in true reality of guilt and folly, all wicked men, who set themselves to oppose GOD's kingdom of righteousness; who, without repentance, amendment and obedience to GOD's commands, expect to escape, and teach others that they may escape his righteous judgment, are, in the Apostle's estimation, *mockers of God.* For,[d] 1. They, as far as in them lies, confound the necessary reasons and proportions of things, and endeavour to take away the eternal and unchangeable difference of good and

a. *Matth.* ii. 16.
b. *Matth.* xx. 19.
c. *Matth.* xxvii. 29.
d. I abridge Dr. *Clark*'s Commentary a little. [Samuel Clarke (1675–1729): "God is not mocked," Sermon 119, in *Works,* vol. 2.]
6. Clarke, Sermon 119, in *Works,* 2:29–31.

evil, which are the general order and rule of GOD's creation, and the very foundation of his government over the universe. For what is government, but the preserving of the order and reason of things, and suiting them to the capacities and qualifications of persons? To endeavour therefore, either in doctrine or in practice, to set aside, or to elude this great and essential distinction of things, without which the *government,* and even the Being of GOD is of no consequence: what is this but in the highest degree, mocking of GOD, and taking away the notion of a supreme Lord and Governor of the universe? 2. It is *mocking God,* because it is an entertaining of very dishonourable and very injurious apprehensions concerning the perfections and attributes of GOD himself. I speak not now of atheistical persons, of such as directly deny either the being or providence of GOD; but of such as either carelesly or presumptuously deceive themselves or others, by imagining that GOD has not so great a concern about moral good and evil, but that they may by some means escape his final wrath, without a life of virtue and true holiness. This, I say, is really and in effect taking away his moral perfections. It is divesting him of those perfections, by which he is (as our Saviour emphatically stiles him) the *great king,* <4> the supreme governor of rational and moral beings, as well as of the natural world. All attempts to elude the great ends of the divine government, by substituting any thing else whatever in the place of virtue and true righteousness, in the place of temperance, equity, charity and truth, is, in the Apostle's esteem, a *mocking* of GOD. It is such a mockery of him, as really tends more to hurt and efface in men's minds the true notion of GOD, and to hinder the efficacy of virtue and goodness in the world, than questioning the very Being of a supreme governor at all. The ungodly has said in his heart, GOD *has forgotten, he hideth away his face, and he will never see it. They say, tush, the Lord shall not see, neither shall the God of* Jacob *regard it.*[a] 3. As such persons (continueth the same Author) are in the true estimation of things, *mockers of God* upon all these accounts: so they are still further guilty of the same charge, in perverting the plain revelation of CHRIST, and overthrowing the whole design of his religion. The great doctrine

a. *Psal.* x. 12. xciv. 7.

our LORD came to preach is this, *The Son of man shall come in the glory of his Father with his angels; and then shall he reward every man according to his works.*[a] And the sum of what his Apostles preach amounts always to the same. *We must all appear before the judgment-seat of Christ, that every one may receive the things done in his body according to that he hath done, whether it be good or bad.*[b]

But let us enquire more particularly into the meaning of this doctrine, to deny which is called *deceiving ourselves,* nay, *mocking God.* "Whatsoever a man soweth that shall he also reap." Because the happiness of the virtuous in a future state is very properly set forth to us in scripture under the notion of reward, and the misery of the wicked under the notion of punishment; therefore men unwilling to part with their vices, are apt to consider such promises and threatnings, as arbi-<5>trary positive denunciations, which may be altered, and which GOD is too good and merciful to execute (as to the punishing part) to the rigor. And to prevent this fatal error concerning GOD, the Apostle gives us to understand, and calls upon us seriously to attend to it in the most urgent emphatical manner, "That the promises of happiness to the good, and the threatnings of misery to the vicious in a future state, are really kind declarations to us of the great end and purpose of the divine moral government, and of the laws inviolably observed by GOD in it: declarations of a law, so founded in equity, and so absolutely necessary to the general good of moral beings, and the perfection of the divine administration, that it cannot be altered in any respect or degree: an universal, immutable decree or general rule, without which there can be no moral government, it being involved in the very nature of virtue and vice; or, which comes to the same thing, it being the necessary result of those essential differences of things, which make actions good or bad. And indeed, what distinction can there be between virtue and vice; that is, between the neglect, misuse or abuse, and the right use or suitable exercise of moral powers, if they have not different effects, quite opposite tendencies, influences and consequences?

a. *Matth.* xvi. 27.
b. 2 *Cor.* v. 10.

The apostle, to enforce and illustrate this great truth, makes use of a figurative expression, than which none can be better adapted to express it with full force, or convey a truer and livelier idea of its extent. "Whatsoever a man soweth that shall he also reap." As men do not gather grapes of thorns, or figs of thistles: as the fruit is always of the same kind with the stock that bears it, and the grain reaped is necessarily of the same sort with the seed that was sown; so mens final state of happiness or misery shall be the proper and correspondent effect of their present actions. *He that soweth to his flesh* (as the apostle expresses it in the following verses)[7] *shall of the flesh reap corruption: but* <6> *he that soweth to the spirit, shall of the spirit reap life everlasting.* "In the present time (saith the incomparable author just quoted, in the same discourse)[8] we frequently see this in some degree verified, in what we usually call the natural course and consequences of things. In the future state, after what manner the effects and operations of nature will proceed, we are now altogether ignorant: and therefore we represent to ourselves, very justly and with the greatest reason, every circumstance of that state, as the immediate effect of GOD's final judgment, and the direct execution of the irreversible sentence. Yet were we able to discern, or had GOD thought fit to discover to us, the *particulars* of the whole proceeding; the difference perhaps of GOD's several ways and methods of acting would not appear so great to us as we are apt to imagine. The certainty at least of the *connexion,* and the proper *correspondency* of the events, would be altogether as *conspicuous,* and appear as far removed from any degree of *arbitrary uncertainty,* in all those things which we ascribe to the *immediate judgment of GOD;* as in any of those which we now look upon as arising from the *natural consequences* and *connexions of things.* For what are the *natural consequences and connexions of things,* but the result of *that order and disposition* of things which GOD originally established in the creation? And the very *same power* which established and preserves this order of nature, has *appointed* likewise the connexion of consequences in the progress of the moral state of the world. However

7. Gal. 6.8.
8. Clarke, Sermon 119, in *Works,* 2:27–28.

different therefore the *manner* and *method* of GOD's operations may be, in these two different governments of such very *different kinds* of subjects; yet the *operation* may in each be equally regular in its kind; and the proper *effect* or *event,* corresponding to the antecedent cause, whether in the *natural* or *moral* world, may be alike *certain* and invariable in both. When in the course of nature, we see grain sown in the earth produce regularly and uniformly, after cer-<7>tain stated periods of time, fruit of the same kind with that which was sown; we are very apt to let the wonder slip out of our minds, and lose the whole force of its impression, merely by affixing to it a word of no signification, and calling it by the name of *natural:* whereas in truth, inanimate *nature* is nothing but an empty sound; unintelligent *agents* and *powers* (as we improperly call them) are nothing but *mere instruments;* and the whole effect is really the *operation* of him, who is the *Author and GOD of nature.* By the *disposition* and *appointment* of the same author and ruler of the universe, the moral consequences and connexions of things do, in *their proper manner,* and at their *proper seasons,* take place likewise in the world. And could our faculties extend themselves to take in at one view those larger periods of the divine dispensations, on which depends the harmony and beauty of the moral world, in like manner as our experience enables us to contemplate the yearly products of *nature;* we should then probably be no more struck with wonder at the seeming *forbearing* of providence to interpose at present, in the ordering of the *moral* state of the world; than we are now surprized, in the *regular course of nature,* to see grain lie, as it were, dead in the earth in winter, and seemingly dissolving into corruption, and yet, without fail, at the return of its proper season, bringing forth the certain particular fruit, of which it was the seed. The apostle's similitude therefore in the text, not only in general is a certain and infallible truth, but very probably may be also a truth which has in *itself* a more *immediate and necessary connexion,* than men are usually sensible of. 'Tis not only true, that GOD has actually set before men such and such promises and threatnings; but probably it will be found true also, at the final issue and event of things, that he has appointed by as *close and regular a connexion* in morals as in naturals, that whatsoever a man soweth, that shall he also reap. <8>

In the natural and material world, the *more observations* men make, and the *greater accuracy* they arrive at, and the *longer periods* of time they are able to take in the *more clearly and distinctly* do they discern, that in that innumerable variety of the works of GOD, all things conspire uniformly, with the most exquisite exactness, to produce (and that sometimes out of the greatest seeming confusion) the properest and most regular effects. The moral world is of infinitely greater importance: it is that, for the sake of which this beautiful and stupendous fabrick of the inanimate universe is created, and without which it is nothing. It cannot be doubted then by any reasonable person, but that the same wisdom, which in the *unintelligent works of nature,* has shewn forth itself in the contrivance of such inexpressible aptnesses and proportions of things; will *much more* in the government of *rational beings* (which are in a far *nobler* and *more proper* sense, the subjects of GOD's power and kingdom) shew forth itself finally, in making every event, through a wonderful variety of different dispensations, terminate at length in most evident and illustrious manifestations of perfect justice, goodness, and truth.

However therefore, melancholy pious persons, patiently persisting in the practice of their duty, may, when they observe how providence, *in the present time* suffers all things seemingly to go alike to all, be thereby sometimes tempted almost to despond; yet in reality their reward is laid up for them with GOD *much more certainly,* than grain which in the winter seems to lie dead in the earth wherein it was sown, may yet be depended upon to bring forth fruit in its proper season. The psalmist expresses this very emphatically: "They that sow in tears, shall reap in joy: he that now goeth on his way weeping, and beareth forth good seed, shall doubtless come again with joy, and bring his sheaves with him."[a] The figure is the same with that in the text: and the *literal meaning* of it is <9> well expressed by the author of the book of wisdom,[b] "Tho' they be punished in the sight of men, yet is their hope full of immortality; for their reward is with the Lord, and the care of them is with the

---

a. *Ps.* cxxvi. 5–6.
b. *Chap.* iii. 4. and v. 15.

most High." And by the apostle himself,[a] "To them who by patient continuance in well-doing seek for glory, and honour, and immortality; to them GOD will give eternal life." And therefore christians are exhorted,[b] "Cast not away therefore your confidence, which hath great recompence of reward. For ye have need of patience, that after ye have done the will of GOD, ye might receive the promise. For yet a little while, and he that shall come, will come, and will not tarry." And St. *James* in like manner,[c] "Be patient therefore, brethren, unto the coming of the Lord. Behold the husbandman waiteth for the precious fruit of the earth, and hath long patience for it, until he receive the early and the latter rain. Be ye also patient; stablish your hearts; for the coming of the Lord draweth nigh." On the contrary, however *presumptuous* and *careless* persons may deceive themselves with numberless vain imaginations, expecting to *reap where they have not sown, and to gather where they have not strawed;* yet as certainly as the *nature of things* is unvaried, and the *perfections of God* unchangeable, the final issue of things in the future state will be *universally,* what *Job* observes it to be *sometimes,* even in the *present* state,[d] "I have seen they that plow iniquity, and sow wickedness, reap the same: by the blast of God they perish, and by the breath of his nostrils they are consumed."

So far goes our excellent author from whom all this is taken. Now indeed 'tis evident, that St. *Paul* in the text is immediately speaking of GOD's rule with respect to a future state; whence it plainly follows, that our present state is, with respect to a future life, a probationary state; a state of education, trial, and <10> discipline; a state in which the foundation is laid for our after happiness or misery; or, to keep to the apostle's excellent similitude, our *seed-time,* to which it is the *harvest.* But it is no less plain, that the same rule must take place in God's government, even in this present state, as far as its being a probationary state, to be compleated in a succeeding life, that shall be exactly proportioned to the

a. *Rom.* ii. 7.
b. *Heb.* x. 35–37.
c. *Ch.* v. 7.
d. *Ch.* iv. 8–9.

foundation laid in this, permits. For it is a rule which an infinitely good and wise Being must adhere to in all his administration. And accordingly the apostle establishes this rule with regard to our future state, upon a principle from which it follows that it must be an universal and perpetual law in the divine government of all moral beings, namely, the absolute moral perfection of the Deity. For his reasoning is briefly to this effect. Think well on the nature and perfections of the Deity, and you must see that it is deceiving yourselves, and entertaining very unjust and unworthy apprehensions of God, to imagine that this is not the method of his administration in the moral world for ever, and therefore in a future state, "That as one soweth, so shall he also reap." 'Tis indeed only in a future state that it can be fully perceived by us to be the rule in God's government, because this is but our moral seed-time, and that our harvest. But this is the rule, which the perfections of God oblige him to observe; and it cannot be frustrated or eluded by us. The apostle seems to express this truth by a similitude taken from the order in natural things, as it were on purpose to lead us to conceive, that there is a perfect analogy between the government of the natural world, and that of the moral, as far as the natural differences of the two allow; and therefore that we ought to judge of and account for moral as for natural things. Now in nature the rule is not only, that the harvest is correspondent and proportioned to the seed-time; but that the gradual advances of things in the seed-time to matu-<11>rity in harvest, are proportioned and correspondent to the seed sown, and the culture and industry bestowed.

But this will be yet clearer, if we attend to what is said in the subsequent verses, to illustrate the general assertion, That whatsoever a man soweth, that shall he also reap. "He that soweth to his flesh, shall of the flesh reap corruption: but he that soweth to the spirit, shall reap of the spirit life everlasting."[a] For here the apostle divides mankind into two classes; or their present conduct into two different sorts of seed-time, each of which shall in a future state have its proper, natural and proportioned effect to the full. Such a division of mankind, almost in the same phrases, is common among ancient moralists. And nothing can be

a. *Gal.* vi. 8.

more just, if we rightly consider human nature. For man, as he is now
constituted and placed, in order to make nature full and coherent, is
neither a merely sensitive, nor a purely rational being; but a compound
of these two natures, strictly bound and united together. From which
constitution it plainly follows, if the end and purpose of a being may
be inferred from its frame and make, that man is made to govern his
sensitive appetites by reason, and to attain to a confirmed love of rational
pleasure above merely sensitive gratification. Now those who, neglecting
the cultivation of their rational part, are entirely immersed in sense, may
very properly be said to sow merely to the flesh, to the carnal or sensitive
part, to make provision for it only. And, on the contrary, they who give
due diligence to improve their rational faculties, to maintain the superiority of reason in their mind, to govern all their sensitive appetites by
it, and keep them in due subjection to it, and thus are endeavouring to
get the ascendant of sensual pleasures, and to establish in their minds
the sincere love of virtue and goodness; such are justly said to sow to the
spirit, to <12> sow good moral seed. But if this be the rule in God's
government, "That whatsoever one soweth, that shall he also reap"; then,
in consequence of this established order and connexion of things, it
must be true, that in a future state, in which our carnal part no longer
exists, and where we are far removed from all sensitive enjoyments, the
means and instruments of them being then quite destroyed, a neglected,
abused, prostituted, corrupted mind, quite a stranger to, and incapable
of rational exercises, and the enjoyments resulting from them, must reap
a harvest of corruption, disappointment, and anguish. And, on the other
hand, those who have given due pains to improve their minds, and prefer
virtuous exercises, and the joys these alone can give, to all merely sensitive
enjoyments, are thus naturally prepared for reaping full bliss from proper
means and occasions of exercising their well-improved moral powers,
which accordingly their harvest shall afford them: a bliss which may be
justly called, *the life everlasting of the spirit,* the proper life of rational
powers that endureth for ever. For though the compleat fruits of virtue
cannot possibly take place till virtue itself be brought by due culture to
its maturity and perfection, no more than harvest can prevent seed-time
in the natural world: yet, as in the natural seed-time things advance in

proportion to culture and industry, and the good seeds sown bringing forth their beautiful pleasant blossoms, bespeak a joyful and plentiful harvest to come in its season; so in our moral seed-time, virtue likewise advances and improves in proportion to the good seed sown, and our diligence to improve it by due culture, and brings forth its pleasant blossoms, which give great satisfaction to the virtuous mind, and plainly betoken a harvest of glorious fruits, and full happiness, to be the natural end to which it is in its progress. Accordingly the immediate fruits of virtue, that is, of rational exercises, and of right culture of the mind, are said in holy writ to be the pre-<13>sent reward of virtue; a reward far superior to what any other pursuits can give. The joy and peace of a good conscience are its present attendants; which being of a kind even with the divine felicity, redounding from no other source but his moral perfection, are to us a faint image of it, as our moral perfection is of his; and a sure infallible prognostick of the fulness of bliss, which the maturity of virtue must needs produce, when its harvest comes, but cannot possibly bring forth before that period. Every thing in nature requires culture and proper seasons to bring it to its proper perfection. And gradual improvement to moral maturity and vigour, by due labour to cultivate virtue, by making the best use one can of all the seasons and circumstances it may now be placed in, is implied in the very idea and definition of virtue. 'Tis here therefore in its state of education and trial; and the pleasures now accompanying its exercises are as natural a presage of the happiness that will arise from its perfection, when placed in circumstances fitted and proportioned to it, according to the established order and connexion of things in the moral world, as the pleasures and beauty of the spring, or of harvest advancing gradually, are of a good one to come in its due season according to the settled order of nature.

This is the plain meaning and sense of the account given by St. *Paul* in the text, of that rule adhered to by God in his government of moral beings; to think of altering, eluding, or disappointing which, is not only a gross deceit, but downright *mocking* of God; since it is a rule necessarily resulting from those moral attributes essential to God, which all his works clearly manifest to every one who will but seriously consider and take a right view of them.

Let me only add, that if this passage should be thought to relate only to charity; because the apostle is speaking immediately before of *communicating to him that teacheth in all good things;* [a] and sowing is a metaphor frequent-<14>ly used by St. *Paul,* for mens laying out their worldly goods in charitable uses: [b] yet what he adds of sowing to the flesh and to the spirit, a way of speaking common in scripture to denote the various conduct of good and bad men, and the different fruits and consequences of good and bad conduct in that future life, which is the completion of things, seems to favour our understanding it in a larger sense, which doth not render it a less proper motive to the apostle's exhortation. Nay, without taking it in that large sense, as expressing a general rule in the divine administration of moral beings, the apostle's reasoning is hardly intelligible. For how can we conceive that it is by charity alone that we can sow to the spirit, and to eternal life, unless charity be taken for the whole of virtue? Can charity supply the want of all the other virtues? May not one give largely of his worldly goods to the poor, and yet be very carnally minded? Can charitable deeds attone for a bad life? Or finally, how can we imagine, that it is mocking God, to suppose that charity shall not be rewarded by its proper fruits in a future state; and yet that it may be supposed, without mocking God, that other virtues shall not also have their own proper rewards in it by their own fruits; or that it is not repugnant to the divine perfections to imagine, this is not the general rule with regard to the conduct of moral beings in the divine government, "That whatsoever one soweth, that shall he also reap?"

But tho' this passage should not be allowed to mean such a general rule in the divine administration of moral beings, yet that rule will be found to be the plain and direct doctrine of the holy scriptures in numberless passages, and very often in the same manner of expression. [c]
<15>

a. *Gal.* vi. 6.
b. *Rom.* viii. 1, 5, 6, 10, 11, 12.
c. *Job* xxxiv. 9, 10, 11, 12, compared with *Job* iv. 8. *Prov.* i. 31. xxii. 8. xxix. 12. *Ps.* lxii. 12. *Eccles.* xii. 14. *Is.* iii. 10, 11. *Jer.* ii. 19. xvii. 10. *Mat.* x. 41, xii. 31, *&c.* xvi. 27. *Luke* xii. 47. xix. 16, 17. *Rom.* ii. 6. 1 *Cor.* iii. 8, 14. xv. 41, 58. 2 *Cor.* v. 10. 1 *Pet.* i. 17. *Rev.* ii. 23. xx. 12, 13. xxii. 11, 12.

This passage doth therefore necessarily presuppose or include in it the truth of the following propositions, each of which will appear, as we proceed, to be the express doctrine of revelation in many other places of holy writ, or a direct consequence from an express doctrine; and, at the same time, to be either demonstratively certain from the nature and course of things, and the perfections of God; or, at least, highly probable.

PROPOSITION I

Revelation supposes the existence of God, and his moral attributes, to be known and understood by those to whom it is addressed.

"For they who have not very clear and just ideas of the divine perfections, far from being able to judge whether a message can really come from him or not, cannot so much as comprehend the meaning of such a pretension."

Insomuch, that if a divine messenger should come to instruct a people quite ignorant of the Deity, he must first open their reason, and lead them gradually, by rational instruction suited to their capacity, to the knowledge of GOD, before he can deliver his message to them, and reason with them about it. The arguments to prove that an embassy is from GOD, must run in this manner. "'Tis worthy of GOD: 'tis suitable to his moral perfections: nay, it hath all the proper evidences and credentials of a divine message." But can such reasoning be understood by those who have no idea of GOD, and do not know what moral perfection, and a supreme creator and governor of the world, signify? <16> To suppose that, is the same thing in effect, as to speak of measuring without some

517

known standard or rule. This is too evident to be longer insisted upon. It is indeed by no means inconsistent to suppose a divine messenger taking pains to instruct in just notions of GOD, and the divine excellencies, that these being well understood, the divine authority he pretends to may be the more evident to those whom he would inform and influence. Nay, it is by no means absurd to imagine a person may be sent by GOD, on purpose to instruct a people plunged in darkness, and ignorance or superstition, in the knowledge of the only true GOD, his moral perfection, and the duties naturally and necessarily resulting from our relation to him, as our maker and governor, and from our relation to one another, as fellow-creatures under the same laws and administration. And such a person being invested for so excellent a purpose with very great knowledge and power, may reason in this manner, "You see, by my works, what an extensive insight I have into the nature of things, or the government of the world: this my power sufficiently evidences: this the works I do fully prove; for they are natural, full and proper samples of such very large and comprehensive knowledge. I may therefore reasonably be judged to be able to give you a true account of the government of the world, since my doctrine, far from having any hurtful tendency, hath on the contrary a very comfortable and beneficial one with regard to every man in particular, and human society in general; and since you have not the least reason to doubt of my integrity and good intention toward you, nor of my knowledge. And I do assure you, that all is made and governed, with perfect wisdom and benevolence, by one all-perfect mind, whom it is your highest excellence and happiness to know, love and imitate."

And indeed, such reasoning would be quite unexceptionable: it is strictly philosophical. For is it not <17> precisely parallel to several ways of arguing, which no man hath any scruple about? Such as this for instance: "Sir *Isaac Newton* gave full proofs of his profound skill in mathematical philosophy, and of his integrity; but he asserts, that he hath accounted for the motions of the celestial bodies by that same law of gravitation, which we know takes place in all the bodies subject to immediate experiment: and therefore we may rest assured that it is so; tho' we be not able to go through all his investigations and reasonings to prove it." Or, to give one other example, "Such a physician hath studied the medicinal art with great application; hath shewn himself to be a very humane, wise, good man; and hath given very great proofs of his skill in the science he professes: we may therefore safely rely upon him, tho' we do not understand the principles upon which physicians reason and choose their methods of treating our diseases." We reason, and must reason, in innumerable instances in this manner almost every day of our life. And indeed, such reasoning, as it cannot be admitted in one case, and rejected in another, without very unaccountable partiality; so it must be universally received, or we must absurdly say, that there can be no such thing as reasoning from samples, specimens or experiments; which philosophers, at least, must immediately see to be giving up with all real knowledge.

But tho' a divine messenger may very justly reason with the people to whom he is sent in this manner: yet it is not to be imagined that he will stop there; and not go on to tell them, that if they will attend to him, he will quickly convince them, that there are many very evident and irrefragable arguments to prove his account of the government of the world (which they have no good reason to doubt of, even as coming from him) to be true. And therefore he would certainly proceed to open and clear up their understandings gradually; and to lead them by proper steps to a <18> full conviction of his doctrine concerning God, by rational arguments, or by reasonings which will be felt to conclude necessarily by all who are made capable of attending to them. And if he should have any other message to deliver, till he hath made this first step he cannot go further; because he could not possibly be understood. It would be talking in the dark, and absolutely to no purpose.

Now, agreeably to what hath been concluded must be the conduct of a divine instructor; we find our Saviour himself, and his Apostles, frequently reasoning from supposed previous knowledge of God. We have a remarkable instance of it in the gospel of St. *Mark*,[a] "Ye err, says he, because you not only do not understand the sacred writings you have so long enjoyed, but you do not so much as understand the first principles

a. Chap. xii. ver. 24, &c.

of natural religion: you have not just conceptions of God, and his divine power." "Ye err not knowing the Scriptures, nor the power of God."

In like manner, St. *Paul* finding the *Athenians* very ignorant and superstitious, before he proceeds to deliver the christian doctrine to them, he argues with them from principles of natural religion. "Ye men of *Athens,* saith the apostle, I perceive that in all things ye are too superstitious: For as I passed by,[a] and beheld your devotions, I found an altar with this inscription, TO THE UNKNOWN GOD. Whom therefore ye ignorantly worship, him declare I unto you. God, that made the world, and all things therein, seeing that he is Lord of heaven and earth, dwelleth not in temples made with hands: neither is he worshiped with men's hands, as though he needed any thing, seeing he giveth to all life, and breath, and all things. And hath made of one blood all nations of men for to dwell on all the face of the earth, and hath determined the <19> times before appointed, and the bounds of their habitation. That they should seek the Lord, if haply they might feel after him, and find him, though he be not far from every one of us; for, in him we live, above, and have our being; as certain also of your own poets have said. For we are also his offspring. For as much then, as we are the offspring of God, we ought not to think that the God-head is like unto gold, or silver, or stone, graven by art and man's device."

So the same apostle, in several other places, as, to name no more, in the epistle to the *Galatians*. "Howbeit then when ye knew not God, ye did service unto them which by nature are no gods. But now after ye have known God, or rather are known of God, how turn ye again to the weak and beggarly elements, whereunto ye desire again to be in bondage?[b] And, in the text, the apostle, when he speaks of mocking God, plainly supposes the nature of God to be so far known by those to whom he writes, that if they would but attend to what they understood of his moral perfections, they must perceive the truth he asserts concerning the divine moral government necessarily to result from it. The author of the epistle to the *Hebrews,* tells them, "That he who comes to God, must

a. Acts of the apostles, chap. xvii ver. 22, *&c.*
b. Chap. iv. ver. 8, *&c.*

believe that he is, and that he is a rewarder of them that diligently seek him."[9]

Our Saviour reasons to the same purpose, when he says, "No man can come unto me, unless the Father who sent me draw him." And when he tells us, that those who having just notions of God, know his will, and set themselves in earnest to do it, they shall be able to discern the truth of his doctrine, its perfect agreeableness to just conceptions of God, and of the Divine will, with regard to our moral conduct; and the truth of his pretension to be sent of God to instruct us in our duty, and the way to eternal happiness.[a] <20> "No man can come to me, says Jesus Christ, except the Father which hath sent me draw him.—And again, Every man that hath learned of the Father cometh unto me."[10] The phrase, *except the Father draw him,* is, in our present manner of speaking, unusual, and therefore it appears uncouth. But it is explained by what follows, "He that hath learned of the Father." The meaning is, no man can effectually believe in Christ, or become a good christian, except he first believes in God. Natural religion is a necessary preparative for the reception of the christian. In the scripture stile, The love of truth and virtue in general is the dispensation of the Father; and The doctrine of the gospel in particular is the dispensation of the Son. Now, as no man can be a good *christian,* who is not first resolved to be a good man; so no one can listen to, understand or judge of revelation, till he hath just apprehensions of the God from whom it pretends to come. That knowing the Father, in the stile of the Scriptures means, the knowledge of the principles of natural religion and morality, is plain from what our Lord says. "And these things will they do unto you, because they have not known the Father nor me."[b] That is, they have no true sense either of natural religion or revealed.

It is in this sense, that "wisdom is said to be justified of her children."[c]

a. St. John vii. 17.
b. John xvi. 3.
c. Luke vii. 35.
9. Heb. 11.6.
10. John 6.44, 45.

That is, those who are wise, having just notions of virtue and God, or of the essential differences between good and evil, will easily discern a wise and good doctrine from a corrupt, foolish and vicious one, and will render justice to that which they know and understand to be true wisdom. But such alone are capable of distinguishing truth from falshood, or wisdom from folly; for such alone have in them the well improved judgment by which only the distinction can be apprehended. They alone have the rule by which the matter must be tried and measured. <21>

PROPOSITION II

The existence of one infinitely powerful, wise and good mind, the Author, creator, upholder and governor of all things, is a truth that lies plain and obvious to all who will but think.

Many very evident arguments prove it, I shall only mention one, and illustrate it. "There must be in nature actually existing some being, the original fountain of all derived power, whose power is underived; or all power is derived from nothing. But an original, uncreated, independent mind, the author, upholder and ruler of that system, of which mankind make a part, must be perfectly wise and good; otherwise the order that prevails in the world, and our capacity of discerning it, and aptitude to delight in it, must either be blindly or maliciously produced. Both which suppositions are equally absurd."

This argument consists of two parts, which must be considered separately.

I. There must be in nature actually existing some being, who is the primary or original fountain of derived power, whose power is underived, or all the power which operates in nature is derived from nothing.

That there is productive power in nature will not be denied; since we ourselves, who begin to exist, are the effect of such power; and many other things are daily brought into being, which did not exist before. But what is it that we call power, efficiency, or productive energy? Tho' in common language, we speak of the powers of matter; yet not only do all philosophers know <22> and acknowledge that matter is absolutely inactive; but every one may perceive it. For did ever matter of itself change its state, whether of motion or rest, without some cause, to which the change is exactly proportioned? Space, in like manner, is clearly perceived, and therefore universally owned to be passive, inert and immoveable. All our ideas are also no less evidently quite passive perceptions, which have no activity, or can produce nothing. Indeed, properly speaking, what we call matter and space, are but certain orders of sensible ideas produced in us, according to established rules of nature by some external cause; for when we speak of material effects and of space, we only mean, and can indeed only mean, certain sensible perceptions excited in our mind according to a certain order, which are experienced to be absolutely inert and passive, and to have no productive force. But to wave all dispute about the existence of an external material world unperceived by us, and in itself absolutely unperceiveable, as all philosophers acknowledge, and with which of course we have nothing to do; it is obvious, that we have no notion, nor can have none by experience of any thing that is active, besides will. For when we experience ourselves to produce any effect, it is by a volition; *i.e.* by an exercise or act of our will to give it existence, that we do it. To produce, is to give being to a thing; and we can only bring things into being by our will to do it. It is therefore will alone that produces, hath power or productive energy. From which it plainly and necessarily follows, that whatever is produced, is produced by some being or principle capable of willing that effect to exist, and between whose volition that it should be produced, and its actual existence, there is a connexion. But there is, there can be no volition without consciousness. And therefore all power belongs to mind: or nothing is powerful but a mind, or a principle of intelligence capable of giving existence to certain ef-<23>fects, by its volition that they should be produced. We ourselves have power, or call ourselves active in no other sense and we cannot pronounce any other being active, but in that sense alone. To speak of any other activity and power, is to speak without any meaning at all. Because experience, the only source of all our ideas, (the materials of our knowledge) does not, cannot lead us to any other conception or idea of power. Blind, unthinking, unin-

telligent, unconscious power, are terms which either have no signification at all; or include an express contradiction.

Thus therefore it is evident, "That whatever operates, acts, hath
power, or produces in nature, is an intelligent conscious principle, capable of willing, and of giving existence to effects by willing their existence, which kind of principle we shall henceforth, for brevity's sake,
conformably to common language, call in one word, *mind.*"

II. But as we immediately feel and experience, that whatever we give
existence to, we give it to it by an act of our will; so we no less immediately feel and experience that our power of producing is very limited,
and that it is derived and dependent. We experience, that our existence
and all our faculties are derived and dependent; and that the connexion
between the existence of effects produced by our will, and our will to
produce them, is not a connexion of our making, or any way subject to
our power: it is therefore a connexion established, that is, willed by some
other being, by some other mind; the same without all doubt to whom
we owe our existence and all our faculties. For to suppose we have derived
our faculty of willing from one mind; and that the connexion between
our will, and certain effects made dependent on it, is established by some
other distinct mind, is very absurd. 'Tis indeed to multiply causes, not
only without any reason, but contrary <24> to all reason. For what can
be more ridiculous or at least more unnecessary, than to attribute our
faculty of willing to one cause, and its power or efficiency to another?
But however that be, the connexion between our will, and the production of any effects whatsoever, which are found by experience to depend
upon our will, as to their existence or non-existence, being evidently
perceived to be an established, derived connexion, by no means of our
own institution or making, because nowise subject to us, or dependent
on us; it must have some institutor or establisher: it must be appointed
and willed by some principle sufficient to produce and establish it; which
principle, it is evident from what hath been just now laid down, must
be a mind.

III. But now how far can we go on and say this and this power is
derived; or the connexion between this and this willing principle and its
effects is derived? Can we say so for ever or to infinity? Are all the con-

nexions in nature between will and effects of this kind? Is every power and principle of power that operates a derived one? Can we say, we are arrived at a real source of derived power, till we are come to some principle, whose power is uncreated, underived, or which never began to be? If there be not really existing in nature some one really sufficient principle of derived power, then is all derived power derived from nothing. But what is derived cannot be an original source of power. There is therefore, in nature, actually existing a primary source or principle, whence derived power proceeds, and whose power is itself unproduced, necessarily existent, and absolutely independent: that is, a source of power between whose will to give existence to the effects brought into being by it, and their production or existence, there is a connexion that cannot but obtain; and therefore is as necessary as the connexion between one property of a triangle, and any <25> other of its essential, unalterable properties: a connexion, which it is as impossible should not take place, as it is impossible that all the angles of a triangle should not be equal to two right angles. 'Tis in vain to say, that because we experience no connexion between will and its effects, but a connexion derived, and consequently instituted by some mind different from ours, that therefore to speak of an underived connexion, is to utter words beyond our ideas, and without any meaning. For knowing what it is to be derived or established by some will, surely we can say with meaning, *negatively,* that a connexion is not such; knowing what it is to be impossible or contradictory, we can say with a meaning, not only that it is impossible or a contradiction to suppose all power derived; but likewise that there must be a principle of power in nature of such a kind, that there must necessarily be a contradiction in affirming that its efficiency is produced or established by any other mind; and no less a contradiction in affirming that the connexion between such will and its effects, is not as absolutely necessary in itself and of itself, that is, in the very nature of the thing, as the connexion between any two properties mutually involved in one another, or essentially and immutably connected together, is necessary.

"There is therefore, in nature, some one underived, unlimited, independent source of the derived powers in nature, which operate and produce by an established appointed connexion, independent of them."

IV. Now how many such minds may exist in nature, is certainly a very idle question. But, which is of much greater consequence to us, it is a very clear point, that the author of the same system can be but one. We are evidently a part of a system related to our earth and all its other inhabitants, which earth is but one of several planets that revolve about the same cen-<26>tral sun, from which they all receive light and heat, according to the same laws, the same centripetal and centrifugal forces. But however large or small a system may be, it can have but one author, contriver, establisher, upholder and governor, because it is as such one effect, and one effect cannot be produced by several independent wills, each of which is sufficient to produce it, or between each of which and its existence there is a necessary connexion; for this plain reason, that the same effect cannot be produced twice totally and independently. If it is said, but may not two or more independent wills make in nature but one cause or producer? Should it not be replied, that this is a very un-philosophical question? For what can be more so, than to multiply causes without any reason, or when all may be accounted for by one? But which is more, two or more independent wills, which make in nature but one cause, are to all intents and purposes, in respect of the effects or system of effects produced by such wills, but one individual cause; for by the supposal, neither of them being separately sufficient to produce the ef-fect; the sufficiency to produce it is really the result of the two concurring wills: or, in other words, it is the concurrence of such wills that consti-tutes the efficiency, and makes the cause.

And after all, what, if it be not a direct contradiction in terms, ap-proaches nearer to one, than to speak of an efficiency to produce, re-sulting from the concurrence of two or more independent necessarily existent principles? For if a principle, having power, be independent, is not its power independent? And how can independent power depend as to its efficiency upon the concurrence of another distinct will in itself also independent of it?

"There is then of that system of which we are a part, one independent author."

Now this being proved, it remains, in the second place, to confirm the truth of the other branch of our <27> argument; namely, "That an original independent mind cannot be void of all notions of general order and good, or having them, be malicious, otherwise the order that prevails in nature, and our capacity of perceiving order, and our aptitude to delight in it, are either blindly or maliciously produced."

That there is order in nature, is not only acknowledged by philosophers, who all agree, that the more accurately we search into the government of all things within our observation, the more and clearer proofs we find of good order, and wise benevolent administration: But it is evident to every one who can think at all. For do not the seasons, the sun, moon, and stars observe their regular courses appointed to them? Is not man fearfully and wonderfully made and preserved? Or what animal, or even vegetable, is not framed with marvellous skill, and does not shew counsel and design to bring about a very good end by most astonishing methods? In one word, the slightest review of the works of nature must convince every one, that there is design and order throughout all nature, good intention, and wise management to effectuate a generous purpose every where in the minutest as well the largest objects, which it is truly delightful to behold, observe, and contemplate. But whence this order, or whence is it that we are capable of discerning order and design, generous intention and good administration, or management, in bringing about a good end by the simplest methods; and of being so highly pleased with the contemplation of beauty, order, and benevolent design, that nothing almost is capable of taking us off from that pleasant reflexion, while our mind is intent upon it, or of giving us half so much satisfaction? Whence is this; or whence indeed can it be, but from our original make? No other answer can be given to this question; but that we are so framed, or that our Maker hath so constituted us and things. Now can we suppose our creator to have < 28 > so formed us either blindly or maliciously? To say, he hath so formed us and things, without having himself any ideas of order, design, good and simple, frugal, wise, generous management, is to assert he hath done it blindly. For could he be imagined to operate without consciousness or intelligence, if he so operates and produces any effect, he produces it without design, without any notion of it, *i.e.* blindly.

And to say, he hath done it with intelligence, not maliciously, is to

assert, that the noblest, the most usefull, the most delightful faculty we
have, or can have any notion of, that capacity and disposition from which
we receive our highest and pleasantest entertainments, and without
which we would be very low and groveling creatures, is implanted in our
minds by a disposition quite opposite to such a make and temper, and
which, where it takes place, naturally intends evil and misery, and not
good and perfection.

To all this we may justly add, that a first independent mind cannot
possibly have any interest distinct from, much less contrary to the general
good of its creation; and therefore it cannot be evil, or be provoked to
be such: it can have nothing to irritate, fret, disquiet, or discontent it: it
can therefore have no malice; but must be in its temper as remote from
all cruelty and barbarity, as it is with respect to its natural powers from
all limitation, confinement, restraint, compulsion, or contradiction.

"There is therefore one universal independent mind, the author of
mankind, and of the whole system of which man is a part, which mind,
far from being ungenerously disposed, must be perfect in goodness as
well as in intelligence and power." His intelligence must reach as far as
his power; for all power is intelligent; and his power being independent,
his temper must be infinitely above all temptation to cruelty: it must
therefore be perfectly benign and generous. And as for our capacity of
perceiving order, general <29> laws, and publick good, and our natural
disposition to rejoyce and delight in it, which is our great excellence, and
the principal foundation of our happiness, as he could not have formed
such a power and disposition in us blindly; so far less could he have done
it maliciously, unless the best of gifts can come from malignity and bad-
will.

"The original independent creator and governor of our system is
therefore infinitely good."

Now this is the very idea the sacred writings give us of God; and of
the plain, full, and clear evidence, all that falls within our observation,
if but attended to, carries with it, of the divine existence and perfection.

How well is all the preceeding reasoning about a first cause, its independent power, and its infinite benignity expressed in the book of

wisdom,[a] "The Lord made all things by his word: therefore the whole world before him is as a little grain of the balance, yea as a drop of the morning dew. He can shew his great strength when he will, and who may withstand the power of his arm. But he hath mercy upon all, for he can do all things, and winketh at the sins of men, because they should amend. *He loveth all the things that are, and abhorreth nothing that he hath made: for never would he have made any thing if he had hated it.* And how could any thing have been or endured, if it had not been his will; or been preserved, if not by his word. But thou sparest all, O Lord: for they are thine, O thou lover of souls." And how strongly doth he plead against those who are not able to discern the perfections of God in his works, but worship the works of his hands; or which is yet more absurd, of their own hands? "Surely vain are all men who are ignorant of God, and could not out of the good things that are seen, know him that is: neither by considering the works did they acknowledge the work-master. <30> But deemed either fire or wind, or the swift air, or the circle of the stars, or the violent water, or the lights of heaven to be the Gods which govern the world, with whose beauty, if they being delighted; took them to be gods; let them know how much better the Lord of them is: *for the first author of beauty hath created them.* But if they were astonished at their power and virtue, let them understand by them, how much mightier he is that made them. For by the greatness and beauty of the creatures, proportionally the Maker of them is seen." What follows against idolatry, and the account of its rise and progress in the world, is exceeding remarkable.

St. *Paul* speaking of the heathen not favoured with revelation says, "That which may be known of God is manifest in them, for God hath shewed it unto them. For the invisible things of him from the creation of the world are clearly seen, being understood by the things that are made; even his eternal power and God-head; so that they are without excuse. Because that when they knew God, they glorified him not as God, neither were thankful, but became vain in their imaginations, and

a. Chap. ix. x. xi. xiii.

their foolish heart was darkened, professing themselves wise they became fools, and changed the glory of the incorruptible God into an image made like to corruptible man, and to birds, and to four-footed beasts, and creeping things. Wherefore God also gave them up to uncleanness, through the lusts of their own hearts, to dishonour their own bodies between themselves. Who changed the truth of God into a lie, and worshipped and served the creature more than the creator, who is blessed for ever, *Amen.*" [a]

The meaning of which reasoning is, that God hath every where given such a clear manifestation of his existence, perfections, and providence, that his divine <31> nature, eternal power, wisdom and goodness may be clearly discovered and understood from the visible beauty, order, and benevolence observable in the constitution and government of the universe, and in all the laws and causes by which all effects are produced in it, by all those who would turn and apply their minds attentively that way (νουμενα καθοραται, if they are minded they are seen) insomuch that every one who is ignorant of God, is absolutely without excuse. And much more are they so, who having such just notions of God as his works naturally lead to, yet glorified him not as God, or suitably to his excellency; nor with due thankfulness acknowledged him as the author of their being, and the giver of all the good they enjoyed; but following the foolish fancies of their own vain minds, set up to themselves fictitious gods, till by such absurd, superstitious practices their understandings were quite darkened. For vice long indulged, renders the understanding first unwilling, and then unable to behold the light. And their understandings being thus corrupted and perverted by evil affections and habits, assuming to themselves the opinion and name of being wise, they became fools; and quitting the incomprehensible majesty and glory of the eternal incorruptible Deity, set up to themselves the images of corruptible man, birds, beasts, and insects, as fit objects of their adoration and worship. Wherefore they, having forsaken God, the God within them, reason, the voice of the true God, that easily leads those who duly exercise and cultivate it to the knowledge of the true God, went from

a. *Rom.* i. 19, &c.

worse to worse, from one vice to another, till the grossest of crimes were no longer monstrous in their sight, but gave them pleasure. He who abandons reason, and consequently God, is precipitated from vice to vice, and soon becomes a reproach to human nature, made for moral perfection, because made capable of forming just notions of it, and of delighting in it, and pur-<32>suing it by the proper means of right culture and exercise, by which alone it can be attained.

Need I stay to put those in mind who are acquainted with their bibles, that God, the creator of the universe, who is emphatically called in scripture the Father of rational beings or spirits, because for them chiefly was an inanimate world created, is said to be a spirit, and said to be omnipotent, all-powerful, and to have made and to govern all things with perfect wisdom and goodness, and therefore to be the only object of our adoration, and to be the model of moral perfection, after which we ought to endeavour to *perfect ourselves?*[a] And what is it that proves and clearly manifests all this, according to the scripture, but his works? The heavens declare his glory; the firmament sheweth forth his praise,[b] the earth is full of the works of his goodness; all things praise him. Man in particular, according to the sacred writings, being created after the image of God; crowned by him with glory and honour, and invested with a very considerable power and dominion by his reason, fully shews forth the perfection of him who made him.[c] The living God, said *Paul* and *Barnabas*[d] with a joint voice, who made heaven and earth, sea and all things therein, though he hath suffered the nations to walk in their own ways; nevertheless, he left not himself without witness, in that he did good, and gave us rain from heaven, and fruitful seasons, filling our hearts with food and gladness.

'Tis to the manifest tokens of perfect wisdom and goodness, as well as of power, clearly stamped upon all the works of creation, which must have a creator, and be the copy of his mind and character, that the appeal

a. *Matt.* v. 48.
b. *Ps.* xix.
c. *Ps.* viii. 5, 6.
d. *Acts* xiv. 15–17.

is solely and constantly made, in the sacred writings, to prove the providence of an all-perfect mind. To this purpose doth the holy scripture reason in several <33> places, "Understand ye brutish among the people: and ye fools when will ye be wise? He that planted the ear shall he not hear? He that formed the eye shall he not see?" He who endowed us with senses to discern good and evil, with reason, with benevolence, and generous affection, is he not intelligent, good, and benevolent? Whence else could he have copied those excellencies which being bestowed upon us by him, constitute the dignity of our nature, and render us indeed the *image* of a creator, who is perfect reason and virtue? This, I say, is the plain meaning of many places in holy writ, and therefore I shall only add a noble account given of God in the book of *Ecclesiasticus*,[a] "we may speak much and yet come short: *wherefore in sum he is all.* How shall we be able to magnify him? For he is great above all his works. The Lord is full of majesty, and very great and marvellous in his power. When you glorify the Lord, exalt as much as you can: for even yet will he far exceed: and when ye exalt him, put forth all your strength and be not weary, for you can never go far enough. Who hath seen him that he might tell us? And who can magnify him as he is? There are hid yet greater things than these be we see, for we have but seen a few of his works. For the Lord hath made all things, and to the godly hath he given wisdom."

Before we leave this proposition, it is not improper to observe that nothing can be more absurd than the doctrine which has sometimes been advanced; that goodness in God is not the same as goodness in men, but something of quite another kind, and which we understand not. This is highly absurd: because were this true, it would plainly follow, we could have no notion, no knowledge of God at all: we should in that case, when we pronounce God wise, just and good, <34> only affirm we know not what, *i.e.* nothing at all. There must be indeed this difference, that goodness, even in the best of men, is short, imperfect, and mutable; whereas in God, and in him alone, it is essential, and incorruptibly or unchangeably perfect. But still the quality is every where of the same nature or kind, though not in the same degree or proportion. The true

a. *Eccles.* xliii. 29–37.

notion therefore of the divine benevolence must be learned by considering what it is in man. And by augmenting the idea of a good man to boundless perfection, we arrive at the nearest conception that is possible for us to frame of the goodness of an all-perfect mind. Thus our Saviour teaches us to argue and ascend in our notions of goodness. "If ye then being evil, know how to give good gifts unto your children; how much more shall your father which is in heaven give good things to them who ask him."[a] All the perfections of the Deity, *i.e.* all his moral perfections, may be reduced to this one, perfect benevolence; for it comprehends in it perfect wisdom and perfect justice, truth, and veracity, and every other moral excellence. And it is that beneficent disposition of the divine nature, which inclines and moves him to diffuse upon all his creatures, through the immense universe, and through a boundless eternity to the uttermost stretch of infinite power, every good thing that is proper for them; every thing that tends to their true happiness; every good, which either they are in their own nature capable of receiving, or which for him, in his all-wise administration of the whole for the greater good, is fit and reasonable to give. Accordingly St. *John* more than once comprehends all the divine perfections in this one comprehensive expression, *God is love;* and all the duties of man, conformably to this account of the divine excellence, in *love or benevolence.*[b] Nay, our Saviour himself often gives us this <35> concise character of God, "There is none good but one, that is God."

Proposition III

If the author and governor of all things be infinitely perfect, then, whatever is, is right; of all possible systems he hath chosen the best, and consequently there is no absolute evil in the universe.

This proposition is obviously so necessary a consequence from what hath been proved concerning the moral perfection of the supreme cause, that it does not stand in need of any arguments to prove its truth.

a. *Matt.* vii. 11.
b. 2 John ver. 6.

"The creation of an all-perfect mind must be the image of its creator; and therefore it must be perfect, it must be chosen by his infinite wisdom and goodness as the most perfect system, that is, the system in which the greatest quantity of happiness and perfection obtain, that can in the nature of things take place; and this being the case, all the seeming imperfections or evils in it, are such only in a partial view; and with respect to the whole system, they are goods; that is, they are absolutely necessary to its greater good, the end of its creation by an infinitely good being, who could have been disposed to create it by no other motive but pure goodness, or in order to communicate as much happiness as he can to creatures, and to be himself infinitely happy in so doing."

To suppose us, who are made capable of acting with intelligence and choice, made by a being who acts either blindly, or without choice, is to assert, that we are more perfect than our Maker, or that we are endowed with a perfection, which if he hath not, he could not possibly have any idea of; than which, as hath been already observed, nothing can be more absurd. Our Creator therefore, who must likewise be the Creator of all things which constitute the same system, and conse-<36>quently of all within our observation, acts with intelligence, from choice and uncompelled unnecessitated affection, towards the greater good of the whole. We are so made, as to be capable of deliberating and performing, of being directed by knowledge; of being guided, or more properly speaking, of guiding and conducting ourselves by reason. But in being determined by motives, or guided by our understanding and judgment, we experience no force, no necessity, nor any thing in any degree analogous or similar to it. The whole operation or influence of motives upon our understanding, or in exciting affections in us, we experience, may very properly be expressed by *perswasion;* which we feel by consciousness to be as distinct from necessity, violence, or compulsion of every sort, as any two things can possibly be.

Wherefore, if we keep to experience, and reason agreeably to it, we must conclude, that our Maker, who hath thus framed us, acts in like manner with intelligence and preference, through the perswasive influence of his just and adequate views of the results of all possible orders and connexions of things; for he cannot want a perfection he hath given to us, which constitutes all our dignity and excellence, because it renders us capable of merit, and consequently of praise, and thus far exalts us above animals, which do not reason and choose. The author of nature therefore hath produced his creation with intelligence and free choice, through the perswasive influence of his full knowledge of its being the best system that could possibly be produced; the richest with good, the fullest of perfection and happiness. As he cannot possibly experience any restraint or compulsion from without, being absolutely independent; so he cannot experience any necessity or compulsion within, contrary to free choice and voluntary self-approving *affection* towards the greater good of his creatures. <37>

All this is as manifest, as it is that we are free agents (to doubt of which we must first doubt of our inward consciousness, from which scepticism there is no possible way of recovery): and that being such, is a perfection which could not have been conferred on us by a creator not free, since being supposed not free, he must necessarily be supposed to have no idea of freedom, and consequently to be incapable of giving it. "We may therefore rest assured that the greater good of the system of which we are a part, is intended and pursued by its author with perfect free choice, and from purely benevolent liking of the universal good."

Whence then comes evil, is the question that hath in all ages been reckoned the *gordian knot* in philosophy? And indeed if we own the existence of evil in the world in an absolute sense, we diametrically contradict what hath been just now proved of God. For if there be any evil in the system that is not good with respect to the whole, then is the whole not good, but evil, or at best very imperfect: and an author must be as his workmanship is. "As is the effect such is the cause." But the solution to this difficulty is at hand, namely, "That there is no evil in the universe." What! are there no pains, no imperfections? Is there no misery, no vice in the world! Or are not these evils? Evils indeed they are: that is, those of the one sort are hurtful, and those of the other sort are equally hurtful and abominable. But they are not evil or mischievous with respect to the whole; for they are the result of powers, and general laws of powers, the uniform uninterrupted operation of which produces the greater good and perfection of the whole. But what is such, is not evil, but good, with regard to the universal system. Because if it be necessary to the greater good of a system that certain laws obtain universally; it is necessary to the greater good of that system, that all the effects of the constant uniform operation of such laws take place; which is in other words <38> to say, that all the operations, effects, or consequences of good general laws are, absolutely considered, goods, whatever they may be in certain particular limited respects.

God hath chosen the best of all possible systems, because it is the best: such therefore is the nature of things, that there can be no system without partial evils, but the best general laws must, by their constant uniform operation, often produce evils. The evils in our system are not evils with respect to the whole; that is inconsistent with the infinite perfection of the chooser and creator. Wherefore the evils in it are not chosen or permitted for their own sake. But they are chosen, or more properly speaking, permitted, because the laws, from the constant and uninterrupted operation of which they flow, are requisite to the greater good and perfection of the system. *Leibnitz,* in my opinion, makes a very proper distinction in the school-language, between the *antecedent* and the *consequential* will of God.[11] The general laws of a system produced by a good creator are established for the sake of the greater good in the whole they produce; they are therefore established for their own sake, or on account of their own excellence and fitness, by the *antecedent will of God.* But the evils are only *consequential effects* of that will; because they are there only, as they are consequences of the general operation of the good laws which render the system perfect. The error of that great genius consists in his saying most unphilosophically, that God could not do otherwise than he hath done; for God always had and has immutably the physical power of making all possible systems: and he gave existence to the system produced by him with perfectly free choice. But this error proceeds from his ascribing to the motives which determine rational beings in their

11. Gottfried Wilhelm Leibniz, *Monadology* sect. 90, in his *Monadology and Other Philosophical Writings,* trans. Robert Latta (Oxford: Clarendon Press, 1898). The scholastic locus classicus for the distinction is Aquinas, *Summa Theologiae* 1, 19, 6 ad 1.

choices a necessary influence which we do not experience, and that cannot possibly belong to motives, which being judgments <39> or perceptions, must therefore, like all other perceptions, be inert and passive things, and consequently can have no productive energy. While we keep to experience, and use words in a determinate, clear sense, as philosophers ought to do; we must, and ever will distinguish between perswasive influence, or directing light and force, compulsion, necessity, and every thing analogous or like to them. But not to enter farther at this time into a controversy, which is become so palpable a *logomachy*, by deserting common language; or at least by confounding words of very different meanings, and by seeking other proofs, besides experience of what experience alone can ascertain; let us consider whether what must be inferred concerning the evils permitted to take place in a system created by an infinitely good being, in consequence of its being the production of such a being, may not be deduced from any other distinct considerations.

It may seem at first sight a very odd assertion to affirm, that there can be no orders or connexions of created beings in which evils will not be the product of certain methods of action. But we ought, as is universally allowed, to reason agreeably to experience and analogy. And it is plain that we can conceive no orders or connexions of things constituting a state proper for free agents to live and act in, in which different choices and actions are not connected with different fruits or consequences, *i.e.* in which as certain actions will produce pleasure and happiness, so other actions will produce pain, suffering and misery. If we allow ourselves to consider matters accurately, it will evidently appear, that the reverse of a method or fixed order, by which pleasure is produced, must necessarily be a method by which pain cannot but be produced. And it is impossible that a being, whether of a different bodily organization, or of a different mental structure from another being, can receive pleasure in the same way, or according to the same order with that other. But as it is fit that there should be <40> variety of beings, so it is fit that there should be methods by which all the different beings in the same system may have pleasure. For thus only can nature be a full manifestation of infinite power, wisdom, and goodness: thus only can there actually be in nature a great diversity of powers, perfections, and happiness. And to a state of agents, capable of improving themselves, and whose happiness is dependent on themselves, in order to its being their own acquisition, that they may have double satisfaction in it as such, it is absolutely requisite that there be connexions productive of pain, and connexions productive of pleasure. Such a constitution of things is included in the very notion of beings made and placed to improve themselves, and to make themselves happy by so doing. Such a state cannot subsist, unless different choices and pursuits have absolutely different effects and consequences: unless the right culture of the mind, and its rational powers, and the abuse or corruption of them have very opposite effects with regard to happiness or misery. All this is implied in the very idea of an active being.

Thus then we see, that as it is a contradiction to suppose an infinitely perfect mind not to choose the best possible system, so the existence of evils in a system is far from being incompatible with a perfect system, and an all-perfect author, contriver and ruler. And indeed this important truth will be yet more plain, if, having distinctly classed in our minds the evils complained of in nature, into physical and moral, we reflect, "1. That there could be no moral evil, unless certain affections, and the actions excited to by them, had hurtful effects, either within or without the mind." "2. And that as all physical evils, properly so called, in our system, are evidently the effects of the general operation of such universal laws as are necessary to the greater good of our system; so moral evils, which have such pernicious consequences within and without us, are deviations from the good order we are sufficient-<41>ly directed and enabled to pursue; misguidances of affections necessary to our dignity and happiness, against which we are sufficiently forwarned." "3. That reason cannot, in the nature of things, improve, but in proportion to culture, and yet, while it is necessarily weak for want of culture, as it must be for some time, we are furnished with excellent instincts or determinations to point and prompt us right." "4. And that our capacity of acting by free choice, and of guiding ourselves, is a priviledge which so ennobles and exalts us above all merely perceptive beings, that it must needs be an excellent constitution by which it is established as a rule, that this our rational power and freedom shall not be encroached upon, thwarted, opposed, or counteracted." If, I say, we consider all these things which necessarily hang together, not separately, but in one united view, we shall quickly see that when we complain of the government of the world, on account of the evils prevailing in it, we foolishly demand absurdities, or ask we know not what.

But all this having been fully considered in the *Principles of Moral Philosophy*, let us proceed to enquire, what revelation teaches with regard to this article. Now the freedom and disinterested benevolence of the supreme author of the universe being so plainly asserted in the texts that have been already quoted, it is not necessary to repeat them, or mention any others. Freedom is necessarily involved in the very notion of benevolence. It is therefore sufficient to observe, 1. That according to the Mosaick account of the creation, God having created the world, and established the general laws, [a] constituting its order and course, and from which all effects in it proceed, pronounced the whole work good, that is, perfect. 2. And the scripture [b] is full of delightful hymns in praise of the wisdom and goodness of the creation. "How <42> manifold, O Lord, are thy works, and they praise thee!" According to all the books of the old testament, all God's works of creation and providence shew forth the marvels of his wisdom, and the boundless perfection of his goodness, as well as of his power. And the new testament runs in the same strain. "The visible things of the creation, all things that are made, shew forth and declare his invisible power and godhead. There is none good but God, and all his works praise him." The inanimate creation, but yet more the constitutions of various orders of moral beings, angels, seraphims, and archangels, praise him. And man, though made lower than angels, is his image, being crowned with glory and honour by him, that is, with immortal rational powers fitted to attain to a very noble end, a very high degree of perfection and happiness. 3. But he is at the same time said to create evil, darkness, confusion, and yet to do no evil, but to be author of good only. He is called the father of light, the author

a. *Gen.* i. 31.
b. *Ps.* xix. *Ps.* viii. 1 *Chron.* xxix. 11, 12. *Nehem.* ix. 5, 6.

of every perfect and good gift, with whom there is no variableness, nor shadow of turning, who tempteth no man, but giveth to all men liberally, and upbraideth not.[a] And yet by the prophet *Isaias*[b] he is introduced saying of himself, "I form the light and create darkness, I make peace and create evil, I the Lord do all these things." What then is the meaning, the plain language of all this, but that the Lord *delighteth in goodness,* and as the Scripture speaks, *evil is his strange work?* He intends and pursues the universal good of his creation; and the evil which happens is not permitted for its own sake, or through any pleasure in evil, but because it is requisite to the greater good pursued. 4. Physical evils resulting from the general operation of those general laws, which constitute the course of nature, or the material world, are not evils, since, according to <43> the scripture, that order is perfectly wise and good; and every thing obeys the laws, the commandments, the ordinances God hath appointed to them, all which are chosen and established with perfect wisdom and goodness. All things, in the scripture stile, obey his voice, his commandment, his law, and word. That hymn to the Creator in the book of *Ecclesiasticus,*[c] is full of beauties; but two or three expressions in it are exceeding remarkable. "A man need not say, What is this? Wherefore is that? For he hath made all things for their uses. All the works of the Lord are good, and he will give every needful thing in due season. So that a man cannot say this is worse than that; for in time they shall all be well approved." 5. And as for moral evils, whence come they, according to St. *James,*[d] come they not hence, even of our lusts that war in our members? "Blessed is the man that endureth temptation, saith the same apostle,[e] for when he is tried he shall receive the crown of life, which the Lord hath promised to them that love him. Let no man say when he is tempted, I am tempted of God; for God cannot be tempted with evil, neither tempteth he any man. But every man is tempted, when he is

a. *James* i. 5.
b. *Isaiah* xlv. 7. *Amos* iii. 6.
c. Chap. xxxix.
d. Chap. iv. 1.
e. Chap. i. 12–17.

drawn away of his own lust, and enticed. Then when lust hath conceived, it bringeth forth sin; and sin when it is finished, bringeth forth
death. Do not err, my beloved brethren, every good gift, and every perfect gift is from above, and cometh down from the Father of lights." The
meaning of which discourse in other words, is plainly this: Circumstances tempting to sin occur in the world; but by these virtue is tried
and improved, and by overcoming them it gains strength, and merits a
great reward, it becomes thus fit for that glorious after state prepared for
the good and virtuous. But it is a vile and dangerous deceit, to be carefully
guarded against, to imagine that <44> when a man is invited or inticed
to sin of any kind by the circumstances he is placed in, even those which
he could not foresee, or foreseeing prevent, he is tempted of God: as
God cannot be tempted to evil; as no evil affection can possibly enter
into, or be excited in the divine mind; so for that very reason it is plain
he can never be disposed to tempt man or sollicite them to sin; nor is
indeed a man tempted by any suggestions or motions, but those which
ungoverned lusts raise in his mind, reason being unconsulted, lulled
asleep, or willfully resisted and contradicted. It is thus that evil motions
spring up in the mind, and those are the sources of all our deviations
from the laws of moral rectitude, which not only our reason clearly discovers to us, but which we cannot, till we be hardened and rendered
callous by evil habits, counteract, without feeling a strong resistance, and
a very violent struggling; without a war between our reason and our sensitive appetites, those members of which we are composed. Let us beware
of this error. For God is the author of every perfect gift; and the Father
of lights hath placed a light within us, sufficient to direct us into the
right path, and hath given us all the powers and faculties requisite to our
becoming like our Father, and to preserve us free from sin, which, when
it is finished, bringeth forth death; to preserve us from sin, the wages of
which is death; from sin, which must result in the total depravation of
our rational nature, and proportioned unhappiness.

But why then is it so often said, especially in the books of the *Old
Testament,* that he is surrounded with darkness, or that his ways are a
dark intricate maze? For that must be the meaning of such phrases, as
clouds of darkness encompass him, *&c.* Now to this the answer is evi-

dent, the scheme of providence will justify itself to us as it advances; it is not yet complete; and even of what is, we have but an imperfect view; and therefore it is no wonder, if we are not able to account <45> for every thing. This is the necessary effect of having but a narrow, partial view of a system: it cannot but be so. This is the scripture-answer to the difficulty. "Here we are as children: we know but little: we see but darkly as through a glass."ª And that it is a sufficient answer is plain: for since the further we are able to advance in the knowledge of God's works, the more we see of wisdom and goodness in his administration, to what else is it reasonable to ascribe our doubts and perplexities about any effects, but to our ignorance, or narrow views? 'Tis not very long since the works of nature might very justly have been said to have been involved in utter darkness with regard to us. But by the late improvements made in natural philosophy, in consequence of pursuing it in the only way of coming at real knowledge, what innumerable instances are discovered to us of perfect contrivance, and the wisest and best order? Have we not then good reason to conclude, that in proportion as we improve in the knowledge of God's works, natural or moral, by searching diligently into them, we shall still find better and better ground to say, with all the writers of the sacred books, "In wisdom hast thou, O Lord, made all things." But if this be intelligible language, it is certainly intelligible to say, that in a future state, when the scheme of providence is further advanced; our faculties are more enlarged in consequence of due culture here; and we are placed in such a situation as will afford us a larger view of God's works than we can have here; that then we shall be more fully satisfied about the wisdom and goodness of the divine administration than the largest knowledge attainable here can make us.

Let me only add upon this head, that there can hardly be a more absurd doctrine than that advanced by some; teaching, "That things are right, merely because they are chosen, established or willed by God." For according to such a doctrine, it was all one what God appointed to be; any one order of things, how-<46>ever different from the present, had it been established, would have been equally good, equally perfect. The

a. *Job* xxvi. 14. 1 *Cor.* xiii. 11–12.

asserters of this most absurd doctrine, seem to be led to it thro' an apprehension, that to say otherwise, is to suppose some limitation on God's independent power. But must we then deny the moral perfections of God, in order to secure to him his natural ones? Or, is power limited, because it is directed not by another, but by wisdom and goodness, as essential to the being itself who works, as his power by which he works? "If absolute sovereignty or power, saith an excellent writer,[a] could suffice, as some sects of men have imagined, to make such a thing, for example, as *absolute reprobation* become good, it would follow, that the word *goodness* had no signification at all, and consequently, that it was neither in itself of any importance, nor of any consequence to us, whether the almighty God was good or no: than which nothing can be affirmed, more unworthy of the Creator of all things; or be more deservedly reckoned among those *hard speeches,* which if not *unrighteous,* yet, at least, *rash inconsiderate* men have spoken *against him."*

"The consequence of such a doctrine is, that there is really no difference between good and evil in the nature of things, but that will and power makes all the distinction. From whence tyrannical men, who have power to do what they will, think that they have consequently a right to do what they please. But this is not only not true with regard to men, but even with regard to God himself also it is plainly a mistake: for not *power or will,* but the reason of things only is the foundation of *right:* and therefore tho' 'tis indeed certainly true, that whatever God does, we are sure is right, because he does it; yet the meaning of this is not that God's *doing or willing* a thing, makes it to be right; but that his wisdom and goodness is such, that we may depend upon it, even without <47> understanding it, that whatever he wills, was in itself right, *antecedent* to his willing it; and that he therefore willed it because it was right."[b]

That power gives right is emphatically represented by the author of the book of wisdom, to be the fatal error of the wicked, and their corrupt

a. Dr. *Sam Clarke.* [The quotation is a rough paraphrase of Clarke, Sermon 10, in *Works,* 1:63–64.]

b. The same author, (Dr. *Clark*) in another place. [Clarke, Sermon 9, in *Works,* 1:55.]

language, "Let our strength be the law of justice, for that which is feeble
is found to be nothing worth." The constant language of the scripture
is, that God delighteth in good, and hateth evil, and that he makes all
things work together in his creation for good: words that have no meaning, if there be no natural immutable differences between things; if some
connexions of things be not in themselves good, and others evil, independent of his will. A doctrine as absurd as to say, that a triangle may
be a circle. For if power and right are not different, no two things are.
And if God can alter moral relations, he can also alter natural ones, for
moral ones are natural ones. Thus then it appears, that the joint doctrine
of reason and revelation is, "That the system of which God is the author,
is chosen by him, because it is the best of all possible systems, and there
is no absolute evil in it." In the text, the law of God's moral government
asserted is inferred from this supposition; it can stand on no other
foundation.

PROPOSITION IV

*If God hath chosen and established all things, as may best conduce to the
greater good and perfection of the whole system; then excellent, full care is
taken of moral beings in that system; or of that part in which virtue is
concerned.*

This truth so clearly results from the former propositions, that it is needless to offer any demonstration < 48 > of it. It is an obvious corollary from
the latter proposition demonstrated.

And indeed when changed into other equivalent terms, it is itself a
maxim or self-evident principle. For who can say, that "the greater quantity of moral perfection and happiness which can exist, is not the greatest
good that can be intended or pursued?" And how can it be pursued,
without due care about moral beings and virtue, which is nothing else
but moral powers suitably improved and cultivated, and thereby brought
to the perfection they are naturally susceptible of? As the perfection of
a horse consists in the perfection of his qualities, which make him that
particular species called *a horse;* or the perfection of a vine, consists in

its being cultivated to the most perfect state its properties are capable of; so the virtue of a man, must lie in the greatest perfection of those powers, which raise him above the brutes to that rank called *man.* Thus the ancients commonly very fully and convincingly illustrate the nature of virtue, and its essential difference from vice. But moral perfections, and the happiness resulting from thence, being greater perfections than vegetable, or even sensitive powers, and their improvements; in order to the attainment of greater good in the whole of things, the greater quantity of moral perfection and happiness must be intended and pursued, as the principal end to which all others must be submitted.

This appears evident, if moral powers be in their nature superior in excellence to mere vegetative, or even animal ones; it is so necessarily involved in that proposition, that to yield the one and deny the other, is to say the same thing is greater or less, more, and yet not more important in the same respect. And to deny the superior excellence of moral powers above all other qualities, is, in reality, to level all things in nature, and absurdly to say, all things are equal, and <49> that there is no such thing as a gradation from lesser to greater perfection.

"Moral powers therefore, and their improvements, must be the chief object of that infinitely good being's care and concern, whose scope in creating is the greater good of the whole."

But from hence it does not follow; that proper, proportioned care is not, or may not be taken of inferior beings; it only follows from hence, that such beings are not the main object of the divine care, to which all other things are subordinated. We actually see wonderful care taken of all beings; in giving instincts to each species suited to its kind, and making proper provision for their sustinence. And we have no *data,* from which we can positively conclude any thing concerning such creatures, but merely, that no changes, or events of whatever kind, can happen even to them which are not requisite to the greater good in the whole system, of which they make a part. We are as sure, as that there is a God, that the greater good of the whole is the end unerringly and effectually pursued by him; and therefore, that tho' every thing must submit to the principal end; the greater good, yet nothing is submitted but in proportion as that glorious scope requires; the happiness of no perceptive

being, however far below the dignity of man, is otherwise submitted.
Far less then can the happiness of any moral being be otherwise submitted to that end, which is the greater good of moral beings, or the
greater quantity of the greatest kind of happiness and perfection; and
much less still can it be submitted to any inferior end. Not only may the
happiness of inferior beings be, very consistently with this greater good
of moral beings, very fully provided for: but, which is more; there is no
contradiction to what hath been said, in supposing several evils to happen, even to man in this his first probationary state, in consequence of
general laws from which he <50> himself reaps several advantages, but
which are perhaps more especially calculated for the interest of the inferior creation. For a mixture of evils is absolutely necessary to a probationary state, *i.e.* to render it a proper school for forming, training,
educating, improving, and trying moral beings. How otherwise could
many glorious virtues be formed, attained to, or exerted? But much less
can it be concluded from what hath been said, that all things in our
system are merely adapted to us; and that mankind may not, in their
turn, pay submission to higher beings, as the inferior animals do to them.
For can we suppose a creation, which rises so gradually to man, without
any perceptible chasm, ascends no higher? It is contrary to the analogy
of nature to imagine the creation so scanty, so limited, so poor and imperfect. What is enough for us to infer, and what we have sufficient reason to conclude from the perfections of the infinite mind, under whose
direction and administration all beings are, as they are his creatures, is,
that man is duly taken care of and provided for, as may best serve to
promote the general good of the whole system; *i.e.* the greater quantity
of the greatest good. And this will more fully and clearly appear to be
the real truth of the matter, the more large views we are enabled to take
of any of the parts of the system we belong to; and of human nature in
particular.

For with regard to man, it is evident, that as no creature can be made
for a higher end in kind than he is, so he is very well furnished, and very
suitably placed here for attaining to that end in the only way it can be
compassed, which is by proper pains to improve his rational powers; and
every advancement toward perfection in this way, greatly rewards itself,

and by so doing, plainly prognosticates a rise in happiness proportional to rise in perfection. This we have fully proved in the *principles of moral philosophy,* <51> let us therefore see what revelation says upon this head.

So extensive is the divine bounty and care, that the Psalmist, and other sacred writers, in magnifying him, and exalting his perfections, do not hesitate to call him the *preserver,* not only of *man,* but of *beast.* The brutes are emphatically said to *wait upon him;* and he to *feed them;* to *satisfy their longings;* that is, their appetites, which he hath himself implanted in them, in a manner and degree so suited to the particular end of each different species, as alone sufficiently manifests infinite wisdom, and *mercy extending over all his works.*

The sacred writings represent God as having filled the heavens with celestial inhabitants, ascending above one another by certain degrees, the lowest of which are as superior to man as he is to the highest rank of brute animals. He hath created angels, seraphims, cherubims, and archangels, and they are all ministring spirits to God. But at the same time, he who hath created beings, that approach much nearer to him than man in the noblest of powers; those rational powers, which by the different degrees in which they are bestowed, each order of them being placed in circumstances proportioned to their end, distinguish moral beings into different orders, ranks, and classes, is far from being unmindful of man:[a] he hath made him after his own image, so as to render him able to perfect himself after that pattern of compleat perfection; having induced him with the senses of discerning good and evil, moral rectitude, and its contrary; and with the power of attaining to a great degree of knowledge, and a very high pitch of moral goodness. He hath made him lower than the angels, but higher than many species of brutes, all well provided for; because it was fit, the creation should be as full as possible of life and happiness; or be a scale rising by due steps <52> from the lowest to the highest rank of being; but he hath crowned him *with glory and honour;*[b] with moral powers capable of ascending to higher and higher perfection for ever, and of rising in happiness in the same proportion; and he has

a. *Gen.* i. 27.
b. *Ps.* viii. 5, *&c.*

invested him with a very large and noble dominion, *i.e.* he has made him capable of extending his dominion both in the natural and moral world, to a degree of which we cannot know the bounds, till we have gone as far in the study of nature as it is possible for us to reach; and that, by his reason and understanding, susceptible of improvements beyond any assignable bounds by due culture in various situations becoming larger and larger as his powers encrease by culture. For does not our dominion and lordship over sea and earth, air, and all the elements, augment with our knowledge of nature: our power over the brutes, to render them subservient to our advantage, does it not encrease with our insight into their constitutions, powers, and instincts? And finally does not our moral power over our appetites, our passions, over ourselves, and over one another, advance in proportion with our knowledge of human nature, and our diligence to establish well-informed reason as our sole ruler and conductor with the full power and authority in our minds, which of right belongs to it as a guiding principle?

Such is the conduct of God towards man, that the higher order of moral beings are not only said to behold God's creation with wonder, to rejoice in it, and sing his praises with joy ineffable;[a] but they are particularly said to search and pry into the administration of God, with regard to man, with great curiosity; to look into it, not with envy, but with wonder and delight, with the highest admiration and complacency. And how emphatically is the satisfaction of God, and his delight in virtue expressed, in innumerable places <53> of holy writ. Tho' our righteousness cannot extend to God, or profit him, as it does ourselves and one another; yet his delight is in the *excellent ones of the earth;* nay in them, it is said, is *all his delight.*[b] He is represented as beholding the virtuous with a glad countenance, and rejoycing in their progress towards perfection. There is said[c] to be joy in heaven among all the celestial beings, when a wicked man returns to his reason and just judgment, and forsaking vice with abhorrence, sets himself with all diligence to become

a. 1 *Peter* i. 12. *Ephes.* iii. 10.
b. *Ps.* xvi. 2, 3.
c. *Luke* xv. 10.

truly good. And God is said to accept the penitent reformer, to admit him into his favour, and to rejoice over him. The apostle St. *Paul* tells us,[a] that all things work together for the good of them who love God: and who are they who in scripture-phrase are said to love him? 'Tis they who knowing the divine moral rectitude, approve it, admire it, love it, and earnestly copy after it, endeavouring with all allacrity and diligence to transplant, as much as lies in their power, all the excellencies which render the Deity so amiable into their own hearts and lives. They love him who are *love, as God is love,* and such *dwell in him, and God in them: i.e.* They have a mutual resemblance, and they mutually love and delight in one another. God is not represented as pursuing any of his creatures with revenge or hatred: but in condescension to human language, or our ordinary way of conceiving and expressing things, God is said to hate and detest the sinner; that is, the deformity of his mind; and to be aggrieved by sin; *i.e.* to desire sincerely that the sinner would duly ponder his ways, and return to a right sense of the depravity and vileness into which vice sinks and degrades man, and of the beauty of holiness.

It would be endless to enumerate all the strong expressions in scripture, concerning God's universal be-<54>nevolence, his extensive care of all his creatures, his particular concern about moral beings, even about man, and his delight and satisfaction with their virtuous improvements.

But how delightful is this perswasion, which reason and revelation unite in enforcing upon the mind of every one who exercises his understanding to consider himself, or any of the things about him! How wonderfully does this belief dilate and expand the mind? How doth the mind greaten, exalt itself, and triumph, while this noble, this sublime, this amiable idea of the creation and its creator is present to it? To what noble attempts does it raise and elevate the soul? With what generous and truly great affections and resolutions does it inspire it? How divine are the feelings, the sentiments, the motions, the desires, the ambition, the effusion of a mind, while it considers God as spreading his blessings as wide as omnipotent bounty can diffuse itself; scattering them not profusely, or without rule, but with infinite discernment, according to the

a. *Rom.* viii. 28.

justest and the best rules, and in the fittest proportions; and when he considers for what a noble end man, capable of forming this idea and rejoycing in it, is made and furnished? 'Tis indeed hardly possible to quit this delightful, this exceeding comfortable subject. O that men were more acquainted with the satisfaction, the divine satisfaction such meditation fills the mind, and with its happy influences on the temper!

For whether riding, walking, or whatever our bodies are employed about, our active mind can pursue such thoughts. And what is there that we behold, which does not call upon us aloud, to think of our Creator, and the end for which he made us? 'Tis the universal language of all nature: it is the voice of the whole creation, which we must hear, if we do not wilfully shut our ears, and resolve not to hearken to it.

But it will be said, if such care is taken of all moral beings; if God is indeed so bountiful, so benign, <55> so full of mercy as he hath been represented, whence those evils which so sadly vex human life, which so cruelly plague the good in particular? If special care is indeed taken of that part of the creation in which virtue is concerned, why is it so bitterly distressed as it often is! Something hath been already said in answer to this objection; and it shall afterwards be fully handled. I shall therefore at present only remark, that the holy scripture very frequently represents the afflictions of the just to be friendly chastisements[a] from a wise Father, who knows what is proper for them, but hath no pleasure in plaguing any of his creatures. And pious men[b] are often found in scripture owning, "That it was good for them to have been afflicted," and praising God for having tried and purified them from much corruption, in the furnace of adversity. This is universally the scripture language. And tho' it be very true, that (which is also the scripture doctrine) according to the natural tendency of things, and in their common course, virtue is the best preservative against many of the heaviest, even external distresses and calamities in human life, and the best security even for temporal quiet, ease, and happiness; and that it is by the vices of our fellow

a. *Heb.* xii. 6.
b. *Ps.* cxix. 67, 71. 1 *Pet.* i. 6, 7. 1 *Cor.* xi. 32. *Rev.* iii. 19. *Wisd.* iii. 5. *Rom.* v. 3. *Jam.* i. 3, 12.

creatures, that the greatest hardships and severest sufferings are brought upon the virtuous: tho' all this be very true, and a sufficient vindication of the divine providence, yet it certainly well deserves our consideration, that, in a probationary state, as ours plainly appears to be from the nature of the thing, and is positively called in scripture, all the circumstances of human life, however divided and distributed, or from whatever external causes they proceed, ought to be considered equally, as means of trying and improving the virtuous disposition. The objection supposes, that adverse cir-<56>cumstances alone ought to be considered in this light. But if our state be indeed designed for schooling, nursing, strengthning, trying, and perfectionating the virtuous temper, it is absurd not to look upon prosperity likewise in the same view. This is the account the wise man gives of riches. "Gold hath been the ruin of many, and their destruction was present. It is a stumbling-block unto them that sacrifice unto it, and every fool shall be taken therewith. Blessed is the rich that is found without blemish, and hath not gone after gold. Who is he? And we will call him blessed: for wonderful things hath he done among his people. Who hath been tried thereby, and found perfect? Then let him glory. Who might offend, and hath not offended? Or might have done evil and hath not done it?"[a] Prosperity is a trial, and designed to be such as well as adversity: and perhaps it is the hardest, the severest of the two. We are to be called to account for the use we have made of the one as well as of the other. And that being the case, what is the evident consequence that follows from it, with respect to man, but that such are the various circumstances of human life as may best serve to form, try, and improve various virtues.

Some are tried by prosperity, some by adversity; or rather all in general seem to have less or more their vicissitudes of both. And why this, but that men may have opportunities of acquiring, exerting, and fixing all the virtues in their turns? Or if some there be who know no adversity during the whole course of their life, and others who are all their days on earth quite strangers to quiet, ease, health, and outward enjoyment— What, even in that case, can be supposed to be the moral use and intent

a. Ecclus. xxxi. 7, 8, 9, 10, &c. See likewise *Deuter.* xxxii. 15.

of such a dispensation, but what is agreeable to the very nature; nay, necessary to the very end of a first probationary state? Namely, that some may have more particular opportunities of <57> exercising one kind of virtues, and others another kind? For what circumstances have not their peculiar class of duties and virtues belonging to them, to which they call and excite, as they give proper opportunity for exerting them?

Some are means of exercising and improving resignation to the divine will; and of recovering the mind from sensual pleasures, and raising its affections to higher objects: and other circumstances are means of exercising and improving compassion, sympathy, bounty, and every generous passion: some afford the means of growing in humility, in fortitude, in patience; and others furnish opportunities of resisting proud emotions of the soul, haughtiness, and vanity, and of conquering and subduing anger, revenge, sensual concupiscence, and many other evil passions, which sadly degrade and corrupt the mind. From what circumstances in life may not a wise and good man reap far greater advantages than all outward ones amount to? For such certainly are the virtues and graces of a well-formed and improved mind. If one is in prosperity, what noble occasions hath he of exerting an equal, modest, humble, nay generous mind; and how difficult is it to behave so! What happiness may he give to himself, by wiping tears from the eyes of the mournful, and bidding misery and affliction be no more!a Is there a more God-like happiness; or can it be surpassed by all the pleasures of sense the most luxuriant circumstances for outward gratification and enjoyment can afford? And, on the other hand, from what kind of affliction or distress, which leaves room for thought and reflexion, may not the good man reap great advantages? And how few, or at least how short are those which, if the mind hath been previously accustomed to rational employments, and is well improved by due culture, do not leave room for useful reflexi-<58>on? How many great men hath the school of adversity formed; how highly profitable is that experience which St. *Paul* tells us it teaches?b And how noble an attainment is that contempt of sensual

a. 1 *Tim.* vi. 17, &c.
b. *Rom.* v. 3. *James* i. 3, 4, 5.

pleasure, nay, of exquisite pain, when it comes into competition with virtue and duty, which it forms and brings to great vigour and perfection in the mind? How glorious is true magnanimity and fortitude? And in the school of affliction chiefly is it nursed, cultivated, and brought to its full force and energy. Truly, in objections against providence, on account of the goods which fall to the share of the vitious, and the evils with which virtue is often distressed, outward things are too much over-rated, and inward ones too much diminished. For the highest ornaments and blessings that man can enjoy, or be possessed of, are the goods of the mind; well-improved reason, and a virtuous temper, contempt of merely sensual gratification, and an elevated, incorruptible esteem of the joys arising from virtuous exercises. To attain to these are we made and placed as we are; and all the circumstances of life are sadly misinterpreted, if they are not understood to be occasions that call upon us to exercise the virtues suited to them, and for exerting which they give us proper occasions. This is the meaning of all those pathetick exhortations to us in scripture, to walk wisely *and circumspectly; not as fools,* but as rational beings,[a] *redeeming the time,* that is, employing every season, opportunity, and condition in life to the best purpose, to the improvement of our mind in knowledge and virtue: to be *patient: and strong in adversity,* and in prosperity to be *meek and humble: to raise our affections,* our desires, our hopes, our fears above this world *to God,* to spiritual objects and exercises, such as afford us the best satisfaction here, the most solid and durable satisfaction; and are therefore an earnest to us of the future bliss <59> kept in store for those who prepare themselves for it. If our light afflictions, which are but for a moment, work us into a rational, a virtuous temper, they work for us an exceeding weight of glory.[b] This is the scripture language. And if we can reason with any certainty from the constitution of a being, and its rank in life, concerning its end; this is the end of our frame, and present condition; even to improve our minds, and to do good to one another, and by so doing to seek and prepare ourselves for glory, honour, and compleat felicity in the state of happi-

a. *Ephes.* v. 15, &c.
b. 2 *Cor.* iv. 16, 17, 18.

ness, to which virtue shall, when it hath been proved and tried, be promoted in an immortal life to come. For why else are we endued with sensitive appetites, but that they may be submitted to our reason and governed by it; why else have we reason, in order to contend with sensual desires, to subdue them and regulate them? Sensitive appetites surely cannot be united in the same constitution with reason and moral conscience, in order to get the ascendant over these higher and nobler powers, but on the contrary to be governed by them. And if so, then are we made to know good and evil, sensible and reasonable enjoyment, in order to attain to the power of preferring with strong affection, habitually, rational pleasures to sensitive ones. But of this more fully afterwards. Mean time it is evident, that the doctrine of reason and revelation is, "That in the creation and government of God, due care is taken of that part chiefly where virtue, *i.e.* moral beings and their improvements are concerned: or that every moral system is administered with perfect wisdom and goodness." <60>

Proposition V

But if this be the universal rule with respect to all moral beings, and all systems of moral beings, "That whatsoever one soweth, that shall he also reap"; then is every moral system very well governed: then are moral beings perfectly well taken care of.

That the general, constant, and uniform observance of such a rule in the government of moral beings must render that government equal, just, righteous, nay, perfectly good is very evident from the explication already given of it. It must therefore be a fixed law in the government of moral creatures, if the administration be righteous, equal, just, faithful, true, and good, or these are words without any meaning: this, I say, will immediately appear, if we recall to mind the explication given of this rule in the introduction to this discourse, which amounts briefly to this: that the happiness of moral beings, and all their improvements, shall be their own purchase and acquisition, the product of their own industry and diligence in exerting themselves to attain to them, according to the laws of nature, fixing the means by which they may, and cannot otherwise be acquired.

Now the law, "That whatsoever one sows, that shall he also reap," thus defined in general, seems to include in it the following particular things, which it is necessary to mention, and consider apart, in order to have a clear and adequate notion of it.

I. It supposes moral beings furnished with powers and faculties, whereby they are capable of certain moral improvements, and of certain proportionable degrees of moral happiness. And indeed, when we speak of moral beings, we necessarily speak of beings thus framed and furnished. For every inanimate thing is a complication of certain qualities fitted for <61> certain ends. Every merely animal being is a being capable of sensitive perceptions within certain bounds. And a being cannot be different from merely perceptive beings, but by means of some superior power, which raises it above them, by fitting and qualifying it for some higher end, for some nobler exercises, and proportionably nobler enjoyments. This, I believe, will be readily allowed to be too evident to need any farther confirmation, or even illustration.

II. This rule supposes moral beings to be placed in circumstances requisite for the exercise of their moral powers, and for having the enjoyments naturally redounding from them. Powers or properties, of whatever kind so placed, as that no use can be made of them, are certainly absolutely useless; they are created in vain. But we see no examples or instances of such bad oeconomy in nature of any sort, even with respect to merely material things; but have good reason to think, they are all made and placed for very advantageous purposes. As to suppose beings endued with moral powers in any degree so placed, that these powers, for want of subjects or materials to be employed about, or of occasions to call them forth into action, have, or can have no business, no exercise, no enjoyment, is to suppose the most idle and foolish, because useless conduct in the Maker and Governor of all things; so we have not the least ground of suspicion from any part of the present constitution and administration of things within our observation, to think it ever happens. 'Tis contrary to the idea of infinite bounty, to imagine any species of moral beings wanting in the universe in its due place and time, which would render nature more rich, more full and great, than it can be, without such a species of being. But it is yet more so, to suppose a moral being so placed as to exist to no purpose; which is necessarily implied in supposing any species of moral beings so <62> placed, as not to be able to exert its powers about their proper objects; not for want of powers, but for want of objects suited to their powers.

III. But, in the third place, the rule principally implies in it the dependence of the happiness and improvements of moral powers upon the moral being itself invested with them. 1. It necessarily supposes the improvement of moral powers to be a progressive work. This is implied in the very notion of moral powers and moral improvements or acquisitions. 2. It supposes the progressive improvements or advances of moral powers to depend upon the will and disposition of the moral being to set itself to make improvements and advances, and its firmness and constancy in applying itself to such a pursuit. This is likewise included in the very notion of a rational or moral creature. For how can any thing depend upon a creature otherwise, than by the dependence of its existence or non-existence upon the will of that creature? Things depend no otherwise upon the supreme being than in that way. He is omnipotent in no other sense but this alone, that all possible things depend upon his will for their existence or non-existence. And we have a sphere of activity, a certain degree of power and dominion, because with regard to us there is a certain dependence of effects, as to their existence or non-existence upon our will. Without such a dependence we would have no power; our will could never operate. And there can indeed be no other dependence of things upon any being, besides this alone. 3. The rule supposes certain fixed laws ascertainable by moral beings, according to which they may attain to certain improvements, the means for making such acquisitions being fixed by these laws. And indeed nothing can be more obvious, than that were there no such laws with respect to moral beings, they could attain to nothing. Every end in an or-<63>derly system must be the natural effect of certain means; the contraries of which must have very different, if not absolutely opposite and repugnant consequences. If the means for arriving at an end be not certain and fixed, they cannot be ascertained by the experience and observation of any being: they are

absolutely unascertainable: which, if they be, it is to all intents and purposes the same, as if there were, with respect to such beings, no means
for attaining to an end; nor no end to be compassed. In moral systems
therefore, where moral beings are capable of pursuing and gaining ends,
there are fixed laws which prevail uniformly, determining the means by
which these ends may be accomplished or brought about. 4. In the fourth
place, the rule not only supposes a certain degree of happiness and improvement to be within the compass of moral beings, by the proper
pursuit of them in the due use of the means correspondent to that end,
according to the laws of nature; but it supposes them so framed as to
have particular satisfaction in improvements so made, so purchased and
acquired; a sense of merit in so doing, and of demerit in not doing so;
a capacity of approving and condemning themselves according to their
conduct. We are so framed that we cannot conceive any joy superior,
nay in any degree near to that of inward well-founded self-approbation.
And indeed beings, not capable of it, must be very inferior to us, and
can hardly with any propriety be called moral beings; for what can that
title mean, but having an inward discernment of moral good and evil,
and being capable of pursuing the one, and avoiding the other, with an
accompanying sense of acting rightly in so doing. 5. The rule supposes,
that finally upon the whole, or in the sum of things, every one shall reap
the full natural fruits and consequences of his behaviour. Virtue must
be acquired gradually. It is a progress, a gradual purchase. And before it
is formed, it cannot have the effects of <64> fully formed virtue, in whatever circumstances it may be placed, *i.e.* however favourable to formed
and improved virtue; because the effect cannot prevent the means or
cause. In its advancing state of formation, trial, and improvement, it can
only have the effects of its advances. But if it hath in its state of education
the natural and proper effects of its exercises towards improvement in
the circumstances allotted to it for its culture, growth, and improvement,
then is it exceeding likely, that when it is formed to a great degree of
perfection by due culture, it shall reap, by being placed in suitable circumstances to such high improvement, the full fruits of so advanced a
state. And if it hath in the present state its proper present effects; and it
shall have in its improved state, the proper effects of such a one, in con-

sequence of circumstances adjusted to that end; then with respect to virtue is administration just; and doth the rule fully obtain, "That whatsoever a man soweth, that shall he also reap." And what may be concluded, with respect to vice, is obvious from the received rule or maxim concerning opposites or contraries; which is, that their natural effects will be as contrary to one another, as the qualities are whence they proceed.

Now if to make beings thus capable of creating to themselves their own happiness; thus capable of providing for themselves; thus capable of perfecting themselves, and exalting their nature to its highest pitch of excellence, be not to make excellent beings; or to constitute and place beings capable of moral improvement well, what can goodness mean; how can wisdom manifest itself; what are justice, righteousness, faithfulness, truth, and bounty? Such beings are equally and justly treated; for the happiness and perfection they may attain in consequence of their frame is thus absolutely dependent on themselves: they are thus, so to speak, their own masters, masters of their own fortunes: 'tis true and faithful to do so, for thus beings <65> may really attain to the end their constitution points out as attainable by them, and so invites them to aim at and pursue. It is highly good and generous to do so, for it is rendering such creatures capable of the highest and noblest kind of happiness; it is to invest them with the most excellent powers and affections that can be conceived: and it is to render them capable of the solidest and most sublime joy that can be imagined: the consciousness of worth and merit. It is finally to observe, with regard to them, a rule which must be just, equal, and reasonable, if equity, justice, and reason have any meaning.

Need I stay to prove, that what we have said of just, equal, and generous administration, with regard to moral beings, is what the sacred scripture means by God's judging, ruling, and governing all things, all beings, whether in heaven or on earth, in righteousness, faithfulness, truth, and mercy. What must be the consequences of not understanding these terms, when applied to God in the same sense as when we attribute goodness, and these other attributes naturally included in it, to men, hath been already observed. And the universal voice of scripture is, that God is a righteous, faithful, merciful ruler and judge; that he hath

formed the inanimate world[a] by *weight and measure,* that is, according
to the best laws: and that the whole universe is full of his goodness: that
he reigneth over all, not as an arbitrary tyrant, but according to the laws
of reason, equity, and goodness, governing every being consistently with,
or agreeably to its nature, and never departing from the end he proposed
to himself, and which moved him to create, the universal good. <66>

We shall afterwards have occasion to enquire, whether limitations of
any kind are consistent with this rule, and the equity, from which the
observance of it results, and may be inferred. The proper place for that
enquiry is, when we come to consider, how this rule is observed here
with respect to mankind. And therefore it is sufficient at present to observe, that as in the natural, so much more in the moral world, it is reasonable to conclude, nay it is a necessary consequence from the infinite
perfection of the Creator and Governor of the universe, that as there
can be no general laws established which are not contributive in the
whole to the greater good; so there can be no limitations, restrictions, or
oppositions to any one good law, but from another equally good law. In
nature, as far as our enquiries have reached, we find no effects, but what
proceed from general laws; but we find, on many occasions, laws thwarting and controuling laws: hence monstrous births, and other such like
productions, in which nature does not deviate, or is not deficient, much
less malign, but is really controuled and conquered, by the superior force
of some other good law. Now as it is in nature, so may it be in the moral
world: there is such an analogy between these two parts of the same
system conspiring to the same end, that it is not unlikely to presume, it
may be found to be so. But whether it is so or not; or however far it is
so, either in the one case or the other, it is equally comfortable and certain, that all the laws of the natural and moral world are fitly established,
because they are chosen and appointed by infinite wisdom and goodness;
for such only could infinite wisdom and goodness choose.

But it is needless to dwell longer upon a hypothetick proposition,
which there will be occasion of further illustrating, when we come to

a. *Job* xxviii. 24, *&c. Ecclesiast.* xviii. 39, 43. *Wisdom* xi. 24, *&c. Ps.* vii. 8, *&c.* xi.
7. xxxvi. 5, 6, 7. xxxvii. 28, *&c.* xcv. 13.

prove, that the rule defined, the rule which is affirmed in the text to be an immutable law in God's government of mankind, is really such: there is however another hypothetick pro-<67>position, which plainly follows from this one we have now been explaining, if we may at all depend upon analogical reasoning; which is,

PROPOSITION VI

If the rule defined be really observed with respect to mankind, in their present state, we have ground to conclude, that it is an universal law in God's moral government.

Now upon this head I would only observe two things.

I. That it hath been inferred to be a rule necessary to good administration, or that makes good administration, from the very nature of good, or even of equal administration of moral beings. It hath therefore been already proved, to be an universal rule in good and equal moral government. It hath not been inferred to be a rule in God's government of man, from any thing particular in man's frame; but from the consideration of properties, common to all moral beings; and from attributes of God, which must influence and guide his conduct universally: it hath therefore been deduced from such principles, as prove it to be an universal law. But,

II. If it can be once proved from experience, to be a rule that takes place, with respect to mankind here in their present state, as shall be proved immediately, it may from hence be inferred to be an universal law in all moral systems, if analogy be a good foundation to reason upon in any case.

Philosophers have so fully explained reasoning from analogy, with the other kinds of evidence, that I need not now do it; and that we must act upon presumptions founded upon analogy, no person who under-<68>stands the term, and the affairs of life, will deny. 'Tis therefore sufficient for my purpose to observe, that we may conclude, any rule, which by taking place among men, contributes to their dignity and happiness as moral agents, to take place also among all other moral beings: Or, 1.

It is absurd to conclude, from the prevalence of gravitation, as far as experiment can reach, that it obtains universally, throughout the whole material system, even though all other appearances of the most remote celestial bodies to us, may be accounted for by it. For the one case is precisely parallel to the other: the former amounting only to this, that a rule which is found to prevail among mankind, or more properly speaking, in the government of mankind, which sufficiently accounts for the equity and goodness of the ways of providence towards man, may be concluded to prevail universally in all systems of beings, which are analogous to man, in respect of our moral powers; since that law being supposed to take place so universally, the administration of beings will be universally equal, just, nay good. And why is gravitation concluded to be an universal law, but because it obtains as far as we carry experiment; and gives an orderly, consistent, harmonious account of the most distant appearances. 2. But which is more, if this rule is found to obtain with respect to mankind, it may be justly concluded to be an universal law in all moral systems: Or all moral beings are analogous as moral beings, and yet not governed by a law, suited to the powers in which chiefly they are, or can be similar to one another. However different moral beings may be from one another in degrees, numbers, and extent of powers; yet beings which are of a moral nature must be like one another in this respect, that they have reason, and are capable of discerning the relations of objects; the fitnesses and unfitnesses of affections and actions, with respect to objects, persons, or other affections and actions, and of conducting <69> their behaviour by this moral sense or moral knowledge. Now to suppose beings so far alike, and yet the happiness and improvements of one sort of such analogous beings, and not of the other, to be conformable or proportionable to their conduct, to their choice and pursuits, is to suppose them to be unlike in the most essential, or at least the most important part belonging to the powers of reason and free agency, in which they are analogous. But why need we insist longer in reasoning from analogy, to prove a thing that is necessarily included, as hath been already shewn, in the very nature of a moral being; or without supposing which, no definition can be given of moral agents, that can distinguish them from inferior beings, who have no sphere of activity,

no guiding or ruling principle in their constitution? I proceed therefore
to enquire, whether experience be agreeable to what hath been inferred
abstractly from the nature of things, concerning man, and all rational
beings; that is, whether it be really in fact the rule in the government of
mankind, "That whatsoever a man soweth, that shall he also reap." For
however convincive abstract reasonings may be, yet such is our make,
who are framed to gather the principal part of our knowledge from experience, that no demonstration is more, if equally satisfactory to our
mind, than plain indisputable experience: an admirable instance of the
care of our Maker to adjust our frame to our circumstances.

Proposition VII

*Experience proves this to be the law, with respect to mankind in their present
state, "That whatsoever a man soweth, that shall he also reap."*

This we have already seen to be the express doctrine of the scripture,
with regard to futurity: it is directly affirmed to be so in the text; and we
may not <70> only justly conclude, that what is the law in the divine
government of mankind with respect to a succeeding life, is the present
law as far as the nature of a preparative state to a future one admits; but,
as hath likewise been observed, the consideration of the divine perfection, which is mocked or injured by denying it to be the rule, whence
the apostle St. *Paul* infers it to be the rule, does as necessarily shew it to
be the present rule, as to be the rule with regard to futurity: and indeed
it is hardly conceivable in the nature of things, how it can be the rule
with respect to our future state, without being the rule with regard to
our present state (which is the preparative or probationary one, with
respect to futurity; or, in the apostle's phrase, its *seed-time*) as far as the
nature of the state of probation permits it to be so.

Let us however leave all these considerations, and impartially inquire
into fact: that is to say, inquire candidly, and without being byassed by
any hypothesis, as philosophers ought to do, what experience says about
the matter in question. 1. One thing only I must premise before I go
farther; which is, that 'tis indeed very unaccountable to hear some phi-

losophers, who confess, that we ought to reason from experiments only in natural philosophy, say, that with respect to the mind, if we appeal to experience, we can never come to certainty; for there is nothing so absurd, with relation to it, for which we shall not find witnesses who will appeal to their feeling and experience for the truth and reality of it. For if it should be retorted, as it may justly be, that there is nothing so absurd that we do not find some asserting to be true from the experience of the joint testimony of all their senses, what would follow from that? Would it follow from hence that experience has not the right of deciding in matters of experience; that the senses are not to be depended upon; and that there can be no such thing as knowledge from outward experience? That surely will not be said by any philosopher; since it is from sensible <71> experience only we can learn the connexions of external pleasures and pains with our actions, a most important part of knowledge to us. But if that cannot be said by any philosopher, I may leave it to any thinking person to determine whether the other scepticism about internal experience be not equally ridiculous. The cases are precisely parallel; and like cases must stand and fall by one and the same judgment. The same rules which, being observed in making experiments in natural philosophy, render them a sure foundation to build upon, must, if observed in moral philosophy, render experiences in it equally certain, an equally solid foundation to build moral conclusions upon. Which rules may be reduced to these two; namely, to take care "1. That the experiments be analogous in kind"; and "2. that they be proportioned in extent and moment to the inferences deduced from them. And experiences taken upon testimony, must all of them, whether concerning objects of the outward senses, or inward sentiments, operations, and affections of the mind, be tried, examined, and admitted, or repelled by the very same *criteria*, or rules of moral evidence."

Having just premised this observation, to obviate rash and inconsiderate cavilling against reasoning from experience about matters of fact or experience; it is well worth while to observe, 2. That experience or careful observation of the animal world, shews us that all animals are directed by proper instincts, to the end for which they are naturally fitted; strength, agility, or whatever it be; and not only to their food, but their medicines; to suitable care of their young, while that is necessary, and no longer; to fly their enemies, or guard against them, and to herd each tribe among themselves. None of their instincts are unsuitable to their condition, unprovided for, or implanted in vain.

Now from such care of animals, so visible throughout all nature, and asserted in the scripture as an instance of the extensive bounty and care of providence, we <72> may reasonably conclude, that similar care at least prevails with respect to higher moral beings: that they are all fitted, each species to its end, duly provided for, and well placed, in order to attain to it: that their powers are not made in vain, and that they do not even want proper instincts and determinations of nature, to assist, direct, or invigorate their reason, as far as instincts are convenient or suitable to them: that all their appetites and affections are well adjusted to the end of the species to which they belong; are inlaid into their nature in such just proportions as may best serve that end; and that the laws relative to their increase or decrease, growth or diminution, improvement or degeneracy, are all likewise admirably adjusted to one another, and to the common end of them all, as may best promote the greater happiness of the whole moral system, which can be nothing else but the aggregate or sum of the happinesses of particular individuals.

But, which is more, what we have so good ground from the consideration of the inferior creation, by analogy to presume, must hold, at least, equally in the government of superior moral systems of beings, is evidently the real case with respect to the constitution and government of mankind.

For, in general, we find that almost all our pleasures or pains are put in our own power; they are dependent on our actions; they are, in the course of nature, the natural, *i.e.* the appointed or established effects and consequences of them. By our own care to preserve our life, is it preserved; and we can destroy it entirely, or render it as miserable as we please, by foolish pursuits, by irregular ungoverned passions, and mad, or, at least, rash and inconsiderate conduct. What we desire to have, we must set ourselves to have, in order to attain to it; and what we set ourselves to obtain, we generally obtain, if we take the proper methods to acquire it; provided it really be among the <73> number of our τα εφ ημιν[12] to know which is our own business, and may be soon understood, if we diligently observe our powers, and the natural course of things. Were every thing in our power, or were our sphere of activity, which consists in the dependence of things on our will, as to existence or non-existence, boundless, we would be omnipotent. Were the connexion between our wills, and the existence or non-existence of any effects, a connexion necessary and independent of any other mind, we would be so far as it extends absolutely independent. But as it is absolutely inconceiveable, how any being can be limitedly independent, or, in other words, absolutely independent only within certain confined bounds; so we may soon perceive, by experience, that the extent of our power is not only limited, but derived, established by another, and not subject to us. But we are free, or have power as far as it reaches. And our interest loudly calls upon us early to apply ourselves to know the real extent of our power. It ought to be a first and principal care in education to instruct youth betimes in this important matter; for without such knowledge, and indeed without accustoming ourselves early to enquire, whether what we desire be possible, we may, as too many do, lose all our time and labour in chimerical, impossible pursuits. There are many other questions, which education, duly calculated to instruct youth in life and right behaviour, would very early inure them frequently to put to themselves very seriously; or rather, indeed, never to choose and act without having maturely pondered. As, whether it be, all things considered, a prudent choice; an expedient one; and above all, whether it be a right or a base one; a laudable or condemnable one; virtuous or vicious; beneath the dignity of man; if not repugnant to it; or agreeable to his rank, powers and end. But the first question of all, in the nature of things, ought to be, Is it possible, is it in human power, in general, or is it in my power, <74> in particular. For here a distinction must be made, since the general extent of human power must necessarily be limited by particular situations and circumstances. That may be in human power, generally speaking, which is not in the power of certain individuals, because of their particular circumstances. Every one must as necessarily have his

12. "things in our power."

own particular sphere of activity, as he must have his own particular point of sight; his own particular place and site in nature. And therefore, beside the general knowledge of human powers, every one ought early to be acquainted, as much as possibly can be done, with the variations the general extent of human power must suffer from various particular conditions and situations, or from whatever causes.

But we are now treating of human power, in general; and it is plain from experience, that almost all our pleasures and pains are brought about by our own actions; they are consequences to be attained or avoided by us, by certain manners of behaviour or action. There may be very different orders of beings in nature, that is, very different spheres of dominion and activity: nay, that there is an immense variety of such actually existing, reason makes, if not certain, at least very probable to us, who are so framed, that we cannot conceive an universe otherwise constituted and filled, without looking upon it, as scanty and imperfect; the effect, either of very restrained power, or of very nigardly bounty; and what naturally is so probable, the scripture assures us is true. But if we had no extent of power, no sphere of activity and rule, we would not be moral beings; there being really, in the nature of things, no difference between beings, which enjoy or suffer merely by passive sensations conveyed into them, independently of their own will; besides, what the number and variety of such sensations, or passive impressions, makes. They are all of the same class, merely passive, merely perceptive beings, to which rank of being, if reason, reflexion, and free <75> choice, with affection and self-approbation, in consequence of a sense of right and wrong, do not render naturally superior, or of greater dignity, then are *perfect* and *imperfect,* or *more* and *less perfect,* words without a meaning: then are all beings upon a level, and there is no such thing as better and worse, higher and lower in nature.

But, in order to have as clear a view of this important matter as we can, let us, 1. Consider our power with respect to external things. 2. Our power with respect to internal things. And, 3. Let us enquire if there are any limitations upon our power, besides those already mentioned, which are essential to creatures as such; and what these are, and from whence they proceed.

Now, in the first place, with respect to external things, it is evident, that when sensible objects strike our senses, they must be perceived by us: these impressions are passive; they are conveyed from without. And it is evident, that the manner in which any being is affected by objects of sense in this passive way, will differ from that in which another being is affected by the same objects of sense; or to speak more philosophically, hath sensations imprinted upon its mind from without, as their organizations differ one from another. That is the meaning of different organizations; it is their end, and must naturally and necessarily be their effect. But then it is evident likewise, that all the sensations we receive from without, are conveyed to us according to a certain, fixed, uniform, established order, which we call the order or frame of the sensible world with respect to mankind, and that renders us capable of mutual commerce and correspondence. If it were not so, we could not converse with one another, or have any intercourse, nay, we could not foresee what would be the course of things in any case; that is, what perceptions would succeed to one another, and consequently we could not act; nature would have no meaning to us; we could not understand it; and, by <76> consequence, we could not imitate it as we do by many useful arts; nor draw any rules from it with regard to our conduct. But nature, being orderly, it may be understood, imitated, reasoned from, and directions for our actions may be inferred from it. And as it is experience alone that can teach us the order of nature, so it is our business early to attend to the course of nature, in order to know it as fully as we can.

Indeed were we not capable, before we can reason, to form very quick and ready judgments of certain connexions in nature, (concerning the magnitudes and distances of objects, for example) as we very early do, we could not possibly get thro' our infant state. And therefore that we form these judgments, or rather that they are formed in us, by the necessary operations of certain faculties belonging to us, previously to our use of reason, or capacity of making observations upon the settled connexions of nature, is a very manifest sign of the care of providence about us, whose reason must, in the nature of things, that is, according to our make, be gradually nursed and cultivated to any considerable degree of strength and vigor; more especially, if we consider the powers, and laws of powers, from which this so advantageous a way of judging of certain connexions in nature results; since these very powers, and laws of powers, which bring it about, are, on many other accounts, of the highest, the noblest use in our constitution, *viz.* the laws relative to association of ideas, memory and habit. But tho' this capacity of attaining, in our infancy, from a few experiences, to so quick a way of judging of certain connexions and orders in nature, be such an advantage to us, that it may very properly and justly be said to be a supplemental power to that of reason; yet the far greater part of the connexions, by the knowledge of which alone our power can be encreased in nature, as far as it may be encreased, are left to be the objects of our diligent enquiries and researches. And that this is a <77> very pleasant employment, every one who is in the least acquainted with the study of nature will readily acknowledge.

We can extend our lordship very far: the increase of our dominion hath hitherto kept pace with our insight into nature. For what discovery in natural philosophy hath not increased our power and dominion by giving rise to some useful, or, at least, some ornamental art? We can only augment our dominion by increase in knowledge. But increase in knowledge, upon which enlargement of our natural dominion depends, is in our power, or dependent upon us, and attainable by us, not only in any sense that any other thing whatsoever can be said to depend upon us, and to be in our hands, if I may so speak; but it is in our power, or dependent upon us, in any sense that any thing can be pronounced to be in the power and reach, or within the acquisition of any being. For dependence upon a being can mean nothing else but having faculties to attain to it, if they are applied and used to attain to it. And thus increase in knowledge is in our power: in our power beyond any assignable bounds. For who can say of it, Hitherto can it go and no further? There are indeed limits to it: there must be limits to it: there are several things which we have good reason to think we cannot know. But who can say how far enquiries into nature, into any part of nature rightly pursued may be carried? Are not the qualities and laws of qualities belonging to any one object, an almost exhaustless fund of pleasant and useful research by experimental enquiries?

There may be various degrees of facility among beings with respect to acquiring knowledge, and to every acquisition. We experience different degrees of facility and quickness with respect to the same acquirement among ourselves. And higher and lower spheres of activity, greater and lesser powers, must comprehend such a difference, and much more in their full mean-<78>ing. And yet after all, with respect to mankind, the acquirement of natural knowledge may be said to be a very easy purchase. For the connexions of nature lie open to every diligent judicious enquirer; every such a one is daily making, in proportion to his assiduity in observing nature, and trying experiments, very great discoveries with ease and pleasure. Our curiosity prompts us to search into nature, and our disposition to imitate, together with our natural desire of power, strongly at once push us to search after knowledge, and direct us how to pursue or seek after it, even by copying after nature, vying with her, and making experiments. And knowledge becomes easier, in proportion to the advances we have made in it. Our faculties enlarge in proportion as they are exercised: And every discovery we make by the pleasure it gives us, and by making us feel the advantages of advancing and improving in knowledge, is a fresh incentive to diligence in the quest of science. Besides, by reflexions upon our mistakes and errors, compared with our successes, we come to be able to form rules for making surer and more expeditious researches, and for avoiding deceits and errors. And these reflexions, being, by frequent consideration, fixed upon the mind, the science or art of comparing, separating, placing in various situations and juxtapositions, and taking different views of the same objects; and, in one word, the whole science and art of reasoning, becomes habitual to the mind; insomuch, that one thus formed to search, and practised in searching, is never at a loss on any occasion, however new, how to go to work. Thus progress in knowledge becomes gradually easier and easier, and in proportion sweeter and pleasanter to the practitioner. And can there be any other way of knowledge's becoming easier to us than this; any other way, at least, more honourable or agreeable to us? <79>

How it comes about, that notwithstanding the truth of all that hath been said, natural science hath made such slow advances, and is yet so

little studied and pursued, is a question that belongs to the general enquiry, why men, notwithstanding their furniture of every sort for improving in knowledge and virtue, are so corrupt as they are; or at least
generally fall so very far short of what they may attain to, in respect of
perfection and proportional happiness. We shall therefore, at present,
only observe upon that head, that in fact, philosophers were long misled
from the plain and evident way of coming at the knowledge of nature
(for what can be more obvious, than that it can only be attained to by
carefully observing nature itself in its operations?) by a vain disposition,
to make or contrive worlds themselves, and to spin a solution of all the
phenomena of nature out of their own brain, that thus they might have
some shew of reason to consider themselves as creators, or as able to *give
counsel to the Most High*.[a] But such arrogance and folly, what is it but the
degeneracy of a greatness of mind, of a noble disposition to augment
our power, extend our capacities, and be as much beholden to ourselves
as possible, implanted in us by the author of nature for many excellent
purposes? since without such a disposition we could not be capable of
great sentiments, great actions, and many eminent virtues, which highly
bless and exalt human society. 'Tis nothing else but this useful disposition misplaced, misguided, or taking a wrong turn, which we not only
have reason to guide to right purposes, but which there are other affections in our constitution, naturally of equal strength to counter-ballance
and point into the proper path, or to its best pursuits, and to keep us
from running into <80> this and other like extravagances. It must be
still owing, partly to this vanity, partly to thoughtlessness, partly to a
false notion of learning, and partly, if not principally, to sensuality, and

a. *Democrates* wished to be blind, that he might the better study the nature and
origin of the world. And such philosophers seem to have shut their eyes against nature, that they might not owe any part of their philosophy to nature. ["Democrates"
is a mistake for "Democritus." Plutarch mentions a story along these lines while re-
jecting it: "It is a falsehood that Democritus voluntarily blinded himself by directing
his eyes to red-hot mirrors and receiving the reflections from them, so that his eyes
would not cause a disturbance by calling his mind to external things, but should allow
it to remain at home and spend its time on intelligible things like windows which
give on to the street and are shut." Plutarch, *Moral Essays, On Curiosity*, 521c3.]

the prevailing love of external pleasure, that natural philosophy, the advantages of cultivating which, glare every thinking man in the face, is not even yet pursued with that earnest and assiduous application it ought to be. But which ever of these wrong turns of mind be the cause of it, it is certain, that every wrong turn of mind is but a corruption of some good affection, against which we are sufficiently provided and armed by nature. For as to sensual concupiscence in particular, is it not manifest, that were not certain sensitive appetites and affections implanted in our mind by nature, we would neither be capable of those sensitive gratifications, which, when pursued and enjoyed within the bounds reason and benevolence permit, are not contemptible enjoyments; nor would our reason and moral conscience have subjects to discipline, govern, and keep in due order: without such a make it could not be our end, as it now is, to contend in opposition to sensitive lusts, to attain to a just esteem of rational exercises, and of the pleasures redounding from them, above all merely external delights. Nor is it less visible that no affections or propensions in our nature become strong and prevalent, but by being frequently exercised and gratified in consequence of the law of habit, which is indeed the law that renders us capable of perfection. For what else is any perfection, but an affection or power improved to a readiness in exerting itself to the best advantage, and in the most convenient and becoming manner? From all which it is evident that to object against our frame, either on the account of vanity, or any other bad turn, any of our natural powers or appetites may take, or of the method in which they are to be governed, ruled, and perfected, is in reality to arraign our author, because we have a stock <81> to improve, and are made capable of improving it to excellent advantage in the only meritorious and pleasant way. Thus then we see, that we are very well qualified by nature for encreasing, by our diligence to improve in it, our knowledge of the connexions of the natural or material world, provided we but take the right way of pursuing after it, which lies open and manifest to every one who can think at all. For to accuse nature, for not having put it in our power to acquire knowledge, whatever way we take to get it, is absurdly to impeach nature for having made knowledge attainable by us; since it could not be so, were not the only means of acquiring it, fixed and certain;

nay, it is indeed, in general, to accuse nature, because an end is acquired by means; that is, to accuse the author of nature, because nature is an orderly system, and there are fixed and established connexions of things, which may be known, copied and reasoned from by intelligent agents.

But knowledge of the natural world being thus in our power, and easy to be acquired; the encrease of our natural dominion is likewise in our power, and easy to be augmented by us. For having intelligent power to procure ourselves any external advantage, or to avoid any external inconvenience or uneasiness, it is, and must be our own fault entirely, if we do not exercise our power to have advantages attainable by us, and to preserve ourselves against pains avoidable by us. We may have intelligent power, and yet not exercise it; one may shut his eyes, and fold his arms, even when he hath nothing to do, but to open his eyes, and put out his hands to take hold of a very great blessing. But all that nature could do for us was to give us faculties, by the due use of which certain blessings may be acquired, with the self-satisfaction of having thus acquired them to ourselves, by the right use of our powers. To demand any thing else is absurdly to demand, that nothing should depend on our will, as <82> to its existence or non-existence; *i.e.* that we should not be at all active creatures, or capable of merit.

But let us now see more particularly, how certain particular, external purchases stand with regard to us. And I think all the blessings of human life may be reduced to these three, peace, health, and competence. The two last only are external, and therefore they only belong to the present question. *Peace, fair virtue, is thine alone!* We shall therefore consider the two other, health and competence, or let it be called *wealth,* tho' 'tis really the other that is the blessing.

I. Now, as to the former, though many external diseases, pains and sufferings, are beyond our foresight, and absolutely inevitable by us, because they are the effects of the general laws of the material world, which must operate uniformly and invariably, which shall be considered afterwards; yet, in general, it is very conspicuous, that by prudence and care, we may, for the most part, pass our days in tolerable ease and quiet: and that it is by rashness, ungoverned passion, wilfulness or negligence, that men, generally speaking, make themselves very miserable. Certain virtues, really coincide with prudence and wise management with respect to health, and outward ease and convenience; and therefore, must at least be owned to be natural duties, if they be not allowed to be moral ones, or to have any further use and excellence. Of this kind are self-government, a deliberative temper, and temperance; they certainly preserve from many terrible evils, which sadly afflict the rash, inconsiderate, irregular, and unthinking, or wilful; and do really give us more sensible pleasure than their contraries, according to the fixed laws and boundaries of sensitive exercises and gratifications, or of outward pleasures and pains. This, I think, was never denied; and therefore let it only be added to it, that the study of nature, which, if it were not <83> left to ourselves, we could not really have any subjects of exercise for our understanding, or intelligent power of the natural kind, were it duly cultivated, it would certainly be able to do more for the preservation or relief of mankind, than it is yet sufficient to do. And this knowledge, being only acquirable in a progressive manner, in proportion to our application to extend and enlarge it; the external pains we feel, as they are excited only by such objects as tend to dissolve, or, at least, hurt or injure our bodily frame, they are thus proper monitors to take care of ourselves: kind warnings, which very happily supply an unavoidably necessary, or, at least, a very fit inconvenience, accruing from the progressiveness of knowledge; if any consequence, that is really in itself so proper for us, as that is, can justly be called *an inconvenience.*

II. Now, as for wealth, the means of all sensitive gratification; in communities, or societies regularly established; How is it acquired by men? Is it not in proportion to their industry, in the use of the means by which it may be purchased? And in a state of nature, or in society, where money is not in use, the case is the same, insomuch that what the wise man says of industry, in that respect, is an universal proverb.[a] "The hand of the diligent maketh rich." How emphatical are his descriptions of the opposite effects of industry and slothfulness? And they are literally true.

"Slothfulness casteth into a deep sleep, and an idle soul shall suffer hunger, the drunkard and glutton shall come to poverty; and drowsiness

a. *Prov.* xxii. 29. xii. 11. vi. 4. xxiii. 21. xxiv. 30.

shall clothe a man with rags." "I went by the field of the slothful, and
by the vineyard of the man void of understanding, and lo, it was all
grown over with thorns, <84> and nettles had covered the face thereof,
and the stone-wall thereof was laid down. Then I saw, and considered
well, I looked upon it, and received instruction. Yet a little sleep, a little
slumber, a little folding of the hands to sleep: so that thy poverty come,
as one that travelleth, and thy want as an armed man." But, on the other
hand,[13] "He that tilleth his land shall have plenty of bread." "He that
gathereth by labour shall encrease." "In all labour there is profit." "Love
not sleep, lest thou come to poverty; open thine eyes, and thou shalt be
satisfied with bread." "Through wisdom is an house builded, and by
understanding it is established." "And by knowledge shall thy chambers
be filled with all precious pleasant riches." "A wise man is strong, yea, a
man of knowledge encreaseth strength." The same rule takes place, in
the brute creation, in many instances; that is, they are directed and
moved by their instincts to provide in summer for winter; and therefore
the sluggard is called upon, "to go to the ant for example, to consider
her ways, and be wise, which having no guide, overseer or ruler, provi-
deth her meat in the summer, and gathereth her food in the harvest."
The general law with respect to encrease in wealth is, that it shall be made
by those who set themselves earnestly to do it. Without this general law,
there would be no encouragement to industry, by which it is fit that
external advantages should alone be acquired; since it being so with regard to internal goods, as we shall quickly see it is, our whole frame is
thus consistent and analogous; since our bodies require exercise as well
as nourishment; and the preservation of man, by requiring many united
labours, lays a foundation, and makes room for many ingenious arts,
many beautiful inventions and employments, and for the mutual exchange of many friendly offices; or, in one word, makes a close mutual
dependence, and so gives rise to all the variety of blessings spring-
<85>ing from that source, which are indeed innumerable. Now, this be-
ing the general rule, tho' in consequence of natural connexions, as be-

13. The following eight Biblical quotes are from, respectively, Prov. 28.19; 13.11;
14.23; 20.13; 24.3; 24.4; 24.5; 6.6–8.

tween parents and offspring, and social ties of various kinds in an established community, or even in a state of nature, riches may drop into the mouth of the sluggard; yet it is plain, they must have been originally purchased by labour. And, if we add to this, that the law being general; putting out the hand, or exerting our force or skill to take hold of certain external objects, will of course be generally successful, whether it is righteous or unrighteous, fraudulent and wicked, or just and good. But all that duly weighed, we have no reason to complain of the distribution of external goods in this life. For not only may a man be very vitious in several respects, and yet be worldly wise and industrious, which wisdom and industry it is fit should gain its end: but let us think what would be the consequence if only lawful art and industry were successful. To demand it is indeed the same, as to demand that the sun should only shine upon the just; and the rain from heaven only water the fields of the pious; and can we imagine greater confusion and disorder than this would produce? Whereas, as things are now constituted and regulated, the means whereby ends may be compassed are fixed and certain, and the course of things being according to general laws, it is truly orderly and regular.

We have no ground to complain of the administration of providence, with regard to the distribution of external goods, since by the law according to which they are purchased, he who applies himself to knowledge, will attain to it; he who seeks virtue or self-government, will attain to a great pitch of perfection in it; and he who merely seeks sensual gratifications, will also have it; but with all its concomitants and consequences, with a carnal mind, ungoverned passions, incapacity of rational exercises, a mean, and <86> mercenary, selfish, ungenerous temper, and consciousness of inward worthlessness. In order to pursue any end vigorously, the heart, the affections, must be strongly bent upon it: thus alone is virtue purchased. And he who is only fit for, and only thinks of encreasing wealth, in order to pamper his sensitive appetites, will, according to the common course of things, in consequence of the same law, gain that end: but he will not be the nearer to true happiness for having done so; for that outward affluence cannot give, without a well governed, generous mind. On the other hand, the good man, whose chief delight is in rational exercises, only desiring wealth, in order to be able to communicate it, and do good, not only cannot with that temper of mind so keenly pursue wealth as it is necessary, in order to make great riches; but he is really apt to fall into an indolence in this respect, which, as it is blameable, when man is considered to be made for society, so it brings its own punishment along with it, by putting it out of his power to do the good on many occasions, he must feel pain for not being able to do; and consequently checks for so utterly neglecting the purchase of such agreeable power, as not at all to mind it, tho' it might be done to a great degree by him very consistently with his superior delight in other exercises, from which tho' valuable advantages spring, yet the means of being liberal cannot. Such, however, generally make up, in a great degree, by their frugality and self-denial, what too great a neglect of seeking after the means of beneficence otherwise puts out of their power.

Thus then we clearly see, how equal and just the general law with respect to the acquirement of external goods is; it is plainly this, "As a man soweth, so doth he reap."

Let us now enquire, in the second place, whether it is not the same with respect to internal goods, <87> with respect to the improvements of the mind, whether of understanding, or of will and temper. And indeed, as it is fit that all the parts composing the same mind, and all the parts constituting the same system of things relative to the same kind of moral beings, should be analogous or consonant one to another; so really it is in our own case. The same law, which obtains with respect to external purchases takes place with regard to moral or internal ones.

All that hath been said of natural knowledge and natural power, is found, by experience, to be equally true with respect to moral knowledge and moral power. And indeed, whatever names to things some people may affect to give, they must be strangers to the very meaning of the words *moral knowledge,* who out of contempt call it *metaphysick,* and will not allow it to be a part of natural knowledge, in the proper sense of *natural.* For what can be more evident, than that the constitution of our mind is a natural and real constitution, which hath its own real economy and symmetry, as well as any body; the human, or any other. And therefore, that an enquiry into that constitution must be carried on in the same way of experiment, and reasoning from experiment alone, as our researches into bodily frames and structures of whatever sort. And sure to deny, that the knowledge of our inward anatomy, by whatever name it be called, is not a part of knowledge that highly concerns us, is absurdly to say, that we are not at all interested in the temper and fate of our thinking part. We shall not dwell longer upon this head, since it would be but to repeat over again what hath been said of natural knowledge, in the common sense of these words; and there will be occasion in another place of this discourse, to treat of moral or practical knowledge. One thing only not yet mentioned is very well worth our attention, that in order to direct and point us into the proper road of getting knowledge, either na-<88>tural or moral, nature hath wisely and generously implanted in our minds, a disposition to delight in order, unity of design, symmetry, simplicity, and consent of parts to a good end, wherever we perceive it; by which means, we are naturally excited to look out for order, wise and generous contrivance, consent of parts, general laws, harmonies and analogies. And he, who thus pursues the study of nature, whether in corporeal structures or moral ones, will not lose his labour; but have success, that will abundantly reward his assiduity, every step it advances, by pleasure far superior to all sensitive gratifications. There is no need of any proof of this truth to those who are acquainted with such researches. And the lovers of the ingenious arts, which imitate nature, as poetry, painting, sculpture, will they not immediately own, that their delight wholly arises from a taste of order, beauty, simplicity, consistency and unity in imitations of nature? We may justly conclude, as hath been done, that a wise and good being does nothing in vain, but always pursues a good end by the simplest means, carefully avoiding all superfluity, and adding force to what is principal in every thing. And it is the observance of this rule by nature throughout all its works, which renders them so beautiful and pleasing to behold, which they could not be to us, had we not naturally a sense of beauty and unity; a capacity of discerning it, and a disposition to delight in it. And, in the same way, are we qualified to acquire a good taste of the polite arts, for as their end is to imitate nature, what constitutes the beauty of their pattern, must constitute their beauty likewise. They therefore can only give pleasure to a well-formed mind, in proportion to their truth, beauty, simplicity, majesty, grandeur and unity, as nature does. And unless a mind be formed to a right, a very perfect taste of these beautiful qualities, the finest and best of productions of the imitative arts, cannot give one any satisfaction: they must be lost upon such. <89>

Now if we consider how a good temper and disposition of mind, and all the virtues which make a man at once beneficial, happy, great, and amiable, are acquired, we shall plainly perceive, that it is by labour and diligence to improve our faculties and affections, implanted in us by nature, by due culture. No labour can give us a faculty or affection, which nature hath not originally implanted in us; no more than it can add to the number of the external organs nature hath furnished us with. Art can only cultivate, improve, enlarge, and bring to perfection the powers, affections, and dispositions of nature's growth. But if it should be asked, what is the meaning of these words, to improve and cultivate? Before we come to consider more particularly the scripture doctrine concerning virtue and vice, it is sufficient to answer, if less or more perfect may be applied to the qualities of a vegetable, or of a horse, or of any thing, it may likewise be applied to moral powers and faculties. If an imperfect and a more perfect or improved state of any one quality be once allowed, it must be universally acknowledged, that there is an imperfect and more perfect state of all qualities whatsoever. And thus the reality of virtue and vice must of necessity be yielded: since whatever is an advancement towards the natural perfection to which moral powers may be brought, is virtue, with regard to them; and contrariwise every step to degrade them below that perfection, or to hinder them from rising to it, is vice, with respect to them. But can any one be at a loss to understand, what enlargement of reason, and power, and mastership of the mind, or self-command, mean, who understands what it is to have weak and strong eyes, and a wilful, rash, inconsiderate, or a cool, sedate, deliberate head? It is therefore needless to expatiate more on this article; and all that remains to be observed, with regard to external improvements and purchases, is, that having <90> reason and certain affections and appetites in our frame, which are so many capacities of enjoyment, we are capable of improving them; in consequence,

I. Of a sense of right or wrong, natural to all men, that can never be totally effaced. It is evident, that if we had not a natural capacity of perceiving right, and distinguishing it from wrong, and of delighting in and approving the one, and of hating and disapproving the other, we could not possibly be capable of any of those sentiments expressed by self-approbation and self-condemnation, good and bad conscience, a sense of merit, and a sense of guilt and unworthiness. We would be utter strangers to them all, in the same way and for the same reason, that without an appetite, affection and capacity suited to any sensitive plea-sure whatsoever, we could not desire or relish it. It must be true in gen-eral, that without appetites and affections no objects could give us more pleasure than others; or, more properly speaking, nothing could give us pleasure. The great business of reason is to cultivate, improve, and then preserve in due force this our rightly improved natural sense of right and wrong, in the same sense that it is a duty in some degree to improve our ear and eye. But it is in vain to say, that this sense is totally acquired by reason, in proportion as it is improved, and becomes able to take in large and just views of the consequences of things. For as reason may find out that it would be a very advantageous thing to have an ear for musick; or that it may be of some use to affect to have it, and to act as if one really had it; but it can never produce it, when it is originally wanting: so reason may find out, that it would be, on many occasions, advantageous to have a sense of right and wrong, especially in a constitution of things, where true advantage, upon a fair and full estimation of things, is always con-nected with the dictates, the first motions of such a sense; or that it may <91> be greatly for ones interest to affect to have it, and to act as if one really had it: but it cannot produce it when it is not originally implanted in some degree. For this plain reason, that as reason could never be em-ployed to calculate external advantages, if we had no senses whereby we perceive outward pleasures and pains; so it could never be employed to compare right and laudable with outward advantageousness, unless it had a sense of both. And let no man say he hath no notion of any thing but external advantageousness in its various degrees and its contraries, unless he can affirm, that in no case whatsoever any thing ever appears to him to be base which is advantageous; or any thing honourable, and generous, and lovely, if it be contrary to a narrow confined self-interest, that only pursues sensible gratifications; which, such is our make and frame, that no man can or dare say. But having sufficiently explained this matter in the *principles of moral philosophy*, I shall only take notice of another thing in our constitution, necessary to our attainment to perfection of understanding or temper, which it is but just necessary to mention, because it also hath been fully handled in the same enquiry; namely,

II. The law of habit, which is indeed the law of improvement or perfection. Were it not for this general law in our frame, we could not possibly improve or enlarge any of our faculties, become more ready and expert at any exercise, or work any natural propension into temper, so as to render it the bent of the soul, and the ruling passion; but our faculties and affections would always remain in their first state, and all our repeated acts would neither make us wiser or better; more strong, more sagacious, more free, more generous, nor in any respect more improved, than if we had never exercised our reason, never enquired into nature, never acted. <92> But being constituted, as we really are in both the respects just mentioned, we have it in our power to improve all our faculties, powers, and affections; and to grow daily in wisdom and in virtue; we have a stock to improve, a rule to guide us in doing so, and we are sure of success to our endeavours.

All that hath been said, is incontrovertible experience: and need I stay to shew, that it is the scripture doctrine, which abounds with commands to improve ourselves; to give all diligence[a] to add to one virtue all the virtues, and to perfect ourselves, even as God is perfect.[b] We are there represented to be made, as man plainly is in every respect, for exercise, and not for inactivity, which soon wastes and consumes our powers, and then preys upon the very substance of the mind itself, so to speak: but chiefly for moral exercise, or for the improvement of our will and temper. I have already shewn what the scripture doctrine is concerning diligence and industry, with respect to external goods: and indeed nothing is more

a. Pet. i. 5.
b. *Mat.* v. 48.

earnestly inculcated upon us in holy writ than diligence and application, each in some particular calling, for which he is best fitted, without fretfulness and anxiety, and without avarice, but with patient resignation to the will of an over-ruling providence, that we may be useful to society in some laudable way, and instead of being a tax and burden upon it, may even have some share of power to do good to others. "Let every man, saith the apostle, communicate[a] and do good to the utmost of his power; and therefore let no man be slothful in business, but diligently do the duties of some beneficial calling or employ, in the most useful way the talents and circumstances put in his power." But the chief thing we are called upon to apply ourselves to, is the improvement of our mind in virtue, to which diligence in some useful business is so far from being an <93> impediment, that it is on the contrary absolutely requisite; or one of the properest means.[b] We are given often to understand, that our improvement in virtue can only be, and always will be proportioned to our endeavours to advance in it. And we are loudly called upon to remember this employment is the end of our creation, and necessary to fit us for the happiness of another life to come. In the book of proverbs how often are we exhorted to seek after wisdom diligently, and to dig for it as for hidden treasures, because in its hand are all the blessings of this life, and the life hereafter. In these exhortations to apply ourselves diligently to the study of wisdom, the wisdom chiefly recommended, is the wisdom that produces a strong mind, self-command, and mastership of the passions: but the study of natural knowledge is likewise comprehended in the description as a very useful part of it.[c] "Happy is the man that findeth wisdom, and the man that getteth understanding. For the merchandize of it is better than the merchandize of silver, and the gain thereof than fine gold. She is more precious than rubies: and all the things thou canst desire are not to be compared unto her. Length of days is in her right hand, and in her left hand riches and honour. Her ways are ways of pleasantness, and all her paths are peace. She is a tree of life

a. *Gal.* vi. 9, 10.
b. 1 *Tim.* v. 8, *&c. Titus* iii. 8. 1 *Thess.* iv. 11. *Rom.* xii. 11.
c. *Prov.* iii. 13, *&c.*

to them that lay hold upon her; and happy is every one that retaineth her. The Lord by wisdom hath founded the earth: by understanding hath he established the heavens. By his knowledge the depths are broken up, and the clouds drop down dew—[a]Get wisdom, get understanding, forget it not, forsake her not, and she shall preserve thee: love her, and she shall keep thee. Wisdom is the principal thing: therefore get wisdom: with all thy getting, get understanding. Exalt her, <94> and she shall promote thee: she shall bring thee to honour when thou doest embrace her. She shall give to thine head an ornament of grace: a crown of glory shall she deliver to thee." And how beautiful is the description given of her in the book of wisdom, "Wisdom reacheth from one end to another mightily; and sweetly does she order all things. I loved her, and sought her out from my youth, I desired to make her my spouse, and I was a lover of her beauty. In that she was conversant with God, she magnifieth her nobility: yea, the Lord of all things himself loveth her. For she is privy to the mysteries of the knowledge of God, and a *lover of his works.* If riches be a possession to be desired in this life, what is richer than wisdom that worketh all things? And if prudence work, who of all that are, is a more cunning workman than she? And if a man love righteousness, her labours are virtues; for she teacheth temperance and prudence, justice and fortitude, which are such things as men can have nothing more profitable in their life. If a man desire much experience, she knoweth things of old, and conjectureth aright what is to come: she knoweth the subtilties of speeches, and can expound dark sentences: she foreseeth signs and wonders, and the events of seasons and times."[b]

This is the wisdom which we are called to give all diligence to attain to, or improve in. But it is very remarkable that this same wisdom which we are commanded to labour hard to attain, is in other places of the same writings said to offer herself to us, to be at hand, nay to take hold of us: to cry upon us to hasten to her; so that we must shut our ears against her not to hear some of her instructions; and shut our eyes against

a. *Prov.* iv. 5, *&c.*
b. *Wisdom* viii. 1, *&c.*

all the objects around us, not to see her beauty.[a] This is the language of
the same sacred book just quoted. And what doth this mean, but what
we <95> have found by experience to be true, even that nature hath not
only well qualified us for the search of wisdom; but likewise hath implanted in us love of knowledge, impatience against darkness, and ignorance; and many other powerful instincts to push and excite us to
apply diligently to the study of wisdom, and to assist and direct us in
the pursuit. And with regard to right and wrong in particular, we are
told, not only that the moral differences of actions and affections are as
essential and immutable as light and darkness, or bitter and sweet.[b] But
that we have natural senses[c] for discerning good and evil. A moral conscience, which, if it is consulted, cannot deceive us, at least in more simple cases, or in the greater outlines of duty: and that the laws of moral
good and evil are written upon our hearts,[d] the hearts of all men universally and indelibly: and therefore that no man can sin or deviate from
right in any degree, without feeling a law in his mind, warring against
his evil concupiscences, till by long habit the mind is become obdurate
and callous, as it may be, but always is slowly, and after very violent
strugglings against an inward sense of what is *praise-worthy, and truly
becoming and honourable;* for thus likewise the scripture speaks of virtue:
phrases that have no meaning, if a sense of praiseworthy and laudable
in itself be not really belonging to us. For as reasonably might an apostle
exhort one who hath no eyes, saying, If there be any beauty, any visible
order, proportion and symmetry, seek after these things, for they will
give you delight; as recommend it to one who hath no sense of honour
or shame, of base or worthy, saying,[e] If there be any virtue, if there be
any praise, seek after these things, and thus shall you have inward satisfaction; your own hearts will not condemn but approve you, and you
shall have that testimony of a good conscience, which is a perpetual

a. *Prov.* i. 20. viii. 1. &c. ix. 1. &c.
b. *Isaiah* v. 20.
c. *Hebr.* v. 14.
d. *Rom.* ii. 15.
e. *Phil.* iv. 8.

<96> feast. 'Tis needless to quote more passages to prove this to be the voice of scripture, since we cannot almost turn up our bibles without finding some precepts to this effect. I shall only add one more; St. *Paul* writing to the *Philippians,*[a] earnestly excites them to work out their salvation with fear and trembling, that is, with all eagerness and concern. Now to work out our salvation in scripture language is, to give all diligence to prepare ourselves for the future felicity which the pure in heart alone can inherit, and into which nothing that is unclean or defiled can enter: to be assiduous and constant to improve in that sanctity of heart and life, without which no man can see the Lord, or be capable of that happiness, which a future state will afford to those who are fitted for it, by placing them in circumstances, which shall give them larger views of the divine perfections than we can now have, and better opportunities of imitating them. And what are the motives by which the apostle enforces this exhortation? "For it is God which worketh in you, to will and to do of his good pleasure."[14] Some are so absurd, as to interpret the apostle's meaning, as if he had reasoned thus, "Work out your salvation yourselves by your own diligence, for you can do nothing, but it is God that must do every thing for you, even will for you." Which interpretation is indeed a complication of absurdities. But the true and obvious meaning is, "Give all diligence to work out your salvation, for it is God, the creator of all things, who by giving you of his good pleasure the power of willing and doing, with a sense of right and wrong, and reason to guide and direct you, hath visibly made it your end so to do. Your frame shews, that to prepare yourselves for great moral happiness, arising from a well-cultivated and improved mind suitably placed, is your end appointed to you by your Crea-<97>tor. Consider therefore that by neglecting this your duty, this your interest, you contemn and oppose the good will of God toward you, and his design in creating you. The other motive he adds, plainly supposes a natural sense of right and wrong common to all men; insomuch that the most wicked cannot choose but admire and approve good actions when they see them, though they loudly

a. *Philip.* ii. 12, &c.
14. Phil. 2.13.

reproach their own opposite conduct. 'That ye may be blameless and harmless, *the sons of God without rebuke,* amidst a crooked and perverse nation, among whom ye shine as lights in the world.' "[15]

III. Let us now consider if there are any limitations upon what hath been found, according to experience and scripture, to be the general law in the divine government of mankind, whether with respect to external or internal acquisitions; "That as a man soweth, so shall he also reap: he who soweth to the flesh, shall reap corruption, and he who soweth to the spirit, shall reap the fruits of the spirit, which grow up naturally to eternal and compleat moral happiness." For this hath been shewn to be the meaning of the text.

We are as certainly sure, as that there is a God who by his infinitely wise and good providence over-ruleth all, that in such a state of things all must be governed by general laws admirably adjusted to the great end of the whole administration, the greater good. For were it not so, what would be the necessary consequence, but that intelligent agents would be placed in a system which they could neither understand, nor have activity in: that is, creatures endowed with powers of intelligence and action would be incapable of understanding and acting. For how can that be understood, so as to derive rules of conduct from it, which is not ascertainable? And what can be such which does not proceed in a fixed, determined, uniform order and <98> method? 'Tis only settled and regularly proceeding connexions that can be traced, comprehended, argued from, or acted upon. For all art and conduct must go upon this principle, that such a rule being observed in the pursuit of an end, that end will be gained.

Thus we reason in agriculture, mechanicks, in every art: and thus also must we reason in the conduct of our life, in all our actions and pursuits. And as government by general laws may be inferred by necessary consequence in this manner from the moral perfections of the supreme all-perfect mind, who made, upholds, and governs all: so philosophers know that we are able to trace effects in nature to general laws in so many instances, that there is sufficient ground, independently of that consid-

15. Phil. 2.15.

eration, to conclude by analogical reasoning, that all is governed in like manner by general laws. Accordingly in the material world, when the general laws of vegetable, and of what is very similar and near a-kin to it, animal growth, and several other powers and laws of powers in nature do not succeed, philosophers readily own, because they plainly see it is so in many instances, that this does not happen because nature is weak and deficient; far less, because it maliciously deviates in such instances from its general good methods of operation; but purely because the formation or production, which is always carried on according to the same law, or agreeably to the same principle, was in that case over-powered by the operation of some other general law, equally necessary to the good of the whole system. Thus bad weather, blasts, plants, and trees, for instance; and a disease or hurt happening to the mother, will occasion an abortion, or a monstrous deformed birth. And when these and other like appearances happen, which may shock those who are not able to take a large united view of the co-operation of many laws, in order to make a good system, they do not startle philosophers, because they know that the laws regulat-<99>ing the weather and its effects, and the laws determining the consequences of hurts and bruises, and all the other laws from which such like effects as have been mentioned proceed, are very fitly chosen, and that the greater good requires their universal, uninterrupted operation.

In the same manner must it be in the moral world, when certain general laws have not their common and regular effects: they are then thwarted, counter-acted, or over-powered by the influence of other good general laws, equally necessary to the greater good, and therefore never the cause of evil in an absolute sense, *i.e.* with respect to the whole system. Ignorant men perceiving that disappointments to industry, labour, and prudence, sometimes happen, are apt to call such events unlucky accidents, and to ascribe them to chance or fate. But if we consider the matter accurately, we shall soon find, that to ascribe any event whether to chance or fate, or indeed to any thing but the course of general laws established and maintained in full force by the author of all things, is to attribute effects to no efficient. For chance or fate opposed to the will of an efficient mind, must mean causes which are not causes, or productions by nothing. Unthinking men likewise frequently speak of the course of nature, as if by that they meant something quite distinct from providence: but in reality it can have no meaning, but the regular operations of qualities and powers produced and upheld by God according to fixed laws of his appointment. But if it be absurd to attribute effects, and the causes of effects, to any thing but the will of a mind sufficient to establish and uphold that course, and by which it really subsists; then are all events reducible, in the nature of things, by such beings as have a large enough view of the system to be able to do it, to general laws of the appointment of the creator of the world: and consequently, if any one general law is at any time disturbed or interrupted in its course, it can only be in consequence of the ope-<100>ration of some other general law of the same system.

Now all this being very clear, let us try if we can trace any of the interruptions or limitations of the general law we are now explaining, which may very properly be called, "The general law of activity, or industry," to the general laws whence they proceed. That there are certain limitations upon it besides those which belong to it as a sphere of activity having certain bounds, which must be the case with respect to the sphere of activity of every creature as such; or limitations upon it within its appointed and regular sphere, is very plain to every one, since, though in the common course of things, "The race be to the swift, the battle to the strong, bread to the wise, riches to men of understanding, and favour to the men of skill,"[16] otherwise prudence, industry, and wisdom would be empty names without a meaning; for there would be no difference at all between one way of conduct and another: yet it is not always so, "but time and chance (as the wise man saith) happen to all men, the wise; and the foolish; and God sometimes turneth wise men backward, and maketh their prudence foolishness."

The evident meaning of all which is not that men ought not diligently to inquire into the regular consequences of second causes, and act agreeably to them: Else whence these frequent exhortations to get wisdom,

16. Eccles. 9.11.

and to act prudently, to industry and application: for the same wise man exhorts us,[a] "Whatsoever thy hand findeth to do, to do it with all thy might," &c: But merely that the events of things do sometimes not answer to the natural probabilities of second causes, because many, even little unforeseen accidents unavoidably interposing, do very often change the whole course of things, and produce an event quite opposite to what, in all reasonable probability, suf-<101>ficient to have determined a wise man to act as he did, was to have been expected. The swiftest runner, upon the least accidental slip, loses the prize to a rival much slower than himself; and the strongest armies, upon the least disorder befalling them in the day of battle, have been defeated by an enemy whose inferior force they contemned: and as strength and agility of body are not always successful in proportion to the degrees of those faculties; nor powerful armies victorious in proportion to their numbers: so the faculties and powers of the mind likewise, understanding and wisdom, dexterity and skill, are not always successful as might regularly be expected in obtaining riches and honours, favour and distinction in the world: but unseen accidents, or more properly speaking, unseen dispensations of providence, unseen effects of other laws which must take place in the government of things, invisibly and surprisingly turn the course of things, and render qualities which are generally attended with success in their right application, successless. The causes of many unforeseen, and at first very unaccountable events, are afterwards discovered by time, and then our wonder ceases; which is sufficient to lead us to conclude, it is always the case, and that it is not fortune or chance, words without a meaning.

Now if all this be not owing to the two following causes, yet so much is certainly owing to them, that we may justly presume that what is not so, and quite unaccountable by us, must however be the consequence of the operation of some equally good general laws; since the world is found in fact to be so governed, and must be so governed, if it be under the administration of a supreme mind; which it must be, or be the effect of no cause, no contriver, no power, no producer.

a. *Eccles.* ix. 11. *Isaiah* xiv. 25.

I. A great part of the disappointments or limitations of the general law of industry, proceeds from the operation of the laws of matter and motion by which <102> the material world, with which we are at present united, is governed. All interruptions, limitations, or disappointments with respect to the law of industry in the exertion of our power about material objects, it is highly probable, flow from the laws by which the material world is ruled and managed. And that very many do so, is visible to every one: such as external or bodily diseases of very various sorts; the effects of storms, earthquakes, deluges, and many others, too obvious to be mentioned. Now let natural philosophers account for the general laws, whence those hurtful events proceed, by which the industry and prudence of the husbandman, the trader, the general, the politician, the philosopher, *&c.* are often disappointed, and are either rendered abortive, or, which is more pernicious, bring about the very contrary of the good proposed and intended. And I think they have done it. For that being done, our business is merely to conclude, that such effects are not evils: which they cannot be, the laws from which they proceed being good; unless it be evil that the general operation of a law necessary to the greater good should take place, which it is a contradiction to say. The laws of the material world, whence these effects proceed, are necessary to render the material system which they constitute that beautiful and orderly one it is, being so fit a habitation for an immense variety of perceptive beings, and of man in particular, furnishing him with many means of enjoyment and pleasant exercise of the sensitive kind; and, which is more, with many means, occasions, and subjects of rational exercises and improvements.

II. But leaving this point to natural philosophers, or the enquirers into the natural world, I shall proceed to consider another source whence many limitations upon the general law of industry take their rise. Which is, "our being made one kind; our being <103> made for society, and in order to that mutually dependent, so that to every external acquirement and to many internal ones, social assistance is in some degree necessary, and the greater advantages of life cannot be attained, but in a well formed and well governed community." That this is our frame and make in general, cannot be denied. For what advantage, a good disposition only excepted, can any man acquire singly, independently, or without social aid and assistance? Can he attain riches, nay, can he attain bread, or but subsist one moment? Can he attain knowledge in any great degree, without any help from others, and quite by himself? And how few are the virtues that can belong to a being out of society, or quite removed from all other beings! Let us consider how we came into the world, how we subsist in it, how much we depend on our parents, how much on education, how much on example, how much on the temper and abilities of those about us, how much upon the government and constitution of the state in which we live: let us consider, in one word, how we are cloathed, fed, supported, brought into the world, bred up, defended, improved in abilities, or how we can gain any end: and no man will dispute the truth now under consideration. But to say, that it is not fit but unkind, nay unjust, to have so framed mankind, what is it but to assert, that it is unkind and unfit that we should have social dispositions, and be one kind mutually dependent: nay, it must land in saying that it is unkind and unjust to have made us any thing, but singly, each by itself an independent, all-sufficient being. The objection, cannot stop till it terminates in that absurd assertion, and so refutes itself.

If our social dependence be acknowledged to be vindicable and not blameable, then many consequences must of necessity be admitted, which will fully justify numerous limitations upon the law of in-<104>dustry already explained. For hence it will follow that we must suffer in mind and body by bad education, by wrong example, and by the ill-disposition of those about us, of those more especially with whom we are more nearly and closely connected: hence it will follow, that we must suffer by the misfortunes of others, whether they be owing to their imprudence, or to some cause they could neither foresee nor prevent: Hence, in one word, it will follow, that to gain almost every end, we must depend upon the abilities, the prudence, the virtue, and integrity of others. In fine, the effects of a social frame, and of mutual dependence with respect to our happiness or misery, our acquirements or sufferings of whatever sort, are almost innumerable. I shall therefore but just insist a little upon one article of very great extent, which is our dependence upon the good constitution and right administration of the state in which we live: and even here I shall but just mention one instance. If men are slaves to despotic lawless power, or have no share in the government, *i.e.* in making their own laws, and laying on the taxes necessary to the support, maintenance, and advancement of their common happiness, they will naturally become abject, mean-spirited, dastardly, and low, groveling creatures. And what a train of vices must spring from this temper every observer of mankind will soon see. Hence naturally pullulate suspicion, jealousy, envy, fraud, revenge, and many other monstrous vices, which sadly depress and sink men below the dignity they naturally rise to in a free state; where a spirit of liberty and independency, a sense of one common interest and publick spiritedness, desire of aggrandizing the commonwealth, and of shining, gaining fame, honour, power, and dignity in it, by being eminently useful to it, must naturally grow up, as generous plants in their proper soil and climate; for there proper care of education, an essential point to free and happy government, cannot be wanting. There <105> not only will trade, and all arts flourish, but likewise all ingenious sciences, knowledge, ingenuity and industry will spread: and, which is more, virtue. For never was an enslaved people generally a virtuous people. Whereas, tho' the best governed state will not be absolutely exempt from vice; yet every state is, in proportion as it is truly not nominally free, a humane, a generous, an industrious, a virtuous one. Honest measures, avowed and openly pursued by the administrators, proceeding from an honest, generous, publick-spirited disposition, do always, in proportion as they take place, diffuse virtue and happiness over a land.[a] Mercenary, mean cunning dares not appear: it can hardly have success: and being once detected, is sure infamy and misery. Righteousness exalteth a nation; but sin, as it makes people abominable, so it is their ruin. For in a righteous constitution, where good laws are impartially executed, righteousness must *run through the nation as a fruitful stream:* industry will never have reason to complain, and vice can hardly escape punishment. The good example of rulers, ever more powerful than laws, will universally awake publick spirit and honest generous industry. And all the blessings of flourishing arts and sciences, and of ingenious, honest, incorruptible virtue, will as

a. See *Eccles* x. 1, *&c.*

naturally prevail, as good seed sown in a good, well dressed soil produces a fruitful generous harvest. And this is the happy state men are well furnished for, and strongly instigated to pursue by nature. For, to what other end can the inventive and all the active powers of man be supposed to have been conferred upon him, under the direction of his social disposition, lively sense of moral order, and delight in publick good, but this, that men may unite together in a proper manner for promoting publick happiness? To imagine us made and framed as we are with any other intent, is as ab-<106>surd as to say, a ship is not made for sailing, but happens by chance to be fit for that purpose. And indeed if one thing may be invented, contrived, and executed without intelligence and design, that is, by chance, all things may.

Having thus pointed out some limitations on the general good law of industry, with their effects; it is proper to consider what in the whole is the amount of them all, that we may be yet more able to pronounce concerning their equity and goodness. But, before we go further, it is proper to observe, that all the laws of the material world, with all their effects, are plainly ascribed in the sacred writings to the will, the choice, the free, wise and good choice and appointment of the Creator. They are all attributed to his pleasure and will; and to general laws so chosen and appointed.ᵃ For what else can be the meaning of the laws and commandments he is said to have given to material beings, which they unerringly obey? What else is the word, the voice, the ordinance by which they are said to be regulated? How otherwise is it true, that it is his directions which even winds and sea obey, to which he hath said, Hitherto shalt thou go, and no further? How otherwise do the sun, moon, and stars, and all the celestial bodies, keep his statutes and ordinances? And how else, or in what other sense, doth the earth obey his will in yielding its regular increase?

And as for our social make, as it hath been explained, it is plainly implied in all the commandments to men, to be benevolent and useful one to another, and to lay themselves out vigorously in promoting the publick good, each according to his abilities, and in the sphere of power

a. *Job* xxviii. 24, *&c. Psal.* civ. cxxxvi.

allotted to him, with which the scripture abounds. It is because we are so made, that the whole of our duty is placed in universal love, charity and benevolence; in minding every one, not <107> his own things, *i.e.* his own interests merely, but in regarding and consulting the good of society, and the advantage of his fellow-creatures.[a] To prove which to be the real doctrine of revelation is very needless; since no one who is acquainted with it, can possibly not have clearly perceived it to be the universal tenor of the scriptures.

But what is the amount upon the whole, as far as we can judge according to reason and revelation, of the limitations now mentioned? In answer to this, I shall take notice of a few very remarkable consequences of them, of those chiefly which have been observed to arise from our social make.

I. First of all, there must be very many differences among men in respect of abilities and talents, either originally, or which comes absolutely to the same thing, in consequence of their being placed in different circumstances, which will naturally, by exercising affections and powers differently, or occasioning differences with respect to exercises of affections and powers, produce various dispositions and powers. This alternative is put, to avoid a philosophical enquiry, whether men have originally different turns, dispositions and talents; or whether all these differences proceed from various exercises in consequence of various circumstances, calling forth affections and powers less or more into action. For it is plain, that it comes to the same thing to all intents and purposes with regard to individuals, or to society in general, in which of these ways differences are naturally produced. Circumstances of various kinds, the powers being originally the same, will have different effects: and as different powers are necessary to social dependence and social virtues; so different circumstances, which must naturally produce differences with regard to affections <108> and powers, are not only necessary to publick happiness in a community; but, in reality, community can no more be conceived without such differences, than any constitution, nat-

---

a. *Rom.* xii. 10, 11, *&c.* xiii. 10. 1 *Cor.* xiii. *Gal.* v. 14, *&c. Eph.* iv. 31. *Phil.* vi. 7. *Col.* iii. 12, *&c.* 1 *Thess.* v. 15.

ural or artificial, can be conceived without different parts, making, by their different qualities and forms well disposed, a good whole: Not to say, (which is likewise very true, and equally evident) that it is absolutely impossible to place various members of one body or community, all of them in the same or quite like situations. The apostle St. *Paul* helps us to a true illustration of this matter, by a similitude he frequently employs to shew, why in the church of Christ, more especially at the first propagation of christianity, different gifts and talents were bestowed on different members.[a] "For, saith he, as we have different members in our body, and all the members have not the same office; so we being many, are one body in Christ." The reasoning must hold equally good with regard to mankind, as one community, system or kind. For as we have many members in one body, and all members have not the same office; so we being many, are one body, one kind, one system, of which God is the head and ruler; and we are every one members of one another strictly united and dependent, even as the members of the natural body are, making one whole. And as the practical inferences he draws from his argument with respect to different abilities and gifts for propagating the gospel, with an easy change, similar to that made in the reasoning, in order to extend it to an account of the natural differences among mankind, may be applied to mankind in their social capacity as one community; so indeed, some of them being of a general nature relative to men, as one body, they must be understood to suppose those natural differences which constitute them such. We may therefore very <109> consistently with the apostle's design thus paraphrase the whole exhortation.[17] "I beseech you, brethren, for all men are such by nature, and no differences can ever change or alter that immutable relation, by the mercies of God extending over all his works, and particularly evident in all his depensations towards mankind, in order to excite and assist them to advance the great end of their creation, that ye remember you have bodies the seat of many sensitive appetites, in order to govern them by your reason; and therefore give all diligence to attain to self-government,

a. *Rom.* xii. 4–5.
17. The next two pages are a paraphrase of the whole of Romans 12.

to command over all your passions, your sensitive ones, in particular, which are the principal means of your trial in this state, in order to your attainment to moral perfection; that so your well governed appetites, or your appetites sacrificed and submitted to your reason and moral conscience, may render you, and your conduct, as it were, a living sacrifice, holy and acceptable to God, who delighteth in this moral discipline of the mind, and will reward it; for this is your reasonable service; this is acting suitably to the dignity of your reason, and the end of your being, and consequently to the will of your Creator, whose will is your sanctification in order to your happiness, to which it is absolutely necessary.

For I say unto you, to every man among you, through the light bestowed on me, not to think of himself more highly than he ought to think; not to forget that he is but a part of a great system, one member of a large body; but to think justly and truly of himself, and consequently soberly and modestly, according to the measure of powers and abilities God hath dealt to every one in his great wisdom, and make the best use of them for your own sake, and for the good of the whole body. For different members, which have each its peculiar use and office, are not more necessary to compose a natural body; than different members, which have each its peculiar use and office, its particular distinguishing powers, are <110> to constitute one community of moral beings. Having then different gifts, let every one know and stir up diligently the gift that is in him, that he may be really useful, whether it be of body or mind; whether it be for teaching, or for ministering in any other way to the publick good: let us wisely choose the business we are best fitted for, and let us diligently wait on it. If one exhorts, rules, teaches or gives, let him do it with simplicity, with candor, with chearfulness, and with a benevolent and compassionate spirit. Let love be without dissimulation, as becometh members of the same body. Abhor that which is evil, cleave to that which is good. Be kindly affectioned one to another. Not slothful in business, remembering that we serve God, do an acceptable work to him, and are building ourselves up in the best manner in virtue, when we are diligent at some profitable praise-worthy business. If tribulation happens to us, while we are thus employed, let us be patient, and not be cast down as those who have no hope: but let us rather rejoice, as becometh those who know that this is but our first state of trial, to be succeeded by another life, in which virtue shall have an abundant reward: let us acknowledge God in all our ways, ever maintaining on our minds a sense of our dependence upon him, and of his moral perfections, and all-wise over-ruling providence. Which thoughts will make us benevolent, active in doing good; disposed and ready to distribute to the necessities of all in want, according to their merit: ready to shew kindness to strangers, nay, even to enemies, and thus to overcome evil with good." This is certainly a true account of the duties resulting from our social make, our relation one to another as one kind, and our common relation to God, as our father, governor, law-giver and judge. And as we are indeed as closely cemented together by many ties and dependencies, as the members of any natural body are; so we could not be <III> capable of those duties and perfections, to which the apostle exhorts us, were we not such a one, closely compacted and united body, as we really are. And being so made, the practice of these duties makes the perfection and happiness of every private person, and the perfection and happiness of society in general.

The same apostle pursues the same comparison in another place,[a] to shew how unreasonable it was to complain of God's bestowing different gifts in the church, for the common good and advantage of all; which reasoning equally agrees to the similar bestowal of different gifts upon men, for the common good and advantage of the kind, and to be the foundation of social happiness and virtue. For thus may we reason concerning that matter almost in the apostle's words, "Be not surprized, or do not murmur at the diversities of abilities and talents among mankind, which are not owing to their own neglect of cultivating their original powers in a proper manner, as all those are which are blameable, or make unhappy to any great degree. For as the body is one, and hath many members; so all the members of that one body being many, are one body: and therefore, if the foot shall say, because I am not the hand, I am not of the body; is it therefore not of the body? And if the ear shall say, because I am not the eye, I am not of the body; is it therefore not of the

a. 1 *Cor.* xii.

body? If the whole body were eye, where were the hearing, where were the smelling? But now hath God set the members, every one of them in the body, as it hath pleased him. And if they were all one member, where were the body? But now are they many members, yet but one body. And the eye cannot say unto the hand, I have no need of thee: nor the head to the feet, I have no need of you. It is so far from <112> being so, that the parts of the body which seem in themselves weak, are nevertheless of absolute necessity. And those parts which are thought least honourable, we take care always to cover with the more decency; and thus our least graceful parts have thereby a more studied and adventitious comeliness. For our comely parts have no need of any artificial ornaments. God hath so tempered the body, that there might be perfect symmetry, and no disunion, but that all the members should have the same care of one another. And whether one member suffer, all the members suffer with it: or one member be honoured, all the members rejoice with it. Now we are one body, created by one Father, the supreme head of the creation, and each of us in particular is a member of this one body, as an eye, an ear, a nose, a hand, are members of the natural body. And God hath set or so placed some, that they are eminent rulers, others are eminent teachers, others eminent artists, some are fitted for one profession, and some for another, some for government, some for languages, some for philosophy, some for the study of medicine, or the *healing art,* and some for mechanical arts, no less useful in society. Are all philosophers, all heroes, all legislators, all teachers, or all great and extraordinary genius's? Have all the same gifts, whether of healing, of speaking, interpreting, or of whatever other kind? Why then do ye unreasonably contest with one another, whose particular gift is best, and most honourable or profitable? Every gift and business that is truly profitable to men is useful and honourable, when exercised with a spirit of benevolent industry. I will shew you a more excellent way, *viz.* mutual good-will, affection and charity, which is the best of all attainments, that which makes the honest man, the man of merit, because it makes man the image of God, in respect of which all other gifts of the highest kind are comparatively vanity. And this disposition of mind, <113> may all attain to, whatever their powers, abilities, talents or circumstances in life may be." This reasoning is not merely analogous to that of the apostle; it is evidently included in it.

So that according to the scripture doctrine of providence, a vast variety of differences amongst mankind is necessary to the greater good of mankind. And in reality the principal effects of all the various circumstances in which men are placed; of all the vicissitudes in life; of all the operations of external causes with regard to man, are the differences these make in respect of abilities, and occasions for exerting them; or of affections, and occasions for exerting them. But it being manifest in general that great variety in these respects is requisite to general good; nay, to the very subsistence of rational community, the presumption must be, that every particular variety is absolutely requisite to the greater good of mankind as one body. If we keep the apostle's similitude in our view between the natural and the political body, we will easily perceive that the latter, as well as the former, must consist of many different members closely united. And indeed if we but reflect a little upon what must be the necessary result of different situations with regard to abilities and tempers, to power, to knowledge, and to all external as well as moral acquisitions, we can no longer be puzled to account for the diversity among mankind, in any of these regards. For if various situations be allowed to be necessary, as they must be, unless all beings could be placed precisely in the same point of time and sight; then must all the variety resulting from different situations likewise be necessary. But any few differences whatsoever, in respect of situation, being supposed, a very great diversity of powers and affections; or, which is the same thing, a very great diversity of operations of powers and affections, immediately presents itself to us as the natural effect of such differences. <114>

II. But not only are the principal limitations of the general law of industry no more than effects of such differences, as are absolutely necessary in the nature of things to promote general good: but, as it hath been already observed, there are no disadvantages arising to particular persons from any laws of nature, with respect to external goods, out of which moral advantages may not be educed by wisdom and virtue, which would abundantly compensate them to the sufferers themselves. And with respect to the attainment which constitutes our principal dignity, well governed affections, or a virtuous temper of mind, all men, not-withstanding all the differences in human life, are upon a very equal footing. Virtue consists in self-dominion; or in command over the interior affections destined to be governed by reason. And this acquisition is in every man's power, in whatever situation he may be placed. It is true, some may not be able to make equal progress with others in knowledge, either not having equal abilities with them for that progress; or, which comes to the same thing in effect, not being in equally advantageous situations for it. But in every situation men may acquire a virtuous temper; or abound in benevolence toward men, and love and resignation to God. And those who have attained to this temper, as they are more happy here than affluence or even science can make those who have it not; so they must enter into another world very fitted by it for exercises of benevolence and devotion; and having this pure, refined, rational cast of mind, they may with the social, friendly assistance of the more advanced in science (a very agreeable employment to a generous mind) very soon make much greater improvements in the knowledge of God's works, or of universal order and harmony, than those can possibly do in any situation, whatever other learning they may have acquired, whose minds are discord and impurity. A mind which is itself all harmony, cannot fail, in a proper situation, to make <115> very quick and large advances in the study of order and wisdom.

It is also true, that in certain circumstances of life there is no occasion of exerting several very noble virtues: very rare situations are necessary to give one such opportunities: but all who have attained to the love of virtue, and to self-dominion in this life, have the *root of the matter* in them; the never-dying root of rational happiness: a principle of virtue, which being placed in proper situations for that end, will quickly bring forth the most glorious fruits of beneficence; the most splendid virtues. So that this state being considered as a preparatory one for futurity, in which various situations, various educations, various means of exercise and trial are necessary, no objection can be made against any present differences among mankind, either with respect to opportunities of improving in science, or of exerting certain virtues, which do not terminate in requiring, either that there be no differences at all among mankind,

but that they should be one kind, one community without any differences of the parts or numbers, that is, without parts; or, which is equally
absurd, in requiring, that a progress should be finished without beginning, and proceeding towards its end and completion.

To illustrate and confirm what hath been said, let me just add, that
the vicissitudes in human life, whether with respect to particular persons,
or to large collective bodies of men, render our present state such a duly
variegated or diversified school for acquiring very large moral knowledge, as it could not otherwise be in the nature of things. Now who will
say that such knowledge can be of no use to beings in another world?
What else can fit beings for extensive spheres of action but large knowledge, joined with benevolence, the natural concomitant of an enlarged
understanding? The farther one is advanced in knowledge, the fitter are
his faculties become to be placed in a si-<116>tuation for taking in more
extensive views, and attaining to higher knowledge. But this is not all,
the wiser one is, *i.e.* the more acquainted he is with moral beings, and
their power and capacities, the better qualified he is for the higher exercises of beneficence, which are the proper rewards to wisdom and virtue. Now in order to get wisdom or extensive moral knowledge, as well
as to have opportunities of exerting several great virtues, moral beings
must be placed in a situation proper for that end. And what situation or
school can be such, but one which shews moral beings to us in very
various circumstances; in many different attitudes; or very variously tried
and exercised?

In fine, when we object against differences among mankind here, we
do not reflect that differences are not only necessary to this state, but to
every state of moral beings. Far less do we consider that the great rewards
of virtue in every state of moral beings can be nothing else but certain
virtuous exercises, which necessarily require differences. It is true, the
differences necessary to a state of trial as such, cannot belong to the state
to which it is preparatory. But even that state which succeeds to a first
state of trial must have its differences: otherwise it could not be a state
of active employments; a state of virtuous and rational exercises.
Though the same differences cannot be equally suitable to every state of
moral beings, yet in every state of moral beings, or at every stage of moral

progress that can be imagined, certain differences are necessary; for the noblest exercises of the virtuous temper necessarily require some differences; rational virtuous exercise cannot take place without differences. It is therefore absurd to object against the differences which take place in our present state, in whatever view we consider it; whether by itself abstractly from the future state to which it is a prelude; or as it is a first and preparatory state with regard to a future one. The objections do really suppose that there <117> may be a whole without parts; and that virtues may be exercised where there are no objects or subjects of virtuous exercise. There are indeed but a very few first principles in morals. And these two, however simple and self-evident they may appear, are however the very principles which are called into doubt by most of the objections against providence; *viz.* that every being must have its own peculiar situation which no other can possess at the same time, and that every affection when it is exerted, is exerted about some object, which if it did not exist, the affection could not be gratified. Let us therefore remember the apostle's reasoning, and the consequences to which it naturally leads. That the body must be made up of many members; and that if there be teachers or rulers, there must be persons to be taught and ruled: when we suppose a state or community, we suppose members constituting that state as different from one another as the eyes, the ears, *&c.* are from one another in the natural body. And whenever we suppose exercises any-wise analogous to ministring good, to teaching, to ruling, or to any other such moral exercise, we suppose persons ministred to, persons taught, ruled, benefited. But because there will be occasion to return to this subject in speaking of a future state, I shall not dwell any longer upon it at present.

From what hath been said, the following corolaries may be inferred.

COROLARY I

That if mankind subsist and pass into any state after this life, it will likewise be the rule there; it will be the rule according to which men will be placed there; and it will still be the rule with regard to their acquisitions and advances there.

We have already reasoned in this manner. That if it be the rule with regard to placing men in a future state, and all their acquisitions in it (as St. *Paul* as-<118>serts in the text it is) it must also be the rule here, as far as the nature of a preparatory state to futurity permits. And we may alternately argue in this manner, that being found in fact to be the rule here in this present life so exactly observed, as that from hence the ways of God to man in it are fully justifiable, it must of necessity likewise be the rule in the state that succeeds to this life, in order to make the conduct of providence towards man compleat; if there be any such after-life. The scripture asserts, that there is a future life; and that this is the rule by which men shall be tried, judged, rewarded, or placed, and have their condition determined in it, all which phrases must necessarily have the same meaning. And that it must be the rule in a future state is demonstrable from the moral perfections of the Deity, from which the apostle infers it in the text. But abstractly from all these considerations it is plain, that if we may reason from analogy at all, as from the state of mankind at one period of time to their condition at another; or from the laws obtaining with regard to God's government of mankind in infancy and childhood to his government of them in riper years; we may likewise conclude that if there be a future state of mankind, the law observed here generally, without any limitations that do not take their rise from sources of a very beneficial tendency, shall be the law in a future state, without any limitations but such as likewise proceed from causes necessary to the greater good.

COROLARY II

But it likewise follows from what hath been proved actually to be the rule here with regard to all acquisitions made by mankind, that there must be a future state; otherwise indeed are moral powers and their acquisitions by labour and industry made to very little purpose; nay, wilfully destroyed in a manner to which we <119> see nothing that bears any likeness or analogy in the whole course of nature. To suppose no future state succeeding to this, is to suppose God to do what no man could do without being limited in power, or extremely capricious, to lay a noble foundation, and not carry on the building; or sow, manure, and cultivate, merely to have the pleasure of destroying things in their blossom, and when they are near to maturity, or when the harvest is at hand. God will, must perfect every good work he hath begun. He must therefore compleat the moral building that may be raised upon so goodly a foundation, and which, as far as it is advanced, promises a very perfect superstructure. Shall there be spring in the moral world, and no harvest? Surely the work is not finished here when moral powers are brought, by due culture, and variety of discipline and probation, to be fit for higher exercises than they could be qualified for before they were come to this maturity and vigor. If it stops here, it is a very imperfect work; nay, it is a cruel work: it is a cruel end to such an excellent beginning and an end it in no respect looks like or threatens. But the works of an infinite good and wise being cannot thus stop short of their completion, they cannot be imperfect. He cannot change or be changed, and therefore the same excellent disposition which alone disposed him to create moral beings capable of high improvements to all eternity, and to place them in a first state where their powers might have the properest means and materials of exercise for their improvement, must excite him to place them afterwards in a situation suited to their improvements made in this state. We know that a state designed merely for probation and discipline cannot always last; and we know this state, as it does not always last, so neither can it in the nature of things; for all material things must wax old, and wear out. But moral powers are of a different kind: they do not wear out; <120> they must be wilfully destroyed, if they cease to be. And can he who is infinite goodness take pleasure in destroying moral powers, and in disappointing all their natural hopes and desires, which are to be placed in proper circumstances to improve, and become more perfect; and in knocking down at once all the acquisitions made by them with much patience and suffering, with earnest labour and struggling? To say so is indeed to think most contemptibly, most ungenerously of the supreme being: it is to mock him: it is to deny all his moral perfections: it is to represent him as the most arbitrary of beings; as the worst of tyrants.

But let such thoughts be far from us: for what instinct prompts us to hope, and reason, to say the least of it, renders highly probable, revelation, by bringing immortal life and the law observed in it to light, hath put beyond all doubt. If we doubt or are diffident about the former reasonings from the divine perfections and analogy, let us no longer be so, but firmly established in the comfortable belief of a future state, in which every man shall reap as he hath sown here; for Christ, who died and rose again from the dead, assures us it is so: and he and his apostles, not content to affirm it by a testimony confirmed by miracles, for our greater comfort and assurance, often reason that it must be so in consequence of the divine moral perfections: that otherwise his work, his providence would be a very imperfect; nay, a very unjust iniquitous scheme. *And shall not the righteous Judge of the world judge and act righteously?* Will he deceive the hopes he hath implanted in us, and which virtue, as it improves, renders more strong and vigorous? *Will he not perfect what he has begun?* But if there be no future state, can we say that providence ends well; ends mercifully; nay, so much as justly? For here certainly tho' virtue hath noble opportunities of improvement; yet it doth not fully appear, that he who hath sown to the flesh shall reap corruption, and he who hath sown to the spirit shall <121> reap the fruits of the spirit; here the effects of virtue and vice are not fully compleat. They cannot be so till after a state of trial. For in it the effects of trial only can appear, and not the full harvest. But effects appear which do indeed promise an excellent harvest; effects which are themselves the first fruits, or at least the beautiful pleasant blossoms that betoken a joyful harvest to come in its due season. Effects which shew us how happy the virtuous mind may, must be, if after its state of formation and trial it is placed in circumstances for which it is become fit: effects which shew us, how happy God can make him, who hath given all diligence to improve the stock of rational powers he hath put in his hands, in proportion to the opportunities he had of making improvement, if he be generously disposed to do it: effects which promise indeed bitter things to carnal, sensual, corrupted minds; but bespeak blessed fruits of the same kind with themselves, only more perfect in degree, to the good and virtuous. Effects, in one word, which are the image of the divine happiness, and an earnest, a fortaste of the improvements in happiness that must arise from highly improved faculties duly situated; and therefore such effects as plainly shew to us what is the natural progress to happiness according to our make, even progress in virtue, progress in likeness to God. And what our make, and frame, and situation clearly points out to be our road to happiness must be such; otherwise our make and frame points us to an end we cannot attain to; and by it *God deceives us.* But we *deceive ourselves and mock God,* when we think, there is not a future state, in which God will render to every one according to his works, and we shall all reap the harvest of our doings, the harvest to which our doings naturally tend. For God, who cannot be mocked, resisted, or eluded, hath unalterably fixed this righteous, this truly generous and kind rule in his government of mankind, and of all moral beings, "Whatsoever a man soweth, that shall he also reap." <122>

∞ SECTION II ∞

The scripture doctrine concerning providence more fully explained, in order to prove a future state, and that this is an established rule in the divine government of mankind, "That whatsoever a man soweth, that shall he also reap."

A necessary observation upon reason premised, by way of

INTRODUCTION

Tho' it be a plain and universally received rule in criticism, that the obscurer passages of an author are always to be interpreted by the plain ones, and not the plain ones made doubtful by those that are more obscure, not to extend which to the sacred writings, in common with all others, would be most unaccountable partiality, to say no worse of it: yet upon some obscure passages of scripture are certain doctrines founded which are inconsistent not only with reason, but with the whole tenor of the scripture in general, or numberless plain declarations therein, in order to banter revelation, and turn it into ridicule. But to all impartial men such railing must indeed appear not merely ridiculous, but highly unjust and abusive; if it be really unjust or ridiculous not to observe the same rules of criticism in interpreting all books: and I now choose rather to take notice of some very false and hurtful opinions about scripture doctrines, into which those who pay a serious regard to revelation are misled through wrong notions of natural religion, by some passages of scripture: opinions by which they are induced to think very meanly of the guide God hath given us, without which revelation could be of no use to even our reason, as if by it we could not attain to <123> any just ideas of the divine moral perfections; far less come at any knowl-

606

edge of his works of creation and providence, or of the equity of his ways to man. The passages by which weak men (for however pious they may be, very weak and ignorant they certainly are) are misled into such injurious notions of reason, and of God the father of lights whose image and gift it is, are such as that in *Isaiah,*[a] who says, speaking of God, "there is no searching of his understanding." But even in the same place doth not the prophet appeal thus both to reason and tradition or revelation: "Hast thou not known? Hast thou not heard that the everlasting God, the creator of the ends of the earth fainteth not, neither is weary?"— And doth he not in a following verse affirm, "that they that wait on the Lord shall renew their strength: they shall mount up with wings as eagles, they shall run and not be weary, and they shall walk and not faint." The plain meaning of which passage must be, That they who endeavour to know God, in order to conform themselves to his image and will (which necessarily implies a capacity of knowing God) shall feel their faculties enlarge, and they shall gradually ascend in knowledge and in holiness, so as to become at last able to make a very swift progress in both, without wearying or fainting.

Or that other passage of the same prophet,[b] "For my thoughts are not your thoughts, neither are your ways my ways, saith the Lord. For as the heavens are higher than the earth, so are my ways higher than your ways, and my thoughts than your thoughts"—Whence some have inferred that we cannot have any clear apprehension of the divine perfections, so as to be able to affirm in any case, that any thing is unjust with respect to God; so totally different is justice in God from what we call such in men—Whereas the verse immediately preceeding plainly shews it can have <124> no such meaning—Let the wicked forsake his way, and the unrighteous man his thoughts: and let him return unto the Lord, and he will have mercy upon him, and to our God, for he will abundantly pardon—Where it is evidently supposed that we can distinguish between righteous and unrighteous ways, between mercy and its contrary; and thus understand what it is not to be like to wicked and unrighteous

a. Chap. xl. 28.
b. Chap. lv. 8–9.

men, but to have justice, goodness, and righteousness higher than the most perfect men, as heavens are higher than earth.

Or that of the Psalmist,[a] Clouds and darkness are round about him—Though it is often repeated by the same Psalmist—That we have full evidence from his works, that judgment and righteousness are the habitation of his seat—And that the whole universe is full of the riches of his bounty and goodness.

Or that of *Zophar* in *Job*,[b] "Canst thou by searching find God? Canst thou find out the almighty unto perfection? It is as high as heaven, what canst thou do; it is deeper than hell, what canst thou know?"—Though there nothing evidently is said, but that finite minds cannot fully comprehend all the ways of infinite knowledge.

Or that of *Solomon*,[c] "As thou knowest not what is the way of the spirit (of the wind it should be translated, according to that of our Saviour, 'Thou hearest the sound thereof, but knowest not whence it cometh, nor whither it goeth'). As thou knowest not what is the way of the wind, nor how the bones do grow in the womb of her that is with child; even so thou knowest not the works of God who maketh all"—Which cannot be understood as if it were absolutely impossible for men to attain to any skill in the anatomy of the human body, or of the ani-<125>mal oeconomy and growth in general; but in the same sense as the wise author of the Book of *Ecclesiasticus,* who having given a noble description of all the parts of the visible creation known in his time, sums up all at last with this judicious exclamation,[d] There are still hid greater things than these, and we have seen but a few of his works.

Or that of the Apostle St. *Paul*,[e] O the depth of the riches of the wisdom and knowledge of God! How unsearchable are the judgments of God, and his ways past finding out! For who hath known the mind of the Lord; or who hath been his counsellor? Where tho' the full ex-

a. *Ps.* xcvii. 2. xcii. 5. cxlv. 5. *Isa.* 40.8. *Ps.* lxxxix. 14.
b. *Job.* v. 9. ix. 10, 11. xi. 7–8. xxvi. 14.
c. *Eccles.* xi. 5.
d. Chap. xliii. 36.
e. *Rom.* xi. 33–34.

tent of the riches of God's wisdom and mercy are said to be beyond human reach, and many of his ways to be past our finding out; yet we are plainly supposed to be able to know and understand not only what wisdom and mercy means; but that they may be in God in the most exalted degree of perfection, and therefore may produce many things perfectly consistent with them which we cannot comprehend.

Or, to name no more, that of the same apostle,[a] Where is the wise? Where is the scribe? Where is the disputer of this world? Hath not God made foolish the wisdom of this world?—The plain meaning of which words and those which follow is, "Where is the philosopher skilled in the wisdom of the *Greeks?* Where is the scribe studied in the *Jewish* learning? Where the professor of human arts and sciences? Hath not God rendered all their learning and wisdom folly, plainly proved it to be so by the discovery of the truths of the Gospel? For since the world, by their natural parts and improvements in what with them passed for wisdom, acknowledged not the only true God, tho' he had clearly manifested himself to them in the wise contrivance and admirable frame of the <126> world, it pleased God, by the plain (which seems foolishness to them) doctrine of the gospel, to bring to true and salutary knowledge, those who understanding it, believe, receive, and conform to it."

As there is no foundation for the doctrines which have been mentioned in these or any other texts of scripture: so the frequent exhortations in scripture to search after the knowledge of God, to prove all things, and hold fast that which is good; to prove God's ways, and carefully to prove and try all pretended revelations from him, and to be ready to give a reason of any faith or hope we entertain or profess: the frequent commendations of those who take pleasure in searching into God's works, God's revelations, laws and testimonies; the severe censures of the ignorant, deceived, blind, and rash; the severe corrections of superstition, idolatry, and of implicite blind faith, and of talking deceitfully even for God: all these together, with the direct assertions of his justice, truth, goodness, faithfulness, mercy, and all his other perfections in scripture, as the ground, the only ground of religious love, hope and

a. 1 *Cor.* i. 20.

confidence; and the frequent appeals to his works, as evidently bearing the marks of his glorious attributes, and loudly calling upon us to study and imitate them, to love, adore, and copy after them, are sufficient refutations of such tenets, which obviously leave nothing to dignify human nature, above that of the brutes, who are only inferior to us in respect of their not being endued with reason, as we are; and leave no foundation for religion or morality. For if we may not understand the justice and goodness of God, in the same sense as we attribute those moral perfections to men, we cannot understand them at all; and consequently, we ascribe them to God without any meaning; and we, in reality, must deny moral differences of actions to be certainly intelligible by us, and consequently say, that we have indeed no rule of acti-<127>on. In truth, if we may not exercise our reason, or are not able to make any advantageous use of it, in studying the works of God, in order to know God, and our relation to him, and the duties resulting from that relation; What are we? Or what indeed is our reason good for? For, how mean, how low, how truly barren, and unprofitable is all knowledge, in comparison of this!

Let us not therefore vilify our reason, which is our glory; but let us *quit ourselves like men,* which it alone makes us to be. Let us look upon it as the image of God in our souls, which renders us capable of delighting in the contemplation of his works, by rendering us able to see clearly the manifest tokens of infinite intelligence, power and goodness, shining so visibly in them; and capable of transplanting these virtues, by careful and diligent imitation, thro' the sincere love of them, into our minds and lives. And let us accordingly delight ourselves, day and night, in searching into his works, and in endeavouring to conform ourselves more and more to the universal language of them all; the plain language of our own truly wonderful frame in particular; that to endeavour to be like God, is our proper study, our end, our dignity, our glory, our happiness. All this is the proper work of reason, and to it must revelation speak. It might be as reasonably offered to the brutes, as to us, had we not reason to understand its voice, and discern its evidences of truth and divine authority. But let us not be surprized, if we are frequently puzled, and in the dark.

For as we cannot judge of a kingdom; nay, not of a small family, unless we know its whole constitution and government; but may presume, that the parts not yet understood by us are of a piece with what we perceive clearly to be good or bad: as we cannot be competent judges of a ship, a watch, <128> or any machine, without understanding its mechanism, or the parts, and mutual references of parts, which compose it: but we may in such cases reasonably presume, because other works of the same artist, which we fully comprehend, are wisely contrived for their ends, that these also will be found to be such, when they are duly considered and fully comprehended.—Or so soon as we begin to discover the uses of some parts, we may infer, that a full insight into the whole would discover the uses of all the parts, and the excellent contrivance of the whole for a useful end.—So with respect to the works of God, if we can no where see any vestiges of good order and contrivance, then are they wholly incomprehensible to us, and we can make no conclusion from them: but, on the other hand, if, as far as we have advanced by the study of them, we have still found more clear evidences of excellent general laws, and of good and wise administration; then have we excellent reason from such samples to judge well of the whole; or to conclude, that all is perfectly good, tho' we know but a part, and can indeed see but a very small part of the scheme which is carrying on to perfection, even so far as it is advanced, in our narrow and limited situation. Thus we must reason concerning God's works, or give over reasoning in such a manner concerning men's works, and consequently give over acting upon prob-abilities, that is, acting upon the evidence on which the management of human affairs absolutely depends. Let us remember, that such conclu-sions concerning God from his works, are agreeable to what we have good ground to think of him from other considerations and arguments, those and such like which have already been considered; and that the scripture account of God is likewise to the same effect. And thus, let us not suffer ourselves to be shaken or startled, that we should at any time be in the dark, who see but a small part <129> of a scheme, that is indeed but a little way advanced. But let us, without fear of displeasing God, who cannot be intelligently loved, worshiped or praised, without clear and just ideas of him, which may be safely depended upon as infallibly certain, exercise our reason with candor, diligence and impartiality: not stand in awe to search, but yet search respectfully; not fear incurring his displeasure, for falling into any errors we can fall into in the diligent honest search of truth, without any biass, or with the pure love of it: far less dread his displeasure for endeavouring to grow in knowledge, in the knowledge of his perfections especially, to the utmost pitch of knowledge, the most enlarged diligent mind can reach. If we cannot clearly comprehend the agreements of certain ideas, or may not safely depend upon our clear conceptions of them, then can we not indeed attain to any knowledge. But if we can discover some agreements of certain ideas, and may depend on such discoveries, we may likewise with equal assurance depend upon our clear perceptions of certain disagreements of ideas: that is, we may depend upon it, that what we clearly perceive to be impossible, unjust, &c. is really what we clearly perceive it to be. Let it, however, be remembred, that very consistently with this position, between which and absolute scepticism there is no medium, (for I now would have knowledge to be understood in its largest sense, comprehending not merely demonstrative truths, but probability in its several ascending degrees) it may justly be said, that many questions may be asked relative even to known truths, to which we are not able to give any satisfying answer to ourselves. No truth can lead by a just chain of reasoning to an absurdity; and therefore there cannot lie objections against any truth, which are in that sense absolutely insolvable, that is, which necessarily terminate in a plain absurdity; for objections, thus terminating, are indeed demonstrations that the propositions from which they necessarily result <130> are absolutely false, because contradictory. But what is it that we know so fully, as to be able to enumerate all its qualities, or powers, and their productions; or that we can answer every intelligible question about it? Do we know any property of any body in this manner? Any law of nature in this manner? Do we know ourselves, or any part of ourselves, in this manner? And as justly may one say, who is ignorant of the particular use of some part of a machine, tho' he knows in general the end of the machine, that the machine is useless, or that part at least useless; that he shall never be able to comprehend it, or that no man can: nay, as justly may he infer, that for that reason, there is no such machine existing, but that his senses are deceived, when he thinks he sees it; as, in any case of natural, or of moral providence, say what he understands is not certain; it cannot be depended on, but must be given up as a deception, because there are several things relating to it he does not yet know, and cannot account for. To argue in this manner, in either case, or indeed at any time in any instance, is in effect to assert, "That because there is one question in a science which we cannot solve, there is no such science." Every impossibility or contradiction perceived to be such is a part of our knowledge: we cannot exclude negative propositions from our knowledge without sadly contracting its bounds: many, very many such propositions, both in natural and moral knowledge, are of the highest use and importance. But a question, which is intelligible, tho' not answerable, is no more than a question, to which as yet we cannot reply: for it would not only be absurd to conclude that no being can solve it; but it would be absurd to say that we ourselves may not afterwards be very capable of giving an answer to it. Otherwise how had science advanced? For how many questions about the government of the material world were but lately deep mysteries in that sense; which are now no more so, but clearly understood, tho' related to, or connected with other properties, and laws of properties <131> not yet understood, and therefore the proper object of search to the curious.

It was not unnecessary to premise this observation in an attempt to explain providence. It might otherwise appear too presumptuous and arrogant to many, tho' it be indeed man's properest and best study.

Of divine providence according to the scripture doctrine.

PROPOSITION I

It is universal, extending not merely to the material, but likewise to the moral world, and is absolutely uncontroulable.

The providence of God, in which the apostle asserts, it must be a law, "That whatsoever a man soweth, that shall he also reap," (because to deny it is to entertain the most injurious apprehension of the providence or government of God; or to mock God) is in scripture frequently asserted to be universal, or over all, and absolutely irresistible and uncontroulable.

That there is one God, who created and ruleth all things, is the express doctrine of the sacred scriptures in many places. Not only did he create, and doth he support and rule the inanimate material world; but he likewise made, upholds in being, and over-rules all perceptive and all moral beings. Nay, he is represented, not only to have created angels, and men, and all the various orders of rational beings, as well as all the various ranks of merely animal ones, and to have given them all their powers, capacities, affections and appetites; but he is likewise represented to foreknow all the actions of all agents. "The ways of man are before the Lord, and he pondereth all his goings.[a] His eyes <132> are upon the ways of man, and he fathometh all his goings."[b] And all things are open and naked before him from the beginning, from everlasting. And indeed this exactness of knowledge is necessary to the judge of all the earth, in order to his doing that which is right in the final decision of men's eternal state; or that he may render to every one according to his works, and thus every one may reap as he sows. This is too evident to need being insisted upon. For it is manifest beyond doubt, that, in order to a just distribution of rewards and punishments, or of happiness and misery in the government of men upon the whole of things, God must not only know the actions of men, but likewise be, as is asserted in numberless places of holy writ, a discerner of the thoughts and intents of the heart.[c] "He must be able to search all hearts, as he is said to be, and to understand all the imaginations of the thoughts." "The Lord must not see merely as man seeth. For man looketh on the outward appearance: the Lord must be able to look into the heart."[d] This perfection is necessary to judge the world in equity, and to render to every one the fruit of his doings; since virtue and vice lie not merely in the outward actions, but

a. *Prov.* v. 21.
b. *Job* xxxiv. 21.
c. *Heb.* iv. 12. 1 *Chron.* xxviii. 9.
d. 1 *Sam.* xvi. 7. *Psal.* xxxiv. 13, 14, 15.

principally in the heart. And therefore in scripture, as the inward truth and sincerity of the mind is represented to be what God chiefly regards; so, on the other hand, the heart of man is said to be deceitful above all things, and able not only to deceive others, but to deceive itself by secret partiality, and very difficultly perceptible flattery: but, at the same time it is said, no man can deceive God, who is greater than our hearts, and knoweth all things.[a] The abstruse, difficult question upon this subject, is not how God knows present and past actions, but how he fore-knows future free actions. And this must be such in the nature of things, <133> in consequence of our being created minds, and therefore not able to judge, but by faint analogy, of the extent and manner of the operation of God's natural powers and perfections: the difficult question relating to this subject is, God's fore-knowledge of future events. "Known unto the Lord are all his works from the beginning of the world."[b] Now, no doubt, God, who gave to us, and all creatures, all the powers they enjoy, and who hath established all the laws, according to which they improve or degenerate, and, in general, operate or admit any changes of whatever kind; and who likewise hath ordered all the laws, according to which external material effects are produced; nay, properly and strictly speaking, immediately produces them; such a being must needs know all the possible results of powers, and laws of powers, which are thus of his own creation and establishment. Here there is no difficulty at all. For such universal knowledge, nay, such an establishment is by none thought inconsistent with liberty of action in men, in any sense of liberty of action. But fore-knowledge of free actions is thought by some an impossibility in the nature of things; and by others, it is judged absolutely repugnant to, and incompatible with the liberty of moral agents: and therefore some have said, that the perfect government of moral beings does not require such pre-science: but that in order to the wise choice of the best system, the full knowledge of all possible connexions, and their results; the perfect comprehension of all the consequences of all possible distributions of powers, and laws of powers, is sufficient. But

a. 1 *John* iii. 20.
b. *Acts* xv. 18.

many predictions of events, which have been exactly fulfilled, recorded in scripture, prove divine fore-knowledge in such instances: and being admitted in some instances, it is not only possible that it may be universal, but it really cannot <134> be supposed not to be universal, or not to extend to all; since no possible reason can be given, why, or how it can take place in any one instance with respect to events depending on free actions of moral agents, and not reach to all, without supposing it to be in such instances, not merely fore-knowledge, but positive decree or appointment, which hypothesis, it is owned, is absolutely incompatible with free agency.

The difficulty therefore with respect to divine prescience of free-actions, as distinguished from consciousness of what is decreed and appointed to happen, is thus accounted for by the best writers[a] on the subject.

I. They observe, in general, that our finite understanding may very reasonably be allowed not to comprehend all the ways of infinite knowledge, as the scripture says we cannot. "Can'st thou by searching find out God? Can'st thou find out the Almighty to perfection?"[b] But this acknowledgement of the incomprehensibleness of God must always be understood, as it really is in the scriptures, and by such writers, with relation to such things only as do not imply any express, clear contradiction: for whenever that is the case, it cannot be said of such things, that they are incomprehensible, or what we cannot understand; but, on the contrary, are such things which we do plainly and distinctly understand that they cannot possibly be. The necessary falsity and absurdity of all such things being as evident to our understandings, as the truth of the plainest principles. It must also be observed, as these authors do take notice, that this acknowledgement ought to be understood only of things expressly revealed, not of any human doctrines or reasonings.

a. Dr. *Samuel Clark,* and Mr. *Woolaston.* [Samuel Clarke discusses this in *A Demonstration of the Being and Attributes of God,* proposition 10; William Wollaston discusses it in *The Religion of Nature Delineated,* 99–110.]
    b. *Job* xi. 7.

II. Secondly, They observe, that in the matter before us, the question is not, whether men's actions be free, but whether or no, and how that freedom of action, which makes a moral agent such, and men to <135> be men, can be consistent with fore-knowledge of such actions. For if these two things were really inconsistent and irreconcileable, it would follow, not that men's actions were not free, (since that would totally subvert all morality and religion, and take away all the moral attributes of God at once); but, on the other side, it would follow, that such free actions as men's are, and without which rational creatures cannot be rational or moral agents, were not the objects of the divine fore-knowledge. And, in such a case, it would be no more a diminution of God's omniscience, not to know things impossible and contradictory to be known, than it is a diminution of omnipotence, not to be able to do things impossible and contradictory to be done.

III. But, in the third place, say they, this is not the case; for these things being premised, we may now answer directly to the question, that fore-knowledge of free actions is not an impossibility or contradiction; *i.e.* is not inconsistent with liberty, because pre-science has no influence at all upon the things fore-known. And it has therefore no influence upon them, because things would be just as they are, and no otherwise, tho' there was no fore-knowledge. Foreseeing things to come, does no more influence or alter the nature of things, than seeing them when they are. What hath no productive energy, or power, cannot make necessary. But knowledge of no kind, neither knowledge of present, past, nor to come, can have any productive efficiency. It is *will* alone that produces, gives existence, or brings into being: independently, if the connexion between the will to produce and the effect be necessary, as it must be between the will of an infinite, independent being, and all the effects willed by such a being: dependently, if the connexion between the will immediately choosing or willing the effect, and the existence of the effect so willed, be established by the will of another mind, as must be the case with regard to all <136> derived beings, and their derived efficiency. Knowledge is merely passive, it can give light, point out the path, the proper road and choice, and so persuade to an election and pursuit; or it merely contemplates and reviews an object; but that is all it can do; it therefore produces or gives existence to nothing. It is the same whether we speak of dependent or independent, finite or infinite knowledge in this case; for being but knowledge, it cannot be active or productive, it can only comprehend, understand, see, or persuade. Further, the manner of God's fore-knowing future free-actions, must not, cannot be supposed to be like his fore-knowledge of things necessary, as all material effects are; for that would be to confound things together, which are totally distinct, and to assert that there is no active power in nature, but the power of God: and perhaps such an assertion does not terminate there, but must really go further. But it is sufficient to our purpose to observe, that to suppose the divine fore-knowledge of free-actions, *i.e.* of the volitions of rational beings, to be necessary, in the same sense that his fore-knowledge of effects produced by his will and decree that they should exist is necessary, is no more to speak of fore-knowledge in the sense we are now considering it, *viz.* as distinguished from consciousness of effects to be produced, in consequence of positive will or decree to give them existence; but is merely to speak of that later consciousness, which cannot without impropriety of speech, or, at least, without departing from the question, as above limited and defined, be called *prescience.*

IV. Now, in the fourth place, they add, That the divine fore-knowledge of free-actions we may have some obscure glimse of, in some such manner as this. What one man will freely do upon any particular occasion, another man, by observation and attention, may in some measure judge; and the wiser the person be who makes the observation, the more <137> probable will his judgment be, the seldomer will he be deceived, and the more may he, or others, depend upon it in their resolutions and actions of the greatest moment. An angel, in the like case, would make a judgment of the future event as much nearer to certainty than that of the wisest man, as the angelick nature and faculties are superior to the human. And therefore, in God himself, whose powers are all, in every respect, infinitely transcending those of the highest creatures, it must needs be, beyond any assignable bounds in respect of certainty, superior to what any the most perfect creature can attain to; that is, it must be certain beyond any chance or hazard of mistake or error;

or, in other words, it must be absolutely certain and infallible; for where there is no hazard of erring, knowledge must be infallible. But however certain it may be, it cannot have any influence upon the fore-known free-actions, unless we say the fore-knowledge of wise men in particular cases, upon the certainty of which their greatest interests may be ventured, and daily are very wisely adventured, can have some proportionable influence upon them; and the more certain fore-knowledge of a higher creature a proportionable greater influence. For will being out of the question, whatever influence knowledge can have as knowledge, cannot belong solely and wholly to the most perfect knowledge; but can only belong to such knowledge, in a degree proportionable to its perfection, and must belong to knowledge, as knowledge, in every degree of it, in some proportional degree. But who ever imagined, that the fore-knowledge of a most perfect creature, however certain, however much to be depended upon in matters of the highest importance, had or could have any influence upon free actions, so certainly foreseen by it. In fine, while knowledge, either of present, past, or to come, as knowledge, can have no influence, the degrees of its certainty can make no alteration in that respect; that <138> is, they can produce no influence. Because this maxim is universally true, "that whatever belongs to any property as such, must belong to it in proportion to the degree in which it is such a property; in proportion, so to speak, to its moment or quantity, in like manner, as what belongs to gravity as such, must belong to every quantity of it proportionally." Another thing I would add, (for what hath been just now said, and what follows I would not have imputed to any other but myself, by whom they are added, lest they should be found not to be true, of which however I have no apprehension) is, that when a ruling passion is established in the breast, good or bad, that being known, and the circumstances in which it is placed being known, the determinations choices, and actions of such persons may be very certainly determined. No wise man, for instance, is at a loss to determine how a thoroughly good and wise man he is thoroughly acquainted with will act in any given case; or how any man, whom he certainly knows to be governed by any given ruling passion, will be swayed in any particular assigned circumstances.

But it is time to leave a subject which hath been so often handled by others.

What remains to be observed concerning providence, according to the scripture account of it is, that it is absolutely irresistible.[a] No counsel, no devise against the Lord can prosper: his will, his power is absolutely irresistible. And therefore when we read of the Devil's setting up a kingdom in opposition to the kingdom of God, great care must be taken that we do not so understand it, as if the Devil had, properly speaking, any power against God. We are <139> sufficiently instructed not to take such ways of speaking in that absurd sense; since, in scripture, wicked men are said to set themselves up against God, resist his will, and exalt themselves in opposition to God's kingdom, which sure no person can understand of natural power in man to resist God. But like ways of speaking about the Devil's opposition to God, without entering into an enquiry what the Devil is, must be interpreted in the same sense, as meaning not opposition of natural powers, but of moral powers and dispositions to God, by doing things wicked and displeasing to God, as wicked men likewise do. Not only is it an absurdity to suppose any created power able to contend, fight against, or oppose God, the supreme Author of all power; but in scripture we read in many places of God's absolute power and supremacy over all malicious wicked spirits; and of his giving power to the good, as such, to discomfit the temptations and machinations of such against them. I beheld Satan, as lightning fall from heaven: behold I give unto you power over the enemy, and nothing shall by any means hurt you.[b] God is faithful, and will not suffer us to be tempted above what we are able, but will with the temptation also make a way to escape, that we may be able to bear it.[c] Resist the Devil, says St. *James,* and he will flee from you.[d] And St. *Jude* assures us,[e] that the angels which kept not their first estate, but left their own habitation, he

a. *Deut.* x. 17. 1 *Sam.* xiv. 6. *Job* xl. 2, iv. 2. *Jerem.* i. 19. *James* iv. 2. *Rev.* xix. 6. *Psal.* lxxxvi. 3. cxv. cxxv. cxlv. *Isaiah* xl. 10, *&c. Dan.* iv. 13. *&c. Ephes.* i. 11, 17.
b. St. *Luke* x. 18–19.
c. 1 *Cor.* x. 13.
d. Chap. iv. 7.
e. Ver. 6.

hath reserved in everlasting chains under darkness, unto the judgment of the great day.

Certain ancient corrupters of religion in the primitive times, from the many evils and wickednesses which are in the world, inferred, there was a supreme evil principle originally opposite to and independent upon the power of God, which monstrous opinion was first taught by some *Persian* philosophers,[18] who <140> called the good principle *light,* and the evil principle *darkness.* And against this absurd opinion it is, that *Isaias,* in his prophecy to *Cyrus,* King of *Persia,*[a] thus declares: "I am the Lord, and there is none else: I form the *light,* and create *darkness:* I make peace and create evil: I, the Lord, do all these things." This doctrine is directly contrary to the whole tenor of the scripture, which expressly asserts one supreme cause the fountain of all power, who is infinitely good and we shall immediately have occasion to shew more fully than hath been yet done, that an independent mind absolutely evil is an impossibility. Mean time, with regard to many ways of speaking in the scripture about the devil and his kingdom, 'tis well worth while briefly to take notice of a very important observation that hath been often made on this subject, which is, that all rational beings whatsoever, capable of good and evil, must be created originally in a state of trial or probation. Answerable therefore to what we see among men, 'tis reasonable to suppose that among all other creatures, likewise indued with the power of willing or choosing, and consequently invested with a certain sphere of activity and dominion, allowing for their respective circumstances, powers, and capacities, there will be proportionally a difference of conduct and behaviour. And accordingly the scripture assures us, that among angels some continued to be the favourites of God, who do his pleasure; and that others of them sinned, and kept not their first estate, but left their own habitation. And concerning the chief of those, our Saviour

---

a. Chap. xlv. 6, 7.

18. Manichaeism, the gnostic religion founded by the Persian Mani (216–77), taught these doctrines. Clarke criticizes Manichaeism in his sermon 10 in his *Works,* 1:62.

tells us,[a] that from the begining he abode not in the truth. What the particular sin of those disobedient angels was, is not distinctly revealed; and therefore it is a vain thing to make conjectures about it. This only we may be sure of, that it was not, as some have incautiously represented it, a <141> rebelling against God, by way of open force; but a presuming foolishly, as wicked men also do, to transgress the laws of their nature and their God: and they are punished not beyond, but suitably to their deserts, or they reap the fruit of their doings. From the figurativeness of the expressions applied to fallen angels, and to sinful men, when they are said to resist or oppose God, as well as from the nature and evident reason of the thing, 'tis plain, that the kingdom of Satan set up in op-position to the kingdom of God, is not literally a kingdom of force or power, but in the spiritual sense a kingdom or party, a dominion or prev-alency of sin, in opposition to the kingdom or establishment of righ-teousness. Departing from virtue and goodness, is revolting from the kingdom of God, and declaring, that we will not have him to reign over us. Hence wicked men are called the children of the devil, and good men the children, the sons of God. The phrase is very elegant, and ac-cording to the analogy of the *Jewish* language, very usual and expressive. For the highest way in that language of expressing any particular quality, similitude, or relation, is by stiling them the children of that thing or person by which any extraordinary quality, similitude, or relation is in-tended to be expressed. Thus men of meek, calm spirits, are in scripture called the sons of peace; and outrageous oppressors, sons of violence. Men of true courage are sons of valour; and in still a sublimer sense, sons of thunder; persons of exemplary virtue, faith, and piety, of what-ever nation they are of, are children of *Abraham.* Men under the sen-tence of death are called sons of death. *Judas* for his singular corruptness is stiled the son of perdition. And persons under any great or lasting distress, sons and daughters of affliction. Many of which figures have a very great grace, nay, give a very extraordinary energy even to modern poesy, as those acquainted with the sublimest of poets, *Milton,* will read-ily acknowledge. <142>

a. *John* viii. 44.

Thus then we have proved that, agreeably to reason and scripture, the divine providence is as universal as is necessary, in order to the exact observance of that rule of just and equitable moral government asserted in the text, "That as one sows, so shall he reap."

PROPOSITION II

The Divine Providence is clearly and expresly asserted in scripture to be infinitely wise and good; so that from hence it may justly be concluded to be a rule strictly observed by it in the government of moral beings; "That upon the whole every one shall reap as he sows."

The knowledge of the supreme fountain of all power must of necessity be proportional to his power; so that if the latter be boundless and infinite, the former must likewise be so. As God cannot know things, or relations of things, but from consciousness of his own power to produce, so his knowledge must be proportionable to his power. Whatever therefore is possible in respect of infinite power, must be clearly known by the infinite mind possessed of that power. But to say the power of an independent original mind, the one cause of all things, is limited, is certainly to say, it is limited without any thing to limit it, there being nothing beyond or without it to limit it; or there being in reality no source of limitation upon it, beside natural impossibility, if that can properly be called a limitation, or a confining and restricting cause; as it certainly cannot. God's power therefore is infinite; and his knowledge, which cannot but be proportionable to his power, is also infinite.

Wherefore though the scripture, the design of which is never to enter into philosophical discussions; but merely to give such clear ideas of the perfections of God and of his providence as are necessary, or of im-<143>portance to the direction of our conduct, doth no where expresly affirm that God knows all possible things and relations of things; yet since it says, that nothing (which does not imply a contradiction) is impossible to God, that he is all powerful and knoweth all things, we may justly say that he fully comprehendeth all possible things, and all possible relations, habitudes, connexions, dependencies, and consequences of things. All power is intelligent power; and infinite intelligent power necessarily implies this in it. So likewise does the free choice of God in choosing what possible system to create, imply it. And from our power of imagining various combinations and distributions of things which never existed to us, we may draw a very probable argument, That the divine mind, from whom we derive this power of conceiving various systems by analogy in our imagination, hath full knowledge of all possible variety of systems or combinations of things.

But though infinite knowledge thus defined be necessary to infinite wisdom and presupposed by it; nay, though infinite wisdom must necessarily belong to such knowledge, yet wisdom in a distinct way of conceiving it, is a different attribute from knowledge. Wisdom, properly speaking, is the right use or exercise of knowledge. And therefore it differs from knowledge, as the use of a power differs from the power itself. 'Tis therefore in the divine nature, possessed of infinite knowledge, the exercise of that knowledge, and the power inseparably connected with it, in the best and properest way, for the best end. Having the infinite knowledge just defined, he must always know the best end, and always clearly see the means that are fittest to produce that end; and knowing both these, he must always be disposed, without any byass to the contrary, to act accordingly. No person will say, that there can be various possible combinations of things, with certain consequences result-<144>ing from them, and yet not better and worse, more fit and less fit; more and less perfect combinations of things. To assert that, is to say that all properties are the same, and will turn to the same account, however they are ranged, placed, distributed or combined. And that God can perceive all possible relations and consequences of things, and yet not perceive what is fitter and worse; since we cannot understand and compare different combinations, without clearly seeing it in these cases, is to suppose God void of a capacity of the noblest and usefulest kind which he hath given us. Nay, which is more, it is supposing him to know all combinations of things without understanding that which alone can render such knowledge either useful or pleasant. And which is yet more absurd, if any thing can be so, it is really to suppose God to know and fully understand combinations of things without understanding them.

For what is it to understand fully any disposition of parts and properties, but to know its natural consequences, results, effects and tendencies; or, in one word, its aptitudes to certain ends. Now if the first mind must know what is best, he must choose it with full delight and complacency; he must prefer it, and preferring it, he must invariably pursue it. That he must pursue what he unchangeably prefers will be owned, since nothing can alter his views of his things, nor his temper and disposition. And to suppose him not to like what is best, that is, what appears to his perfect understanding such, is to imagine him, without liking and approving the best, capable of giving us a disposition to distinguish the appearances of things, and so to delight in what appears best to us, that however corrupt we may have rendered our minds, yet we cannot choose but approve what is best, while it is perceived by us. Strong passions may quickly obscure our view of it, and hurry us into pursuits very contrary to it; but we cannot reflect upon or view it without approba-<145>tion. And it is impossible we can be so framed by a being, who, knowing the best, does not like or approve it.

It may very justly be questioned whether any being can be capable of perceiving beauty, order and proportion, whether in material or moral objects, without being pleased with it, and naturally delighting in it. There may be creatures, who have no ideas of beauty. But to assert, that a mind may perceive beauty without being delighted by it, seems to be absurdly to distinguish between an agreeable perception and the pleasure perceived. For whatever qualities we may find, by enquiry into natural connexions, to be united with beauty, order and proportion, in material or moral objects, which, when discovered, may, by associating or blending themselves with the ideas of beauty, order and proportion, greatly heighten our pleasure in contemplating them; yet beauty, order, and proportion, are names for certain agreeable ideas, distinct from any others that may be connected with them, either by nature, or by voluntary association: *i.e.* they are names for certain pleasures. And surely pleasure of whatever kind cannot be perceived without perceiving pleasure.

There are certain ideas, which we express by the words, *harmony, proportion, order, beauty,* even in material objects, which give delight to all mankind, quite distinct from their affording any gratification to any of our sensitive appetites; and from quite another view of them, than as being for their interest and further advantage; but merely as such intellectual forms, images or ideas immediately, and by themselves. The faculties from which we receive these pleasures, and the pleasures themselves, are as natural, and as easily to be accounted for, as any sensual appetite whatever, and the pleasures arising from its gratification. There is no question that can be asked about them, as, "How they give us pleasure?" "Whence it comes? And what it is?" that does not <146> likewise belong to all our other pleasures, and the faculties by which they are perceived, and in the same sense; and that may not therefore be resolved in the same way: which will ultimately be in all cases, "That we are so constituted, or such is our nature and frame." Otherwise we must run into the same absurdity with respect to the causes of our pleasures, as some do in speculation about efficient causes; that is, suppose an infinite series of them.

To explain this subject a little more fully, because the argument, I think, is not very common; let it be considered what is meant when visible beauty is said to be connected with regularity in objects, and with utility; that regularity and utility are the foundation of visible beauty, or the qualities whence it results: or, in other words, that it is regular objects composed of various parts, conspiring by their mutual respects, and close union, to some proper or good end in the simplest manner, which alone excite the perception of beauty in us. For what is the meaning of this, but that where we perceive beauty, we shall always find, by proper enquiry, that there is regularity, unity of design, simplicity and utility? Perhaps it must be so in the nature of things. But whether it must be so or not in the nature of things, we constantly find by observation, that it is so in fact with regard to us. Yet the perception of beauty is distinct from the regularity and utility with which it is connected. So distinct, that beauty may, and frequently is perceived, where there is no notion of regularity, or of unity of design. Nay, beauty is so distinct from regularity, that the latter is discovered by proper rules and measures, which we are excited to apply to a beautiful object, by the agreeable perception of beauty with which it immediately strikes us. And as for utility, in many cases, where beauty is perceived and admired, it is not easily discovered. They are therefore said to be connected together, because they are found to be so in fact; or because we learn from ex-<147>perience, that beauty being always connected with regularity and utility, in order to produce it in human workmanship, we must study regularity and utility, and take the proper methods to produce them. They are therefore connected together, as other ideas of different senses are, which by their connexion or co-existence make the same object. And consequently, to confound visible beauty with any other perception, is the same absurdity as to confound smell with any other sensation. And as it would be absurd to distinguish the agreeableness or disagreeableness of a smell from the smell itself; so it is the same absurdity to distinguish the agreeableness of beauty from the beauty perceived.

If therefore we suppose the Author of our nature to have any conception of proportion, order and beauty, in natural or moral objects, he must necessarily have pleasure and delight in perceiving them; for not to suppose it, is to suppose him to have pleasant conceptions and not to have them. But if he have not conceptions of proportion, order and beauty, then hath he produced, and made us capable of perceiving what he knows not, or has no idea of.

If we pursue this argument but a little farther, since we not only perceive beauty and order, moral and natural, with immediate delight; but are capable of making such perceptions the objects of our reflexion, and thereby of receiving new delight from them, as objects worthy of our approbation and pursuit; and thus are capable of determining to set ourselves to improve such a capacity with all diligence, by our reason, into what is called, with respect to natural beauty, a good taste of nature, and of the arts which imitate nature; and what is called, with respect to moral beauty, a good taste of the harmony and consistency of life and manners; or, in one word, of virtue, and a good moral temper. This being our constitution, for the very same reasons just mentioned, the Author of our nature must have in him a perfect love and approbation of natural and moral beauty, he must delight in <148> it with a delight of approbation, and therefore must steadily pursue it in all his operations and works. I thought it not improper to shew, that the Author of our frame must have delight in beauty and order, natural and moral, analogous to ours, in the same way that any of our other powers or perfections are analogous to his. And what hath been said, may very easily be applied to the perception of the greater good in a system, and delight in it, or approbation of it, if these two be not really co-incident. For that perception must be a beautiful and agreeable one to every mind who can form it; and must be approved as the best pursuit by every mind who can reflect upon it: it is so at least with regard to us. And God, who hath so constituted us, must himself have the perception of best, and having it, he must have delight in it, and approve it, as the best, the worthiest end. He who hath implanted in us our capacity of discerning the best in certain cases, and our determination to like and approve it, must have, analogous to it, a perfect conception of best and worthiest in every possible case, in all circumstances, in the whole of his creation, and full delight in it, and approbation of it as such. It cannot but be so in the nature of things, unless ideas of beauty and order, and love of them, and delight in them, can be blindly, *i.e.* fortuitously produced.

Now it is remarkable, that God is said, in scripture, to delight in the beauty of his visible creation; to rejoice in it; to review it with full complacency and satisfaction. And indeed, it is as certain, that God cannot give, or render capable of any one faculty, without a distinct adequate conception of it; as that he cannot give any other without a distinct adequate idea of it. If he can blindly produce any thing, every thing may be blindly produced: chance may be the author of every thing: nay, with regard to what is supposed to be produced, without a clear and distinct understanding of it by the supreme cause, the supreme cause and chance are the same thing. <149>

"Tho' we could not possibly have any glimpse of the way and manner how God can have clear conceptions of all the pleasures and pains of which he hath rendered his creatures capable, and which are the effects of his laws; yet it is not in this case alone, that we cannot fully account for the divine manner of knowing or perceiving things: that is often the case, and must necessarily be so, even with regard to minds far superior to ours, because they are not infinite." But for the sake of what is obscure and unknown, we must not give up with clear and certain truths.

Such as this, "that what is not perceived or known, cannot be intended, aimed at, designed; or, in one word, produced with intelligence: and what is not so produced is really produced without a producer, which is absurd."

We are indeed sufficiently warned by the holy scripture, as well as by reason, not to ascribe any imperfection to God; yet we are sufficiently authorized by the sacred writers to ascribe eyes, ears, hands, and all our senses, and all kinds of affections to God, so far as these ways of speaking only serve, or are only employed (as they are in scripture) to denote that God must have clear adequate conceptions of all his works, and cannot be the blind Author of any thing. For to ascribe blind production to him, is not only to attribute imperfection to him, but it is to assert an impossible thing, or a down-right contradiction. With regard to the affection we are now speaking of, it is ascribed to God in direct terms. He is said to delight in moral beauty, the beauty of holiness; nay, in all beauty and order, even that of the inanimate material creation, for he pronounced it good; and he is said to abhor all deformity, moral deformity[a] in a more special manner. The argument we have been now using to establish the holiness, <150> the goodness, the purity of God, or his supreme love of order, beauty, proportion, publick good; and, in one word, what his infinite knowledge perceives to be best, is *Job*'s: "Shall mortal man be more just than God? Shall a man be more pure than his Maker?"[19] The angels are higher than men, yet even the most perfect of them must be infinitely inferior to God, in purity, sanctity, and every perfection; for from him is all derived that they possess or are capable of. And another inspired writer reasons, as hath been observed, to the same purpose: He[b] that planted the ear, shall he not hear? He that formed the eye, shall he not see? This emphatical solid reasoning is ushered in by a most awakening solemn preface, "Understand ye brutish"; to give us to understand, how absurd it is to imagine any capacity or perfection we possess, must not be derived from one who possesses it, and all perfection in the most compleat degree and manner; since were

a. *Habak.* i. 13. *Job* iv. 17, xv. 15, 16.
b. *Psal.* xciv. 9. *Prov.* v. 21. *Jer.* xxiii. 23, *&c.*
19. Job 4.17.

any thing so produced, it would be produced without intelligence, than which there cannot be a greater absurdity supposed.

Thus then, tho' whatever imperfection attends or may attend any affections in us, or in any order of created beings, cannot belong to God; yet not to ascribe to him delight in beauty and order, moral and natural, is to ascribe to him the greatest of all imperfections, want of capacity of discerning order and beauty; or, which is yet worse, if it be at all conceiveable, ill affection towards what he perceives to be orderly, beautiful and best. This proposition is therefore true in general, that God knows what he has made, and knowing beauty, natural and moral, and the best in every possible case, is naturally and immutably well affected towards it, and steadily and unerringly pursues it. <151>

But, in order to infer the wisdom of God, as it hath been above defined, no more is necessary than merely to reflect, that every unwise action, or circumstance of action, must necessarily proceed, either from shortness of understanding, from defect of power, or from faultiness of will. It is either because the agent knows not, or that he cannot, or that he will not do what is best. But from each of these defects and imperfections, the divine nature is infinitely removed. Therefore, every action of God, must of necessity, (in the moral sense of the word *necessity*) be what is absolutely in itself, and upon the whole most wise. "By wisdom therefore, as the scripture speaks, hath the Lord founded the earth, by understanding hath he established the heavens; by his knowledge the depths are broken up, and the clouds drop down dew."[20] Or, as the prophet expresses it, "He made the earth by his power, he established the world by his wisdom, and stretched out the heavens by his understanding."[21] Who can express the mighty acts of the Lord, or shew forth all his praise? How manifold, O Lord, are thy works; in wisdom hast thou made them all. This wisdom of God do all his visible works speak aloud, says St. *Paul.*

The providence of God, if it be infinitely wise, must also be infinitely good; for an infinitely wise being cannot be maliciously disposed, but

20. Prov. 3.19–20.
21. Jer. 51.15.

must be of the most beneficent disposition, or be disposed to extend happiness as far as his omnipotence can: Goodness being nothing but a fixed disposition to do always what in the whole is best; and, so far as is consistent with right and justice, what is most beneficial to all. It is evident, that the supreme, universal, original mind, having all knowledge, his understanding can never mistake or err in judging what is best; and having no want of any thing to complete his own happiness, no private good distinct from the exertion of his power to communicate happiness, his will can never be influenced by any wrong affection, or have any allurement, temptation, or pro-<152>vocation laid before it to act otherwise than according to what he knows to be best. But hence it is very obvious to reason, that he could not possibly have any other motive to create, but only that he might create all the various capacities of perfection and happiness, which it was fit for infinite wisdom to produce, in order to display its riches and fullness; and for infinite goodness to produce, in order to give existence to the greatest quantity of good that could possibly exist; and that he might dispense happiness to moral beings in proportion to their different improvements and deserts. In proportion, I say, to their different improvements and deserts: For it is necessary to equal or just administration, that happiness should be approportioned to goodness or merit; depend upon it, or result from it, in consequence of the constitution and administration of things. Goodness does not mean profusion without rule, but according to the best rule and measure; but proportion to merit, or good desert, must be the best rule in dispensing happiness, or a measure and rule or proportion in dispensing it, must be words without a meaning; which cannot be said, while an essential difference between moral good and evil is allowed.

In truth, an independent, all-powerful evil mind, is a complication of absolutely incompatible and repugnant qualities. It is a complication of infinite power and infinite knowledge, which are in the nature of things inseparable, and of infinite blindness, darkness and ignorance: it is a compound of independence and self-sufficiency and happiness, and of insufficiency to happiness, absolute discontent and uneasiness. For what else are envy, hatred and malice, but absolute misery? And to perfect the absurdity, it is a combination of freedom from all provocation, want, distress or injury, implied in independence, and of envy, resentment and cruelty, which ever suppose dependence, distress and injury, or provocation.

To be satisfied of the truth of these reasonings, we need only reflect, that our nature (and every moral be-<153>ing must be by its constitution the image of its Creator) is no less a stranger to self-hatred than it is to ill-will, emulation and resentment being away; but, on the contrary, there is deeply inlaid into it, benevolence or good-will. There is no such thing as love of injustice or oppression for their own sake: there is no such thing as delight in mischief as such: no such thing as disinterested malice. As corrupt and irregular as men sometimes become; we perceive nothing in the world that is vicious or hurtful, but what is really the fruit of eager desires after external goods, which all observers of human nature have acknowledged there is reason to think the most abandoned would choose to obtain by innocent means, if they were as easy and as effectual to their end. Emulation and resentment, by any one who will take a right view of human nature, as we shall see afterwards, will not be found to be arguments of any thing like pure malice in our frame. And indeed all the principles and passions in the mind, which are equally distinct from self-love and benevolence, (of which there are very many) do primarily and most directly lead us to right behaviour with regard to others, as well as ourselves, and but accidentally to what is evil. Now can such a nature be the production of a being of pure malice. As well may we suppose benevolence to aim at nothing but evil, as disinterested malice to have carefully and designedly thus produced a very complicated frame, so evidently calculated for the generous pursuit of the good of its kind, in many different respects, all concurring to the same good end, and mutually strengthening and exciting one another for that effect.

Nor need I stay to prove, that the scriptures assert the infinite goodness of God in the strongest and clearest terms. It is the universal language of the Bible. And indeed it would be in vain to recommend to us the love of God, without representing him as such. For it is this perfection alone that can render him the object of love. And this is the character given of God in the scriptures, *that he is love.* <154>

I shall therefore upon this head only make two very important re-marks, and then proceed to enquire into a particular character given of God in scripture as merciful, which seems to imply something distinct from the general notion of goodness.

I. In opposition to reasonings to prove the goodness of God from his works, to which the holy scriptures are ever appealing as manifest evidences of it, it hath, or may be said, that he who knows not the whole, and cannot see the final issue and tendency of all things, can pronounce no certain judgment of it.

Let it therefore be observed, first of all, that the issue of such an objection is not atheism, but mere doubt or scepticism: for it goes no further than this; what tho' we can count many goods, yet because we cannot number all, we cannot positively say whether the ballance lies upon the side of cruelty or benevolence; for may not all the goods we can count be finally conducive to evil, which, upon the whole, is perhaps far superior in quantity to good, as it must be, if the goods that are in it be but subservient means to evil.

Now, it seems sufficient to take off this scepticism, that we can easily imagine to ourselves a system in which there is nothing but pain; and a system in which there is nothing but pain, and no pleasure, must be a worse system than one, in which there are many pleasures. But a being delighting absolutely in ill, would produce the worst system that could be. But if it is said, in pursuing the objection, that we can also conceive a system in which there is nothing but pleasure, and therefore, if a good being must choose the best, the author of a system, in which there is any mixture of pain, must be at best but a very imperfect being, or cannot be absolutely good. The question being thus reduced to its ultimate terms, it may be answered, in the first place, by appealing to any one, "what a spectator of any complex piece of work, ignorant in a great measure of the various parts, and <155> references of parts by which it is constituted, and consequently of its general end, whatever that end be; but who, upon the first sight, and partial view of it, plainly saw several things to be just and beautiful, while others appeared to his eye disproportionate and wrong; what such a spectator would infer from these appearances to his eye in this imperfect view of the whole?" Would he not immediately conclude there was a probability, that a full sight and knowledge of the whole frame would wholly destroy the appearances of wrongness and disproportion? But that there is no probability, that a complete view of the whole, that is, of all the parts, and all their mutual respects constituting the whole, would destroy the particular, just, beautiful, and right appearances? Would he not conclude, that such a view might shew the parts already appearing good and just, to be so likewise in another manner, and higher degree, by subserviency to greater goods or nobler ends? He would not certainly conclude that the right appearances perceived were not intended? And as for irregularity and disorder do we ever suspect it to be designed? He would therefore infer, that the wrong appearances are not really such, but appearances which even good and just parts must have to a spectator who has not a full view of the whole.

Thus are we necessarily led or determined by our make and frame to reason concerning men, human actions, human inventions; and every thing we see and are determined to act by in the way of probability: and which of our affairs in life admits of any other evidence or manner of determination and choice? And if it be so, we are made to reason so likewise concerning the whole of nature; that is, we are made to conclude well of the works of our Author, the Author of all things, from the samples of beauty and good we see. But would an evil being have so made us? There are many evident reasons why a good <156> being should make us so, of which this is principal, even that we may thus be naturally led to conclude his goodness, and to love and imitate it. But no reason can be assigned that could move pure malice to make us so, unless it be merely to disappoint us terribly at last, which if it be the aim of the Author of nature, its accomplishment is reserved for a future state, in such a way that the further we are able to advance in the search of his works at present, the more and clearer evidences we see of good order, and wise and beautiful administration in it; and the more appearances of evil are destroyed. For this is known by all philosophers to be the truth of the case with regard to this system of which we are a part. The only thing that can be disputed in this reasoning is a fact, for the truth of which we must appeal to experience: which is, the determination in our nature to reason, or rather to choose and act in the way mentioned. But let every man try himself fairly whether this is not the way he reasons and is naturally disposed to reason about men and things, as well as the government of the world. For who does not naturally judge of men in this manner, never presuming they are evil, unless there be very evident instances in their conduct, which clearly demonstrate they must be bad; but, on the contrary, ever presuming with great assurance, that the good things they do come from a good heart, and are not snares to deceive? Thus do all men reason, till they have quite corrupted their minds, and have studied and struggled themselves in opposition to nature, under the specious shew of acquiring prudence, into a resolution to suspect all men, and to treat them as if they were knaves: and even then they must sometimes judge contrary to this unnatural, affected rule, and very frequently do so. 'Tis in vain to say, that beings of another make will judge differently; for the question is, how we are formed to judge, and what must be the final cause, and consequently the motive <157> for implanting such a disposition in our nature; or so constituting us. We have no reason to imagine there are any such beings in nature as have not the like disposition: we know none such. And if we are really so made, we must either own that we are designedly so made, in order to judge well of our Creator, and in order to have a benevolent idea of our fellow creatures, and a kind disposition towards them, which design can only be the design of a very generous creator; or we must say that we cannot know the final cause of any thing, or conclude any thing from it when known; not of the eye or ear, for example; for their final causes are not more evident than the final ends now mentioned of our natural determination to assent to or be satisfied with probability, in the manner described, in judging of complicated works, and of all appearances in men or things.

What renders the answer to the preceeding objection compleat is, that though we can conceive a variety of beings perpetually entertained by agreeable sensations in a passive manner, yet we can only conceive it to be in a passive way, and in a way not reducible to general laws; and we cannot possibly conceive a regular system of great moral happiness, in which certain choices and actions are not attended with evil or hurtful consequences; because moral agency supposes capacity of prudence and folly, virtue and vice, good and ill desert, and such agency cannot take place, as hath been often said, but in a state where if certain methods be chosen and pursued, certain pains will be the consequence. Moral agents justly treated, are agents so placed that they shall upon the whole reap as they sow; reap the fruits of their doings; that is, beings of good desert shall have proportional happiness, and beings of bad desert shall have proportional misery. But such a system does ours, as has been proved, plainly appear to be even at present; whence it is highly reasonable to conclude, that <158> as revelation teaches us, it shall more fully be found to be such the farther it advances, that is, in an afterlife, to which this is as spring to harvest in the natural world. But let it be observed, that when abstracting from the arguments which demonstratively prove the moral perfections of God, and consequently a future state, or in other probable reasonings we say, it is highly reasonable to conclude so and so; or it is natural, it is likely; if in such cases we ask what that means: the only answer that can be given to the question is, that we are, because our circumstances require such a frame, so adjusted or constituted that when we perceive no necessary connexion, but mere likelihood, we are determined to acquiesce in such perceptions according to the various degrees of likelihood. It does not follow from hence that rules may not be laid down by careful observers of the course of things, and of the different consequences of venturing to act upon different degrees of probability, for assisting and directing us in judging of degrees of likelihood, and of satisfaction or acquiescence proportioned to them, in the same manner as it is necessary, to try and examine the real values of objects, in respect of any good or advantage they are fitted to afford, least we should imagine more in them than there is, and so act with affection not proportioned to their real, but to a false imaginary value. That by no means follows. For in effect it is but observing how appearances of likelihood, which in fact do influence the mind, all of them in some degree, turn out in the ordinary course of judging and acting upon such appearances. But if the mind had no disposition to confide in certain degrees of likelihood, nothing but demonstration could satisfy us: that is, nothing but clear perception of necessary agreement or disagreement of ideas could determine us to act: nothing else indeed can produce what is properly called assent of the understanding: it really means that perception: like-lihood or probabi-<159>lity produces properly a disposition to act with more or less hope or assurance; with more or less diffidence about the event; which, to treat accurately of it, will be best measured by the quantity of interest one would stake or risk upon acting on hope or assurance so produced.

Our being so made is necessary to our situation, and it is therefore an argument of the care of our Maker about us; and being so made, not to be satisfied about the wisdom and goodness of the Author and Ruler of the world, in the manner it teaches and prompts us to reason and acquiesce, is really doing violence to our nature; and accordingly we feel it to be so. For no fact is more certain, than that whatever pains men may take to think ill of the Author of nature, or even to doubt of his moral perfection, in opposition to the plain evidence we see every where of wisdom and goodness, they can never attain to their end. Nature will often tell them, by making them feel the violence they do to a very proper determination in their nature, that they act a most unaccountable, unnatural part. Were this determination merely given us to satisfy us in enquiries after the character of our Maker and Ruler, it might perhaps, by opposition, be at last quite overpowered. But being by our circumstances necessitated often to yield to it, and act conformably to it, and frequently feeling the advantages of it in these respects, opposition to it in that single instance is too bare-faced partiality, or dissonancy and inconsistency to be palliated to ourselves with any specious shew by all the cunning artfulness of the most deceitful heart, ever so much practised in cheating itself by giving things false colours; the most dangerous of all wicked dispositions to ones self, as hypocrisy is the most dangerous of all vices in respect of society.

II. A second observation I would make is, that though wisdom and goodness may properly be said to constitute the moral character of the Deity, which ren-<160>ders him the proper object of religion, love, esteem, hope, gratitude, and confidence; yet there are several other attributes ascribed to the Deity in holy writ, which we have good reason, from the contemplation of ourselves and our situation, to conclude really to belong to him: attributes that may be deduced from wisdom and

goodness, being really included in them; but which however we can consider distinctly from them; and must so consider, in order to have a clear
conception of them. These attributes are truth, or faithfulness and veracity, purity or holiness, and equity and justice.

Sure I need not stay to prove that the scriptures frequently ascribe
these perfections to the Deity, and that reason leads us to ascribe them
to the Deity will be evident, if we attend to our own make. For it is as
manifest as that we are made to approve benevolence in ourselves and
others, that our moral understanding or moral sense is not indifferent
to every thing but the degrees in which the benevolent disposition seems
to prevail, and in which it seems to be wanting. For were we so constituted, we should neither approve of benevolence to some persons preferable to others, nor disapprove injustice and falshood upon any other
account than merely as a greater share of happiness was observed likely
to be produced by the first, and of misery by the last. Both of which
suppositions are contrary to manifest experience in our situation. There
are numberless cases in which, notwithstanding appearances, we are not
competent judges whether a particular action will upon the whole do
good or harm; this will in all very complex cases be a very difficult enquiry, for which the bulk of mankind at least are not qualified. And
therefore it is fit that in a system where the greater good of the creation
is the end of its Author, we should not only be indued with benevolence,
and reason to guide it in its properest exercise; but likewise be immediately determined by our nature <161> to certain methods of acting
which upon the whole will produce the greatest good, by a sense of fitness in them, and unfitness in their contraries, quite distinct from a perception, that the observation or transgression of them is for the happiness or misery of our fellow-creatures; but as directly and immediately,
and by the same approving and disapproving faculty, as we are determined to approve benevolence, and disapprove its opposite, or all de-
partures from it. And as this is fit, so in fact, this is the case with respect
to us, for there are several dispositions of mind and several actions which
we cannot but approve or disapprove, abstracted from the consideration
of their conduciveness to the happiness or misery of the world: several
dispositions and conformable actions which are naturally and necessarily

approved or disapproved by conscience, by that power within us, which is the judge of right and wrong, without any reflection on their consequences with regard to publick or private interest. Numberless instances of this kind will occur to every thinking person. All pieces of falshood, deceit, and treachery do thus appear base and detestable to our approving and disapproving sense: some to every person, even those whose sense of right and wrong hath been most industriously perverted. Nay, there are even certain actions which we can hardly give any other name to, than the general one of indecencies, which yet are odious and shocking to human nature.

Upon the supposition that strict observance of truth, veracity, decency, and other such rules of conduct, which we are naturally determined to approve, quite distinct from all consideration of their conduciveness to the greater good or ill of our kind, be really contributive to such ends, it plainly follows, that there is a good reason for so constituting us, with regard to them, who really are not in all cases able to judge of the tendency of actions, in respect of the over-ballance of happiness or misery they may produce: nay, upon that supposition there is a very good reason for so con-<162>stituting us, even though we were always able to judge easily and readily of the tendency of every action; *viz.* in order to strengthen the benevolent principle, and to be, if not directors and guides to it, yet assistants and corroboratives of it. And if the world be the contrivance and production of an infinitely good being, as we have found it to be, as the principle of benevolence, so these other dispositions, and the approving sense of them, cannot be implanted in us, but for the greater good; or for their amiableness and usefulness. Whatever be the reason of implanting them in us, they are to us a natural rule of action. But they cannot be given us to be such by an infinitely wise and good being, unless they be really worthy of the approbation with which we are determined by him to contemplate and reflect upon them. And nothing can have amiableness or approveable worthiness to such a being, but what is really in itself by its observance conducive to the greater good, his only end of creation and government. Now though we could not determine whether those rules of veracity, truth, and justice we are made to approve, be rules that God himself observes, and must observe in the government of the world: yet if we cannot prove the contrary; since we are so made, the presumption will naturally lie that they are such, even to him. And that it is so revelation expressly declares. But that the observance of those rules must be necessary to government, whose end is the greater good of moral beings, is almost certain. For what is truth and veracity but acting according to the truth, the reason, the real fitnesses and proportions of things? And whence else can the greater good of a system result? What is purity and holiness, but moral rectitude, or a disposition of mind conformable to the truth and reason of things; from which if the greater good in the whole do not necessarily ensue, there is and must be a contrariety between the disposition of things most conformable to reason and <163> truth, and the disposition of things most conducive to good, happiness, and perfection, which is absurd. Though we are not competent judges in every case of the necessary means to the greater good of a system of which we know so small a part; yet we are sure in general that no conceivable transgression of truth and veracity can be such; as for instance, "giving the marks of a revelation to what is not"; and far less, "deceiving hopes implanted in moral beings by nature," and yet far less, "punishing or making them miserable for pursuing what is evidently the end of their natural frame when justly considered": the not rendering upon the whole to every rational agent according to his good or ill desert: the inflicting any evil or misery for the sake of plaguing the innocent. Now if by induction we find that every instance we can imagine of violation of truth and veracity is contrary to the pursuit of greater good, we may justly conclude, that the universal observance of them is necessary to the greater good. And to all these reasonings we have yet this other to add, that God our Author, who hath given us such a moral understanding, by which we are not indifferent to veracity and truth, and other moral qualities, and their contraries, must have clear conceptions of them, and of their appearances to our moral understanding, as he hath constituted it. He therefore so formed our understanding, either because he perceives a real absolute amiableness in these qualities, which, if it be owned, they are then allowed to be really, absolutely, and immutably amiable in themselves to all moral understandings; and therefore they must be so to the Deity, and of consequence they must be a rule of action with regard to him: or because they have, though not an absolute amiableness in themselves, yet a relative fitness with regard to mankind in their situation, in order to direct them in their conduct for the greater good of their kind: upon which last supposition, at the same time that it must <164> be owned, that great goodness alone could have so constituted us, we must needs be very much puzzled to explain, how an appearance of amiableness and approveableness can be given to intelligible objects or images, not essentially belonging to them, or what that means. If it be not co-incident with the absurdity already mentioned of separating an object or quality perceived from the perception; it is at least, but a puzzling, perplexing hypothesis; whereas the other is a simple and consistent one, liable to no difficulties: since it goes upon no other supposition but this self-evident principle or fact, that all intelligible forms or images have essentially some appearance to the moral understanding, capable of reflecting on them, which necessarily excites either approbation or disapprobation as such, abstracted from all other considerations, as visible forms do of beauty or deformity, regularity or irregularity. All appearances to the eye produce either the one or the other of these sensations, though 'tis only more remarkable or striking ones that are very much attended to, others being in comparison of them comparatively as nothing. And all moral appearances must in like manner affect the mind, when they are reflected upon, and so made objects to it, either with a perception of beauty or of deformity; though 'tis in like manner only the principal kinds of such appearances in respect of which others are comparatively as nothing, that are much attended to.

Now truth and simplicity are in all instances so inseparable, that we may safely always prefer the more simple hypothesis to all others. And indeed we are naturally framed so to do; and while we are influenced by this disposition to look out for the simplest hypotheses, where looking out for any is either necessary to assist and direct in our choice with regard to action; or to quiet our minds, by taking off uneasy and perplexing difficulties and doubts, we never have in the event reason to repent so doing. The physician, the natura-<165>list, will always before experiment presume the truth of the simplest hypothesis; for experiments always turn out in its favours; and thus shew, that our determination by nature to embrace the most simple hypotheses, is by no means a deceit: But this, as it is a very strong argument of the care of nature about us, so it is an instance of that strict regard to truth or veracity, which is one of the divine perfections we are now enquiring about. For to give an instinct or determination which deceives us, is falshood; and to give one that does not, is veracity. And thus again we have another argument to prove what we are contending for. For all our determinations being right guides, or guides which do not deceive, or lead astray from our proper pursuits to disappointment, they are really so many samples of the adherence of the Author of our frame, and of all things, to truth and veracity in his government of mankind; from which, according to all the rules of analogy, it is reasonable to conclude the rule to be universal in the divine government.

III. But what hath been said of the truth and faithfulness of God, naturally leads me to take particular notice of what is taught in holy writ of the mercy, the compassion, the patience and long-suffering of God, attributes under which he is peculiarly represented to us by the inspired writers. Whatever evils befal men in this life, yet the holy scripture declares, that God always affords men sufficient provision for their eternal happiness, if by their own perverseness they neglect not the means which he gives them for that end. Nay, the sacred books often tell us, that one great end of temporal evils is the advantage that may be reaped from them, with regard to advancement in virtue, and thereby laying a foundation for great future felicity. God has endowed men with reason and natural conscience, to distinguish between good and evil, and to forwarn them, as it were, by an inward and per-<166>petual instinct of the certainty of a future state, in which it shall be rendered to every one according to his desert. And revelation confirms this by declaring expresly, that according to the several degrees of men's knowledge in these matters, he will require of them a severer or less severe account in such a manner as becomes the judge of the whole earth, to do right. And that in the mean time, in order to bring sinners, if possible, to repentance, and a just sense of their duty; he with much patience, long-suffering, and forbearance frequently, nay, generally defers their punishment or misery; and if they do repent, he forgives and pardons them, as a father receives a returning child; or a shepherd rejoices over one of his flock that had been lost: for so the scripture speaks.[a] And this is that part of goodness which is strictly and properly distinguished in the holy scriptures by the name of *Mercy.* The character or description there given of the divine mercy, patience, and long-suffering consists in this, "That God is not willing that any should perish, but that all should repent and live; or be restored to his favour by returning to the ways of truth and holiness, without which it is impossible in the nature of things to be happy in a future life; that he is ready to forgive the penitent sinner; and that sentence against an evil work is not speedily executed,[b] that the sinner may have space, opportunity, and inducement to repent."

How emphatical are the words of the Psalmist to this purpose,[c] "The Lord is full of compassion and mercy, long-suffering, and of great goodness—He <167> hath not dealt with us after our sins, nor rewarded us according to our iniquities and wickednesses—Like as a father pitieth his own children, even so the Lord is merciful unto them that fear him; for he knoweth whereof we are made, he remembereth that we are but dust." And the particular instances given us in scripture of this patience and forbearance of God toward sinners, shew us that this is the meaning of it.

And indeed the general conduct of providence towards sinful and corrupted men and nations, shew that the mercy and patience, ascribed to God in scripture, do really belong to him. A very wise *Heathen*[d] in his enquiry "Why the wicked, whose ways God must abominate, are not immediately destroyed," among many other reasons gives these. 1. That

---

a. *Luke* xv. 7.

b. *Rom.* ii. 4. *Eccles.* viii. 11. 2 *Peter* ii. 15. *Rom.* ix. 22.

c. *Ps.* ciii. 8. The Book of *Wisdom* says (Chap. x.) Thou, Lord, hast mercy upon all; and winkest at the sins of men, that they should amend. This is the way of his merciful providence. He chastises by little and little them that offend, and warnest them, by putting them in remembrance wherein they offend, that leaving their wickedness, they may believe in thee, O Lord.

d. *Plutarch.* [Plutarch, *De his qui sero a numine puniuntur,* 550D–551C, 552D, 554B.]

in general, this world is the state of our probation, and the next the state of rewards and punishments; that many vitious men are led to repentance at last, and become exceeding good; remarkably virtuous and useful. [Upon which head I can't but remark, that the *Jews* had a proverb, that no man could equal the zeal of a sincere penitent: And St. *Paul*'s description of such a person is very well worth our attention.[a] "Behold this selfsame thing, that ye have sorrowed after a godly sort, what carefulness is wrought in you; yea what clearing of yourselves; yea what indignation; yea what fear; yea what vehement desire; yea what zeal; yea what revenge?"] The other reason, he adds, 2. is, That very wicked men are fathers of good and worthy children; that by the bad the virtuous are exercised and tried; and other wicked persons are punished. 3. That they themselves, far from being happy, are really miserable, however dazzling to unthinking eyes their outward prosperity may appear. 4. That the world being governed by general laws, or in a regular manner, and not by partial wills, God brings about the punishment <168> of wicked men and nations very often in such a manner, as must be more instructive to all thinking men, than positive interpositions can be, by shewing wickedness to be in the general and natural course of things the ruin of individuals and of states. And 5. That such are the natural connexions and dependencies of mankind, that no wicked man can be destroyed without involving others, perhaps good, or at least not so bad, in his ruin. An excellent author gives these reasons for God's forbearance, in not suddenly destroying, or very visibly punishing wicked men as their sins deserve, from the consideration of the general conduct of providence; all of which are justified by revelation. 6. But another remarkable reason he gives is directly the language of scripture, which is,[b] That men in general are qualified and fitted to contemplate and understand the government of God in the world, as the divine behaviour and conduct, in order to make it the model or pattern of their own. And this patient, merciful, tender, compassionate conduct of God in the course of his providence towards sinners, shews us how compassionate, how tender,

a. 2 *Cor.* vii. 11.
b. 2 *Peter* iii. 9, 10.

how forgiving, we ought to be; we, who after our best endeavours are liable to so many weaknesses, which require mutual indulgence from one another; and fall so far short of our duty to God, that we greatly need pardon and mercy from him who must hate iniquity. A patient, meek, compassionate, forgiving spirit, so necessary to happiness in human life, is frequently urged upon us in the new testament, from the consideration of the mercy of God, and his readiness to pardon us; his tender compassion for all our weaknesses; and his not exacting rigidly of us all that duty requires at our hands, and we are really qualified to perform, would we but set ourselves with all our might to do it. And how can the cruel, unforgiving man presume to ask pardon <169> of God? The natural notion of equity must first be forgot by us, before we can choose, but yield to that remarkable reasoning of the son of *Sirach*,[a] "He that wrongeth shall find vengeance from the Lord, and he will surely keep his iniquities in remembrance. Forgive thy neighbour the hurt he hath done to thee, so shall thy sins also be forgiven when thou prayest. One man beareth hatred against another, and doth he seek pardon from the Lord? He sheweth no mercy to a man which is like himself, and doth he ask forgiveness of his own sins?" I have mentioned this emphatical reasoning, because not a few thro' very imperfect notions of natural religion, imagine a forgiving, meek, patient temper is no part of it.

But to prevent mistakes upon this head, let it be observed, 1. That in the administration of a God of infinite purity and holiness, or of absolute moral rectitude, the only road to true happiness must be virtue, or purity and sanctity of manners. Nay, in the nature of things, rational happiness cannot arise but from well improved rational faculties: virtuous enjoyment virtue alone can give: none can possibly partake of a happiness bearing any likeness to the happiness of the divine mind, but by becoming partakers of that divine nature, or like to God in that moral rectitude from which his felicity results. 2. Whence it follows, in the second place, that till the sinner repents, he is naturally, and according to the essential differences of things to which the divine government is and must be consonant, quite out of the road to true happiness, and in

a. *Eccles.* xxiii.

the direct natural way to misery, the proper, natural and necessary misery of a rational moral being; a mind confirmed in depravity and vice. 3. But then, thirdly, When a penitent sincerely reforms, and returns to virtue, he puts himself into the natural and the appointed way to rational happiness, the result of ratio-<170>nal perfection. 4. And yet, in the fourth place, God's sparing very wicked sinners, and putting means in their way for their reclamation from vice; and his freely pardoning them, are in a proper and strict sense, acts of grace, of patience, mercy, and forgiveness; in the same manner that a man's not merely forgiving his enemy, but restoring him to his favour and confidence upon his sincere repentance, and taking proper methods to bring him back to a sense of his vice, and a better mind, are what a man is not strictly obliged to do in justice, and could not be blamed for not doing; but is truly and properly not mere lenity but benignity; the highest generosity. And indeed, such goodness is called among men, God-like, from a natural sense of the divine compassion and forbearance, of which we are all monuments. 5. In the last place, as such compassionate administration is not inconsistent with government by general laws; but supposes compassion and mercy to have moved God in the choice of his conduct towards men, and to have determined him to the methods by which he is really found to govern the world; so, on the other hand, it is plain, that to a generous mind, continuance in sin will be highly aggravated by the consideration of such tender and merciful government. Sinful conduct, in proportion as wicked men have less or more shared of it, according to different circumstances, all of which were the choice of infinite mercy in order to greater good in the whole, does certainly heighten in proportion their guilt, and render their wickedness more inexcusable, if ingratitude be a sin: And the truly good, or all who ever come to take a just view of things, will look upon it as doing so; and therefore far from having any disposition to indulge vicious appetites in hopes of forgiveness, they will be more unwilling to offend. This goodness will lead them to repentance; it will engage them to double watchfulness and diligence, not to offend God, whose laws are really but so many rules for our <171> attainment to true and unchanging happiness; and to recommend themselves to his favour by duly grateful behaviour. This is the meaning of the *Psalmist,*

when he says, "There is forgiveness with God,[a] that he may be feared."
To whom among men is one who hath any sense of honour most desirous to be acceptable; whom does he most fear, most reverence, and
most love; the person who tho' he exacteth nothing but what is just, yet
hath no compassion, no lenity; or he who, tho' he be strictly good and
virtuous, and cannot be reconciled to vice, is however of a kindly generous disposition, and taking all pains to reform the bad, is willing to
accept of them when they sincerely reform? This patience of God is a
truly amiable quality; and among the many good ends it evidently serves
in order to promote the greater good, this one is none of the least, that
this patience, duly considered, exciteth toward God such a filial reverence, as is indeed an excellent virtue even with respect to society by its
natural fruits: for it naturally produces a generous regard to those who
are wisely merciful; and a compassionate forgiving temper toward our
fellow-creatures when they hurt or wrong us.

I shall conclude this article with observing, that as to think of abusing
goodness and mercy, is the worst, the most irreclaimable of vitious tempers; so there cannot be a falser or more pernicious mistake in speculation, than to imagine, that there is no reason to fear the goodness, the
mercy of a pure and holy being, who must have the strictest regard to
moral rectitude in his conduct. For, on the contrary, such goodness, such
mercy, is the natural and just object of the greatest fear to an ill man.

A humourous, capricious being may change. And a being, who is
rather malicious than good, may be appeased by cringing and flattery.
But such a goodness <172> or mercy as hath been defined, is a fixt, steady,
unmoveable principle of action; which, tho' it may bear long with sinners, in order to give them space to reform, and in order to excite them
to it, by a sense of the gratitude and respect naturally due to such forbearance, which is the good principle in our natures that is last corrupted
or quite defaced; yet it cannot alter the nature of virtue and vice, or of
moral perfection and happiness; A connexion, which, if God could alter,
yet he would not change on any consideration; far less to gratify vitious
men who are unwilling to forsake their wicked pleasures. Every one may

a. *Psal.* cxxx. 4.

observe how much greater chance of impunity an ill man has in a partial administration, than in a just and upright one. And no attribute of God which we can consider, does not prove to us, that virtue alone can recommend to his favour, or put us into the road to true and lasting happiness under his administration.

Now having thus briefly considered the scripture doctrine concerning the principal attributes of God, to which his government of mankind, and all moral beings must be agreeable, it is evident, that whether they are considered as parts of the divine goodness; as belonging to the idea of it, or necessarily resulting from it; or separately, as distinct perfections; they all shew us, that this must be an unalterable rule in it. "That whatsoever a man soweth, that shall he reap." Denying it to be such, is ultimately to deny every one of his moral perfections.

If he hath a strict regard to moral rectitude, then must the serious pursuit of it be the only way under his administration to happiness; and by consequence its opposite must have an opposite effect. If he be good, he must pursue the general good of moral beings; that is, he must conduct all things so, as may best serve to promote the greatest quantity of moral happiness, resulting in the nature of things only from moral perfection. If he be true and faithful, his administration must be <173> correspondent to what the nature and frame of man, as a moral being, shews to be his end, even to attain to happiness by attaining to moral perfection: for this is plainly the natural language of our whole frame with regard to our end; that man is here, in order to lay a foundation for future unchangeable happiness resulting from a well-improved mind, suitably placed, by the sedulous pursuit of virtue: this his frame and make duly considered, as clearly points out, as any other constitution whatsoever indicates its end by the disposition and combination of the parts which constitute it. If God be pure, holy, just and good, then will he certainly upon the whole render to every moral being, suitably to the use he makes of the stock put into his hand for improvement in his circumstances. And if God be patient and forbearing toward sinners, it is to lead them to repentance,[a] and thereby into the road to happiness;

a. *Rom.* ii. 4. *Ezek.* xviii. 21, *&c.* xxxiii. 11. *Acts* xxvi. 20. xvii. 10. 2 *Tim.* ii. 25, 26. 2 *Pet.* iii. 9.

because he is not willing that any should be miserable, but that all should, by acting agreeably to their nature, at last find the reward, the advantage of so doing, which cannot be obtained any other way.

The apostle had therefore good reason to say, it is a gross deceit, because it is mocking God to imagine, "That whatever a man soweth, that shall he not also reap."

PROPOSITION III

The divine, infinitely wise, just, good, faithful, and merciful providence, governs the whole universe by general laws: and what is said in the sacred writings of the ministry of angels, and of special miraculous interpositions of providence on certain occasions, is not inconsistent with government by general laws.

It hath been already more than once observed, that the phrases by which God's government of the mate-<174>rial world is expressed[a] in scripture, plainly mean the production of all natural effects according to established general laws.

And in holy writ several general laws in the moral world are mentioned or acknowledged: as the law of habits, or the improvement and degeneracy of the mind in consequence of that general law; or the established power of usage, custom or habit; the law of industry, according to which all acquisitions, external or internal, are made: and finally, this important law in the text, that it shall be rendered to every moral being, upon the whole of things, according to the foundation they have laid in their first state of probation; that every one shall reap as he has sown, or according to his behaviour: he shall reap the natural fruits of the seed he sows. Government therefore throughout all by general laws, throughout the moral as well as the natural world, is the doctrine of the scriptures. And indeed, as, seeing we can trace government by general laws in very many instances in nature, we have hence reason to presume, that the government of the moral world is analogous to it, and likewise by general laws; so were we strangers to the material world, if we can trace

a. *Psal.* xxxiv. 4, *&c. Psal.* iii. 7, 8. cxlviii. 5, 6, 7, 8.

the observance of those general laws which have been mentioned in the moral world, we would have in like manner good ground to infer, that the material part must likewise be governed by general laws analogously to the moral; and that from this single consideration, which is evident at first sight, that the material and moral do make one system, or are intimately and closely blended together, and have but one Author, and one end or scope.

But this subject is of great importance, and therefore it is well worth while, in the first place, to shew more particularly than hath been yet done, how, or <175> upon what grounds we may reason so from the material world to the moral, as to infer government by general laws in the later from government by general laws in the former. And then, secondly, to consider, whether marvelous interpositions are not repugnant to the doctrine of government by general laws, whether in the material or moral world.

I. Let us enquire how, or in what manner, and upon what ground, we may reason from the government of the material world to that of the moral. For some consider these two as so quite distinct, that good order may appear in the one, and yet there may be nothing but disorder and confusion in the other. They think, that as one may have a very good taste of architecture, gardening, and laying out fields, and yet be a very bad head of a family in other respects; so the contrivance of the material world may shew excellent taste of beauty and order in that kind, and yet an equal good taste of moral order and harmony may be wanting. And therefore they conclude, that it is only from moral administration, that the moral character of any being can be inferred with any degree of certainty or assurance.

Now, in answer to this specious reasoning, it might be shewn, that the taste of beauty in architecture, and the other ingenious arts, is so analogous to and connected with good taste of beauty and harmony in moral conduct, that if one who hath the former be irregular and dissolute in his morals, he must be so in down-right contradiction to the sole principle upon which his delight in the ingenious arts and works of taste is founded; and so be at perpetual variance with himself. And therefore we naturally presume, that one who shews perfect good taste in the external oeconomy of his house, gardens, &c. cannot fail in his moral conduct thro' ignorance, but thro' the strength of ill-grounded appetites, in opposition to frequent reproaches <176> of natural conscience, not seldom excited, and always exaggerated by the exercises of his other taste, or rather of the same taste about inferior objects, which, when it is duly cultivated, naturally leads to right moral conduct: a ground of suspicion that cannot take place with regard to the Author of the universe, or any original, universal, independent mind.

But not to insist upon what would unavoidably lead us into a long enquiry into the principles of the polite arts, and the nature and foundation of good taste in them, we shall only observe, that tho' *moral philosophy* be distinguished from natural, and the moral from the natural world for several good reasons; yet it would be a very great mistake, if any one should be led by that distinction to consider them as two distinct or separate worlds, or two distinct spheres of action: for not only are they but parts making one world or system; but strictly speaking, there is but one possible object of divine care or providence, which is the happiness of beings capable of happiness in their several degrees; and therefore the whole constitution and government of what is called the material part of the creation is, properly speaking, a moral constitution and government; being nothing else, but a constitution and government, according to which perceptive beings are affected in such and such manners by certain sensations. But this being true, it is unreasonable to speak of the government of a material, and the government of a moral world as distinct systems: the more proper and philosophical way, is only to speak of a moral government, or of the government of beings capable of happiness and misery. And therefore, if in tracing and examining this moral government, certain universal laws are found out; and, in general, if as far as we are able to carry our enquiries, the moral government seems to be carried on by universal and not partial laws; we have certainly reason to conclude, that universally throughout the same moral government, all is governed by gene-<177>ral laws. When we speak of arguing from the material world to the moral, it sounds at first like arguing from conduct in one sphere to conduct in an absolutely different one. But it is not really so; for it is only arguing from some parts of one and the same sphere to other parts of it; or from some samples of conduct in one and the same sphere to conduct universally in that same one sphere or system. No doubt, we may reason in many instances very justly from one's conduct in one sphere to what might be expected of the same being in another sphere. But in the matter now before us, we do not argue from one different sphere to another, but we conclude from samples of conduct in several instances what may be judged of the conduct of the same being universally throughout the whole of that one government. But if it is said, that all being granted which is demanded, yet when we have found in the moral government of providence only general laws and good order with respect to the conveyance of sensations into our minds from without; or, in other words, with respect to the manners in which we are affected by sensible pleasures and pains; can we from thence alone conclude, that general laws and good order are universally observed with regard to every thing upon which the greater good in the whole administration depends? May not a scheme of government be well so far, and no further? And that order just mentioned, with regard to the conveyance of sensible ideas, may be, and is likely to be but a very small part of the whole scheme. True. But certainly if general laws are clearly perceived to prevail to any degree in a government, there immediately arises a presumption that they prevail universally throughout the same one government. Suppose two absolutely distinct independent governments are found at the first comparison to have a similitude, will not a presumption immediately arise, that there may be throughout the whole a similitude between them; and will not this <178> presumption strengthen in proportion, as the comparison advancing, greater likeness is found between them: and if these two governments are known to be contrived and under the administration of the same head and ruler, will not the presumption from the beginning be yet stronger on that account, that a very great resemblance will be found between them by acurate inspection and comparison? By parity of reason therefore in a government which appears plainly to be one, to be contrived, effected and governed by one and the same head, there must arise a very strong presumption, because it is such, that throughout the whole of it there is analogous or similar government; and this presumption will grow stronger in pro-

portion to the new instances of analogy and likeness, or of similar government by general laws, that are discovered, even tho' all these instances
should be of the same category, as all instances with regard to the conveyance of sensible ideas are. But, no doubt, the presumption will become yet stronger if general laws are found to prevail likewise in some
instances that are not of the same category with sensations, but so remote
from them, as to belong to quite a different rank or category of effects.

II. Now, in the second place, government by general laws is no less
obvious in many other instances, than it is with respect to the methods
in which sensible ideas are conveyed, which are properly called the laws
of nature; or the connexions between certain means and certain ends in
the material part of God's government of moral beings. In our enquiry
into the moral world, several laws are proved to be general in it from
their effects, in the same manner as natural philosophers have proved
certain laws in the sensible world to be general. But not to repeat what
hath been said there, let me but just suggest here that there is a <179>
much more exact correspondence and analogy between the natural and
moral world, (in what sense we understand this distinction, hath been
just now explained) than superficial observers are apt to imagine or take
notice of; so that it may be justly said of the whole of the divine government, as far as we are able to extend our enquiries into it, with the
son of *Syrach,*[a] "All things are double one against another: and God hath
made nothing imperfect." The inward frame of the human mind, all its
affections and powers, and all their laws correspond to the external condition and circumstances in which man is placed, *i.e.* to the laws of the
sensible world, which we are at present capable of enjoying in various
ways, and consequently of being variously affected by it; these two constitutions are so analogous, so correspondent, so nicely adjusted to one
another, that had we no other argument to prove them to be one system
directed to one end, by one Author and Ruler, by similar methods of
government, that single consideration would be sufficient to evince it.
For as we must either not admit final causes at all, or we must admit
them wherever we perceive them; so, we must either admit similarity

a. *Ecclus.* xiii. 4.

and correspondence, wherever we perceive it, or not admit it in any instances. And there are no where in nature, clearer instances of analogy
in nature, than between several laws of the natural world, and several
laws of the moral world.

A careful examiner will find, that all our affections and passions are
not only well-suited to our external circumstances; but that they themselves, and all the laws or methods of exercising them, with their different consequences, have a very exact correspondence with, and analogy
to the sensible world, and its laws. Is there not an obvious similarity
between the principle of gravitation toward a common center, and universal benevolence, in their operation? And what is self-love, but the
attraction by which a private system is constituted, preserved, and kept
together, in like manner, as by close cohesion of parts, particular bodies
<180> are formed and preserved. Nor is there any more inconsistency
between the co-existence of the two principles of self-love and benevolence in the same mind, than between the attraction of parts by which
every particular body is formed, and its gravitation toward the common
center of the whole system, in order to the coherence or support of the
whole. Homogeneous bodies more easily coalesce than others: and so is
it with minds. For is not friendship a particular sympathy of minds analogous to that particular tendency we may observe in certain bodies to
run together and mix or adhere? Compassion, or a disposition to relieve
the distressed, is it not similar to that tendency we observe in nutritious
particles of several kinds, to run to the supply of wants in bodies which
they are respectively proper to supply. Hunger, and other such appetites,
are with regard to our conservation what a disposition in all plants to
attract their proper nutriment is to them; which, while they want, they
droop and seem uneasy like famished animals. Minds repel injuries in
the same way that bodies do, (our eye-lids, for example) instantaneously,
by a similar, innate, repelling force. And which is yet a more remarkable
instance of similarity between the natural and the moral world, dominion is proportional to property, as gravity to quantity of matter; so that
all *mutations in the orbs of civil government,* if one may so speak, are
resolvable into that moral law of dominion, in like manner as all the

motions and variations in the celestial orbs are into the natural law of gravitation.[a]

But since no one can be acquainted with nature, or indeed with the imitative arts, with poetry in particular, without perceiving and admiring the <181> correspondence between the sensible and moral world, from which arises such a beautiful, rich source of imagery in poetry, and without which there could be no such thing; I shall not insist longer upon it than just to observe, that we are excellently fitted to admire the beauty of the natural world, and to trace that connexion between beauty and utility, every where prevailing in nature, confessed by artists, who imitate nature as the foundation of their arts; and which is the chief source of all the natural philosopher's delight: and there is the same connexion in the moral part, between the moral beauty of affections, actions and characters, and real advantage, real soundness and usefulness, whether with respect to the private system; *i.e.* the good of each individual, or the publick system, *i.e.* the good of our kind. And, to add no more, as every thing in nature requires culture, in order to its arrival to its perfect state; so likewise does every quality of the mind require proper diligence to bring it to proper maturity: and as the power of man in the natural world, extends no further, than uniting and disuniting elementary unchangeable bodies; so in the moral world, all his power likewise consists in uniting and disuniting; or associating and dissociating elementary unchangeable ideas and affections. So that, upon the whole, from the consideration of nature, there is good reason to conclude, that all is governed by general laws very analogous or similar.

a. All the mutations which have happened in the most considerable states, of which ancient history gives us any tolerably exact accounts, may be reduced into effects of this law, and of inequality in the rotation of power, as the phenomena in the mundan system are resolved into effects of gravitation. See the ingenious Mr. *Harrington*'s works. A careful consideration of the principles he goes upon will lead us to a solution of many great moral phenomena from very simple and excellent principles or laws in the moral world. [That power should rotate is a key idea of James Harrington's. See especially his *Commonwealth of Oceana*.]

III. But if any one should say, why lay such a stress upon government by general laws; for is it not sufficient, that all things be disposed, placed and adapted for the greater good, whether the author of nature works by general laws or not: *i.e.* whether effects are reducible to certain harmonies and analogies, or stand single, and have no relation to one principle: or, in other words, tho' no two effects are instances of the same manner of operation: for those are the <182> different phrases by which philosophers explain their meaning when they speak of general laws. To this an answer hath already been given, *viz.* that were that the case, nature could not be called an united system; it would be a loose incoherent heap of effects, without any cement or union, like a heap of independent unconnected stones. And how one end can be pursued in such a case, or what meaning the pursuit of general good can have upon that supposition, I am entirely at a loss to conceive. But one thing is certain, beyond all doubt, that no intelligent creature could ever understand such a course of things, perceive beauty in it, comprehend it, or form rules of conduct to itself from it. From which it plainly follows, that all the interests of intelligent beings, all their rational exercises of understanding, of will, or of affections, absolutely require government by general laws: knowledge, contemplation of beauty, activity, prudence, virtue, are impossible attainments, but in a state where general laws do obtain, and are traceable to a certain degree. But this hath been already observed, and is only repeated now, because it is necessary to be put in mind of it, in order to our being able to answer the other question with regard to providence, which it was proposed to discuss under this head, namely,

II. Whether miraculous interpositions of providence are consistent with government of the world by general laws. An excellent author reasons to this purpose on this subject. "It is from analogy that we conclude the whole of nature to be capable of being reduced into general laws. It is from our finding, that the course of nature in some respects, and so far, goes on by general laws, that we conclude this of the rest. And if that be a just ground for such a conclusion, it is a just ground also, if not to conclude, yet to apprehend, to render it supposeable and credible, which is sufficient for answering objections, that God's <183> miraculous interpositions may have been, all along, in like manner, by general laws of wisdom. Thus, that miraculous powers should be exerted at such times, upon such occasions, in such degrees and manners, and with regard to such persons rather than others; that the affairs of the world, being permitted to go on in their natural course so far, should just at such a point have a new direction given them by miraculous interpositions; that these interpositions should be exactly in such degrees and respects only; all this may have been by general laws. These laws are unknown indeed to us: but no more unknown than several other laws from whence certain effects proceed are, though it is taken for granted, they are as much reducible to general ones as gravitation. Now, if the revealed dispensations of providence, and miraculous interpositions be by general laws, as well as God's ordinary government in the course of nature, made known by reason and experience; there is no more reason to expect, that every exigence, as it arises, should be provided for by these general laws of miraculous interpositions, than that every exigence in nature should by the general laws of nature. Yet there might be wise and good reasons, that miraculous interpositions should be by general laws; and that these laws should not be broken in upon, or deviated from by other miracles."

This reasoning from analogy is certainly very just. But it is not from analogy merely, that we have reason to conclude, that the whole of the divine government must be by general laws; and consequently, that even miraculous interpositions must be all along carried on by general laws, tho' unknown to us. Because the scheme of providence which is carrying on, whether in a way we can trace, as we do when we are able to reduce certain effects into their general laws; or in methods unknown to us; must be a scheme, all the parts of which were chosen by the divine creator and <184> ruler of all things, as the best and fittest in order to promote his sole end, universal good; an end called in scripture very properly his glory. It cannot therefore be a scheme which frequently requires interpositions, at certain points, till then never thought of by the ruler of the world, and maker of all things. That is inconsistent with his perfections. And yet between such instantaneous, extemporary, and before unthought of interpositions to serve particular exigencies, and a scheme in which all is carried on according to a general order and method; or, which is the same thing, according to general laws established by him from the first, or more properly speaking, from all eternity, there is no middle. The one or the other must be the case; but the former being absurd, the later must be true. But if miraculous interpositions cannot mean such extemporary, unpremeditated or casual interpositions, *pro re nata;*[22] 'tis plain, miraculous interpositions can be in no other sense miraculous to us, than any other effects are really such, whose laws are unknown to us, tho' we do not call all such miraculous. A miraculous interposition, the effect of a general law, is not miraculous, if by miraculous is meant anomalous; because that would be to say, it is an anomalous effect of a general law. But as the commonalty of mankind, who have no notion of general laws, call nothing miraculous but what is uncommon, and do call all uncommon effects such; so even the philosophers, whose daily employment it is to trace general laws, do not however call effects which they daily or often see miraculous, merely because they know nothing of their general laws; but such only as are either contrary to general laws they are acquainted with; or are, at least, at the same time extremely uncommon, and extremely unlike the common course of nature. In this sense, do they who believe the truth of the dispensations recorded in holy writ, say many things in them are contrary to known laws, and many are very unlike the common <185> course of nature, and they are therefore miraculous. But when that is said, nothing is said that is contrary to the doctrine of the divine government throughout all, from the beginning, and for ever by general laws. For all these dispensations may have been carried on by general laws unknown to us, as many laws of effects, which being very common, do not startle us, are: and if they be really what they are represented to be in the scriptures, that is, if they be really true, or if they really happened, they must have been brought about by general laws, since providence works in no other manner.

But here it will be said, is not all this directly repugnant to what you have been endeavouring to establish; for of what use can miraculous interpositions be, if no rules can be inferred from them for our conduct; but rules for conduct can only be deduced from known general laws, or

22. "In these circumstances" or "as things stand."

effects reducible into general laws: and is it not very contradictory to talk of an established order of nature, and at the same time of effects or interpositions contrary to this order of nature: And yet what do miraculous interpositions mean, but dispensations suspending or counteracting and conquering general laws of nature? In order therefore to take off all those difficulties and clear this matter as fully as we can. Let it be observed,

I. That if there are created beings in nature higher than man, as it hath been often said nature and reason render highly probable there are, of very various ranks, gradually ascending in knowledge and power one above another, in such proportion that the lowest of them transcends man, as man does the highest class of brutes; upon that supposition, every order of such beings will have its peculiar sphere of power, activity, or dominion alloted to it, as man hath his appointed to him. But the exertions of power natural to a rank of beings superior to man, or accord-<186>ing to the laws of their nature, and of their sphere of activity, will be in respect to man miraculous in the strongest sense of the word, that is, impossible, or absolutely beyond his reach. To such beings the laws which limit human power in the natural world may be no confinement; but it may be in their power to act quite contrary to them. For hence it will not follow, that the same nature admits repugnant laws, since what we call the laws of matter and motion, or the laws of the sensible world, are the laws according to which sensible effects are produced to us or in us, and according to which we must operate, in order to gain certain ends; and while these remain the same to us, nature remains the same of us. Thus, to explain the matter by an example or two, though the law of gravity prevail universally through the natural world, insomuch that all the appearances of the planets are reducible into it, together with that centrifugal force, which is the result of the inertnes of matter; and that we cannot suspend or change it, but must act and work conformably to it; yet very consistently with this order of nature it may be in the power of beings, superior to us, to act contrary to this property which is to us a rule and boundary of power, so as to be able to walk upon the water, and to suspend heavy bodies in the air, &c. In like manner, though it be not in our power to cure any diseases but gradually, and by certain methods discovered to us by experience; yet it may be in the power of beings of a superior sphere of activity immediately or instantaneously to cure or remove certain diseases by methods altogether unconceivable by us. All this may be, and yet order in nature may be preserved; for order is preserved while the laws belonging to every particular class of beings prevail invariably, making to each class their peculiar spheres of power and rules of action. Nay, various orders of beings cannot possibly take place in nature, but it must be true, that with respect to every lower kind there will really be in nature as various <187> exertions of power quite miraculous, as there are orders of beings higher than them, that is, exertions of power, which being perceived by them, would necessarily appear quite miraculous to them. And if we suppose it possible, as there being no contradiction in it we must allow it to be, that beings superior to man belonging to the same system, may operate upon the same material objects, and render at times their operations visible to us, then will in all such cases real miracles happen to us; that is, operations performed, either contrary to the laws of matter and motion we cannot suspend or alter, but must invariably conform to in all our operations; or though agreeably to them, yet, which comes to the same thing, without such a visible intermediate progress as all our operations are and must be performed in; for both of these ways of operating are equally miraculous with respect to us. But as if ever such productions of superior beings visible to us have happened, or shall happen, they are productions of power derived from God, according to spheres of activity and laws of powers appointed by him, and so make a part of the general scheme of providence: so whether they be a part of it or not, human power, and the laws of human power, or our sphere of activity and dominion can suffer no alteration; nor consequently, our rules of conduct pointed out to us by our make and sphere, or deducible from it. We must suppose beings of superior ranks to man either to have no power in the material world to produce sensible effects; or we must needs suppose many effects may be produced by them, which are not miraculous, but reducible to the general laws of nature, and therefore in no degree surprising to us. But whatever their powers and operations may be, all that is, is according to the will of one cause the Author of all things, from whom all powers and laws of powers are derived, and who hath appointed all things for the greater good. And there is really no more reason to say that the world is not the same uniform <188> system, if we consider it as the theatre in which various beings with different powers exert themselves variously; than there is to say, that nature or the world is not the same uniform system, because different men have different degrees of knowledge, and consequently of power; or because in ages of science men have vastly greater power than they had in ages of ignorance, and before certain laws of nature, and properties of things were known, which being discovered, augment man's power. The scripture asserts that there are various orders of beings superior to man, who have vast powers, and are not inactive, but are continually employed in exerting their powers. But they are said to be created by God, and to be subject to him; *to be ministring spirits to do his will.* And there is no inconsistency with what is said there, of their being employed or employing themselves to the service of good men, or in any other way under the superintendency of providence, or agreeably to the great end providence proposed and unerringly pursues, in giving to beings various powers, and appointing to each class its peculiar sphere and bounds. For so far every thing is carried on with infinite wisdom and goodness, and according to general laws. And man, though he knows not the spheres of other beings, yet in proportion as he knows his own sphere, which with regard to him is never altered, may know his duty or rule of conduct, which, with regard to every being, can be nothing else but what its make and sphere points out, and renders always the same to it. But when it is said, that the sphere of man remains always the same, let it not be inferred from hence, that a man may not be endued with power, the exertions of which will be truly miraculous to his fellow-creatures, and shew him to be endued with knowledge and power superior to them, or to be directed and assisted in certain operations by some being of a superior rank to man; for though that may be, yet the natural sphere of mankind will remain <189> the same even in that case, and while it remains the same, the duties resulting from it must also be the same.

II. Now this being understood, it must be obvious, that interpositions or dispensations of providence, said in scripture to have been particular, extraordinary, or miraculous; as in delivering a particular person or nation, in conveying certain blessings, or inflicting certain evils at certain times upon persons or nations, in sending a preacher of his will invested with power to give it an evidence of an authority more than human, and in other such like instances, are by no means contradictory to the doctrine of the government of the world by general laws; because we may evidently comprehend how all such may be produced by general laws, as making parts of the vast scheme of providence. And though we should never be able to trace these effects to their general laws, yet some other created beings superior to us, may in their larger situation be able to do it; and in that way may be capable of deducing to themselves very useful observations for their conduct from such laws, in the same manner as we do rules for our conduct, from what we are able to discover of the connexions and laws of things in the world, by our experience and reason.

But if it be said, of what use can such dispensations be with regard to man? It may be answered, No exertions of the powers of other beings; no particular miraculous interpositions of providence, can alter the rules of conduct, which are deducible from our make, our sphere of activity, and the connexions and laws of things with regard to us. So that it will always remain to be our business to know these, that we may not by any means, by any false reasoning, or specious shew of supreme, divine authority, be deluded into the reception of rules contrary to them. For nothing inconsistent with them can be a true rule to <190> us; a rule that will not misguide us. But then a certain part of providence, which we cannot discover by experience or reason, being made known to us by divine revelation, or, which comes to the same in the present case, by a being superior to us, who is acquainted with it; though the general rules according to which it is carried on be not laid open to us; yet by such information of certain facts, if there be reason to depend upon it, we may be led to the knowledge of certain rules of conduct, or certain duties otherwise not known to us; because these may as evidently result from the knowledge of that part of providence thus discovered to us, as our other duties knowable by reason and experience do result from those parts of providence whence they are inferred: and if the former be not inconsistent with the latter, that is, contradictory to them, we can have no reason to object against them upon the account of the manner in which we are brought to the knowledge of them; but in such a case, the whole question will turn upon the credibility of our information concerning that part of providence from which they result and are inferred. Did rules thus made known to us clash with those deducible from experience and reason, we would have sufficient ground to reject the information. But if they do not, the credibility of such information, as hath been now supposed, will doubtless be a question well worth our considering; nay, a question we cannot refuse to consider with close and candid deliberation, without transgressing one rule of conduct, which reason and experience clearly teaches us; namely, not to despise any information concerning the conduct of providence, and our duties resulting from it, which hath any likelihood of truth: for those beings, who are invested with superior knowledge to us, or who have larger views of nature than we, are certainly able to instruct us, who are not so wise and knowing; and we being made to receive our knowledge for the direction of <191> our conduct, not wholly by immediate experience, but in a great measure by testimony, ought to examine instruction in nature or providence offered to us by testimony. It is not now my present business to enquire into the particular miraculous dispensations of providence mentioned in scripture; but merely in general to shew how such are not inconsistent with the government of the world by general laws, which hath been done. And this was necessary, in order to reconcile them with what the scripture says, as we have seen of fore-knowledge, and of an universal providence, by which general laws are established, which all things invariably obey; or according to which all effects are produced for the greater good. For in such a manner do the holy writers speak of all things animate and inanimate; of all beings of whatever orders and ranks.[a] "The works of the Lord are great, sought out of all them that have pleasure in them. His work is honourable and glorious: and his righteousness endureth for ever. He hath made his wonderful works to be remembered: the Lord is gracious and full of compassion. The works

a. *Ps* iii. civ. cxiii. cxv. cxlvii. cxlviii.

of his hands are verity and judgment; all his commandments are sure. They stand fast for ever, and are done in truth and uprightness.—The Lord is high above all nations and his glory above the heavens. The heavens are the Lord's; but he hath given the earth to the children of men.—Great is our Lord, and of great power; his understanding is infinite.—Praise him from the heavens, praise him in the heights. Praise him all ye angels, praise ye him all hosts, praise ye him sun, moon, and stars, praise him all the stars of light. Praise him ye heavens, and ye nations above the heavens. Let them praise the Lord, for he commanded, and they were created. He hath also stablished them for ever and ever: he hath made a decree which <192> they shall not pass—Let all beings praise the Lord, for his name alone is excellent, his glory is above the earth and heaven, for all, even fire, and hail, and snow, fulfil his will. The Lord hath prepared his throne in the heavens; and his kingdom ruleth over all. Bless the Lord, ye his angels, that excel in strength, that do his commandments, hearkening unto the voice of the Lord, the voice of his word. Bless ye the Lord, all ye his hosts, ye ministers of his that do his pleasure. Bless the Lord all his works in all places of his dominion. Bless the Lord, O my soul. Bless the Lord, O my soul: O Lord, my God, thou art very great, thou art clothed with honour and majesty—Who maketh his angels spirits, and his ministers a flaming fire—He appointeth the moon for seasons; the sun knoweth his going down—O Lord, how manifold are thy works! In wisdom hast thou made them all: the earth is full of thy riches." "He that liveth for ever created all things in general. The Lord only is righteous, and there is none other but he who governs the world with the palm of his hand, and all things obey his will, for he is the king of all by his power. As for the wondrous works of the Lord, there may nothing be taken from them, neither may any thing be put unto them, neither can the ground of them be found out."ᵃ So likewise in a few words the apostle St. *Paul,*ᵇ For of him, and to him, and through him, are all things, to whom be glory for ever. *Amen.*

a. *Eccles.* chap. xviii.
b. *Rom.* xi. 36.

Proposition IV

The providence of God always works agreeably to, or consistently with the liberty of moral agents.

The doctrine of predestination having been often shewn to have no foundation in holy writ, and to be ut-<193>terly subversive of all morality and religion: and the doctrine of fore-knowledge having been proved not to be inconsistent with free-agency, I shall only here briefly take notice what it is in which the holy scripture places moral liberty, and what it, as such, includes in it, or necessarily presupposes.

I. According to the scripture,[a] The man who is not governed by reason, but by caprice, humour, fancy, or appetite, is unable to controul his desires, or never exercises the power and authority of his reason to examine them, and keep them within reasonable and becoming bounds, is a slave, in bondage, or a stranger to moral freedom. It describes the miserable slavery of such persons by many excellent ways of expression: telling us, they are[b] servants of sin: servants to uncleanness and to iniquity, and servants of corruption. That they cannot cease from sin: that sin hath dominion over them, and reigns in their mortal bodies, while they obey it in the lusts thereof. That though in their mind they cannot choose but approve the laws of God clearly pointed out to them by their make and frame, and therefore the law of their nature, yet they feel another law in their members warring against the law of their mind, and bringing them into captivity to the law of sin; so that they cannot do the things that they would, or that they approve. That which they do, they allow not; for what they would, that they do not; but what they hate, that they do. All which is comprised in one expressive word afterwards. They are sold under sin: that is, they have by long ill habits and corrupt practice, as it were, given up themselves, parted with their liberty, and yielded themselves absolute-<194>ly into the snare of the Devil (the

---

a. Dr. *Sam. Clark's* Sermons. [The passage is part quotation from, and part paraphrase of, a portion of Clarke's sermon 35, in *Works,* 1:215–22.]

b. *John* viii. 34. *Rom.* vi. 19. 2 *Peter* ii. 19. *Rom.* vi. 14. vii. 2. *Gal.* v. 17.

snares of vice) to be taken captive by them at will. This phrase is twice applied in the old testament to *Ahab,*[a] that he did sell himself to work wickedness in the sight of the Lord. And twice to the people of *Israel;* in the days of *Hosea,*[b] that they sold themselves to do evil in the sight of the Lord: and in the days of *Antiochus,*[c] that they were sold to do mischief.

II. The true liberty of a rational agent is placed by the holy scripture in his being able to govern all his appetites, and his whole conduct, by reason, with delight and complacency. It consists therefore in a just un-byassed judgment, and in a power of acting conformably to its dictates. Man therefore, in the scripture sense, is free, when his reason hath the place or authority due to it in his mind, and gives laws to all his appetites and choices. And he is then free, because he is master of himself; his better part rules, the guiding principle within him has the power and authority which of right belongs to it, and all the parts made to be ruled by it are under proper subjection to it. He is then neither awed by base, mean, unreasonable fears, nor bribed by foolish, fantastick hopes: he is neither tumultuously hurried away by blind, rash, precipitant, unruly lusts and passions, nor imposed upon and cheated by false appearances of present good, but considers impartially, and judges soundly, and acts effectually, and with manly resolution. This is *to quit ourselves like men:* to act like reasonable beings. For to what other end can reason be given us: what else is its use or dignity? This, in the scripture language, is the freedom of a man, of a christian, of an angel; of every rational agent. How emphatically do the scriptures speak of it.[d] The law of the spirit of life <195> hath made me free, saith the apostle, from the law of sin and death; and delivered me from the bondage of corruption, into the glorious liberty of the sons of God. Such a person is said to be dead to sin; that is, to have destroyed the power of vitious appetites,[e] that he

a. 1 *Kings* xxi. 20, 25.
b. 2 *Kings* xvii. 17.
c. 1 *Maccab.* i. 16.
d. *Rom.* viii. 2, 21.
e. *Rom.* vi. 7. 1 *Peter* iv. 1, 2. *James* i. 25.

should no longer live the rest of his life in the flesh, to the lusts of men, but to the will of God. He is said to live to God, and to live after the spirit. The truth is said to have made him free, and the law according to which he regulates himself is called the perfect law of liberty.[a] His delight is in this law, and it is his meat and his drink to do the will of God. O Lord, saith the Psalmist, I am thy servant, and the son of thine handmaid: thou hast broken my bones asunder, and I shall walk at liberty, for I seek thy commandments.

III. Now this true moral liberty implies in it a just sense of right and wrong; a well-informed understanding; or, in one word, a clear, strong, and sound reason, able to distinguish what is fit and becoming in every circumstance. 'Tis the understanding that guides us. And therefore our Saviour says,[b] "The light of the body is the eye; if therefore thine eye be single, thy whole body shall be full of light. But if thine eye be evil, thy whole body shall be full of darkness. If therefore the light that is in thee be darkness, how great is that darkness." 'Tis therefore our principal business to take care, that this light within us be not corrupted, or even weakened, so as not to be able to serve the purpose of a guide; but that it burn strong and clear. 'Tis only a sound and just judgment of things, that can shew us clearly the right road. And therefore in the scripture lan-<196>guage it is truth that sets and maintains us free; it is truth that is the light of life: and our principal interest is to get wisdom, discretion, and a sound understanding. If we look into our mind, and consider how our affections are excited or subdued, how they are taken off from certain objects, and placed on others, we shall quickly perceive that we are influenced by our opinions and fancies. And that in order to act wisely, we must first be able to judge truly and wisely. "No man, says an excellent philosopher,[23] sets himself about any thing, but upon some view or other, which serves him for a reason for what he does: and whatsoever

a. *Ps.* i. 2. *John* iv. 34. viii. 32. *Ps.* cxvi. 16.
b. *Matt.* vi. 22, 23.
23. Locke, *Of the Conduct of the Understanding* §1, in his *Some Thoughts Concerning Education; and, Of the Conduct of the Understanding,* edited by Ruth W. Grant and Nathan Tarcov (Indianapolis and Cambridge: Hackett, 1996).

faculties he employs, the understanding, with such light as it has, well or ill informed, constantly leads; and by that light true or false, all his operative powers are directed. The will itself, how absolute and incontroulable soever it may be thought, never fails in its obedience to the dictates of the understanding. Temples have their sacred images, and we see what influence they have always had over a great part of mankind. But in truth the ideas and images in men's minds are the invisible powers that constantly govern them, and to these they all pay universally a ready submission. It is therefore of the highest concernment, that great care should be taken of the understanding to conduct it right in the search of knowledge, and in the judgments it makes."

We shall have occasion to treat more fully in another place of the conduct of the understanding, and the duties of that class. Mean time, 'tis obvious from what hath been said, that nothing can be more false than to assert that men are not accountable for their understanding; for if men are not accountable for their understanding, they cannot be accountable for their actions: if it is not in their power to have sufficient light to guide them, they cannot have it in their power to direct themselves aright. 'Tis, on the contrary, properly speaking, for our understanding, that is, for <197> our right use of it that we are chiefly accountable. Or if any do not like that way of speaking, 'tis to our right or wrong conduct, in consequence of our following a right or wrong judgment of things, that we owe and must owe all the consequences that come upon us, by our conduct in this world: it is according to it we fare. And if there be another world, our fate in it must depend, in like manner as in our present temporal affairs, upon the road we take and pursue; and what is it that directs us to the road we take, good or bad, what points it out to us, or prompts us to go in it, but our opinion or judgment of things. So that whatever way we consider things, or whatever view we take of them, it is to our right or wrong understanding chiefly that we are beholden for all the consequences of our choices and pursuits.

IV. Yet, in the fourth place, in order to have freedom, inward liberty and mastership of the mind, and of all our appetites by our reason, 'tis not sufficient to have a sound and well-informed reason; but reason must actually reign in our minds, and exert its authority in governing us according to the dictates of right judgment. Now how does reason acquire or maintain this ruling and governing authority, which as naturally belongs to it, as it does to the eye to see, or the ear to hear? It must acquire it by actual practice, and maintain it in the same way. 'Tis by repeated acts that bad appetites acquire a ruling power, which does not belong to them. And it is by repeated acts that reason can alone acquire or preserve its rightful power and authority of governing. This is the consequence of the law of habits, which renders us capable of improvement to perfection. So that without such a law man would not be a free-agent; or his free-agency would be of no use to him: for without it he could never, by all his repeated labours, attain to habitual command <198> over himself, or to the power of acting habitually under, or by the direction of his reason. As this will soon appear to be the truth of the case to any person who gives the least attention to the human mind; so it is manifestly implied in the descriptions given by the sacred writings, of liberty and slavery, which have been just mentioned; and in all the commands and exhortations to govern our unruly appetites, and to act like reasonable creatures.

V. Now that it is in every man's power to improve his understanding, and to attain to the government of his affections, passions, and actions, by his reason, by setting himself seriously to do it; and in every man's power to set himself to do it, no man doubts while he consults his inward feeling and experience. It is only called into question by some pretended philosophers, who do it by asking questions which really have no meaning. If a created agent can be free, says a philosopher, man is certainly so, for he has all the appearance of it: he has the same consciousness as if he were; and all things are so constituted with regard to him, as if he were; for his happiness or misery, in the far greater part, are of his own procuring: almost all he suffers or enjoys is the product, the consequence of his own different pursuits; of his own conduct and behaviour. In one word, all the appearances, all the sentiments and feelings we experience, inward and outward, are owned to be appearances of freedom in man, in any conceivable sense of freedom. What therefore is doubted of, if man's free agency be doubted of, is doubted of contrary to experience, from which alone we can learn what man is or is not, what man hath or hath not. It is therefore doubted of in opposition to that evidence, upon which we sufficiently rest in all cases, when experience is known to be the evidence that must decide. Moreover, certain absurd consequences are owned to result <199> from the contrary supposition. For it is owned that if a man allows himself to act as if he were not free, he will soon repent his folly, and return to the common rules of action, which suppose man to be a free and accountable agent. Now what is the amount of all this, but that experience, or, in a word, consciousness, far from affording us any ground of doubt about our freedom, assures us of it in such a manner, that freedom, were we possessed of it, could not otherwise make itself known to us by consciousness; and that outward experience shews the constitution of things about us to be such, as they would be if we were free; such as it is really unjust they should be, if we are not free; because that for us to act in any instance upon the supposition of our not being free, would be to involve ourselves in inextricable miseries: to act, for example, as if we were neither capable of praise or blame, good or ill desert, of reward nor punishment, &c. what madness would it be?

'Tis true, some philosophers, who assert necessity in opposition to free-agency, have endeavoured to shew, that men, though not free agents, are nevertheless capable of praise and blame, and may be justly rewarded and punished. And without examining how consistent or inconsistent with their account of necessity these assertions are, lest that should appear invidious, let me only observe, that if we are really and truly, in a proper sense, owned to be capable of praise and blame, of good and ill desert, and of reward and punishment, then must the dispute, in all practical respects, be at an end; and be indeed in speculation but a logomachy. For free-agency cannot be better described than to be "That power of acting with choice, the consciousness of which in ourselves naturally leads us to apprehend ourselves to be capable of praise and blame, good and ill desert, reward and punishment, and therefore accountable to ourselves, to <200> society, to our fellow-creatures, and to our Creator, for our conduct." Now this liberty being owned, whatever inconsistency there may be between such an assertion, and certain ways of speaking about our freedom, the foundation of morality is safe and entire; and such ways of speaking must be classed with other inaccuracies philosophers fall into in other very important matters; philosophers who affect to depart from common language, and to subtilize into perplexing intricacies, things, in which common sense finds no difficulty at all. And indeed the consciousness of such free-agency cannot be denied, without saying that a sense of merit or demerit in ourselves or others, never apprehended but where choice and freedom is supposed, and always unavoidably apprehended in all such cases, is a mere delusion; to say which, what better is it than with the *Pyrrhonists,* [24] to doubt of the reality of every thing, and whether we dream or are awake?

VI. But after all, what is this mighty dispute about? Is it whether we have perceptions or not? Or whether we will or not? Or whether our volitions are our own or not? Or is it whether we form judgments or not? Or whether our judgment guides us or not? Yes, they will tell us, here lies a part of it; for if our judgments necessarily determine our choices, then are our choices necessary. Now to this I answer, that experience, to which alone we can appeal, because nothing else can decide the matter, tells us, that though our choices are always guided and influenced by our opinions or judgments; yet, 1. In the first place, our opinions or judgments do not produce our choices. They act no otherwise upon us than the light or guide does, which being offered to conduct us to a place, perswades us to accept of the opportunity, and go to that place. Knowledge can produce nothing: and it is only experienced to give light, to direct and perswade. And, 2. As it is in our power to get know-<201>ledge by seeking after it in a proper way, so it is in our power to remain in darkness by avoiding light and knowledge, if we choose it. And therefore, though it should be granted (contrary to all feeling and experience) that there is no difference between the last judgment of the understanding, and volition, or nolition, that is, the choice of the mind to do or forbear doing, which some have asserted, in order to secure their darling notion of necessity; yet we are still free or have power, because to be rightly informed in order to judge right, or to be in utter ignorance,

24. Pyrrhonists were followers of the Greek skeptical philosopher Pyrrho of Elis (ca. 365–270 B.C.).

is in our power. Experience tells us we must set ourselves to get knowledge in order to have it, and that by setting ourselves to get it, we may attain to it: we are sure of attaining to it in a very great degree, especially in matters of conduct, if we seek after it. But how is it the mind is experienced to set itself to get knowledge, but by an act, a firm resolution of its own will, to seek after it?

But they will not quit us here: they will reply, Must not the mind be excited to will the acquisition of knowledge by pursuit; and what excites that volition, is it not a judgment of the mind about the importance of knowledge? These volitions themselves therefore are the necessary consequences of judgments, that is, perceptions, in all which we are passive, as all philosophers own.

That we are passive in our judgments, in this sense, that we must see things as they appear to us, is owned by all philosophers; and that judgment itself is passive or can produce nothing, shall be as readily owned. But what can they conclude from all these concessions against our freedom, or our having it in our power to get knowledge, to direct us in our choices by our endeavours to get it, if we set ourselves to do it in earnest; and our having it in our power to direct our choices by our knowledge? There cannot indeed be a progress of causes, nor even of means, to infinity. That is absurd. But the way how we are excited to exert ourselves to acquire knowledge will be evident <202> to those who look into what passes in the human mind. All things about us speak out loudly to us the importance of knowledge; and nature hath not only made knowledge agreeable to the understanding, as light is to the eye; but hath likewise implanted a strong curiosity after knowledge, and an impatience under ignorance or darkness, in order to move and excite us to set ourselves seriously to get it.

What then, after all, is it that remains to be discussed in relation to this dispute about our free agency, but this single question, which is also a question of experience; namely, Whose act, exercise, or production is our volition, choice, or preference? Now to this experience plainly answers, it is our own totally: it is wholly the act, the exercise, the production of our own mind. What do they who assert that we are not free agents say? They own, and must own, that if we consult experience, it tells us so. And why then may we not, trusting to experience, rest satisfied it is so; and so put an end to a question which is plainly about a matter of fact, and inward experience. For if it is said, reason tells us the contrary; here is an opposition acknowledged between reason and experience, which if yielded, puts an end to all reasoning and all experience, as very idle foolish employment. Yet it is to reason the appeal is here made from experience, which is so far from being allowed in other matters of experience, that to speak of appealing from experience to theory, or reason not founded on experience, would be reckoned the grossest absurdity by all enquirers into nature or fact. But what are these reasons? It would be endless to trace the defenders of necessity, or the deniers of free-agency in man, through all their subtle sophistical resorts. Let it therefore suffice to take notice of their capital much boasted of argument, which I think is of that species of sophistry called, *petitio principii,* begging the question.[25] <203>

Whatever is not produced by a cause (say they) is produced by chance, which it is absurd to suppose any thing to be. But whatever is produced by a cause, is the necessary effect of that cause which produces it. Therefore every thing that is produced is a necessary effect. From which it follows (continue they) that whatever is effected or produced in our mind, is a necessary effect: not only our ideas and affections, but our volitions, for these begin to be, or are produced, and must have a cause, and are therefore necessary effects of their cause.

This is their capital argument,[a] upon which I beg leave to make the few following remarks.

I. If by the maxim, whatever is produced must have a cause, be meant, that whatever is produced must have an external producer, it is the maxim of those who plead for an infinite series of external causes, and assert, that the production of all things which exist may be accounted for by that supposition.

---

a. See a philosophical enquiry concerning liberty and necessity. [Thomas Hobbes, *Of Liberty and Necessity* (1654).]

25. *Petitio principii* is the fallacy of "begging the question"; that is, using as a premise the proposition that is to be proved.

It would be invidious to imagine that to be their meaning, since they own the existence of one supreme cause of all beings. But if that be not the meaning of the maxim, it can be no injury to their argument against liberty or free-agency to change it thus.

Whatever is produced must have a producer, but whatever is produced is the necessary effect of its producing cause; therefore whatever is produced within or without a mind, is a necessary effect.

II. Now when the argument is thus stated, it is plain, that to say whatever is produced is the necessary effect of its producing cause, is begging the conclusion it is brought to prove, if by necessary effect be meant the opposite to free production: and if by neces-<204>sity be meant any thing else, the argument concludes nothing at all. If by necessity be meant a production which is not free, their argument, in other words, stands thus, whatever is produced must have a producer: but nothing that is produced is a free production; or, in other words, whatever is produced is quite the contrary or opposite to free production. Therefore, nothing produced within or without a mind is a free production, but is a necessary effect in a sense destructive of free production, or free agency. And who does not see that this is to beg what is to be proved, *viz.* That there is no free agency, no free production? That to reason thus is to beg the question about our free-agency is plain; for if it proves any thing, it proves that the volitions of the divine mind are not free actions, exertions, or productions of its activity. And yet they are either free actions; or motives, *i.e.* judgments must have a physical productive power (which none will assert) for they have no external producer. They therefore who reason thus, can bring forth no conclusion from their reasoning, till they have shewed what none of them have yet attempted to do, that free production or action is a contradiction: for sure it is not sufficient to prove it to be so, merely to assert, that whatever is produced must be necessary; while in reality, for all they say about it in their definitions,[a] that assertion amounts to no more than to say, whatever is produced must be unfree, which is plainly begging the question.

---

a. The writers for necessity never give any other definition of *necessity*, but that it is the opposite to *freedom*.

III. But if by necessity they mean any thing else but what is expressed by the words *unfree* or *not free*, what is it they mean? Surely, they cannot merely mean by it power sufficient to produce its production; for then their argument would be a mere paralogism, amounting to this, whatever is produced, is produced by a sufficient producer. But whatever is <205> produced, is produced by sufficient power to produce it; therefore, whatever is produced within or without a mind, is produced by sufficient power to produce it; of which nobody will say any thing, but that it is an idle unmeaning repetition of the same proposition three times. And if by necessity they mean power between the exertion of which to produce something, and the actual production of that something, there is such a connexion as cannot but take place; or to suppose which not to take place, is a contradiction. That there must be somewhere in nature such power, will be readily granted; for were there not in nature some such power, all power would be derived from nothing. But doth it follow from that single consideration that no exertions of power are free? Does it follow that the exertions of creating power are not free? Or does it follow that by such power minds may not be produced, which though productions by their volitions be effected in consequence of a connexion established between them and their volitions by the power which created them, and gave them their sphere of derived power or dominion; yet their volitions are the free actions of their own minds, in consequence of their having had conferred upon them by their author the active power, *will*, the only faculty or power that can be called active, and a power which cannot be active or called so without being at the same time free, and called so; free and active being really but synonymous words? To prove that something else must be advanced besides, that there is and must be necessity some where in nature, meaning by necessity, underived power, between the productions of which, and its exertions to produce them, there is a necessary connexion, or a connexion, the non-existence of which is a contradiction. For that it does not follow from that single consideration will be plain, when taking necessity in the meaning above defined, the argument is stated thus. <206>

"There must be somewhere in nature a power, between the productions of which and its exertions to produce them there is a necessary connexion; but whatever is produced by such power, within or without a mind, is not active or free, but necessary, that is, unfree or unactive. Therefore nothing in our mind is active or free." Now when the argument is thus stated, who does not immediately see that the thing to be proved is begged? *viz.* That underived power cannot produce an active mind, whose volitions are its own, not produced in it by an external cause, but its own efforts or exertions. It follows indeed from the maxim, that whatever active being begins to exist, is created by underived power of the kind defined. But does it follow from that maxim, that underived power cannot communicate the power of willing? Or that it can produce no being that is active; nothing, in one word, distinct from passive impressions; such as our sensible ideas, for instance, are felt and universally acknowledged to be. None of these consequences follow, at least without some other intermediate steps which I have not yet seen offered by any writer for necessity. And far less then does it follow from hence, without some other intermediate steps, that if an active being can be created, its volitions will not be its own volitions, its own efforts, totally its own acts. But it is really to no purpose to dwell longer on such an idle dispute. [a]

Let us keep to experience in all natural and in all moral enquiries, which are all of them equally about matters of fact. And if we do so in this question, it must soon be determined, for we all know, we all feel, we are free agents, and that praise or blame is due to us for our conduct, when we are free from external restraint or compulsion: that it is in our power to get knowledge to direct us in the way wherein we <207> ought to walk; and having got knowledge, it is in our power to choose and walk in the right path. This is matter of experience. And the scripture treats us as such free beings, with a certain moral sphere of activity, and tells us, that our happiness for ever depends upon our conduct; for every one shall reap the fruit of his doings: and that the governor of the world in all his dispensations, preserves our liberty free and unencroached upon; or acts with us, and toward us, always as free agents. Whatever assistances we may have in the course of providence for doing good; or whatever

a. After all *freedom* properly belongs to the agent, and not to the faculty of willing, and it signifies *to have power.*

temptations to do evil; the good we do is our own doing, and the evil we do is our own doing; and it shall finally be rendered unto every man according to what he hath done, whether it hath been good or bad, with such allowances for different circumstances, not only as justice obliges to make; but, which is more, with all the allowances that mercy can make consistently with the great purpose of providence, universal good, and the unchangeable nature of moral rectitude; the unalterable moral differences of things.

This is the substance of the scripture doctrine concerning divine providence, with which reason and experience exactly agree. And hence arises this plain consequence.

COROLARY I

From the proceeding accounts of divine providence, it plainly follows, that all is conducted by infinite wisdom, goodness, veracity, faithfulness and mercy: all therefore is right or perfect. But how is it right or perfect?

I. Not in such a sense, as if by the corruptions of mankind several miseries were not introduced into the world, without which it would be a much happier, a much better, and more perfect state; but because the <208> general laws by which all is governed, and whence proceed all the consequences of corruption among mankind, are excellent, are perfect, and cannot be changed but to the worse; being the choice of infinite wisdom and mercy, because they are the best. In a moral government, the consequences of vice and corruption must be very different from those of virtue. But consequences of all sorts in our system are the effects of general laws, admirably calculated for the best, and by the observance of which the greater good in the whole will be effectually accomplished. The government of the world is perfect, because all the powers, and all the consequences of all the powers, and laws of powers belonging to it, are such as they ought to be in order to greater good, the sole end of an infinitely wise and good being in all his administration. Yet after all,

II. Let it be remembered, that when all that is, is said to be perfect and right, it is only said to be so as a part of an excellent or perfect whole, carried on by providence for the greater good in the sum of things. All is perfect, considered as a part of an advancing scheme, which is absolutely good. But considered as a whole ending with this life of man, it is not then perfect, but very imperfect. And therefore it cannot end in that manner; but it must be only a part that hath a much further respect even to an immortal life to come. The work, the contrivance of an infinitely perfect being must be perfect; and upon supposition, that this life is not the whole of providence with regard to man, but a part only, as it plainly appears to be, we can sufficiently account for every thing. What therefore remains to be concluded, but as instinct or natural hope prompts us to expect, and as the scripture fully assures us, "that this is not the whole of our existence, the whole of providence with regard to us, but a part, a very small part only." There must be, in the nature of things, a very great difference between <209> a part of a whole considered as a part, and considered as a whole; What, in the later sense or view, would be very imperfect, very incomplete, nay, very bad, may, in the other sense or view, be very perfect and good. Now as the arguments *à priori,* which prove a divine providence over-ruling all, plainly lead to this consequence, that the present state cannot be the whole, but only a part of an excellent whole, which is gradually advancing: so if we abstract from all those arguments, and confine ourselves merely to what we see of things, and argue only *à posteriori,* it is plain, that our present state hath no appearance of a whole, but, on the contrary, hath all the appearances or signs of its being but a part; and if we consider it as a part, it hath all the evidences and signs of a well administered part, so far especially as virtue, or the improvement of moral beings, are concerned. It must therefore be such a well governed part of an excellent whole, if we can at all reason from analogy; for whence can we conclude good order in the whole, but from what we see of good and wise government? And what else can we infer from thence, but the continuance of perfectly good order for ever, or throughout the whole?

III. This is the doctrine of experience, of reason and revelation; and hence we may easily see what we ought to think of what the scripture says of evils and miseries introduced into the world by means of sin and corruption; while at the same time all is affirmed to be good, as all the parts of the government of an infinitely wise and good being must be:

as, for instance, of the deluge, whether universal or partial, whether the effect of a comet, or of whatever other cause, (for all which enquiries the ways of speaking about it in scripture leave sufficient latitude;) for it and every event must be the effect of good general laws; the universe being so governed. Upon the whole therefore, from the beginning, order hath been kept in nature, <210> and also in man. And therefore tho' the apostle not only groans, but represents all good men, nay, the whole creation, as groaning for the immortality which is to succeed this state;[a] yet he expressly asserts, that even in this present state all things work together for the good of the pious and virtuous; and that present miseries are, in a great measure, the effects of the corruption of mankind; so that whatever obscurity there may be in some particular phrases in these parallel passages, they in general amount to no more than what may be said of an architect, or master of a house, who, tho' he longs earnestly to have the building finished, and to be free from all the evils and incumbrances which attend the carrying on of his scheme, is however highly pleased with the foundation that is laid, and the work so far as it is advanced; and is only earnest to have it compleated, that he may enjoy all the pleasures and advantages of it: or, more properly still, of a founder of a state, who rejoicing in the hopes of compleating at last his noble scheme, bears patiently with all the evils and hardships attending the laying the first foundation, and yet earnestly longs for the completion of it, and the happiness that will then accrue to him, and all the members of that state.

This Corolary is necessary to prevent mistakes, and clear up the true sense in which the present unfinished state of things may be properly called *a perfectly good part of providence.* It is such, because it is a proper part of a perfectly good whole; or is such a part as plainly manifests, that the whole which is carried on is good, being governed by excellent general laws, which produce the greater good in the whole.

Now all this being very obvious from what hath been said, may it not be inferred, <211>

---

a. *Rom.* viii. 20, *&c.* 2 *Cor.* iv. 17, *&c.*

COROLARY II

That the highest love, praise and adoration, must be due by all moral beings to the supreme infinitely perfect Creator and Ruler of the universe; by man in particular? Every character, in proportion to its perfection, naturally raises our esteem, love and praise. And what then must be due to a character infinitely perfect, upon whom we absolutely depend, the author of all things? Can we believe there is such a being, and not take pleasure in meditating upon his perfections; or not think it our duty frequently to meditate upon them? And can we contemplate them without feeling the warmest motions of love and adoration towards him? Meditation upon his perfections will naturally excite love and adoration, and love and adoration will naturally excite earnest desires and endeavours to imitate such a perfect character, and become like to it. Meditation on God will naturally produce praise and resignation to his all-perfect will, and the most serious longings after greater and greater conformity to his amiable, beautiful, perfect image, in order to have the most comfortable inward consciousness of being acceptable and agreeable to him; the object of his favour and delight. And in those acts of the mind, which must be in themselves exceeding pleasant, and have a very happy influence upon the temper, doth the holy scripture place devotion, praise and prayer. This is evident, if we attend to the acts of devotion recorded in the scriptures, many of which have been already quoted; and to the many exhortations to maintain and keep alive upon our minds, a strong sense of the divine perfections, and of our dependence upon God, and the infinite obligations we are under to him; the many exhortations to *pray without ceasing,* and *to rejoice in God evermore.* [a] And indeed an habitually pious <212> regard to God, consisting in love and resignation, can only be produced or preserved by frequent meditation on God, and the repeated acts of praise, and resignation, and prayer, to which meditation naturally leads. But not to insist long on this subject, three things are very evident from that excellent pattern, or model of devotion, or prayer

a. *Luke* xxi. 36. *Rom.* xii. 12. *Phil.* iv. 6. *Col.* iv. 2, 3. 1 *Peter* iv. 7. 1 *Thess.* v. 17. 1 *Peter* i. 17.

recommended to us by our Saviour. 1. That we ought to praise God with the most serious warm affection. 2. That we ought to resign ourselves, with respect to all external events independent of our own foresight and care, to his all-perfect will, which ordereth and disposeth every thing to the best. 3. That we ought to indulge ourselves in acts of benevolence towards all men; in acts of forgiveness to our enemies, under the serious perswasion of God's readiness to forgive the penitent, and of the need we stand in of his patience, forbearance, and tender mercy: and in asking or breathing after more perfect virtue, to ask which is indeed to have.[a]

This is plainly the meaning of our Lord's prayer, as it is commonly called; for if we attend to what is said in scripture of God's glory, more especially manifested in the government of higher orders of moral beings; or in the heavens: to what is meant in holy writ by his kingdom; namely, the advancement of piety, righteousness and virtue in the world;[b] and to what is called there the bread of life, namely, the doctrine of eternal life. If we attend to all these things, and to the general tenor and genius of scripture language, this will be found to be a just paraphrase upon it. *Our Father which art in heaven.* O Lord, whose supreme excellency and glory appears more and more illustriously in the government of moral beings, in proportion as they approach nearer to thee in power and perfection; thou art also our Father, the Father of mankind; we also all are the object <213> of thy care; thou art not unmindful of us, for tho' thou hast made us lower than the angels, yet thou hast crowned us with glory and honour, and given us a very noble dominion; for we are capable of knowing thee, loving thee, and imitating thee, and of growing in happiness, as we advance in conformity to thy moral rectitude, and become more like to thee, are more desired of thee, and delighted in by thee. *Hallowed be thy name.* O let all beings capable of understanding thy infinite perfection, and magnifying thee, praise and exalt thy infinitely pure and holy name, for all power is derived from thee, natural or moral; and all the inanimate things by obeying the infinitely good laws thou hast appointed to regulate their motions, do shew

a. 1 *Kings* iii. *Matth.* vii. 7, &c. *Luke* xi. 9, &c. *James* i. 5, &c. iv. 2, 3.
b. *John* vi. 27, 33, 35, 51. *Matth.* iv. 4.

forth thy praise, the infinite excellency of thy nature, and that perfection which all moral beings ought to love, cannot but love and adore while they meditate upon it, and ought to imitate in order to the attainment of their proper perfection and happiness, and the sense of thy love and approbation, to which no other enjoyment bears any proportion. Let angels, and archangels, men, and all rational beings, reverence, adore, and hallow thy wonderful character and name, and purify and sanctify themselves, as thou art pure and holy. *Let thy kingdom come.* O may the righteousness, the benevolence, the purity, the virtue, in which thou delightest, and for advancing in which all moral beings are made, and well fitted and qualified by thee, each order of them in its sphere, encrease and spread, that the world of rational beings may be such as thou made and intended them to be, such as it is in their power to be, and such as thou wouldst rejoice to behold them. *Let thy will be done in earth as it is in heaven.* O that men were such, that so thy will might be done in earth their habitation, as it is done amongst the higher orders of celestial beings, who perfectly obey thy will, and are perfectly happy in so doing. *Give us this day our daily bread.* We were made by thee, we are preserved by thee, and from thee we receive every thing that we enjoy: <214> O may a sense of our dependence upon thee, and of our infinite obligations to thy bounty, be ever present with us, that we may walk humbly and piously with thee; and receive from thy hand whatever comes to us as of thy ordering; as the bread fittest for us, as the food most convenient for us. Let us ever remember what we are, and that the nourishment of our spiritual part in virtue is the chief thing that concerns us; the bread of life to our souls; that thus we may make the best use of every event that befals us, which we could neither foresee nor prevent, for the advancement in us of those divine qualities, which are our chief excellence, and from which alone true happiness can accrue to us. *Forgive us our trespasses, as we forgive them that trespass against us.* O how far short do we every day fall of our duty, and of the improvements we might have made in virtue; but thou, O Lord, art full of mercy and compassion, and will graciously forgive the infirmities and weaknesses of men, who are seriously pious and virtuous, who have the root of true virtue in them, and who, tho' they are not indulgent to their own faults and miscarriages, yet are very tender and compassionate toward their fellow-creatures, and very ready to forgive them; ready, as all who study to be like God must be, to bless them who hurt them, to heap coals of fire on the heads of their enemies, who use them wrongfully and despitefully, and to overcome evil by good. Without this right temper of mind, it would be the most wicked arrogance to hope to share of thy mercy; for to such only can the compassion of the holy God, who hateth iniquity, extend. But having this temper, and an earnest desire to improve in it, we have confidence towards God, who, like a tender Father, pitieth his children, and generously remembreth that they are but here in a state of trial and probation, for the improvement of the faculties and dispositions thou hast implanted in them, to perfection. *Lead us not into temptation: but deliver us from evil.* <215> Let us remember the great end of events with respect to us in this our first state of trial; or the use we ought to make of them, that they may not tempt us to sin; that neither prosperity nor adversity may ever seduce us from our duty, but that we may look upon them both as means for our building ourselves up in holiness by our right use of them. The world is full of snares and temptations; so thou hast thought proper it should be. And indeed such must a state for acquiring virtue be. Let it be to us, not a state of temptation to sin, but of education in virtue, by our proper use of every thing that befals us. This is the earnest desire of our souls, under the sense of thy perfection who ruleth over all; whose kingdom the world is, and to whom as belongeth all power, so is due from thy rational creatures all honour and glory for ever. *Thine is the kingdom, the power, and the glory.* Now, that the mind must be much improved by such exercises, is evident at first sight: and will fully appear, when we come to consider more particularly the doctrine of the scripture concerning virtue, and its agreeableness with reason.

The scripture doctrine concerning virtue and vice, and its agreeableness to reason and experience.

INTRODUCTION

A preliminary observation upon the essential difference between virtue and vice.

Having thus got clear of the more thorny part of our subject, it being that which is most perplexed with abstruse, subtle, knotty questions, commonly called *metaphysical ones;* the remaining part will be found more easy and plain. <216>

It was indeed impossible to treat of the divine moral perfection, or answer the objections made against providence, the ways of God to man in particular, without entering a good deal into the explication of virtue and vice; or of the perfection and imperfection belonging to all moral beings: but it is highly proper to take this important subject a little deeper, or at least to consider of it more fully. And here it will of course fall in our way to vindicate more at large than hath been yet done, the frame, constitution and situation of mankind. All the parts of this subject we proposed to handle are so intimately related and connected together, that wherever we set out, in order to explain that particular part as it ought, we are of necessity led to treat of all the rest. We shall, however, endeavour to avoid repetitions as much as is possible, without being delicate to a point of nicety and affectation, unbecoming the gravity and importance of the question under consideration, and of *philosophy* in general; because it ever indicates a mind more taken up about the form and dress, than the substance; or more desirous to flatter the ear by smooth periods, than to enforce truth on the mind by strong close argument. I shall only, before I go further, premise one observation, which amounts to a demonstration of the essential difference between virtue and vice, and a full refutation of those who make the morality and immorality of actions dependent on the arbitrary will, whether of God or of society: for some, on the one hand, have asserted that it is the will of God which constitutes right and wrong; and some others have taught, that it is human laws which make all the difference between just and unjust, or moral good and evil. Now independently of all consideration of the will or nature of God, or of human society and its civil laws; from the mere consideration of the nature or constitution of any thing that exists, whether natural or artificial, it is necessarily and evidently true, <217>

"That there is a perfect and imperfect state belonging to every thing, to a ship, a watch, or any other machine of human invention; to a plant, a tree, or any other inanimate thing; to a lion, an elephant, a horse, or any other brute animal." This cannot be denied, without saying every ship is as well contrived and built for the end of a ship as any other; every watch is as well formed for its end as any other; every plant or tree is in as natural and perfect a state as any other; every horse is as sound and good as any other, &c. which is absurd. Now if that be really absurd, it must be equally so to assert, "that there is no such thing as perfection or imperfection, a better or a worse state with respect to moral beings; that is, beings endued with the faculty of reason and reflexion, and invested with a certain sphere of activity and power; but that it is all one whether such a being exercises its moral powers, or not exercises them; exercises them right or wrong; employs them well, or abuses them; is fit to pursue no end at all by them; or fit to pursue this or any other end, all ends being alike, and all means alike." But if that be absurd, "Then while by virtue is meant, operation with choice and self-approbation, by the best, that is, the properest means, toward the soundest and most perfect state of moral powers, and by vice the contrary, there must be as natural, essential, and immutable a difference between those two, as between being distorted or maimed, and entire or sound; between sickness and health, pleasure and pain; a fresh, vigorous, beautiful tree, and a decayed withered one; a vitious and deformed, or an infirm and ugly horse, and a good, tractable, sprightly and handsom one." For can it with any shew of reason be said, that there are no such powers in nature as reason, and reflexion, and will; or that these powers alone, of all powers or qualities, have this particularity in them, that every state, and condition of them, is equally good, equally sound, equally beautiful and perfect? Yet if that cannot be said, it must necessarily <218> follow, that no will or law of any being whatsoever, attended with whatever degree of power to make one suffer pain or enjoy happiness, can make that to be the perfect state of moral powers, which is really, in the nature of things, its imperfect state; or those exercises of moral powers tend to produce the former, which are really, in the nature of things, steps towards the production of the latter. Power may as well attempt to make darkness light, bitter sweet, a triangle a circle, a ship a watch, a tree a man, as to make reason and understanding not reason and understanding; or strong, vigorous, clear, well improved reason the same with weak, feeble, dark, unexercised, unimproved reason; or benevolent, generous self-command the same with an ungoverned, mean, mercenary, low, groveling spirit; that is, make it the same excellence, the same perfection in respect of reason, understanding and temper. Suppose any of these two opposite states of moral beings, no matter which, to be attended with ever so great sensitive pleasures constantly, and the other as constantly to raise the greatest, the acutest, the most exquisite sensitive pain; yet such a connexion, whatever disposition it might shew in the Author of such a constitution of things, would not, could not alter the nature of these two opposites; make them not opposites; or render the perfect, the imperfect state, or, *vice versa,* the imperfect the perfect one; no more than supposing, the perceiving any truth to be such, as, for instance, perceiving all the angles of a triangle to be equal to two rights, to be attended with the violentest pains of body; and ignorance of it, or a mistake about it, to be accompanied with the most delightful bodily sensations; that odd constitution of things could alter the nature of a triangle, or the nature of truth and falshood in general. If the operations of a moral being tending, in the nature of things, to produce the most perfect state of its powers, were attended with bodily sensations of the most painful sort; and the op-<219>posite operations had always accompanying them a train or succession of the most pleasant bodily sensations; such a wretched state of things, would indeed shew the contriver and former of it to be an enemy to moral improvements, and a friend to the neglect or abuse of moral powers; and moral beings so situated, would be under the miserable necessity of laying themselves out to act as contrary to their improvement toward their perfection as possibly they can: but still, even in that situation, certain qualities would as necessarily, in their several degrees, be with respect to moral powers, degrees of perfection and imperfection; as various degrees or forces of giving light, for instance, are various degrees of perfection with respect to a candle, or any other body, the end of which is to give light. In such an odd situation of moral beings, interest and virtue, as it hath been defined, would be diametrically opposite to one another. But their being so would not alter the nature of virtue, no more than it would alter the nature of interest: so far from it, that in such a case, it would be as immutably true, that the interest of moral beings is, by being so placed or constituted, basely, vilely placed or constituted; as it is, that he would be a base, a vile, a cruel father, who should choose to make the happiness of his children, or their exemption from constant, violent tortures, depend upon their care to distort their bodies into monstrous forms; for if distortion cannot be the perfect state of the human body, though a tyrant should positively order all his subjects, who were sound or not distorted, to be cruelly tormented all the days of their life; by parity of reason distortion of the mind cannot be its perfect state, though it should be commanded under the severest penalties. Now, having premised this observation, it is manifest, that in treating of virtue, there are two questions to be discussed; the first of which must be, what is the perfect and most excellent state of our <220> powers which constitute us men, and what are the exercises by which that perfect state is acquired or attained to: which enquiry being dispatched, the other that naturally offers itself is, how our interest stands, according to the constitution and connexions of things, with respect to our moral perfection or virtue. And to both these, I hope, a satisfying answer shall be given conjointly in the following explication of the agreeableness of the scripture doctrine concerning virtue and vice with reason, which will be found clearly to shew virtue to be the private good, and vice the private ill or misery of every man, all things fairly considered, even in this present life; which being proved, it must of necessity follow, that the Author of mankind, upon whose will, or whose disposition of things here and hereafter, all our interests depend, is himself supreme virtue, supreme moral perfection, or infinitely good and perfect: And hence it will also follow, that we are not only obliged to pursue virtue, or the perfection to which our moral powers are naturally fitted to attain, by certain means and exercises, as it is our perfection or the dignity and excellence of our nature; but likewise, in the sense of *Civilians,* when they speak of obligation, *i.e.* that we are obliged to it in point of interest, in consequence of the connexions of things, constituting our interest by the will of our Creator and ruler; virtue being in this respect properly speaking his law; as it is in the other sense, or considered by itself, our excellence; and, as such, the law of our nature. So St. *Paul* calls it;[a] for when the *Gentiles* which have not the law, do by nature the things contained in the law, these having not the law, are *a law to themselves,* i.e. they themselves are a law to themselves: their constitution is to them a law, or rule of conduct, clearly pointing out to them the part they ought to act with regard to their reason, or guiding and ruling principle. <221>

Proposition I

The moral perfection we are called by revelation to pursue and seek after may be reduced to those two general heads. 1. The perfection of our understanding. 2. But more especially of our will or temper.

We are commanded by revelation to do no injury to our bodies in any of its members; but to take care of our health, and to preserve ourselves in a sound state of body. And indeed all our duties, and all our perfections may be reduced to those two, *a sound body,* and *a sound mind.* Now, as for the first, I need not stay to shew it is duty and interest, or that here

a. *Rom.* ii. 14.

there is no competition between duty and interest; and how far the care of our bodies belongs to us, and what are the excesses or the negligences to be avoided in this respect by us, will appear as we go on in the explication of those duties which belong to the other head, a *sound mind*.

These duties shall be considered in various lights. But because it is evident, that our principal powers, as men, naturally divide themselves into these two, understanding and will, it is not improper to make some general observations, first of all, upon these two powers, and the perfections belonging to them, which we are exhorted or commanded by revelation to seek after with all diligence.

That we have understanding, and are frequently commanded to cultivate and improve it with all diligence by revelation, are two things too evident to be insisted upon. For what else do all the precepts in the holy scripture already mentioned to get wisdom, discretion and understanding; to love knowledge, to prefer it to all worldly treasures; to search for it with all assiduity and earnestness; to dig for it as the most valuable of riches; to search and prove all things im-<222>partially, fairly and diligently, that we may fly from evil, abstain from every appearance of it, and hold fast to that which is good, to that which is excellent or praiseworthy in itself, and therefore good or acceptable to God; to be able to give a reason for our conduct, for our hopes, our fears, and all our pursuits, for the truths we profess to believe, and to govern ourselves by: what is the meaning of all these precepts if we have not an understanding faculty which we can prove; and if we are not by those precepts exhorted diligently to improve it by suitable exercises, in order to its being cultivated to due vigor and perfection?

But, in order to illustrate the perfection of our understanding; shew the proper means for attaining to that end; and that it is our duty and interest to give all diligence to improve our understanding, (or, in the scripture language, *to grow in wisdom*) according to revelation and reason, it is necessary to make the following observations.

I. If we would have a clear notion of what makes the perfection of the understanding faculty, or of reason and judgment, let us but reflect what makes the perfection of the body or of any of its members; of the eye, for instance, from the perfections and imperfections of which, on account of its analogy to the understanding, are almost all the words taken, which are used to signify to us the infirmities, diseases, or imperfections of the latter, and their opposite perfections: such as strength, clearness, liveliness, quickness, penetrating, discerning, distinguishing force; justness, accuracy, acuteness, truth, &c. Our Saviour admirably illustrates the use, extent, and perfection of the understanding, and consequently our duty and interest with regard to it, by an alegorical reasoning taken from the use and perfection of the organ of sight.[a] "The <223> light of the body is the eye: therefore, when thine eye is single, thy whole body is full of light: but when thine eye is evil, thy body also is full of darkness. Take heed therefore, that the light which is in thee be not darkness. If thy whole body therefore be full of light, having no part dark, the whole shall be full of light; as when the bright shining of a candle doth give thee light." His meaning is: what the eye is to the body: that very same thing in proportion, the moral judgment and understanding, the directing principle, is to a man's mind. And by considering the eye of the body, and its use, and wherein its perfection or imperfection lies, we cannot but be led to conceive, wherein consists the analogous use and perfection or imperfection of the understanding, the eye of the mind, which guides our conduct, as the eye does the motions of our hands and feet, according as it is less or more fit for doing its natural office and function. If the moral judgment of the understanding be clear, pure, unbiassed, and untainted, or incorrupt, as a sound vigorus eye, and be exerted with simplicity and sincerity, as a man uses his eye, and trusts to it when he knows it not to be tainted with any unnatural colour, that can deceive him by representing objects in a false hue, it will direct and preserve men in the paths of truth and right, wherein they ought to walk; or be perpetually calling upon them to return into them, if they depart from them, as the eye, when it awakening from sleep or inattentiveness, calls upon a man, at the brink of a precipice, to stop and turn aside into the safe and right road. But as when a man's eyes are blinded, put out, or hood-winked, his whole body must of necessity move in darkness: so if the moral judgment of the mind, the principle

a. *Luke* xi. 34–36.

which ought to guide and direct mens actions, and which alone can shew us either our interest or our duty (in whatever sense that last word be taken) be itself perverted by false prejudices, and corrupted by unruly appetites and passions, which render it as un-<224>capable of judging well, as certain diseases do the eye of seeing things in their true light and genuine colours; there is no hope but such persons must mistake their way, stray from their best interest, and act contrary to the nature and reason of things: that is, contrary to the plain dictates about our behaviour, which are the natural language of the properties and relations of things duly considered, in the same sense, that one way duly attended to by the eye in a sound state, appears to it the worst or improperest road to a certain place or end, or contrariwise the best, easiest, and safest. For all properties and relations of things, by whatever names they are distinguished, natural or moral, must have their natural influences, with regard to our conduct, so far as they are concerned in it. We cannot deny that in one case, and own it in any other, without falling into a gross contradiction and inconsistency. "Take heed therefore, adds our Lord, that the light which is in thee be not darkness." Let every man think himself at least obliged to take as much care of his moral understanding, as of his eye, to preserve it sound and entire, able to do its functions well, and consequently, to be a true guide, that will not deceive or mislead, but represent things fairly to us; take care that it do not fall into a lethargy or drowsiness, and so leave us often without a guide, and yet more that it be not vitiated or corrupted in any manner to such a degree, as to lead us wrong, by setting things before us in false colours, and not as they really are in themselves: take care that it do not obscure, magnify, diminish, or double objects, nor give them the appearances of properties they have not; but may shew every thing to us which it concerns us to know, in order to right action, or action no wise contrary to the real nature, tendency, and consequences of things, as it really is, in its true shape, magnitude, hue, and proportions. All the diseases of the understanding, and all the preservatives against them; all the good qualities, and all the <225> means of attaining to them, and preserving them, might very aptly be illustrated by pursuing this similitude. But what hath been said is sufficient to our purpose at present, which was merely to shew, that there must be a perfection belonging to the understanding as well as to the eye; and that this perfection must consist in its being able to direct our conduct, for that must be true, if there be any such thing as fitness or unfitness of conduct, any such thing as acting agreeably or disagreeably to the nature, that is, to the properties, relations, and connexions of things; or finally, if there be any such thing as interest and happiness, or pleasure and unhappiness, resulting from action and conduct. Leaving it therefore to those who write professedly on the conduct of the understanding, to explain the rules of it more minutely, I proceed to a second observation upon the duties of man, with respect to perfectionating the understanding, which is evidently our guiding principle, or the light by which alone we can be directed in our conduct,

II. That it is in every man's power to improve his understanding faculty to a very great degree of soundness and perfection, in order to its being a sufficient and a right guide in conduct; or to improve in knowledge of every sort, to a very considerable pitch; but more especially in that knowledge which is requisite to direct his moral behaviour, and that it is our interest and excellence so to do. Sure, I need not stay to prove, that knowledge, or a state of mental light, is more agreeable than a state of inward darkness; or, which is the truth of the matter, that knowledge is exceedingly agreeable to the human mind by its constitution, and ignorance very painful and uneasy to it. This none will refuse: it is therefore our interest, even in respect of immediate delight, abstracting from all other considerations to get knowledge, and to deliver <226> ourselves from a state of darkness, or even of doubting, which is really a sort of twilight, or rather mist in the mind, and proportionably disagreeable to the understanding, as it is to the natural eye. Hardly will any one who is in the least acquainted with searches after truth and knowledge say, that however pleasant knowledge may be when attained to, in any considerable degree, yet the labour with which it is acquired makes it too dear a purchase; for every step towards knowledge abundantly rewards itself. So agreeable hath the author of nature, who hath made us for exercise, made the exercise of our guiding principle to us, that every glimpse of truth as it begins to dawn upon the mind, wonderfully chears and awakes it: The employment of our faculty of judging, comparing, enquiring and finding out truth is a most pleasant one in itself, even abstracting from the agreeable hopes of success, and the unspeakable delight accruing from hence, with which our natural love of truth and light, our strong desire after it, and our consciousness of our power to attain to it by proper application, are ever animating and enchearing us in the pursuit; all which affections likewise grow stronger and more lively, in proportion to our conquests and advances in the search of truth. Now as it affords pleasure to us, and is therefore, even in that respect, abstracting from the necessity of it to guide us, our interest, or a large part of our natural happiness; so that it is an attainment, the earnest pursuit of which highly becomes human nature, as being capable of it, is no less evident than that it is better to see than to be blind; better to have a sound, entire, unvitiated eye, than a weak, infirm, and diseased one. If there be any such thing as perfection, this must be one. If the words becoming, suitable to nature, excellent and desirable for its own sake, have any meaning at all, this must be such. And to decide this question, which must ultimately terminate in asking, "What are <227> we necessarily disposed to approve, prefer, esteem, or value, abstracting from all considerations of conveniency and advantage, the understanding that is able by due culture to judge quickly and soundly, or that which is not." Let us examine what necessarily passes in our mind, when we make this comparison. For surely, no one can put this question to himself who will not immediately say, "The excellence of understanding is to understand."

But the important question now to be considered is, How or in what measure it is in every man's power, by his frame, to improve his understanding, and acquire knowledge; in answer to which let it be observed, in the first place.

I. Let us observe with an excellent philosopher, in whose words I am to go on very nearly, or with a few variations, for a considerable time.[26] "We are born with faculties and powers capable almost of any thing; such at least as would carry us farther than is imagined; but it is only the exercise of those powers which gives us ability and skill in any thing, and leads us toward perfection. A middle-aged plough-man will scarce ever be brought to the carriage and language of a gentleman, though his

26. Locke, *Of the Conduct of the Understanding* § 4, 6.

body be as well proportioned, and his joints as supple, and his natural parts not any way inferior. The legs of a dancing-master, and the fingers of a musician fall, as it were, naturally and without thought or pains into regular and admirable motions. Bid them change their parts, and they will in vain endeavour to produce like motions in the members not used to them, and it will require length of time and long practice to attain but some degrees of a like ability. What incredible and astonishing actions do we find rope-dancers and tumblers bring their bodies to! Not but that sundry in almost all manual arts are as wonderful; but I <228> name those which the world takes notice for such, because, on that very account, they give their money to see them. All these admired motions beyond the reach and almost the conception of unpractised spectators, are nothing but the mere effects of use and industry in men, whose bodies have nothing peculiar in them from those of the amazed lookers-on. As it is in the body, so it is in the mind; practice makes it what it is, and most even of those excellencies which are looked on as natural endowments, will be found, when examined into more narrowly, to be the product of exercise, and to be raised to that pitch only by repeated actions. Some men are remarkable for pleasantness in raillery; others for apologues and diverting stories. This is apt to be taken for the effect of pure nature, and that the rather because it is not got by rules; and those who excell in either of them, never purposely set themselves to the study of it, as an art to be learnt. But yet it is true, that at first some lucky hit, which took with some body, and gained him commendation, encouraged him to try again, inclined his thoughts and endeavours that way, till at last he insensibly got a faculty in it without perceiving how; and that is attributed wholly to nature, which was much more the effect of use and practice. I do not deny, that natural disposition may often give the first rise to it; but that never carries a man far without use and exercise; and it is practice alone that brings the powers of the mind, as well as those of the body, to their perfection. Many a good poetick vein is buried under a trade, and never produces any thing for want of improvement. We see the ways of reasoning and discourse are very different, even concerning the same matter, at court and at the university. And he that will go but from *Westminster-hall* to the *Exchange,* will find a different genius and turn in their ways of talking, and yet one cannot think, that all whose lot fell in the city were born with different parts <229> from those who were bred at the university or inns of court. To what purpose all this, but to shew, that the difference, so observable in mens understandings and parts, does not arise so much from their natural faculties, as acquired habits. He would be laught at that should go about to make a fine dancer out of a country hedger at past fifty. And he will not have much better success, who shall endeavour at that age to make a man reason well, or speak handsomly, who has never been used to it, though you should lay before him a collection of all the best precepts of logick or oratory. No body is made any thing by hearing of rules, or laying them up in the memory; practice must settle the habit of doing, without reflecting on the rule; and you may as well hope to make a good painter or musician, *ex tempore,* by a lecture, and instruction in the arts of musick and painting, as a coherent thinker, or strict reasoner, by a set of rules, shewing him wherein right reasoning consists.

This being so, that defects and weaknesses in mens understandings, as well as other faculties, come from want of a right use of their own minds; I am apt to think the fault is generally mislaid upon nature, and there is often a complaint of want of parts, when the fault lies in want of due improvement of them. We see men frequently dexterous and sharp enough in making a bargain, who, if you reason with them about matters of religion, appear very stupid."

"The reason why men do not choose surer principles to argue from, or argue more accurately and justly, is, because they cannot: but this inability proceeds not from want of natural parts, but generally from want of use and exercise. Few men are from their youth accustomed to strict reasoning, and to trace the dependence of any truth in a long train of consequences, to its remote principles, and to observe its connexion; and he that by frequent practice has not been used to this employment of his understanding, <230> 'tis no more wonder, that he should not, when he is grown into years, be able to bring his mind to it, than that he should be on a sudden able to grave or design, dance on the ropes, or write a good hand, who has never practised either of them. What then should be done in the case? I answer, we should always remember what

I said above, that the faculties of our soul are improved and made useful to us, just after the same manner as our bodies are. Would you have a man write or paint, dance or fence well, or perform any other manual operation dexterously and with ease, let him have never so much vigour and activity, suppleness and address, naturally; yet no body expects this from him, unless he has been used to it, and has employed time and pains in fashioning and forming his hand or outward parts to those motions. Just so it is in the mind; would you have a man reason well, you must use him to it betimes, exercise his mind in observing the connexion of ideas, and following them in train. What then, can grown men never be improved or enlarged in their understandings? I say not so; but this I think I may say, that it will not be done without industry and application, which will require more time and pains, than grown men settled in their course of life will allow to it, and therefore is seldom done. And this very capacity of attaining it by use and exercise only brings us back to that which I laid down before, that it is only practice that improves our minds as well as bodies, and we must expect nothing from our understandings any farther than they are perfected by habits."

"The *Americans* are not all born with worse understandings than the *Europeans,* though we see none of them have such reaches in the arts and sciences. And among the children of a poor countryman, the lucky chance of education, and getting into the world, gives one infinitely the superiority of parts over the rest, who continuing at home, had continued also just of the same <231> size with his brethren. He that has to do with young scholars, especially in the mathematicks, may perceive how their minds open by degrees, and how it is exercise alone that opens them. Sometimes they will stick a long time at a part of a demonstration, not for want of will or application, but really for want of perceiving the connexion of two ideas; that to one, whose understanding is more exercised, is as visible as any thing can be. The same would be with a grown man, beginning to study mathematicks, the understanding, for want of use, often sticks in a very plain way, and he himself, that is so puzzled, when he comes to see the connexion, wonders what it was he stuck at in a case so plain."

I have quoted this excellent piece of experimental reasoning from an admirable, justly esteemed philosopher. 1. To give strength to what I had before said, that though society requires diversity of gifts, talents, tempers, or, in one word, genius's; and though such diversity may be in some measure natural, yet for the greater part it is owing to different kinds and degrees of exercise or want of exercise, in consequence of the law of habits; a most useful and essential part in our constitution. 2. But chiefly to shew, on this occasion, in what sense it may be justly said to be in every man's power to improve his understanding to a very great pitch of perfection. And in this sense it plainly is so, that generally defect in knowledge is not from want of natural parts; but from want of proper exercise to cultivate natural parts. 3. And in the next place, to give me an opportunity of remarking, how much the improvement of our understanding depends upon education, and consequently upon the care, not only of our parents, but upon the care of society about education. The many beneficial advantages of that close social dependence among mankind, of which this is an essential, or *necessary* part, are very evident, and have been already treated upon. All therefore I <232> would now observe on this head is, that a state which does not take proper care to put and keep the education of the youth of the higher ranks in life upon a good foot, neglects the most essential thing to the well-being of every private person, and of society in general; the most essential thing to the end of government, if that be publick happiness; and when that is not the end, and the proper means to it are not carefully pursued, a state of government is indeed much worse than a state of nature. This needs no proof; for it is indeed with the consent of all thinking men, in education, that the foundation stones of private and publick happiness, private and publick virtue, things in their nature absolutely inseparable, must be laid; according to it will the superstructure be. As for those that have time and the means to attain to knowledge in a well-governed state, it is indeed a shame for them to want any helps or assistances for the improvement of their understanding, that are to be got. Those who by the industry and parts of their ancestors have been set free from the constant drudgery to their backs and bellies others lie under, should bestow some of that time, which commonly is either very foolishly, if not wickedly spent, or lies very heavy on their hands, on the improvement of their heads, and to enlarge their minds with pleasant and useful knowledge. 'Tis certain that the power of being really and extensively useful in society depends upon a well-improved understanding; upon ability to judge of the interests of mankind; the fitness of laws and the propriety of expedients in different emergencies; which knowledge cannot be acquired without study and deep thinking, as well as reading, and will never be sought after but by a good heart, and always will be sought after by such. And let but any one consider, whether riches give merit, without a disposition to employ them well, and skill how to do it? They do really otherwise render one but more contemptible; because having them points one out <233> to publick view, and makes his virtues or vices more conspicuous; and if one be not able to use them to their best purposes, every one who wishes well to society, or to himself, will naturally say of such, How ill is such wealth placed! How unworthy is the possessor of it! How shamefully incapable is he of doing the good such affluence puts in his power!

But the publick care of education ought to extend yet further, and comprehend in it the whole body of the people, in such a manner, as that not only all useful arts and crafts may be understood and brought to perfection; but that all, even the meanest may have opportunities of being instructed in the principles of virtue and true religion. Now, here I cannot but observe, that the one day of seven, besides other days of rest, allows in the christian world time enough for this (had they no other idle hours) if they would but make due use of these vacances from their daily labour, and apply themselves with as much diligence to the study of religion, as they often do to a great many things that are useless, and yet more difficult. This is certainly true, provided any care were taken of the common people in their infancy; or those whose sacred business it is to instruct them, would take due pains to enter them according to their several capacities into a right way to this knowledge, and to assist and encourage them in their endeavours to improve in it. And this shews us what an excellent institution it is, by which a convenient portion of time is thus set apart from labour, to be dedicated to the improvement of the mind; and teachers are appointed for that beneficial end. None can choose but approve such an institution, if they have a just sense of the dignity of human nature, and of the common unalienable rights and privileges of mankind, and of the chief end of society and government; or unless they inhumanly and barbarously, as well as impiously think, that the bulk of mankind are made to be mere beasts of burden, whose understandings ought <234> to be put out, as certain *Scythians* are said to have done the eyes of their slaves, or kept in darkness that they may be more tame drudges; less apt to rebel, because less sensible of bad usage; and that if they are allowed so much as any diversion, or respite from labour, it should be for the same reason as bells are hung about the necks of pack-horses or mules. Experience shews us, that the original make of their minds is like that of other men; and they would be found not to want understanding fit to receive very useful instruction, if they were but a little encouraged and helped in it, as they should be by those who in christian countries are employed and maintained for that most beneficial, noble end. There are many instances of very mean people, who have raised their minds to a great sense and understanding of religion, and likewise of other parts of science. And tho' these have not been so frequent as could be wished by all the lovers of mankind; yet they are enough to take off the imputation of incapacity of knowledge charged upon the bulk of mankind, by some who delight to paint human nature in the worst colours they can devise; and to prove, that it is the fault of those whose business and profession it is to instruct the people, if more are not brought to be very knowing, especially in matters of religion. They might very easily by proper methods be put into such a right way of considering the works of creation, that even while they are employed about their manual occupations, their minds might be very busy in admiring the wisdom and goodness of the Creator, in some object or other within their observation. This knowledge is capable of being conveyed in a very pleasing, agreeable manner to every capacity. And the original end of the sabbath is forgot, when due pains are not taken at that time to lay open, in a way suited to the meanest capacity, the invisible perfections of God, which are clearly manifested by every part of nature we see. But <235> this leads to observe, with relation to the improvement of our understanding,

II. That such is the make and frame of the human mind, that it is in every one's power, with a very small degree of assistance from their teachers, easily to attain to a very clear and distinct notion of all the duties of life, of all moral obligations. Let it not be said here, that this is to take for granted what we have not yet proved, the reality of moral obligations. For not only did we set out in this *section* with an observation that sets the reality of morality beyond all doubt; but in proving what is now asserted, it will at once appear, that there are really moral obligations; and that these lie open and plain to every one's understanding, who will but think at all. In reality, man is so made, that he must perceive, or rather feel, certain moral obligations, or shun himself, and all reflexion. Moral obligations may be proved and illustrated in various ways, some, if not all, which are very intelligible to the meanest understanding. But this is not all the care that the Author of nature hath taken of us: this is not all the Author of nature hath done to shew us our duty, our happiness, our excellence, and what ought to be to us the rule of all our conduct. For there is a natural principle of benevolence in man, which is in some degree to society, what self-love is to the individual, that is, the same security for our right behaviour towards it, that self-love is for our right behaviour to ourselves. This we all feel we cannot divest ourselves of; and it as naturally points us to proper behaviour in any case whatsoever toward our fellow-creatures, as any instinct in an animal directs it to its end. We cannot deny, that there is such a principle in our minds, without asserting that there is no disposition to friendship; no such thing as compassion, no paternal or filial affections in our nature; or, in one word, no affection in us which hath the <236> good of another for its object and end. Which is, if any thing be, to deny evident matter of fact. For what property of a body manifests itself more plainly than these qualities of our minds. We shall afterwards have occasion to explain at greater length the real consistency between self-love and benevolence, which some affect to represent as two principles that cannot subsist in the same breast, or if they do, must be at perpetual war the one against the other. Mean time, let any one attend to his own mind, and the motions or affections, which bestir it most agreeably, and say, whether the greatest satisfaction to ourselves does not depend upon our having a benevolent disposition in a due degree: 'tis this which makes the cheerful, the happy temper, without which the most prosperous circumstances of outward enjoyment cannot afford any considerable satisfaction; for without it the mind is found peevish, and discontented with itself, and every thing about us: and all its exercises touch the mind with more exquisite and more durable joy, than any sensual gratification or selfish indulgence can give us, as we may feel even when the mind is tenderly and benevolently moved by probable fiction, as in a tragedy. So that a due consideration of our best pleasures, or most valuable enjoyments, *i.e.* of those which are the remotest from all grossness and remorse, would be an effectual security for that right behaviour towards society, to which benevolence prompts us. Further, the several particular affections in our minds contribute and lead us to publick good, as really as some others do to private. That there is not one principle only in our nature, but that we have many different passions or affections in us, each of which hath its own particular object and end, will be evident to any one who will but take the slightest review of his make and frame. There is in our minds a herding principle, or love of society, distinct from affection to the good of it, in common to us with all animals who flock and herd together, desire of esteem from others, immediate impulse to <237> compassionate and relieve the distressed, indignation against injuries done to others: and these may justly be called publick affections, because they have an immediate respect to others, and as naturally lead us to behave in such a manner as will be of advantage to our fellow-creatures, as hunger prompts and directs us to seek for proper food and nourishment to our bodies. For as persons, who never made any reflexions upon the desirableness of life, or if they ever did, do yet of course preserve it, merely from the appetite of hunger, without making any such reflexion at the time they are instigated by that appetite; so by being influenced merely from regard to reputation, or by some other publick affection, without any consideration of the good of others, men often work to publick good by mere impulse of nature. Now, if it is said, that when all this is owned, what is it to moral obligation, for so far 'tis only instinct that acts? The answer is obvious, here first is a plain evidence of the care of nature about us to make us social. For as the instincts or appetites by which we are led or compelled to self-preservation, are instances of the care of providence about the preservation of the individual; so the instincts and affections by which we are impelled to mind the interests of our fellow-creatures, and to act agreeably to them, are instances of the care of our Maker about the preservation and commonweal of society. In both cases, they are plainly instruments or means by which kind providence carries on its good ends, which they themselves have not in their view. But this is not all; for this being our constitution, if we take a view of it, and reflect upon it, as we are able to do, and cannot avoid doing, (for who can avoid reflecting upon himself, and what passes within him) we must needs see that we are as immediately and naturally intended for society and benevolent exercises, as a watch is made for measuring time; and that we act at once contrary to the end of our make, our greatest <238> happiness, and the will and intention of our Maker, if we endeavour to root out of our minds all the publick affections; and to shut as it were our ears against their dictates, or harden our hearts against their calls and impulses. This is a reflexion we cannot evite making, if we look into ourselves, and consider our frame ever so slightly. For in this manner do we reason about the end of every machine we use or see; and being inur'd to make such reflexions on many occasions every day, how can we escape making it, when we think of or review ourselves, and attend to the impulses of our nature, and the different ways in which these affect us? But in whatever sense moral obligation be taken, that sense of it is necessarily comprehended in this natural reflexion just mentioned, to which the slightest consideration of our frame must lead us. For what can it mean, if it neither means obligation to act agreeably to the end of our frame, and to the intention of our Maker, nor to our interest?

This however will be clearer, when we have considered, that according to our make we cannot take a view of our affections, or actions, and remain indifferent, or neutral to them all; but, on the contrary, tho' there be some to which we are almost quite indifferent, being very little moved or affected by them; yet there are others which we cannot choose but approve, or disapprove. There is in our mind a principle of reflexion, which passes judgment upon our heart and temper, and all our affections and consequent actions, pronouncing some to be in themselves just, right, and good, and others to be in themselves evil, wrong, and unjust; an approving and condemning faculty, which without being called upon or consulted, exerts itself with authority; and which, if not forcibly resisted and opposed, never gives us quiet while we act disagreeably to it; but gives us the supremest peace, satisfaction, and joy, when we behave conformably to it, and set ourselves to maintain its authority in our mind, <239> as our ruler and law-giver. Now by this faculty natural to man, he is a moral agent; *he is a law to himself;* he is conscious of moral obligation, and is never at a loss to find out how he should conduct himself. This principle carries along with it a consciousness of its supremacy in our constitution, or of its right to give law to us, and pass sentence upon us. If any one would be satisfied at once, that he hath such a principle in him, and how it directs him how to behave towards his fellow-creatures; let him but ask himself sincerely, and attend to the answer of his mind or conscience, or of this approving and condemning faculty, "Have I indeed no guide, no rule of action, and may I give full swing to every appetite, every fancy, that sollicites or importunes me, without running the risk of any condemnation, but from self-love, if I bring more pain upon myself by the pursuit than all the pleasure was worth—May I do any injury in my power to my neighbour, that I can do with impunity, or which instead of my suffering by it will procure me some sensual gratification"—and so on—For we may fairly put the whole of moral obligation upon this one point, *viz.* The reply that the mind, thus seriously searched and examined, will give to itself: and to what can we appeal in any question about inward experience but to experience? To refuse to put the issue of the question on this footing is absurd, and at the same time it is a secret confession of the inward forefeeling how it must be determined, if this trial is yielded to. To say, what we call conscience, moral sense, or the approving and condemning faculty, is owing to prejudices of education and custom, is indeed to ascribe a power of creating to art: for were we not endowed by nature with such a faculty, it is as evident, that affections, actions, and characters could never be made to appear to us under any other image, but <240> that of advantageous or disadvantageous, and not under the semblance or shew of worthy or base, fair or foul, comely or abominable; as that musick can never be made to appear to one who wants an ear, to be any other than an art from which some pretend to receive a pleasure he has no idea of; or as what some make a very profitable trade of. 'Tis in vain to say, May not the idea of shame be connected with what you will by education. For first of all, education can never make a man really and truly ashamed of himself for consulting his reason before he acts, or for doing a generous action at the expence of several sensitive pleasures, even in themselves innocent, the money so generously bestowed would have procured him. And, in the second place, if a sense of shame and honour, however misguided it may be by education, does not originally suppose in our nature an approving and disapproving faculty, which naturally of itself, previous to all instruction, approves certain actions and disapproves others, so soon as they are presented to its sight or consideration, then may all our natural appetites be resolved into education and custom: nay, consistently with that assertion, there can be no reason to call any sentiment or feeling of the mind natural. But if what hath been said be matter of fact, then is man, every man so formed, that in order to know moral duties or obligations, right or wrong, he needs only exercise his inward conscience, or his faculty of reflexion, his approving or condemning sense.

Now that this part of our constitution is acknowledged in scripture, as what constitutes us moral agents, and as a sufficient guide to all men, with respect to their behaviour to themselves, their fellow-creatures, and to their Creator and Governor; and that as such it is frequently recommended to our sedulous culture and improvement, is plain. St. *Paul* speaks of it in the <241> strongest terms.[a] "For not the lovers of the law are just before God: but the doers of the law shall be justified. For when the *Gentiles,* which have not the law, do by nature the things contained in the law, these having not the law, are a law unto themselves. Which

a. *Rom.* ii. 13–15.

shew the works of this law written in their hearts, their conscience also bearing witness, and their thoughts the mean while accusing, or else excusing one another." So St. *John,*[a] "And hereby we know that we are of the truth, and shall assure ourselves before God. For if our hearts condemn us, God is greater than our hearts, and knoweth all things. Beloved, if our hearts condemn us not, then have we confidence towards God."

And what is said in the book of *Wisdom,*[b] of wisdom, moral knowledge, and a sense of duty, is very remarkable. "Wisdom is glorious and never fadeth away; yea, she is easily seen of them that love, and found of them that seek her. She preventeth them that desireth her, in making herself first known unto them. Whoso seeketh her early shall have no great travel; for he shall find her sitting at his doors. To think therefore upon her is perfection of wisdom; and whoso travelleth for her shall quickly be without care. For she goeth about seeking such as are worthy of her, sheweth herself favourably unto them in the ways, and ruleth them in every thought. For the very true beginning of her is the desire of discipline, and the care of discipline is love. And love is the keeping of her laws, and the giving heed to her laws is the assurance of incorruption. And incorruption maketh us near unto God."

This is the real state of man with regard to the knowledge of moral obligations, or to our capacity of finding true wisdom. So that with respect to this most important of all knowledge, all men, with very little <242> assistance from proper instructors, may make very great advances in it, or be perfect masters of it as far, at least, as the ordinary duties of life require.

III. Tho' I have resolved to leave it to those who professedly write on the conduct of the understanding, to point out fully the rules to be observed in the search of truth, and to avoid error; yet men, in the search of knowledge, are so often misled by some very good and useful principles in our frame, that I cannot choose but offer a few reflexions upon some of the sources of error, or impediments to the acquisition of true

---

a. 1 John iii. 19–21.
b. Wisdom vi. 12–20.

knowledge. First, the very eagerness and strong bent of the mind after knowledge, if not warily regulated, is often an hinderance to it. It still presses after new discoveries and new objects, and catches at variety of knowledge, and therefore is too desultory, and stays not long enough on what is before it, to look into it with the acurate attention it should, and must in order to understand it fully, thro' haste to pursue what is yet out of sight. Hence it is, that so many are too superficial in their examination of objects, ever to get to the bottom of any one thing, or be thoroughly masters of it. For tho' truths are not the better or the worse for their obviousness or difficulty, but their value is to be measured by their usefulness and tendency; yet the discovery of most truths requires close attention and acurate search; and one can no more make great proficiency in knowledge by proceeding in a hasty desultory manner, and leaping from object to object, without fastening long enough upon any one to draw any solid fruit from it to the understanding, than one can learn much of a country from the transient view he has of it by riding post thro' it.[a] But there is another haste, that does often, and will never fail to mislead the mind, if one is not warn-<243>ed, and upon his guard against it. The understanding is naturally forward, not only to encrease its knowledge by variety, (which makes it leap from one to get speedily to another part of knowledge) but is also impatient to enlarge its views, by running too fast into general observations and conclusions, without a due examination of particulars enough to found them upon. This seems to augment their stock, but 'tis of visions, not real truths: for theories built upon so narrow a bottom, are not knowledge, but rash precipitant presumptions. General observations drawn from particulars, are indeed as agreeable to the mind on account of their universality, as they are extensively useful; but great care must be taken not to be deceived in admitting general observations; for if the foundation be not solid, what must the whole superstructure built upon them with great care and labour be?

That many are misled in both these ways is too evident from expe-

a. See *Lock on education.* [Most of this page and half of the next is part quotation and part paraphrase of Locke, *Of the Conduct of the Understanding* §25.]

rience to be proved. But few have sufficiently adverted to the sources whence all this proceeds. It will however soon appear, if we consider a little the structure of the human mind, how both these kinds of haste and rashness come about. They do really take their rise from very useful passions or principles in our nature. For, in fact, they proceed partly from our natural love of exercise and progress, and our love of variety or novelty, affections, which if they be really distinct, must however of necessity go together; and are all of them absolutely requisite to beings intended for exercise, exercise of body and mind, and for progress, insomuch that they can attain to no perfection, but gradually, and in proportion to diligence and activity to make progress or improvement: and partly from a principle of no less usefulness in our frame, or with respect to our situation, which is our natural delight in analogy, harmony and order. For hence a tendency to draw general conclusions from particular observations necessarily results. And yet without <244> such a disposition we could never make any considerable advances in knowledge, but our heads or memories would ever remain a magazine of separate materials which could not be called *knowledge,* but continue to be a collection of lumber not reduced to use or order. 'Tis the business of education to guide these principles right; or to exercise and practise them in a useful way, that would prevent their becoming hurtful in either of those respects that have been mentioned. In the moral enquiry, I have said a great deal of the utility of the associating principle, or aptitude in our nature, and likewise of the errors of which it must necessarily be the occasion, if education is not calculated, as it ought, to warn us of, and put us upon the watch against such misguidance. But I can't choose but add here, that 'tis this useful disposition in our minds, which in a great measure gives rise to our precipitancy in drawing general conclusions, and in admitting principles. In an orderly uniform world, ideas must often be presented to our minds conjointly, which however have no other connexion or correspondence, but merely that of their having been often presented together to the mind. And minds made so as to be able to associate, will, during their whole life, find it very difficult not to judge, that things really and naturally are what they have often appeared to them to be, provided education doth not early interpose to teach and accustom them to separate and dissociate, both with respect to natural and moral appearances. And indeed it is the chief business of education, if its end be to fit us for life, and to teach us to think justly of things, and act well, to inculcate upon youth from their tenderest years, in a way suited to their capacity, the necessity of never suffering any ideas that have no natural cohesion to be joined by appearances in their under-standings: or, in general, of never allowing any ideas to be associated in their minds, in any other or stronger combination, than what their own nature and corespondence give them; and for that reason, <245> edu-cation ought not only to recommend it to youth, but actually to inure them to examine the ideas that they find linked together in their minds, whether their association be from the visible agreement that is in the ideas themselves, or merely from the habitual and prevailing custom of the mind, in joining them thus together in thinking; or from their having often occurred to the mind closely connected, either in consequence of the course of nature, if they be natural appearances, or in consequence of the practice of the world, if they be moral ones. But how contrary to this, and all the other ends of education, is, as an excellent writer on the subject has long ago observed, that prevailing custom among all sorts of people of principling their children and scholars; which in reality amounts to no more, but making them imbibe their teacher's notions and tenets, by an implicite faith, and firmly adhere to them, true or false.[a]

But all this may perhaps be thought too long a digression from my present subject, which hath been, I think, sufficiently illustrated; and will be yet more so, in considering the other general class of our duties, or perfections, to which we are exhorted by revelation, agreeably to rea-son; to which I now therefore proceed.

IV. How easily moral knowledge, which is the most important of all knowledge, may be acquired by all men, will yet more clearly appear, if we consider what is that right moral temper of mind, and correspondent conduct, which we are commanded by revelation to labour to attain to as our happiness, our interest, our most reasonable and becoming dis-position of mind, and so much the end of all knowledge, that without

a. Mr. *Lock.* [Locke, *Of the Conduct of the Understanding* §41.]

it all science is vain and unprofitable. Now what is this temper? It consists in the presidence of reason over <246> our mind, and all its appetites and passions, to such a degree of stable authority, that no fancy, no appetite, no passion, is able to hurry us away with it into any pursuit it may paint to us in the most tempting colours, till reason and moral conscience have examined the matter, and pronounced sentence? It consists in self-government or mastership of the mind; and in being so strong, as never to act contrary to reason, or even without a very good reason. It consists in being able to subdue and conquer our strongest appetites, when to yield to them would be to act a base, or ungenerous, or even an unmanly, effeminate part. It consists in having benevolence so predominant in our mind, as to be disposed on every occasion to consult the good of our fellow-creatures; and to prefer it to our own selfish sensual indulgences. It consists in sweetness, goodness, and what is properly called *humanity, or benignity of temper.* It consists in an habitual love of the supreme being, and cheerful resignation to his will; and finally, in that fortitude and magnanimity of mind, which enables one to suffer with due resolution and bravery any evil, rather than forego his integrity, and act contrary to his inward sense of right and wrong; and generously to forgive injuries. This is the substance of what the holy scripture recommends to us as our chief study. It often reduces all our duties to love; the love of God, and the love of our neighbour. It often exhorts, not only to compassion and mercy, but to a meek and forgiving temper. It commands us to overcome evil by good. It frequently exhorts to patience under affliction, and resignation to the divine will, which orders and disposes all things to the best. It abounds in precepts, to subdue our unruly passions, to strive for the mastership and command of them: and what it represents as the principal thing, is to maintain the authority of reason, as our guiding principle in our mind, that we may live and act like reasonable beings; may be habitually able on <247> every occasion to prove what is agreeable to reason, and therefore acceptable to God; that we may always enjoy the testimony of a good conscience, telling us, that in all simplicity and godly sincerity, we have had our conversation in the world; and that when our hearts, being void of all consciousness of offence, do not condemn us, but approve us, we may have confidence toward God, whose voice conscience is. I shall have occasion afterwards to explain more particularly all those duties, and then the particular places of scripture where they are recommended to us shall be pointed out. Let me only at present mention two: one from St. *Paul* writing to the *Romans.*[a] "For the kingdom of God is not meat and drink, but righteousness and peace, and joy in the Holy Ghost. For he that in these things serveth Christ, is acceptable to God, and approved of men. Let us therefore follow after the things which make for peace, and things wherewith one may edify another." The other is from the epistle of the same apostle to the *Ephesians,* much to the same purpose.[b] "Be ye followers of God as dear children. And walk in love as Christ also hath loved us—Let no man deceive you with vain words; for because of the unclean works of darkness cometh the wrath of God upon the children of disobedience. Be not ye therefore partakers with them. For ye were sometimes darkness, but now are ye light in the Lord: walk as children of the light. For the fruit of the spirit, is in all goodness, and righteousness, and truth, proving what is acceptable to the Lord. And have no fellowship with the unfruitful works of darkness, but rather reprove them.—But all things that are reproved, are made manifest by the light: for whatsoever doth make manifest, is light."

The meaning of which two excellent exhortations amounts plainly to this: "Tho' christians are ex-<248>empted from the bondage of the *Jewish* law with respect to meats and drinks; yet the more valuable privileges and advantages of that kingdom, which Christ came into the world to establish, do not consist in the enjoyment of a greater variety of meats and drinks, but in uprightness of life, and in peace, and joy of mind, resulting from a good conscience, and the use of the most advantageous gifts and benefits of the Holy Ghost under the gospel, for our advancement in true virtue and piety. For he that by the study of purity, holiness and peace, obeys the commands of Christ, is acceptable to God, and must be approved by all men, who have their natural sense of right uncorrupted. The things therefore that we set our hearts upon to pursue

a. *Rom.* xiv. ver. 17, *&c.*
b. *Eph.* v.

and promote, let them be such as tend to peace and good-will, and to instruct, and build up one another in the holiness and goodness of temper, to which we are called by Jesus Christ."

"Let all bitterness,[27] and wrath, and anger, and clamour, and evil speaking, be put away from among you, with all malice. And be ye kind to one another, tender-hearted, forgiving one another, even as God forgiveth you. Be ye thus followers, or imitators of God, as those who are under special obligations to his mercy, and who would approve themselves to him, as dear obedient children to an affectionate parent. Propose no less an example to yourselves to be imitated by you, than God your Father, who is in heaven. And let love conduct and influence your whole conversation, as Christ also hath loved us, and hath given himself for us, an acceptable offering of a sweet-smelling favour unto God. Let not the works of darkness, those works, which, conscious of their baseness and impurity, hate and avoid the light, be named among you without abhorrence. For let no man deceive you with vain words; all works which dare not stand the test of light are highly abominable in the sight of God, and those <249> who obey these wicked lusts, and practise these self-condemned wicked deeds, will God bring to judgment. Be ye not therefore partakers with such. For if God will punish the heathen nations for such works, because tho' they are not favoured with revelation, yet they have a law in their hearts, which condemneth these abominable practices, to which they do not hearken; but which, on the contrary, they have, as it were, quite defaced and obliterated; how much more aggravated must your guilt be, if ye are guilty of the same abominations, who are no more in the state of darkness the *Gentiles* had brought on themselves;[a] but have, by the gospel of Christ, clear light and knowledge given to you. Walk therefore as in a state of light. For the fruit of the spirit of Christ, and of his gospel, is in all its sincere followers, goodness, righteousness, and truth; and these good fruits, due examination, or bringing things to the light, and a fair trial, will shew and prove to be acceptable

a. See *Rom.* ii.

27. The paragraph begins with Eph. 4.31–32; the remainder is a paraphrase of Eph. 5.

to God. Do not partake in the fruitless works of darkness, but rather reprove them. For that is light, which sheweth what things are reproveable, and what things are good and honourable: whatsoever doth make things manifest is light. And this light ye now have, that you cannot consider wicked works, without seeing how condemnable they are."

Now let us consider this temper of mind a little, and see whether any man can think of it, without approving it as the perfection of his will and affections; of his reason and heart, which he ought to labour to attain to; and which tho' it can only be acquired by repeated acts, or by diligent exercise of the temper itself, yet may thus be attained to by every one. Can any one think, that man does not sink below the dignity of his nature as a reasonable being, in proportion as he degrades his reason, and suffers himself to be governed by blind appetites, which he never calls to account? <250> Can any man doubt, that a benevolent, humane, generous disposition, is in itself, amiable, lovely, praiseworthy? Or, finally, Can one ever persuade himself, that love of God, and resignation to his all-perfect will, is not the disposition which the belief of God dictates to us, as suitable to such a perswasion, and highly reasonable and becoming us? Who is not capable of understanding what is meant by governing himself by reason, instead of suffering himself to be hurried and transported by appetite or passion into any pursuit, without knowing its consequences; Or what benevolence to man, and love to God mean? And can any man, who understands what is signified by these qualities of the mind, wrought into habit by due practice, in the same manner as all propensions are rendered habitual; or as all our faculties are perfected, and yet not approve it as the greatest perfection of a rational being? Let him but paint to himself this character, and oppose it to its reverse, and then say which he thinks the most laudable and becoming. And if he cannot choose, but highly esteem and approve it in others, even in distant countries or ages, from whom no advantage could possibly accrue to him; how can he choose but approve it in himself, and condemn its opposite, and every step towards the settling it in the mind? In order to judge of what is becoming, there is no need of computation, as in questions about interest or disadvantage depending upon the remote consequences of actions. It is a matter of immediate sensation or feeling. As the eye discerns beauty in outward objects immediately, tho' one be not acquainted with the rules to be observed in imitating or copying it; or the ear distinguishes concord and discord in sounds immediately, tho' one be unacquainted with the theory of musick, and the principles of composition: so, in this case, does the approving and disapproving faculty of the mind, by whatever name it be called, immediately and distinctly discern the fair and <251> foul, the odious and amiable, the right and wrong in affections, actions and characters, so soon as they are presented to the mind. And we cannot avoid seeing them, because the actions of others are ever presenting themselves to us; and we must be conscious of our own actions, and of the affections by which they are produced. Indeed so powerful, so absolutely ineffaceable, is this sense in all men, that however corrupt any age hath been, however ignorant, however perverted and misled by superstition, yet every man in it, as far as we can judge from history, even the most abandoned hath felt at times, the severest checks and remorses of conscience arising from this sense in him; which, if any man will but consult his own heart, he will feel to speak to him with an authority, that he can't help thinking to be, what it really is, *divine*. We are told by historians, that *Felix* governed the *Jews* in a very arbitrary manner, and committed the grossest acts of oppression and cruelty: and *Drusilla* his wife, without any good reason to justify a divorce, had left her former husband, and given herself to him; and consequently was an adultress.[a] Now when St. *Paul* was sent for to explain to them the nature of the christian religion, then newly published, and therefore a matter of curiosity; he first discoursed to them on the eternal, immutable laws and obligations of justice, temperance and charity, without a right and deep sense of which, it is impossible to be a sincere convert to christianity; because these must be an essential part of every revelation that is of divine original. Upon this the natural conscience of this wicked man was alarmed. It was sadly darkened and perverted, as appears from his character; but it was not quite lost or defaced. And therefore on this occasion, it was quickly rouzed and moved to speak that natural awful language, which on many

a. *Acts* xxiv.

occasions, makes the boldest <252> to Christ, with regard to mankind; or what that part is which he is employed in carrying on in God's universal government; it is very manifest, 1. That his commission was given to him on account of his worthiness, his consummate virtue. The plain language of the scripture, of all that is said in the holy writings, about Jesus Christ, his commission, the power, the authority given to him of the Father, is, that true virtue is the only valuable consideration that prevails with God, the only power or quality, in heaven or in earth, that can be honoured and rewarded by him. 2. That as in this world, or God's visible government, all is carried on chiefly by the instrumentality of men; so the invisible government of God is carried on by the instrumentality of agents superior to man. And, indeed, we must suppose the happiness of other rational agents to arise in a manner analogous to the happiness of good men, though in a superior degree, from their instrumentality in doing good; from their virtuous employments in promoting universal happiness. 3. It is no less evident from what is said of Jesus Christ, and his glorious commission and charge from the Father, and of the angels being ministring spirits to the heirs of salvation, and to execute other great purposes of God's universal benevolence, that beings of the noblest and most perfect orders may have occasion for fortitude, for magnanimity and resignation to the divine will, in order to their noble employments, in the execution of which they are happy beyond all expression. The patience, the magnanimity, the resignation to God, and the benevolence to mankind, with which Jesus Christ bore the contradiction, the raillery, the persecution of sinners, is set before us in scripture, at once as an example of, and a strong motive to our sedulous study of those virtues. And they shew, that there may be occasion for these virtues in the most perfect state. But my design being merely to shew the consistency of the principles of religion discoverable by reason, with the fundamental <253> doctrines benevolence and self-government? Is not the mean, mercenary, selfish man, universally contemned, nay, hated? And what can we do in the world, what scheme can we carry on, or what enjoyment can we really have without the assistance of others, and when we are really the object of their hatred and detestation? Next to inward self-approbation, and the sense of the divine favour and love, the supremest of all joys is certainly consciousness of merited esteem and affection from all good men, which can only proceed from the same source with these other joys. And sure it is a much easier, as well as securer way to get and maintain goodwill, esteem, and love from our fellow-creatures, by real uncounterfeit goodness, than to be continually upon the guard and watch, lest our mask should drop or fall aside, and the fatal discovery be made of our real vileness and baseness.

And with respect to bodily sensations, did ever benevolence, temperance, the presidence of reason in the mind, and self-government, produce an uneasy one, that was not doubly compensated by the consciousness of the goodness of the action, in the eyes of God, and all wise beings. But how innumerable are the pains brought upon us by intemperance and all ill-governed passions? It is needless to insist upon this article, since temperance, nay, abstinence, are universally acknowledged to be necessary means of health and bodily pleasure. And the cheerful, benign, humane temper, is unanimously pronounced by all *the happy one.* With respect therefore to fortitude, patience, magnanimity, and resignation to the will of God, who is it that hath evidently the advantage in the calamities which happen alike to all men, (for I do not now speak of those of our own making, all which belong to vice) the man who is able to support his mind by agreeable reflexions, or he who hath no comfort; nothing to keep up his spirits, nothing to relieve or strengthen his mind? <254>

To be able to judge of the obligation to virtue, even in point of interest, meaning by that the securest way to outward ease, to health, and sensitive pleasure, not succeeded by far greater sensitive pain, is not a matter that requires deep computation: it is a plain truth, universally acknowledged by most expressive proverbs in all nations from the beginning of the world, which demonstrate at once the indisputableness of that point, and the universality of good sense. The men of pleasure, commonly so called, are not the men of pleasure. *Epicurus,* whom they pretend to follow, however false his method of proceeding was in deducing moral obligations, hath clearly proved, that a virtuous life is the life of pleasure; and that without it there is no solid lasting happiness, even in this life, abstracting from all consideration of God or futurity.

In fine, the matter now under consideration, is so evident, so incontestable, that all sorts of philosophers have agreed in it, "That temperance, self-government, or regular passions, and a benevolent humane temper, together with fortitude, able to bear up under the inevitable distresses human life is subject to, are necessary to self-enjoyment; necessary means of happiness." Even those who have laughed at the notion of moral obligation, properly so called, have acknowledged a natural obligation, in respect of self-interest, or private good, to those virtues; or that, abstracting from the inward peace they give by a sense of their agreeableness to the dignity of human nature, and the intention of its maker; or, supposing these to be groundless fancies and prejudices; they are however such qualities as every wise man will endeavour to attain for his own sake, in order to evite the greatest of pains, and to have the best of pleasures. That emphatical saying of old *Homer,*[28]

Never, never, wicked man was wise. <255>

seems to have been a proverb in that ancient time, and there are many such like ones almost in all countries. The *Proverbs, Wisdom of Solomon,* and the *Sayings of the Son of Sirach,* abound with such strong, nervous sentences in favour of virtuous conduct.[29] "He that walketh uprightly, walketh surely; but he that perverteth his ways shall be known." "The integrity of the upright shall guide them, but the perverseness of transgressors shall destroy them." "The righteousness of the upright shall direct his way, but the wicked shall fall by his own wickedness." "The righteousness of the upright shall deliver them, but transgressors shall be taken in their naughtiness." "He that diligently seeketh God shall procure favour; but he that seeketh mischief, it shall come unto him." "He that trusteth in his riches shall fall, but the righteous shall flourish as a branch." "The light of the eyes rejoiceth the heart, and a good report makes the bones fat." "He that followeth after righteousness and mercy,

---

28. Homer, *Odyssey,* trans. Pope, II.320.
29. The following quotations are taken from, respectively, Prov. 10.9; 11.13; 11.5; 11.6; 11.27; 11.28; 15.30; 21.21; 28.6.

findeth health and honour." "Better is the poor man that walketh in his uprightness, than he that is perverse in his ways though he be rich."

The useful maxims expressed in these emphatical proverbs, every one must consent to who attends to their meaning, which is so well explained by an excellent author,[a] that I cannot forbear laying it before my readers. The paths of virtue are plain and streight, so that the blind, *i.e.* persons of the meanest capacity with an upright intention shall not err therein. The ways of iniquity and injustice, of fraud and deceit, are infinitely various and uncertain, full of intricate mazes, perplexity, and obscurity: It requires great skill and industry to find out such methods of over-reaching our neighbours, as will have any probability of success; it requires much study and intentness to manage the design to the best advantage; and it cannot but cause much sollicitude of mind, to <256> be always in fear of being disappointed by a discovery. How many do we meet with in the world, who (out of a greedy desire of a little greater gain) endeavouring to over-reach and deceive their neighbours, have, for want of laying their contrivances cunningly enough, and managing them with secrecy and advantage, fallen short of that gain which they might, without farther trouble, have gotten in the plain way of honesty and uprightness. But now uprightness and sincerity is a plain and a smooth road; and though perhaps not always the shortest way to riches and honour; yet he that keeps constantly on in this path, is surer not to mistake his way and lose himself, than he that climbs over rocks and precipices, in hopes of coming sooner to his journey's end. The upright man lays no projects, which it is the interest of his neighbour to hinder from succeeding; and therefore he needs no fraudulent and deceitful practises, to secure his own interest by undermining his neighbour's. He frames no designs (if he be in a private station) which depend much on secrecy for success, and therefore he is not in a continual anxiety and sollicitude of mind, lest a discovery should make them abortive. In a word, as the ways of iniquity are rough and slippery, dark and crooked, intricate and perplexing; so the paths of uprightness are clear and even, plain and direct, that the way-faring men, though fools, shall not err

a. Dr. *Sam. Clark.* [Clarke, Sermon 134, in *Works,* 2:117–18.]

therein. The way[a] of the wicked is as darkness, they know not at what they stumble; but the path of the just is as the shining light, that shineth more and more unto the perfect day. "And he that walketh in right paths—when he goeth, his steps shall not be straitned; and when he runs he shall not stumble."[30] That the way of uprightness is the freest from danger in itself, and according to the constitution of things, least liable to misfortune and disappointments, must needs be con-<257>fessed by every one that considers the nature of things, the general causes of men's miseries and calamities, and the true and natural tendency of uprightness and sincerity. If the constitution of things be evidently such, that the society of mankind, and the peace of the world cannot possibly be maintained without some degree of faith and sincerity amongst men; and that the less of this uprightness there be found in the world, so much the nearer things draw to confusion and dissolution: if the general causes of mens misfortunes and disappointments lie manifestly in their own irregularities and disorders; and the ruin of most men be evidently owing to their own deceitful and indirect practices; as (I think) it cannot be denied to be: then is uprightness undeniably the securest and least dangerous course. If the securing our good name and reputation in the world; if the gaining the generality of mankind, the best and wisest of them at least, to be our friends; if the making our private interest the same with the publick, and founding the hopes of our own advantages not on the ruin but prosperity of our neighbours, be the likeliest way to prosper in the world; then has uprightness clearly the advantage. For what certainer method can a man take to secure his credit and reputation, than to do nothing, but what the more nicely and exactly it be scanned, the greater approbation it will be sure to receive? And what better and more effectual means can a man use to secure to himself lasting and beneficial friendships, than to lead *"An uncorrupted life, and to do the thing which is right, and speak the truth from his heart: to use no deceit in*

a. *Proverbs* iv. 19, 18.
30. Paraphrase of Prov. 4.11–12.

his tongue, nor do evil to his neighbour, but to swear to his neighbour, and disappoint him not, though it be to his own hurt." [a]

Thus then it is evident, that the principal duties revelation calls us to practise, are in themselves easily discoverable to be our best, our wisest, our safest, <258> and our most becoming course; as well as declared to be so in it, in the strongest terms. But it is proper to consider some other views which revelation gives us of our duty, dignity, and interest.

Proposition II

According to revelation, we are made and placed here in our present state, chiefly to endeavour to attain to the love of the pleasures arising from rational, virtuous exercises; and to the contempt of mere sensual pleasure, in comparison of them; and this reason itself plainly proves to be the chief end of our being from the very nature of our frame, and from our present situation, which are admirably well adapted one to another.

What revelation teaches us to be our end and duty, will clearly appear, if we attend to the character given of the vitious in scripture, or the temper and character that is there condemned, and the description that is there given of the good, or of those who act suitably to the dignity of their nature, and the end of their creation in their present state. The wicked are said to be lovers of pleasure more than lovers of God. [b] And in the text, and several parallel places of holy writ, mankind are divided into two classes, [c] one that soweth to the spirit, and reaps the fruit of an everlasting, rational or spiritual life; and another that soweth to the flesh, and reaps the corrupt fruit of a depraved mind, sold under sin, and a slave to the flesh, to fulfil the lusts thereof. As the whole of what the sensitive world perceives may be ranked under the two general heads of pleasure and pain, of happiness and misery; so the whole rational and moral world may very properly be distinguished under those two op-

a. *Psalm* xv.
b. 2 *Tim.* iii. 4.
c. *Gal.* vi. 8.

posite and most impor-<259>tant characters of good and evil. Now in
the scripture language, the one of these is the kingdom of God, the
kingdom of light, the kingdom of truth and righteousness; the other is
the kingdom of Satan, the power of darkness, the dominion of slavery
and sin. The one of these is the way that leadeth unto life, rational life,
the true life of a man, and his proper happiness that shall endure for
ever. The other is the way that leadeth to destruction;[a] to the death and
destruction of the rational powers, a vitiated depraved temper, and proportionable misery and corruption. The former live after the spirit, the
other live after the flesh;[b] and what is the life of the flesh, but a carnal,
sensual life; for what are the lusts of the flesh, but violent desires after
mere bodily gratifications, which by St. *John*[c] are reduced to the lusts
of the eye, the lusts of the flesh, and the pride of life? St. *James* tells us,[31]
that the pretended wisdom of wicked men descendeth not from above,
but is earthly, sensual, devilish, full of envy, strife, confusion, and every
evil work. But, on the contrary, he who lives to the spirit, hath his affections, saith St. *Paul,*[d] on the things that are above, the things which
make the happiness of the higher orders of celestial beings, the proper
happiness of our powers, and the happiness of a future spiritual state.
And the wisdom which directs and influences to this wise choice, is from
above, says St. *James;*[32] and it is first pure, then peaceable, gentle, and
easy to be intreated, full of mercy and good fruits, without partiality,
and without hypocrisy. And the fruit of righteousness is sown in peace
of them that make peace.

Now this being plainly the doctrine of the christian revelation concerning virtue and vice, and the duty and dignity, or the degradation and
corruption of the human mind, let us consider what may be inferred
<260> from our constitution and rank; or whether it is agreeable to it.

a. *Rom.* iii. 16. vi. 16, *&c. James* i. 15.
b. *Rom.* viii. 13.
c. 1 *John* ii. 15, 16, 17.
d. *Coloss.* iii. 2, *&c.*
31. James 3.14–16.
32. James 3.17–18.

For it is hence alone that human duty, interest, or perfection, can be known; and whatever doctrine is repugnant to that, cannot be true.

Let us therefore look a little into our frame and constitution.

I. Now nothing can be more evident than that we are capable of various pleasures, various gratifications and pursuits, being endowed with many various capacities of enjoyment; many various affections and appetites, each of which hath its proper object toward which it naturally tends. And indeed without appetites and affections suited to objects we could have no incentive to action; we would be utterly incapable of pleasure; no object could be more satisfactory to us than another: nothing, in fine, could give us any enjoyment. It is no less obvious to experience, that our affections and appetites grow keener and stronger by habit. So true is this, that many of our appetites are ascribed entirely to habit, and called appetites, desires, or cravings of our own making. Not that any thing can be produced in us of which the seeds are not originally implanted in our minds by nature. But because in the same manner as habit, accustoming the nose to irritation, renders snuff necessary to the quiet and happiness of some; may any thing else be made requisite to our ease and pleasure, a title, a ribban, any the merest gew-gaw; what we have inured ourselves to, by way of amusement, becomes, in proportion to our idea of it, and our accustomance to it, an essential to our satisfaction and contentment. So are we made, because the power of association of ideas and habit is requisite to our well-being and perfection.

But then, on the other hand, have we not reason, a reflecting, judging, and governing principle in our composition, to manage our affections and appetites, <261> to regulate all our exercises, by the repetition of which our affections are strengthened, and habits formed? Are we not capable of estimating and appraising things; of discovering the fitness and unfitness of actions, and of weighing the different consequences of our pursuits? The same consciousness which assures us that we have certain appetites and affections which grow stronger by indulgence, likewise assures us, that we have in us a ruling principle to govern our exercises and pursuits by. And what can it be intended for; or what is its end and use, but to govern and rule our actions; or to shew us what we ought to pursue, and what to avoid, and with what degrees of activity and carefulness, according to the different moments of things? Surely we cannot say, that the spring of a watch is intended to give motion to its wheels; a ship to sail it; or that the eye is made for seeing, and the ear for hearing; and deny, that understanding is made to discern, judgment to judge, and reason to regulate. If we would know the natural end of any frame or constitution, we must consider its parts as making, by their mutual respects one to another, a whole. And if we consider the parts which make up our frame, it is plain, that we consist of capacities of pleasure, appetites after certain enjoyments, and affections towards certain objects, together with a principle capable of judging of the natures, consequences, and values of things, and therefore of giving law to us with regard to our choices and pursuits. But if so, then are we made to govern our appetites, affections, choices, and exercises by reason; then are our appetites, affections, and choices made to be guided and ruled; and our reason is intended to guide and rule. Our business therefore is to endeavour to establish and confirm reason in our mind, as the governing principle, to which we ought not only to attend, but to conform ourselves in our conduct and behaviour. And <262> he alone, for that reason, acts agreeably to his make, and is in a natural or sound state, who endeavours to maintain his governing principle in its natural and legitimate authority and power. He who does not, is a rational agent disordered, or out of its right and natural state, in the same sense that we say a watch, a ship, or any machine is not in due order, when it does not answer its end. Either perfection and imperfection have no meaning in any case; or man is perfect or imperfect in proportion as his reason maintains or not maintains its influence and dominion in governing him, *i.e.* in regulating all his appetites, affections, and passions; all his desires, choices, actions and pursuits. If we take a just view of things, and own any thing like a scale, or rising in perfection and excellence of beings one above another, we must acknowledge that to have reason is a more noble and excellent endowment, than not to have it. But this cannot be acknowledged, without owning at the same time that there must be such a thing as exercising reason in more and less perfect degrees. And of consequence, wherever reason takes place, the highest perfection and excellence belonging to that frame must lie in giving all diligence to improve reason to its highest degree of power and vigour by due culture. Seeing therefore we have reason implanted in us, capable of being improved to great perfection, our excellence must consist in diligently improving it; and we can only be said to grow in the perfection belonging to our frame, in proportion as our reason advances in perfection; in proportion as it becomes fit to govern; and in proportion as being fit to govern, it does actually exert itself in governing. This is too manifest to be longer insisted upon, since it cannot be denied, without asserting there is no such thing as perfection and imperfection belonging to any thing. We may therefore now advance a step further; and therefore, <263>

II. Let it be observed, that the natural happiness of a being must be similar to, of a kind with, and the result of the qualifications and exercises for which it is fitted by its frame and composition. The happiness of one constitution cannot be the happiness of another constitution, for this very reason, that the constitutions are different. The happiness of an insect can only make the happiness of an insect. A being with other powers and capacities must have other objects, other exercises and enjoyments, to make it happy, *i.e.* objects, exercises, and enjoyments, suited to its particular powers, capacities, and affections. This general truth is likewise too clear, to stand in need of any further illustration. Yet if it be true, it must of necessity follow, that the happiness of a being, constituted as man is, must consist in the exercises of his reason, in governing all his appetites, affections, and pursuits. Such is his make, and such must be his happiness, unless the happiness of a being can be of a kind quite opposite to its frame and constitution. Man indeed is not merely a rational creature, but he has sensitive appetites and affections to be governed by his reason; sensitive appetites and affections implanted in him, together with several other affections and appetites, not surely to prevail and triumph over reason, but to be directed and ruled by it. If therefore it be true in general, that the proper happiness of a being can be nothing else but the result of the just and proportionate exercises of its powers and affections about their proper objects; it must be true with respect to man, that his proper happiness can consist in nothing else but the exercises of his reason in regulating the pursuits of his affections and appetites. It must consist in the exercises of his reason, in regulating his affections and appetites, and their pursuits, because reason is in its nature the guiding and ruling principle; and with respect to us, our appetites and affections are the sub-<264>jects to be governed and regulated by our reason. And it cannot consist in gratifying our appetites without any rule, or, contrary to all rule, without exercising our reason about them, as their director and governor, unless reason be in us to no purpose; be in us not to be exercised; or, contrary to what we experience in the make and frame of every thing, we be supposed to be made with reason to govern our affections and appetites, on purpose that we may have happiness, by neglecting and despising our reason; in proportion as it is useless and insignificant in us; or trampled upon by our appetites and passions, which is to suppose a very contradictory and inconsistent constitution. If we attend to our frame, we shall immediately find, that our sensitive appetites and affections are but a part of our constitution; there is not only distinct from them the governing principle in us, reason; but they are not the only affections or appetites in our minds. There are others very different from them which do likewise make a part of the affections and appetites to be governed by our reason. Now as the proper and natural happiness of a being cannot result from the gratification of a part of its nature only; so much less can it result from the gratification of that part only, which in itself hath the most distant relation to the principal or ruling part; as of all the affections and appetites in our constitution, our sensitive ones most evidently have. For our moral appetites or affections, though made to be governed by our reason, as well as our sensitive ones, have however, in the nature of things, as being moral appetites or affections, a nearer relation to the governing principle in us, than sensitive appetites or affections. The appetite, for instance, after knowledge, implanted by nature in our minds, though it be one of the appetites or affections in our frame which reason ought to govern, yet it hath in its nature or kind a more immediate or nearer relation to our governing intelligent principle, than hunger, thirst, or any such like <265> sensitive appetite: it is in respect of all such appetites a moral principle in us. The love of beauty, order, and harmony, and affection towards the objects which present these ideas to our mind, is also, in respect of any merely sensitive appetite whatsoever, nearer a-kin, so to speak, to our reason, whose business it is to maintain good order, beauty, and regularity in our mind and conduct. And, to name no more, the desire of society so strongly inlaid into our constitution, though but an appetite or affection, is however, in respect of any sensitive appetite, *lust*, for instance, much more nearly allied to reason, whose chief use and business it is to govern all our appetites and actions in such a manner, as is most contributive to the upholding and well-being of society among mankind. Such appetites, and many others that might be mentioned, are in their nature compared with sensitive appetites on the one hand, and with reason on the other, really moral appetites, more nearly allied to reason, and consequently of a higher kind. And therefore of all the parts of our constitution considered singly, our sensitive appetites have the least pretension to be looked upon as the chief means of our happiness: *i.e.* of the happiness resulting from our complete frame; far less have they any right to be considered as the sole means or instruments of it. The preference, on the contrary, in this respect, if there can be any with regard to part of a frame considered singly, must of right belong to the affections, which in their nature have the nearest or most intimate relation to the governing principle in us; otherwise we must say, that the greater and better share of a being's happiness may arise from its least valuable parts, the parts which have the remotest relation to its principal end or to that part which being placed to preside over and govern all the others, constitutes its chief excellence as a whole. To assert so with regard to man's frame, is to affirm of it what will be owned not to hold with respect to any other constitution within our <266> cognizance: and it is to deny an abstract truth, which, if there be any that are indisputable, is certainly of that class, *viz.* That the principal or main happiness of a being must be of a kind with its frame and make. But if that abstract truth cannot be denied, and if experience, as far as we can carry observation, confirms it with respect to all sorts of constitutions of beings capable of enjoyment, "Then have we reason to conclude, previously to the particular examination of our pleasures, that our chief happiness must be the result of moral perfection, *i.e.* of the perfection of our reason, as a governing principle over all our affections, appetites and passions."

III. But, in the third place, as from what hath been said, it plainly follows, that because to endeavour to attain to the government of our minds by reason, is endeavouring to attain to order and perfection in our constitution, in the same sense, that order or perfection is ascribed to any other frame, natural or artificial, in its kind; and it is acting agreeably to our natural make and constitution, and its end, in the same sense that any other constitution is said to be in its natural state, or to answer its end, therefore man is in this sense a *law to himself;* that is, he hath naturally a principle belonging to him, whose right and proper office it is to give law to all his appetites and affections. As this plainly follows from what hath been laid down; so that being granted, it necessarily ensues, that the Author of our frame (for it must of necessity have an author, the same who is the Author of all things, constituting the same system with it) must have intended, that we should act in this manner, which hath been found to be agreeable to our constitution. This we must infer, or not pretend to speak of any final causes, and absurdly say, a constitution may be fitted for an end, and yet not be designed for that end; or that the intention of its Author may be, that it should <267> act quite contrary to that end. But if it be yielded, that to govern our appetites by reason, is the end for which we are fitted, and consequently designed and intended by our Maker; then have we reason to consider our constitution, which hath been found to be, in a very proper sense, a *law to itself,* with regard to our manner of acting, as carrying along with it the force of a *law* in the strictest sense, *i.e.* of a law enacted by our law-giver, our maker, and upholder, the sovereign disposer of all our concerns and interests. In other words, we have good reason to argue thus with ourselves: "Our make and frame declares the will, the intention of our Maker, with respect to our rule of conduct; and therefore if there be any reason, either from reverence or interest, to conform ourselves to the will and intention of our Maker, our rule of conduct in that respect is plain: it is that which the end of our make, or our whole constitution declares to be such; that is, to maintain the presidence of reason in our minds over all our appetites, affections and passions. It is then our duty, and our interest, in every sense of these words, to set ourselves with all application to act conformably to this end."

And indeed, since there is no reason to suspect, that the Author of such a make, could have any evil intention in so forming us; but there are, on the contrary, many excellent reasons to conclude from the consideration of all his works, to the order prevailing in all which such a constitution is very consonant, that he is perfectly good, or absolutely removed from all malevolent design:—we must infer, that our acting so, as hath been described, must, according to the constitution and connexion of things, upon the whole, be our greater good and happiness. But this conclusion being once fixed, it must necessarily be allowed, that to endeavour after moral perfection is our duty: or that we are obliged to it in every sense that can be put upon *obligation*. For to suppose such a Maker as hath <268> been described, and as ours must needs be concluded to be, from the consideration of our make, together with all his other works, not to have made our happiness in the final issue or result of things, to depend upon our acting conformably to our end, is a contradiction. We cannot know the intention of our Maker with respect to our conduct, but by knowing the natural end of our frame: but that being discovered, we may infer, that the way to our greatest good in the whole is, by acting agreeably to our natural end, with the same certainty, that we can infer our Maker, not to be malicious, but good. And this principle being established, it will of necessity follow, that tho' our acting so, should at present be some time attended with an over-ballance of pain, yet it must still be our interest to act so, because that cannot possibly be the case for ever, or upon the whole under good administration. But how mightily is this argument strengthened, when we come to consider that it is singly in the extraordinary case of persecution for the sake of adhering to reason and conscience, that there is the least shadow of ground for saying, that acting agreeably to reason, or maintaining it in our mind as the ruler of all our appetites, affections, and pursuits, and yielding obedience to it as such, is contrary to present interest. For in all other circumstances of life, as hath been proved, to be governed by reason is really private interest, or what self-love, rightly informed, will persuade and induce us to choose. And in that single, very uncommon case, there is a satisfaction attending the firmness and constancy of the mind, in cleaving to what reason dictates and approves, in opposition to the violentest temptation to forsake reason, and act contrary to it, which to such sufficiently presages the kind regard of heaven to virtue, even while it suffers it to be so severely tried; and thereby gives a peculiar force in their minds to all the arguments above-mentioned, from which it may be inferred, that upon the whole, or in <269> the final issue of things, acting agreeably to our nature and end, must be our greater good; and therefore, that virtue, which eminently suffers in this life, shall, by such sufferings, be fitted for a peculiarly glorious share of after-happiness, by which those its present distresses shall be most abundantly compensated. This is the language of reason, as well as of scripture, That to him who overcometh, God will give a distinguishing crown of glory: a proportioned reward: they shall shine as stars in the kingdom of recompences. Blessed is the man, says St. *James*,[a] that endureth temptation: for when he is tried, he shall receive the crown of life, which the Lord hath promised to them that love him, To him that overcometh will I grant to sit with me in my throne, even as I also overcame, and am set down with my Father in his throne.[b]

IV. But, in the fourth place, as it cannot be asserted, that the exercises of understanding, reflexion and reason, are not the higher and more noble exercises of beings endued with those powers, without absurdly denying, that the faculty of perception is a greater perfection than imperceptivity; so, that these exercises are according to our make, attended with the purest, most durable, and most exalted enjoyments we are susceptible of; and consequently, that we are in every sense, or with respect to interest and happiness, as well as perfection and dignity, made for those exercises, and the satisfactions accruing from them, and not merely for the pursuit of sensible gratification, will appear from the few following considerations.

a. St. *James* i. 12.
b. *Rev.* iii. 21.

I. If we attend to our constitution and experience, we shall find, that the pleasure any sensible gratification affords us, is naturally in proportion to the violence of <270> the craving nature excites in us, when it is really necessary to the upholding of our bodily frame. So it is with eating, drinking, and every other bodily satisfaction: insomuch, that the vulgar saying, *that no sauce can give such an excellent relish to food, as hunger does,* holds with regard to them all. Luxury may rack its invention as much as it pleases to irritate appetite, or to give things a tempting taste and flavour; but if we abstract from the pleasures of the table, of love, or of dress and equipage, all regards to society, all that having its foundation in a nature made for community and social participation, and consequently belongs not to sense, but to affections of another class, very little will indeed be found to remain of real satisfaction, which is not truly no more than deliverance from a keen appetite or desire after what is wanting to bodily support. If we therefore judge fairly of matters, the intention of nature in so constituting us, cannot be understood to be that we should wholly abandon ourselves to sensuality; but, on the contrary, that we should only mind bodily gratification, so far as the present order of things requires for the preservation of our bodies; or, at least, not in any considerably higher degree. And this is yet more evident, when we consider,

II. That, in fact, we are so far from being framed for giving ourselves up entirely to sensual delights, that when these are pursued or pushed to any considerable degree beyond the use, or rather necessity, just mentioned, they not merely clog us, and produce violent loathing and nauseating at the very sight or mention of them; but very commonly occasion severe pains and uneasiness; very grievous and distressful diseases. And can such constitutions be said to be adapted for debauchery, for luxury, and wallowing in carnal voluptuousness, even supposing there were nothing in them otherwise contrary to our dignity, or misbecoming us? But, <271>

III. On the other hand, how pure and uncloying, how equally remote from all disgust and remorse, are the exercises of understanding? And what are the pleasures of this kind, but the contemplation of order and harmony? The foundation for which is laid in our minds, by our natural

capacity of delighting in harmony, proportion and concord; that we
might, by means of it, derive from our senses an enjoyment far superior
to what the acutest, robustest organs of sense, can afford in the mere
vulgar way of outward enjoyment, by the contemplation of those numbers, that harmony, proportion, and concord, which supports the universal nature, that whole immense material fabrick, the object of our
sight, and touch, and all our other senses, and is essential in the constitution, and form of every particular species or order of beings; and that
we might be led by this speculation to turn our eyes inward, and see
whether a correspondent harmony, proportion and concord, prevails as
it ought, in the discipline and government of our affections. How ready
are even the voluptuous, if they have any notion of poetry, of painting,
architecture, or of any other of those called *the fine arts,* to own, that
the enjoyments of this kind are far preferable to the highest of mere
sense? And,

IV. Need I stay to prove to those who have ever known the condition
of the mind under a lively affection of love, gratitude, bounty, generosity, pity, succour, or whatever else is of a social or friendly sort, that
speculative pleasure, however considerable and valuable it may be, or
however superior to any motion of mere sense, must yet be far surpassed
by virtuous motion, and the exercise of benignity and goodness; where,
together with the most delightful affection of the soul, there is joined a
pleasing assent and approbation of the judgment, to what is acted in
this good and honest disposition, and bent of the mind. "We may ob-
<272>serve withal, says an excellent moralist, in favour of the natural
affections, that it is not only when joy and sprightliness are mixed with
them, that they carry a real enjoyment above that of the sensual kind.
The very disturbances which belong to natural affection, tho' they may
be thought wholly contrary to pleasure, yield still a contentment and
satisfaction greater than the pleasures of indulged sense: and where a
series or continued succession of the tender and kind affections can be
carried on, even thro' fears, horrors, sorrows, griefs, the emotion of the
soul is still agreeable. We continue pleased with the melancholy aspect
or sense of virtue. Her beauty supports itself under a cloud, and in the
midst of surrounding calamities. For thus when by mere illusion, as in

a *tragedy,* the passions of this kind are skilfully excited in us, we prefer the entertainment to any other of equal duration. We find, by ourselves, that the moving our passions in the mournful way, the engaging them in behalf of merit and worth, the exerting whatever we have of social affection, and human sympathy, is of the highest delight; and affords a greater enjoyment in the way of *thought* and *sentiment,* than any thing besides can do in a way of sense and appetite."[a]

V. Another proof that we are not made for self-indulgences, but, on the contrary, for submitting our sensitive appetites to reason, and for enjoyments accruing from the exercises of higher powers about their proper objects, and chiefly from the exercises of social affections, is at hand: for daily experience shews us, that as it happens among mankind, that whilst some are by necessity confined to labour, others are provided with abundance of all things by the industry and labour of inferiors; so, if among the superior and easy sort, there be not something of fit and proper employment raised in the room of what is wanting in common labour; if, instead of an application to any <273> sort of work, such as has an useful and honest end in society, (as letters, sciences, arts, husbandry, publick affairs, or the like) there be a thorough neglect of all duty or employment; a settled idleness, supineness and inactivity; this must of necessity occasion, and never fails to do it, a most disorderly and unhappy state of temper and mind; a total dissolution of the mind, which breaks out in the strangest irregularities, and ends in proportional fretfulness, discontent and misery.

VI. Let me just add, in the last place, that a being endued with understanding and reflexion cannot avoid looking inward on itself, and surveying its own temper and conduct. And there scarcely is, or can be any creature, whose consciousness of injustice, insociability or villainy, *as such merely,* does not at all offend. If there be such a one, it is manifest, he must be in his constitution totally indifferent towards moral good or ill. And that being the case, he can no way be capable of the pleasures redounding from social affection: he must be utterly insusceptible of all

a. See this, and the following argument, charmingly illustrated in the *essay on virtue, Charac.* T. 2. [Shaftesbury, "Virtue" II.ii.1, in *Characteristics,* ed. Klein, 203–4.]

the delights arising from benign and kindly exercises: and consequently must be a stranger to all the best satisfactions of human life; if not absolutely miserable. But where conscience, or sense of good or ill desert is, there consequently, whatever is committed against candor, truth and honesty, must of necessity, by means of reflexion, be continually shameful, hateful, and grievously offensive. As for conscience of what is at any time done unreasonably in prejudice of one's real interest, this disquieting reflexion must still attend, and have effect, wherever there is a sense of moral deformity contracted by injustice. For even where there is no sense of moral opprobriousness, *as such merely;* there must be still a sense of the ill merit of it, with respect to God and man. But where there is a conscience of worth, and its contrary; a sense of base and good con-<274>duct; of a well disciplined, and an irregular, tumultuous, riotous mind, then it is impossible there can be any lasting self-enjoyment, any solid contentment, even amidst the greatest affluence, without the consciousness of serious endeavours to preserve good order, in our affections, and harmony and consistency in our life and manners. A man who lives dissolutely, and abandons himself to outward voluptuousness, without any regard to society, and without taking the least care of his moral part, hath no chance for ease or quiet, but by stupifying his reason, shunning himself, and living in a perpetual hurry and fluster. And is not this really the case with those who are vulgarly called *men of pleasure?* Nothing can bear the review of thought and reflexion, but the earnest endeavours of a good man to maintain the power and authority of his reason over his appetites, and to improve in his contempt of mere sensitive enjoyment, and in his relish for rational exercises; the exercises of understanding, and of social, generous affection. I have said nothing but earnest endeavours, because virtue is a progress, it is the effect of long management and sedulous art; much discipline and severe self-controul. No man is here arrived to perfect virtue, he is but in the progress towards it. And he is the best man, who hath made the greatest proficiency in the conquest of his appetites after carnal objects, and in delight in rational satisfactions. Why is virtue a struggle in moral fictions; or why is there no perfect character in poetry; or why would such a portraiture be thought unpoetical and false, but because in reality there is no such thing in life? Virtue is a warfare, because our appetites grow up, and become very strong, before our reason is able to exert its power, before indeed it knows, or can know its duty, and rule, and its proper functions. But the man, who is diligent in making progress to virtue, is not only in the road to future happiness, if the administration we are under be good; since, in that case, when moral perfection is ar-<275>rived by due culture and severe struggling to a perfection, fitted for being placed in circumstances that can afford it complete happiness, by administring to it objects suited to its perfection, then will it certainly be so placed: he is likewise at present in the only way that can give any true or solid pleasure to such a constitution, as is framed for advancing to moral perfection by due trials and diligent culture. And such is our constitution. Wherefore the holy scripture considers human nature in a right view; and addresses itself to man as he is really formed and constituted, when it calls us to set our affections not on things below; not on things on earth, but on things that are above: not to live and sow to the flesh, but to live and sow to the spirit.

It were easy to shew, that the best heathen moralists likewise considered human nature in the same view, and exhorted to the study and practice of virtue in the same strain. But it is sufficient to have shewn, that if the end of any creature can be inferred with any certainty from its make and constitution, this is the scope for which we are fitted; even to make progress toward moral perfection; that is, the perfection of those powers which entitle us to the character of rational or moral agents. It is for this end, that we have reason to govern, and appetites and affections to be governed: it is for this reason, we have a capacity for sensitive pleasures and sensitive appetites united with reason and a sense of order, beauty and proportion in an external world, and in the management of our own affections and actions; or the conduct of our life. This frame cannot be intended for any other purpose; and accordingly when that end is seriously pursued, the mind is easy and contented with itself, or is in its truly natural state; it thus brings no evils on itself, which can create the greatest of all uneasinesses, remorse and bad consciousness; but, on the contrary, it reviews itself with pleasure, and reviewing its merit, is inspired with double zeal to advance in its proper perfection,

<276> cost what it will; whereas the neglect or abuse of our rational powers and sensuality fill with uneasiness, proportional to corruption and filthiness; often create the violentest bodily disorders, and never fail to render a being utterly averse to all inward thought and correspondence, or to the sight of itself. We are therefore made for the end we are exhorted by the sacred writings to pursue; and in pursuing it does the only true happiness this life can afford us consist. And indeed as the notion of man's being made for a happiness in a future life to arise from his progress in virtue here, and proportioned to it, is a most comfortable idea; so if we do not suppose this to be the end of our frame, what consistent account can we give of our make? What account of it that is consonant to what it really is, or to the character of its author stamped upon all his other works? For if man be not made for that end, which the scripture expresly declares to be the end of his creation, and for which his present frame and situation are very well adapted, then he is the most inconsistent, absurd, nay, the most maliciously contrived piece of workmanship that can be imagined. For he is made for an end, on purpose that he may never attain to it, but may be cruelly disappointed if he aims at it, and pursues it. His whole frame points and prompts him to set a mark before him, which he shall never attain to, but be then most maliciously frustrated, when he thinks he is at the very point of obtaining it. All, according to the scripture account of man, is coherent, hangs well together, and gives a consistent as well as a joyful idea of the moral creation. But if it be not true, that man is made for progress in virtue and for a happiness, which is to be the result of improved virtue suitably placed; all nature, as many evident marks as it bears upon it every where of wisdom and benevolence, is truly but a deceitful appearance of goodness, under which lurks the most cruel malignant intention with regard to all moral beings. To con-<277>clude, the perfection of a being endued with reason must be of the rational kind; and rational perfection is in the nature of things, a gradual acquisition, in proportion to culture, or diligence to improve in it. But man is a rational creature, capable of attaining to a very great degree of rational perfection by due pains to improve himself in it; and therefore diligence to improve in moral perfection is man's present duty, whatever difficulties and strugglings it may

cost; and such virtuous labour must terminate in happiness proportioned to the perfection so acquired, otherwise the rational world, that is, moral beings are under the worst of governments. But since even here, notwithstanding all the hardships virtue during its culture may meet with in order to its improvement, it carries along with it the only happiness suited to our frame in a very high degree, even tho' there were no other signs of goodness in the administration of present things; why should virtue be imagined to be the object of our Creator's hatred, detestation and revenge? As it must be supposed to be, if moral beings are not really made and intended for immortal progress in virtue, proportioned to their care and diligence to improve their moral powers; and virtue, which must in the nature of things be gradually perfectionated by culture and means of probation, after it is arrived to a great degree of perfection in its state of trial and discipline, perishes for ever, is rendered miserable, or is not placed in circumstances suited to its improvements, and from which it can derive to itself, by its exercises about proper objects, very full and complete happiness. For every one of these suppositions can have no other foundation, but in the imagination of a malignant maker and governor of all things, who is an implacable enemy to moral or virtuous improvements. <278>

COROLARY I

From the preceeding account of human nature, and the perfection which man is made, formed and intended to pursue, we may plainly see, why man is so often exhorted in scripture, to mortify and subdue his bodily appetites. Mortify therefore your members which are upon the earth, says St. *Paul*,[a] fornication, uncleanness, inordinate affection, evil concupiscence, and covetousness, which is idolatry. For which things sake the wrath of God cometh on the children of disobedience. And, in another place, the same apostle exhorts us to the same purpose in these words.[b] Let us therefore cast off the works of darkness, and let us put

---

a. *Col.* iii. 5, 6.
b. *Rom.* xiii. 12, 13, 14.

on the armour of light. Let us walk honestly, as in the day, not in rioting and drunkenness, not in chambering and wantonness, not in strife and envying. But put on the Lord Jesus Christ, and make not provision for the flesh, to fulfil the lusts thereof. And he tells us, that if we live after the flesh we shall die; but if we thro' the spirit do mortify the deeds of the body, we shall live. For to be carnally minded is death, but to be spiritually minded is life and peace.[a]

And indeed they must not have attended, neither to the nature of virtue, nor to the close dependence of our body and mind, who think such precepts unnecessarily harsh, and that progress can be made in virtue, which is properly called in scripture, *sanctifying our body and mind,* without strict bodily discipline, without thwarting, opposing, denying, and subduing our carnal appetites. They must not have attended to the nature of virtue, or of progress towards moral perfection. For virtue, as it properly signifies strength and magnanimity of mind, so it properly consists in power and dominion over our appetites; in self-command and ma-<279>stership of the mind: so it was defined by the best ancient moralists. And this is the virtue or perfection we are made to attain to. Our senses grow up first, because reason is a principle, which in the nature of things must be advanced to strength and vigour by gradual cultivation; and their objects are continually assailing and solliciting us; so that unless a very happy education prevents it, our sensitive appetites must have become very strong, before reason can have force enough to call them to account, and assume authority over them. But being endued with reason, in its nature a governing principle, we are made to cultivate it into a capacity of governing, and to set it up, and maintain and support it as a ruler in our mind. In this does our perfection lie. And therefore it must be our duty to exert ourselves to acquire sufficient strength of mind; not only not to allow ourselves to be transported into any pursuit by any of our appetites till we have examined it soundly and carefully; but to be able on every proper occasion to contradict and oppose them. Self-command and strength of reason cannot be otherwise attained to. For he who doth not accustom himself to submit his appetites, and to

a. *Rom.* viii. 6, 13.

deny them their requests, cannot but be a prey or dupe to them; he cannot be master or have dominion over them. But that habitual firmness and magnanimity of mind is attained, as all other habits, by repeated exercises, and must therefore be attained by frequent self-denials. And accordingly it hath been recommended by the wisest philosophers, contrary to the ordinary way, to inure children to submit their desires, and go without their longings; because the principle of all virtue and excellence lies in a power of denying ourselves the satisfaction of our own desires, where reason does not authorize them. And this power is to be got by custom, and made easy and familiar by an early practice. The very first thing therefore, say these writers, that children should learn to know, should be, that they were not to have any thing, < 280 > because it pleased them, but because it was thought fit for them. This is certainly the proper method of forming early in young minds the truly virtuous temper, real magnanimity, and strength of mind, or the habit of self-command. But this disposition is not surely to be formed in young minds by proper discipline and exercise, in order to be destroyed and effaced as soon as we grow up by opposite practice. We cannot take a right view of our make and present state, without seeing the necessity of continuing this discipline over ourselves throughout our whole life; without considering ourselves always as children, with respect to the perfection we may attain to, and ought to be continually aspiring and contending after. For what is the highest attainment in virtue or moral perfection, which is in other words the contempt of sensual delight in comparison of rational satisfaction; what is it in proportion to the perfection that may yet be arrived at by the continuation of proper care and culture?

But they must also be indeed great strangers to our make and constitution, insomuch as to have quite forgot the close and intimate reciprocal communion between our minds and our bodies, who imagine, that the temper which hath been described can be attained or upheld, if we pamper our bodies, and give full swing to all our corporeal appetites; or if contrariwise we do not live in the strictest habitual sobriety, and frequently deny ourselves even innocent gratifications, in order to make self-denial easy, when noble ends call for it at our hands; friendship, the love of our country, or any other such virtuous and generous affection.

It does not follow from hence, that severe fastings, penances, and bodily chastisements at stated times are necessary, or even that they make any part of religion and virtue. They are commonly enjoined and undergone by way of attonement for habitual irregularity, and to make amends for the want of a true principle of virtue, which <281> always works regularly and uniformly, than which opinion nothing can be more absurd. Nor does it follow from what hath been said, that men are to live a rigidly abstemious life, and to deny themselves the necessaries to sustenance; habitually to starve and emaciate themselves, and live in downright contradiction to all that sense and sensitive appetite demands. Every thing hath its extremes; and therefore virtue and truth may be justly said in general to consist in the middle. We are commanded to raise our minds above all sensual gratifications, and to set our affections chiefly upon moral exercises, and the pleasures accruing from them; and we are as certainly made for that end as we have reason to govern our appetites. And therefore, far from making sensual enjoyment our main end, we are to submit all our sensitive appetites to reason, and to inure them to yield easily and readily to what duty requires, to what the improvement of our rational faculties, and the interests of mankind and society require. But this cannot be done, not only without habituating ourselves to sobriety; but without frequent acts of self-denial, even where the indulgence would not be in any degree criminal, nor even so much as indecent. And in this case, because different constitutions require different management, every man must be left to his own prudence: general rules cannot be laid down. It is every man's business to study his temper and complexion, that he may know what is necessary for him to do, in order to maintain and improve in that spiritual turn of mind, which is the perfection of a rational being. I call it spiritual turn of mind, because it is called in scripture, the life of the soul, or *living to the spirit,* being properly the life of our rational powers, the life of all those powers and dispositions in our constitution, which exalt us to the rank of moral agents; our understanding, our judgment, our reason, and our sense of good and evil, orderly and disorderly, becoming and unfit. The pleasures that <282> result from the exercises, which improve these faculties and dispositions, are the noblest we are capable of; they are of a kind, not only with the enjoyments which make other moral creatures superior to us happy, but with the felicity of God our Creator himself, whose happiness results from the exercises of his infinitely perfect moral powers.

But the reasonableness of those christian precepts, by which we are commanded to subdue and mortify our bodies, and to quicken our spiritual part, and to make provision for it, will yet more plainly appear, if we attend to some other ways of speaking in holy writ on the same subject. "Now the study of virtue is there called, putting off the old man, and putting on a new nature, or becoming a new creature." And the meaning of these phrases, with the reasonableness of the view that is given by them of the virtue belonging to men, as the excellence they ought to pursue and aspire after with all diligence, will be evident,

I. If we reflect, in the first place, that, though some few may, through the good influence of virtuous example, and of a wise and happy education, be said to be *sanctified from the womb,* so liberal, so generous, so virtuous, so truly noble is their cast of mind; yet generally speaking, men are so corrupt, the whole world always hath, and still *lieth in such wickedness,* that with respect to the far greater part of mankind the study of virtue is beginning to reform, and is a severe struggle against bad habits early contracted, and deeply rooted. It is therefore putting off an old inveterate corrupt nature, and putting on a new form and temper: it is moulding ourselves anew: it is being *born again,* and becoming as *children,* to be formed into a right shape; becoming docile, tractable, and pliable, as little children, in order to be instructed in, and formed to the temper which becomes rational creatures, and in order to have another set of affections <283> and appetites established in us than those which lead the wicked captive to their gross and impure pursuits. This is the case when the habitually corrupt are called to turn from their wickedness, and to change their ways. They are really called upon to change their hearts, and to form a new spirit within them. And how few are there in the world, who escape its pollutions, so as not to be early in that class; or to be among those *righteous* who *have not need of repentance;* nothing to reform in their temper or conduct; or nothing to do but to advance in the perfection they are already in the train of pursuing. Those to whom the apostles addressed these exhortations were plunged in vice

and sensuality, as appears from the character given of them. And an exhortation to every man who is a slave to his appetites, and hath not yet
attained to the power of right self-government by his reason must run
in that strain. "Wash you, make you clean; sanctify yourself; purify your
heart; mortify the body, and make provision for your spirit, that you
may enter into the holy, virtuous, and spiritual life, which will end in a
life everlasting of virtue and rational virtuous happiness."

II. But farther, let it be considered on this head, that not only are we
so made, that unless a very virtuous institution prevent it, our sensitive
appetites must become very strong or rather very impetuous, before our
reason can have attained to the authority it must have to govern them
as they ought, which can only be acquired by gradual culture and exercise: but as all rational creatures can only attain to moral improvements
in the same way of gradual culture; so it is probable, that all reasonable
creatures have, tho' not affections and appetites of the same species with
ours; yet such as are in this respect analogous to ours, that they are implanted in them to be the subjects of their rational government, as ours
are <284> to be the subjects of our reason and moral discipline; and thus
to be to them, as ours are to us, means or materials of exercise and trial.
We cannot conceive moral beings to be formed to virtue, but by the
discipline of reason; nor can we conceive a state of discipline and probation, when there is nothing to tempt or try; nothing to seduce, nothing
to be conquered. And yet, whatever may be as to that, it is certain, that
our sensitive powers and appetites, and the sensible objects suited to
them, at the same time that they afford us means and materials of rational employments, on account of the order, harmony, and concord
that prevails in the disposition and government of the sensible world,
and in other respects, are really to us means of probation, because they
give occasion to a competition between sensual and rational pursuit; they
lay a foundation, as it were, for a warfare, and give opportunity for
strength and conquest. Our senses do in fact strongly importune us, and
yet because we have reason, and are capable of ruling, subduing, and
conquering sense, and of pursuing rational delights, preferably to those
of sense, we must certainly be made for that end; it must certainly be
our perfection, and it must likewise be the sure way to our greatest hap-

piness, unless our reason be made to be frustrated in pursuing the only end it can be thought to be made for, consistently with our way of judging about the end for which any frame whatsoever is intended. This being our make, we must necessarily conclude, that we are made to conquer sense, and to improve our reason; or to establish in our minds an habitual preference to rational delights, as those from which our happiness is to redound, when we have arrived by due culture in our state of discipline and probation to considerable perfection of the moral kind. For not to infer this from our make, is really to assert no less an absurdity, than that we are endued with <285> reason capable of being improved, and yet are not intended for rational improvement and perfection.

Corolary II

Now if all this be true, then we may see that our present state is justly represented in scripture, as our state of education and trial; our probationary state, in which we are to be schooled and disciplined; or rather are to school and discipline ourselves into a capacity for being perfectly happy in a future state, in the rational or moral way, that is, in consequence of the natural exercises of well-improved moral powers about their proper objects. I need not stay to prove that to be the scripture representation of our present and future state. I am afterwards to inquire particularly into the account given of our future life by the sacred writings. And the whole tenor of the exhortations to mankind in the scriptures runs in this strain, to sow to the spirit now, that we may in a succeeding state reap the happy fruits of that moral or virtuous seed we now sow; to lay up for ourselves treasures in heaven; and to purify ourselves as God is pure, that we may dwell with him, and see him as he is. Consistently with this account of our present state, we are commanded to put on the whole armour of light, and to fight so that we may overcome. And virtue is every where represented as struggling for victory; as contending for a prize: as wrestling and battling against strong and powerful enemies. Nor is it so represented to us by the scriptures only, but likewise by the best antient moralists. And what else can it be with respect to those who have any evil habits to undo; any corrupt passions to submit to reason, and conquer? And who are not less or more in that case? What else can it be with respect to beings whose senses are continually importuning them to throw off the bondage of reason, <286> and give full swing to them? And who is there among mankind, who doth not often feel a law in his members, that is, some unruly head-strong appetite, warring against *the law of his mind,* the law of his reason and moral conscience?

COROLARY III

But though this be true, yet the holy scripture is neither inconsistent with itself, nor repugnant to the nature of things, when it at the same time represents virtue as pleasant and agreeable; as man's supreme happiness even here, and as what can only be rewarded by itself. In order to illustrate this, it seems proper to make the two following observations.

I. As in learning any art or science we distinguish two periods, the first of which is harsh, and attended with a great mixture of uneasiness, but the other exceeding pleasurable: so is it with regard to virtue, the first steps to it, like the first steps towards science or art, are painful, laborious, and in a great measure irksome; especially when the appetites to be subdued are very imperious, and the evil habits to be destroyed are very firmly rooted; but as science or art becomes easier and pleasanter in proportion to the advances made in it, so likewise does virtue: and, at last, when any considerable degree of perfection is attained to in it, then all goes very smoothly and very easily on; then its commands are not *grievous, but light and sweet;* nay, all *its paths are pleasantness, and all its ways are peace.* Virtue must become natural in the same way that any habit becomes natural, that is, by practice, before it can have that pleasant effect in its exercises, which that alone can have, that is, become habitual or natural, in proportion as it is such. <287>

II. But let not this be so understood as if it were quite so difficult a matter to conquer the most inveterate habits, as it may at first be imagined. The greatest difficulty in conquering bad habits arises from this natural language of that habitual unwillingness to exert ourselves in self-government, which must grow upon us with every habit that is otherwise established in our mind, then by force or dint of reason, or with its actual consent and approbation, with which language our natural inclination to extenuate and excuse our faults to ourselves very readily falls in; *viz.* That it is in vain to struggle against an old habit, or, at least, that it will cost a great deal of trouble and pain to gain the ascendant over it. If we can but once attain to force enough of mind to resist this natural suggestion of every bad habit in favour of itself, and to resolve upon asserting the dominion of our reason, the whole work almost is done. Vice is driven out of its strongest hold, and the victory is at hand. And for this reason all good moralists, as well as the scriptures, represent the whole, or, at least, the chief point in reformation, and the study of virtue to be *daring to be wise* (*sapere aude*) or taking the resolution not to be a dupe to every foolish appetite or fancy that may attack us, either with fair promises of pleasure, or specious representations of great trouble and uneasiness; but to act with reason, or upon rational deliberation, and always for very well and maturely weighed considerations. And what man, who is convinced that it is more becoming a reasonable being to act rationally than irrationally, may not easily upbraid himself into this resolution, by but considering frequently with himself, that not to have it is not to be a man; and that there is hardly any thing that human resolution may not master, as we may see from very various effects of it. <288>

III. Notwithstanding what hath been said of virtue, that it is not only a progress, but a progress that requires violent struggling, great magnanimity and resolution; yet it is certainly true, that this laborious progress is man's great happiness here, and that virtue alone can be the reward of virtue.

I. The progress towards virtue or moral perfection, as troublesome as it can possibly be in any case, is however our chief happiness here. It carries along with it a delightful consciousness of becoming strength and greatness of mind in pursuing our chief excellence. It not only can comfort itself with the hopes of attaining to happiness of the highest kind, when the mind is by due culture prepared for it; but it knows itself to be acting the right part, the part suitable to our nature, and which God and all wise beings must approve. And in what other consciousness can a man rejoice: for what other exercise can he approve himself: upon what else indeed can he reflect, without condemning, hating, and abhorring himself, and all his ways? The virtuous man, that is, the man who assiduously sets himself to improve his mind, and to act a becoming part on every occasion; a part suitable to, and worthy of his rational nature, is conscious to himself of having inward strength and courage, true greatness of mind, and of being master of himself, and not a mere slave to every shameful lust, or cowardly fear: and what power, what dominion, what conquest can give joy equal to this? In this alone doth true independency and genuine heroism consist. So true is it, that the exercises of understanding, reason and generous affection, yield a satisfaction which none of the pleasures of mere sense bear any proportion to; that if we ask the truly virtuous man, what reward he would desire for any of these, and he will naturally tell you, other higher exercises of the same kind? Will he say sensual pleasure of what-<289>ever kind? No surely; for he places his chiefest joy in sacrificing these pleasures to benevolence, or some other such virtuous principle.

II. And therefore it is, that virtue is justly said to be its own reward, or in other words, that the glory prepared for the virtuous, in a future state, is called grace, or virtue made perfect, and placed in circumstances for exercises adequate to its perfection. We shall have occasion afterwards to shew that this is the account given of the glory promised to the virtuous in a future state; and therefore we shall only take notice here, That those who say, virtue can have any reward but from virtuous exercises, must mean, if they speak consistently, that something like what is commonly called, the *Mahometan Paradise*, is to be the reward in a future state, for our care in this to improve our rational powers, and to attain to a contempt of sensual pleasures, in comparison of those accruing from moral or rational exercises; which is to say, that virtue is to be rewarded by sensuality; or that we are made and obliged to live godly, righteously, and soberly here, and to make provision for the spirit, and not for the body, to fulfil the lusts thereof, that we may be qualified to wallow in sensual pleasures in another life. The whole question about virtue is, whether rational exercises are not of a nobler kind than mere sensual indulgences. And the moment they are acknowledged to be such, it is granted that virtuous exercises can only be rewarded by virtuous exercises of a higher kind; or, in other words, by more improved virtue exercised about objects proportioned to its excellence and perfection. The moment the reality of virtue is owned, sensual gratification is given up as a low, mean, and sordid part of happiness, in respect of rational exercises and the enjoyments resulting from them. But if the mere delights of sense cannot be the reward of virtue, nothing can be its reward but <290> itself. The moment the happiness of the Deity is acknowledged to result from his moral perfection, moral perfection is owned to be, in the nature of things, the only source of happiness to moral beings: and that being owned, various degrees of moral powers and their exercises must make the only difference amongst moral beings in different states, or of different classes in respect of happiness. Virtue therefore is its own reward. And those who assert, that there is no obligation to virtue independently of the consideration of future rewards and punishments, do absurdly assert (in whatever sense they take obligation) that there is a happiness hereafter for the virtuous, not of the virtuous or rational kind, which makes the only good reason for the study of virtue here: or, in other words, that it is wise and prudent to be virtuous here, merely because in another life the virtuous may be as unvirtuous as they please; because they shall then be released from their obligations to troublesome, virtuous exercises, and shall have their[a] belly full of other delights far superior to all that virtue can by its noblest exercises afford to a rational mind. Their assertion must ultimately determine in this gross absurdity. And from what considerations they can ever infer such obligation to virtue, or such a succeeding reward for it, I cannot imagine. Sure they cannot reason from the excellence of virtue to prove such a state of rewards and punishments to come. And sure they cannot reason to prove it from any of the perfections of the Deity. From what other principle therefore can they conclude the probability of their future state, which

a. It is impossible to speak of enjoyments which are not virtuous or rational in phrases that are not as low as the enjoyments spoken of: it is not to give a gross air to the opinion I am refuting. I use this phrase; some such thing as coarse must be its meaning.

according to them constitutes the sole obligation to virtue? There is indeed none, nor can there, in the nature of things, be any argument to prove a future <291> state, which does not suppose rational exercises to be the best, the noblest, and pleasantest exercises of reasonable beings, and which for that reason does not suppose, that, if there be a state of rewards for virtue, it must be a state in which virtue shall reap happiness, proportioned to its perfection from exercises about objects suited to it; and consequently, tho' higher than any happiness virtue can afford in its first state of education and trial, yet of a kind with what it now gives, and alone can give: virtue therefore is its own reward, and only can be such.

All this will be yet more evident, when we come, in the succeeding proposition, to take a more particular view of the rational exercises recommended to us, by the christian religion, as our duties and excellencies, and to shew, in treating of them, how well man is furnished for the practice of them, or improvement by them. But before I leave what I have been now considering, it is fit to obviate an objection that may be made against what hath been said concerning our natural end, duty, and excellence: which is, That if the case be as hath been represented, then by the necessary state of human affairs, are men upon a very unequal footing, with respect to their ultimate end; since few have time and opportunity, if they have capacity, for moral improvements.

Now in answer to this, I shall not stay to prove, how much of this unequality among mankind with regard to present rational happiness is owing to ill-constituted society, or bad government. Though that be true, yet it is incontestible that the exigencies of human life do require, that more should be employed in manual labours, than in study. And therefore allowing as full force to the objection as can be required, I would only have it observed,

I. In the first place, That in all countries, where true science has made any progress, were men of <292> knowledge as generously and benevolently active in instructing others, as several of the ancient sages, *Socrates* in particular, are represented to have been; the commons, who are under the necessity of drudgery for the backs and bellies of others, as well as their own, and more for the gratification of the luxury of others, than for their own necessities, would be much more knowing than they are in the nature of God, and of moral obligations, in the wisdom of providence, and in the duties and rights of reasonable beings. And in countries where christianity being established there is an order of teachers set apart, chiefly for that noble, generous use, it is not the fault of the commons, if they are not very well instructed in the more important parts of science, those which have been just mentioned.

But, II. Every man may, by himself, if he would duly employ his mind in the contemplation of the works of God about him, or in the examination of his own frame, even while he is working at his lawful and useful business, make very great progress in the knowledge of human nature, and of the wisdom and goodness of God. This all men, generally speaking, might do with very little assistance, for they have all sufficient abilities for thus employing their minds, and have all sufficient time for it, tho' their work did not admit of such reflexions, while they are engaged in it, as many of the more ordinary lower occupations in life plainly do. And indeed in all countries, some of the lower ranks are known to have made by themselves very great proficiency in such knowledge: and many more are known to have made wonderful progress in sciences, much more difficultly acquired.

III. The man who exercises his understanding with benevolent intention, in order to improve any useful <293> art; in order to encrease the lordship of man in nature, or his power and property; to abridge human toil, or add to the happiness of society in any respect, every person who thus employs himself, prefers the exercises of his understanding and the good of society to merely selfish and sensual enjoyments; he is therefore virtuous. Now that more men have not this excellent turn of mind, and greater abilities to gratify it, is the fault of society, in neglecting so much the education of the commons. For were it on a right footing, that industrious, benevolent turn would be early produced in them all; and every various genius being invited and assisted to disclose and improve itself, every one would be at once extremely happy and extremely virtuous, in laying himself out, each according to his genius, to invent or improve in some way that would be greatly advantageous to mankind. In one word, man's lordship over nature, and happiness in consequence of such dominion, can only be enlarged by the knowledge and imitation of nature; and he who benevolently delights in the study and imitation of any part of nature, in order to extend human knowledge and human dominion, is rationally and virtuously employed. Now the same establishments with regard to the education of the commons, that are necessary to the advancement of our dominion and our happiness by the improvement of knowledge and arts, would make true virtue among mankind almost universal. But I propose to treat this subject fully in an *Essay on Education*. [33] Mean time it is evident that christianity calls upon every man to choose to himself some particular calling, profession, or business, in which he may be most useful to mankind; and represents diligence, benevolent diligence and assiduity in it, as serving the Lord; as approving ones self to him; as acting a virtuous, a laudable, a praise-worthy part; and a part that qualifies for, and will be rewarded with a very happy situation in an after-life for the exercise of high <294> virtues. This is manifest from many exhortations to that effect, which have been already cited.

IV. But which is still of greater moment, even those, who, as things go at present in society, have almost no opportunity or advantage for improvement in knowledge, have, however, capacity and opportunity of attaining to command over their passions, and of exercising generous, or honest and benevolent affections. None want opportunities of improving their moral temper; and that being well formed, there is no difficulty in conceiving how such as have made progress in that chief part of moral perfection, may, in another world, be placed in such circumstances as they may soon and easily acquire very great knowledge of God, divine providence and moral obligations; especially with assistance from others, who being far advanced in such useful science, can hardly have an employment more suited to a generous mind, than instructing others, who are well-disposed and fond to learn.

And, in the last place, let what we shall have occasion to shew more

33. Turnbull's "Essay on Education" eventually appeared in 1742 with the title *Observations upon Liberal Education*.

fully afterwards not be forgotten here, that there is no reason to suppose the rewards of a future state to consist merely in the happiness resulting from contemplation. And as for active employments of various sorts, from which unspeakable enjoyments may accrue, they are sufficiently well fitted for them, who have self-command, and a generous disposition thoroughly established in their minds, together with that attentiveness to circumstances which is necessary to discover the best and wisest conduct, that a little practice in good offices soon produces in one of a beneficent turn. God, who knows all men fully, knows how to reward proportionately and adequately every degree of sincere virtue; and therefore the particular kinds of happiness in a future state proportioned to various abilities, not being specified to us by revelation, it can be no objection either against <295> the truth of it or the probability of a future state, if we are not able to form any idea of the matter. Yet if we give but a little room to our fancy, we may, consistently with analogy to the present life, while at the same time we make full allowances for diversity between this and a future state, easily imagine to ourselves as many very happy exercises and employments in it, as we can conceive differences among the virtuous in respect of scientifical improvements, or even with regard to several practical virtues, which require very particular circumstances for their formation or improvement here. But of this afterwards.

Proposition III

Man is well furnished for attaining to the moral perfection he is commanded by revelation to labour to attain to: and revelation considers man in a true light; or gives a just idea of human nature in the representation it gives of human duty and happiness.

After having enlarged at such length on the principles whence all moral obligations must take their rise, a very few observations on the scripture doctrine of virtue will suffice to illustrate and confirm this proposition. Let me therefore only insist a very little on each of these three observations.

I. *The scripture no where sets a mark before man too high above him; or no where represents human nature in a too favourable and flattering light.*

II. *The scripture doctrine of virtue no where sinks too low; or no where gives too low and mean a view of human nature.*

III. *In the christian morality no moral duty or virtue is overlooked or excluded.* <296>

If all this can be proved, it must follow, that the christian doctrine concerning virtue is perfect; and that frequent reading the scriptures must be of great use to fix a sense of our duty on our minds, and *to furnish us for every good work.*

I. The sacred writings do not set a mark before us, too high for man to aim at; or represent human nature more perfect than it is. To prove this, we need only shew, that when the scripture exhorts and commands us to set the perfection of God before us, and to imitate it, it does not set a mark before us, too high for man to aim at; or represent human nature capable of attaining to a degree of moral perfection above its reach: for it will be owned, that a higher, a sublimer, a more perfect pattern cannot be proposed to our imitation. Let us therefore attend a little to the scripture doctrine about imitating God. The whole of virtue and religion is placed by the scriptures in imitating God. At the delivery of the law to *Moses,* the particulars of duty by which the worshippers of the true God were to be distinguished from all other nations, are introduced with this general preface to the whole.[a] "The Lord spake unto *Moses,* saying, speak unto all the congregation of the children of *Israel,* and say unto them, ye shall be holy, for I, the Lord your God, am holy." And the apostle St. *Peter*[b] exhorts christians to holiness, confirming his own argument by the citation of these words, spoken thus from the mouth of God himself to *Moses,* "As he which hath called you is holy; so be ye holy in all manner of conversation: because it is written, be ye holy, for I am holy." I need not tell any who are acquainted with the scriptures, that holiness signifies originally in the *Jewish* language, *sep-*

a. *Levit.* xix. 1–2.
b. 1 *Peter* i. 15–16.

aration from common use: in that sense all the <297> utensils of the temple are in the old testament stiled *holy.* And in the same sense 'tis used of persons also employed in the service of God. But the word is often transferred from this literal to a moral signification, expressing purity and sanctity of manners, distance and separation from all corrupt and vitious practices. When applied to God, it signifies his infinite distance from every kind and degree of moral evil: his infinite moral perfection: the spotless rectitude of his nature. And when we are exhorted to imitate God, it is to imitate him in his love of virtue, his love of truth and righteousness; his benevolence and goodness; his hatred of sin, and his making to himself the eternal immutable rules of justice, goodness, and truth, the measure of all his actions. Accordingly the apostle St. *Paul* commands us,[a] Let us cleanse ourselves from all filthiness of the flesh, and of the spirit, perfecting holiness in the fear of God. And our Saviour calls upon us thus, "Be ye perfect even as your father which is in heaven is perfect."[b] And in the same discourse he tells us, that the pure in heart only shall see God. In other passages of scripture particular moral attributes of God are set before us, as a pattern to follow after and copy. St. *Peter* in the passage above cited sets forth the justice of God as such,[c] "Be ye holy in all manner of conversation, calling on the father, who, without respect of persons, judgeth according to every man's work." And in the sermon on the mount, our Saviour directs us to imitate the goodness of God as the most essential means to obtain a share in his favour, and a part in his most perfect happiness. Love your enemies, saith he, that is, desire and promote their amendment, and then be ready to forgive them; do good to them that hate you, and pray for them that despitefully use you: <298> that ye may be the children of your father which is in heaven: that is, that ye may be like him who maketh his sun to rise on the evil and on the good, and sendeth rain on the just and on the unjust. In the epistle to the *Ephesians,*[d] those who are immersed in

a. 2 *Cor.* vii. 1.
b. *Matt.* v. 48.
c. 1 *Peter* i. 16–17.
d. Chap. iv. 18, *&c.*

sensuality and impurity, whose understandings are darkened, and who live in sin and corruption, are said to be alienated from the life of God, thro' the ignorance that is in them, because of the blindness of their heart. And the design of christianity is, saith the sacred penman, to restore them who are thus ignorant and *past feeling,* or who have quite, as it were, lost all sense of the difference between moral good and evil to a right understanding and judgment of moral things, and to perswade them to put off, concerning the former conversation, the old man, which is corrupt, according to the deceitful lusts, and to be renewed in the spirit of their mind, putting on the new man, which, after the image of God, is created in righteousness and true holiness: and in the succeeding verses this righteousness and holiness is shewn to comprehend all moral excellencies.[a] St. *Peter* represents those who by true repentance and real amendment of life return to their duty, as being restored, and made partakers of the divine nature. The manner of speaking is figurative, and very elegantly expressive of that moral likeness to God, which is elsewhere stiled literally, being partakers of his holiness.[b] And to add no more on this head, the perfection of that glory and happiness in an afterstate, which is set before us in the christian religion, principally consists in our being like to God in purity and holiness.[c] "We shall be like him, for we shall see him as he is." <299>

But now, as high as this mark may appear to be, yet it is not too sublime an end to be proposed to beings indued with moral powers, and in this sense created after the image of God, as man is said to be in scripture, and really is. 'Tis needless to observe, that our imitation of God, of the moral perfections of God, is always to be understood as signifying an imitation of likeness, and not of equality. A perfect and most complete example is set before us to imitate, that aiming always at that which is most excellent, we may grow continually, and make a perpetual progress in virtue. Our business here is to give all diligence to advance and improve in moral perfection. Virtue is, in the nature of things, a progress,

a. 2 *Peter* i. 4.
b. *Hebr.* xii. 10.
c. 1 *John* iii. 2.

and it is represented to be so in scripture. But towards what is it a progress, but towards the highest perfection our reason and the temper of our mind are capable of? And what else can that be, but progress or advancement in greater and greater resemblance to him, who is absolute moral perfection? Progress therefore in virtue is, in the nature of things, progress in likeness to God, or imitation of God. And under this notion accordingly is it represented by the best and wisest heathen philosophers, as well as in the sacred writings. Nor can there be a more proper way of conceiving to ourselves our duty, our dignity, our happiness, the end of our creation, and the perfection we ought to be continually labouring to attain to, in any respect, than under the notion of imitating God, or improving in likeness to him. It is the properest way of conceiving to ourselves, and of keeping before our eyes the high dignity and excellency of the perfection of moral powers, the beauty and amiableness of virtue; and it is at the same time the properest way of conceiving to ourselves the true happiness belonging to moral beings as such. For thus we have before our eyes the perfection of virtue, and the happiness resulting from that perfection. <300> Thus we at once perceive the intrinsick excellency of moral rectitude, and the natural immutable connexion between advancement to perfection, and advancement or growth in happiness. While this idea therefore is before us, every thing is present to our minds that can excite us to the most earnest pursuit of virtue. The amiableness of virtue, its agreeableness to the character and will of our creator; its connexion with our happiness, the necessity of it to render us acceptable to God, and his love of it, and care and concern about it, all these considerations are implied in it, and must be present to us while we consider our end under the idea of becoming like God, of imitating him, and by becoming partakers of his nature, becoming partakers of his excellency and of his happiness.

All this is too evident to be insisted upon after what hath been already said of the very nature of moral powers. And indeed it cannot be denied, that imitation of God, as it hath been defined, is the proper end of moral beings, without denying that the perfection of moral powers is their proper end; or what they are intended to pursue and seek after. Man cannot be said not to be capable of imitating the divine moral excellencies, or not to be made for that noble end, unless it is affirmed that he can have no notion of moral perfection; or that it is above his reach to make any advances towards it. But will any affirm that we cannot form an idea of progress in moral improvement; we, who have naturally so quick and lively *a taste of perverse and upright things,* as *Job* expresses it?[34] We, who cannot look upon any sin without abhorrence. We, whose consciences so strongly upbraid us for every debasement of our nature, for every vice. We, who cannot paint to ourselves, or behold any virtue without admiring, approving, and loving it. For all this is true, even of the worst of men. No man can absolutely lose all sense and discernment of moral good and evil while he <301> retains his understanding. No person can exercise his judgment about moral things, about affections, actions and characters, without perceiving moral differences. And however little some men exercise their thinking powers; however little they care to reflect upon themselves and their conduct; or however much they lay themselves out to avoid serious thoughts; yet, in fact, so is man constituted, and such is the order of things, that moral ideas are ever coming across even those who fly from them; and are at the greatest trouble to keep them out, in such a manner, that they are often made to see their deformity, whether they will or not, and are stung with the sharpest remorse. The heart of man cannot be corrupted to such a degree, but it will continue to tell him as often as he looks into it, that sin debases the human nature; and that man was created a reasonable being, that he might, by assiduous care to improve his mind, become pure as God is pure; benevolent as God is benevolent; like God, and fit for a share of that same kind of happiness, which, in its perfect degree, is the felicity of the supreme being, in consequence of his absolute moral perfection.

It cannot be said to be above our power to make gradual progress towards that high degree of moral perfection we are made capable of conceiving and approving. For in the corruptest ages of the world, there have been eminent examples of virtue, which *upbraid the wicked with their offending the law; and object to their infamy the transgressions of their lives, which reprove their thoughts, and abstaining from their ways as filth-*

34. Job 6.30.

iness are grievous unto them even to behold.[a] Such examples shew us at once what is the true glory of human nature; and that it is in our power to attain to it; and that to say otherwise is the language of a mean heart immersed in the love of gross pleasures, which sadly degrade, and sink all that is noble and manly in our minds: for, in order to be virtuous, no more is <302> necessary than to rouze our souls to the pursuit of virtue, as the only worthy scope we can set before us. By this noble ambition, by this courage, this magnanimity did all they, whose glorious example casts us at such a distance, become such bright patterns of every virtue that truly exalts human nature: and by the same brave and vigorous resolution of mind to perfect themselves, may all men become images of God on earth, and worthy of *dwelling with him for ever:* for so is that state of high dignity and glory in an after life, to which the arduous and perseverant pursuit of virtue leads emphatically expressed in scripture.

None can reflect upon the high epithets and compellations bestowed on the virtuous in sacred writ, such as *children of God, sons of God, heirs of his kingdom:* none, I say, can reflect upon these high compellations, without being excited to endeavour to merit them, if he hath any seeds of generous ambition in his soul: for what is worthy of our emulation; or what can stir up our ambition, if to be in favour with the highest of beings, and to be crowned with glory and honour, and to be invested with a noble rule, or placed in some high sphere of action by him, make no impression on us? Now to deserve these compellations, and all the honour and felicity enveloped in their comprehensive meaning, men must exert themselves to improve their minds into a likeness to God, the Father of minds. And all reasonable beings, as such, are capable of so improving themselves. It is the capacity of such improvement that denominates one a reasonable being. In order to palliate and excuse to ourselves, our meanness, our pusillanimity, in not daring to aim at very high moral perfection, at likeness to God, we may represent to ourselves, our faculties, our sphere of action, our circumstances in this life as very disproportioned to so high an ambition. But to what virtue have not some men attained? And to what virtue may not all men attain in this

---

a. *Ecclus.* ii. 13, *&c.*

life, if the love of virtue be not dead and languid; or if strength <303> of mind be not wanting. The universal language of nature to us, as well as of revelation, is a call to glory and virtue; for whether can reasonable beings turn their eyes, and not see that their dignity consists in despising the corruptions that are in the world thro' base and ignoble lusts; and in sanctifying themselves, that they may be like to that infinitely perfect being, the Father of spirits, whose works proclaim him to be holy, just and pure; perfect reason, perfect goodness. And while this idea is present to the mind, what is it not able to do; what difficulty is it not able to surmount; and how mean and base do all impure pursuits appear to it? It is indeed want of ambition, and a cowardly, dastardly disposition, that alone hinders men from making progress in virtue. None ever fell short of perfection who persevered in the pursuit of it. And since nothing can be gained but by labour and assiduity; we must either say to ourselves, that likeness to God in virtue is not worthy our pursuit; or we ought to awaken ourselves out of the ignominious sloth into which sensual indulgence plunges; and say, as for me, *I will set the Lord before me,* and will content myself with no lower aim, than to become, by adding virtue to virtue, every day more and more like to him. And *while the Lord is before me I cannot be moved:* no wicked, corruptive lust can have dominion over me.

As much as some seem to delight in vilifying human nature, by representing it as originally under bondage to sin, and unable to rise to the pursuit of virtue; Nay, averse to all that is truly good and great; yet if God hath indeed called us to holiness, we must certainly be capable of attaining to it; and *be ye holy as God is holy,* is the universal voice of revelation. It is a language which cannot proceed from an impostor: and if it be indeed the language of heaven, then must man be created after the image of a holy God, and be furnished with all that is necessary to perfect himself as God is perfect. Accordingly, if we look into our <304> frame, we shall find, that as high as the virtue is which is set before us in scripture as our duty, we have all the affections, dispositions, powers and faculties, which progress towards it pre-supposes or requires. We have not only a benevolent disposition; but a sense of beauty and order; a strong sense of the beauty of holiness, and of the deformity and vileness of vice; and together with this we have strength of mind, if we will but exert it, which is able to cleave to virtue in spight of all temptation or opposition. What therefore is wanting to us, in order to our making immortal advances in virtue, if we are not wanting to ourselves? What human resolution is able to do, we may often see, not only in history, but in our own experience. And this is the reflexion we ought to make upon all instances of it, even that the human mind is furnished with all that vigour and strength, in order chiefly to its progress in virtue, in likeness to God; in order to a perseverant, undaunted, unconquerable pursuit of moral perfection. Shall we shew our resolution and firmness of mind, and what that is able to do in other instances, and yet allow the pleasures of sin, which are all softness and dissolution, to deceive us into an opinion of the impracticability of temperance and self-command, of generous self-denial for the sake of the publick good, of patience and resignation to the divine will? Do not other exercises and acquirements of our assiduous, unwearied application and resolution, tell us, that this is the language of that sloth, which, if indulged, will soon efface all that is noble in man, all that exalts him above the brute creation, and leave nothing in him who is created after the image of God, but impotence, slavery and corruption, darkness of mind and monstrous passions, ignorance and deformity? To be satisfied of this important truth, that we are fitted for the immortal progress in virtue, to which God calls us by revelation, if we but set ourselves to advance and improve in it; let us but reflect, whether what must be owned to be <305> the difficultest of all the precepts of revelation, doth appear so to us, while we set the Lord before us; even cheerful approbation of the divine will under the severest afflictions for the sake of virtue and a good conscience. If we are able to attain even to this pitch of divine fortitude, surely no other virtue is above our reach. But who can reflect upon the excellence of virtue, the necessity of its being severely tried, in order to its shining forth with all its glory, and the unerring wisdom and goodness with which the world is governed, without feeling himself enabled, not only to sacrifice every thing in life to virtue, but even desirous to be brought upon that theatre, on which alone the greater virtues can have opportunity to shew forth all their power and excellence? Now the same thought continually present to the mind, would render such resolution, such magnanimity, habitual to it. It is the presence of such reflexions to the mind that constitutes patience, resignation, fortitude, truly virtuous heroism. This is the *faith,* the perswasion that *overcometh the world.* It cannot but produce true fortitude and steady perseverance in virtue: it hath as natural a tendency to produce it, as any other cause hath to produce its effect; any other idea or opinion hath to produce its correspondent affection. And therefore, in order to attain to this sublime pitch of virtue, this exalted magnanimity of mind, our whole business consists in keeping this perswasion ever before our minds. If we would imitate God, and adhere immoveably to truth and virtue, *let us set the Lord always before us,* as the pattern we ought to endeavour after greater and greater likeness to; and as the protector, defender, and lover of those who sincerely cultivate virtue; as the model or pattern, the author, the judge, and the rewarder of holiness; for then shall we be *strong in the Lord,* strong in his cause, in consequence of our love of him, and our faith, trust, and reliance upon him. This idea, this faith, or perswasion, deeply rooted and established in the mind, is <306> its strength; it gives life and vigor to it, and all its noble efforts to improve in grace, in goodness, in virtue: and to overcome all temptations to immoral indulgencies. This is the meaning of this, and other such like ways of speaking in the *old testament,* "they that wait on the Lord shall renew their strength: they shall mount up with wings as eagles: they shall walk and not faint: they shall run and not weary."[35] This is likewise the meaning, when in the *new testament* our faith is said to be, "the victory whereby we overcome the world, and are enabled to escape its pollutions, and to raise our affections towards heavenly objects." It is the belief of the doctrine of revelation concerning God and providence, and the happy ultimate tendency of virtue, that gives us strength to adhere firmly to duty. And indeed to deny that piety is at once the perfection, and the chief support of virtue; or that to consider virtue, as conforming ourselves to the image of God, who being perfect wisdom and goodness, must have so constituted things, that the study of virtue here shall have glorious effects or fruits

35. Isaiah 40.31.

in another life; is not to take the view of it, that is, in the nature of things the most animating, encheering, and invigorating to virtue, is to deny the most evident truth in the world. There may be virtue without piety, and where there are great doubts about the government of the world; and there is an obligation to virtue independent of all consideration of the supreme being: but he who loves virtue, must delight in the idea of an all-perfect providence; it must be exceeding agreeable to him. And the motives to virtue, arising from the perswasion of an all-perfect providence, that must delight in virtue, and take care of it for ever, are truly insurmountable, by whatever difficulties or temptations, while the eye of the mind is stedfastly fixed upon them.

The scripture therefore does not talk to men in too high a strain, when it represents the imitation of God, in order to become partakers of the divine na-<307>ture, and of the divine felicity; that is, of perfection and happiness of the same kind with it, as the mark we ought to set before us; but it thus gives us an idea or representation of the dignity our nature is capable of, and of the noble pitch of perfection we ought vigorously to aspire after, which is the properest to excite and animate us to, and to invigorate, comfort, strengthen, and uphold us in that glorious pursuit.

II. To shew that the scripture doctrine of virtue no where sinks too low, or no where gives too mean a view of human nature, which is the second observation I proposed to enlarge a little upon, in confirmation of the proposition now under our consideration; to evince this, it will be sufficient to observe, 1. That no injustice or indignity is done to human nature, by representing it as capable of becoming corrupt to the greatest degree of depravity. 2. That the humility and poverty of spirit recommended by christianity, are truly noble and sublime virtues. 3. That the exhortations in scripture to be upon our guard against the subtle wiles, the deceitfulness of sin; and to watchfulness, and jealousy over our own hearts, are founded upon principles very consistent with our natural ability to improve in virtue, that hath been asserted, and is indeed supposed in all precepts to the study of it.

I. In the scriptures we have very moving descriptions of the depravity into which men may degenerate. There is no error so absurd, no vice so monstrous, into which men may not be corrupted and seduced by evil concupiscences. "Even those[a] who have made great advances in virtue may go astray, and forsake the right way, and so sadly degenerate as to prefer the wages of unrighteousness to the pleasures of virtue, which they have tasted, and to allure into vitious practices, through the lusts of <308> the flesh, those that were clean escaped from them who live in error; and boast of their liberty, tho' they be the slaves of corruption. Even those who have escaped the pollutions of the world through the knowledge of the truth, may be entangled again therein and overcome." "Even those,[b] who, as another apostle expresses it, were once enlightened, and had tasted of the heavenly gift, and were made partakers of the Holy Ghost, and had tasted the good word of God, and the powers of the world to come, may fall away, and become monsters of impurity and iniquity." In these, and such other descriptions, the sacred writers are not merely speaking of what may happen, but they are setting forth what had really happened; actual degeneracy and wickedness. And there is no need of staying to prove, that, in reality, there is no imaginable degree of corruption to which men may not, nay, do not actually proceed. But let it be remembered, that the scripture speaks to us likewise of the apostacy of moral beings of a higher order than man. And there is indeed no inconsistency between the original integrity of a reasonable nature and peccability. The original integrity of a moral being does not consist in having no temptations to vice, but in being able to subdue and conquer them; which every reasonable being, as such, is. For a reasonable being, signifies a being, which hath reason and moral conscience, or a sense of moral good and evil, to direct it to what is right and fit to be done, and which hath the power of acting according to its right judgment of things. A being thus constituted is made *upright whatever inventions it may seek out;* into whatever error or depravity it may go astray. In this sense we are told God made man upright.[c] And in this sense every reasonable being is formed upright. We have no reason to imagine, that

a. 2 *Pet.* ii. 15–20. *&c.*
b. *Heb.* vi. 4. *&c.*
c. *Eccles.* vii. 29.

any beings are formed by the father of spirits, with a depraved sense of moral good and evil, or <309> with such a natural bias and propension to vice, as to love evil, and to hate good: but, on the contrary, we have good ground to believe, that all beings capable of reflexion are so constituted by their Creator, that their moral sense can never be totally effaced or perverted, tho' it may be sadly over-powered by vitious appetites; and thro' wicked practices, joined with false philosophy, may be at last extreamly vitiated and corrupted: for such a formation is directly repugnant to the very notion of a good Creator. But that reasonable beings may become exceeding wicked and depraved, only proves, that reason and moral conscience may be contradicted; that the love of unlawful pleasures may prevail and get the ascendant in the mind; or, in one word, that moral powers may be not only not cultivated and improved as they ought, but abused and perverted; and that according to the constitution of things depravity, thro' continuance in it, will grow to a most monstrous pitch of vileness and deformity.—All which is involved in the very notion of a reasonable creature, that is, of a moral agent, whose improvement or degeneracy depends upon himself. To suppose a creature who cannot exercise his moral powers amiss, or who cannot act contrary to reason, and a right judgment of things, if he would, is certainly to suppose a creature, at the same time endued with the power of choosing, and yet not endued with it; or invested with a certain sphere of activity, and thereby capable of virtue and merit, and, at the same time, not invested with any such power or dominion, in consequence of which any thing can be called his own acquisition, and so be either, with regard to himself, or others, subject of praise or blame; which is a contradiction. But not only is it impossible, in the nature of things, but beings endued with reason, and with the power of judging, choosing and acting, may not only err in their judgments, but also act contrary to their sense of right and wrong: not only is this an impossibility: not only is this impossible, but it is likewise absurd to suppose <310> it necessary to the perfection of the universe and providential government, that every state in which moral agents are placed should be quite free from all temptations to vice; or so constituted, that pleasures of all sorts and degrees should be solely the consequence of virtuous choice; and nothing but pain should accompany any the least vitious indulgence; such pain, as would effectually deter, and restrain from every vice, and necessitate or force to virtue. For, in such a state, what would temperance, or self-denial, patience, meekness, magnanimity mean? How could these virtues have their theatre, their trial, their conflicts, their victory? Whence have the virtues their names, their being? What merit except from combat? What virtue without the encounter of such enemies, such temptations, as arise both from within and from abroad? To be virtuous, is to prefer the pleasures of virtue to those which come into competition with it, and vice holds forth to tempt us; and to dare to adhere to truth and goodness, whatever pains and hardships it may cost. There must therefore, in order to the formation and trial, in order to the very being of virtue, be pleasures of a certain kind to make temptations to vice. And then is a first state of moral beings well constituted, when it affords such occasions for the trials and triumphs of virtue, as shew it to be a school of discipline, a theatre for exercise, and conflict to various virtues, that moral beings may thereby be made meet for a higher and nobler sphere of action in a succeeding life; meet for rewards and honours in it, which God, the righteous judge, the chief object of whose care must be virtue, or well-improved moral powers, will then certainly render unto all, who have rendered themselves worthy of them by their diligent culture of all the virtues in their minds, their contempt of sensual pleasures, and their firm adherence to the dictates of reason and moral conscience, in spight of all allurements to sin, or the most violent opposition to and persecution of vir-<311>tue they may be tried by in their first state. In this our first state many temptations to vice of various sorts are continually assailing us; but there is no pain we can suffer, nor pleasure we can forego for the sake of virtue and a good conscience, which is not abundantly compensated by the present consciousness of our having acted the best and worthiest part; the part suitable to the dignity of our nature, and that is highly pleasing to our Lord and Creator, the governor of the universe, who *will never leave nor forsake the virtuous, but will make all things work together for their good;* it being evident from the very idea of a good creator and administrator of the world, that he must love virtue, and have had the suitable treatment of it principally in his view, in the constitution and frame of things. Now our state at present, considered in this light, is an excellent state. And every state of moral beings must be a good state, with regard to the general interests of moral beings, if the administration be in favour of virtue or moral improvements, as the administration of the world must be, if it be perfect.

Whether there may not be temptations to vice, and trials of virtue, in a state succeeding to a first state of probation, which, with respect to it, is properly a state of rewards, is another question that shall be considered afterwards, when we come to inquire into the scripture doctrine concerning our future state: but temptations are certainly necessary to a state of trial, to a state of education and discipline; for virtue must be exercised and proved in various manners before it can be brought to perfection. The first state of moral powers must be a school, a theatre, for forming and exercising them, because virtue is and must be a progress.

Human nature has indeed been represented by some in so base, disagreeable, and monstrous a form, that the contemplation of it must needs be frightful and shocking to a generous mind; as having lost its noble powers of reason and liberty, and being the seat of no-<312>thing but irregular and mischievous passions, as a complication of mean-spiritedness, sensuality, ill nature and corruption; in one word, as incapable of any thing that is good and virtuous, and prone to all manner of vice and wickedness. And upon this foundation, injustice, cruelty, ingratitude, pride, revenge, and the worst of villanies have been represented as natural to mankind; and not imputable to them, but chargeable upon the necessary corruption and depravity of their nature; or, which is yet more absurd, imputable to them, and to be severely punished, tho' they be inevitably necessary effects of our depraved make and formation.

The grand foundation of this error has been either that they have taken their estimate of human nature from the force of perverted passions among mankind, and represented to their minds as the original state of it such evil dispositions and wicked habits as are of their own creating, and cannot take place originally in a reasonable nature, all the habits belonging to which are formed, and can only be formed by repeated exercises; or else that they have understood particular passages of scripture, which give the character of the most profligate and abandoned sinners, as describing the natural temper of all mankind. But were this a true picture of human nature, religion falls to the ground. For upon that supposition, what must we think of our Creator? Would it not be a contradiction to speak of his goodness, or his regard to virtue, and concern about it, the belief of which alone can render the Deity that amiable, that all-perfect character, which piety or religion must have for its object; and which revelation must, in the nature of things, pre-suppose as acknowledged to belong essentially to the Deity? There is indeed no foundation for this doctrine in the sacred writings. And if we search into our constitution, it will immediately appear, that virtue is natural to us. For does not nature teach us to be just and charitable, to <313> compassionate, and relieve the distressed? Does it direct us to prey upon our own kind, to delight in oppression, and in injustice, and in the misery of our fellow-creatures? Are not, on the contrary, cruelty, in-justice, and oppression, naturally so hateful to us, that we cannot look upon them without detestation and abhorrence? Does our nature impel us to hate the Author of our being, to conceive an evil notion of him, and to spurn and rebel against him as an enemy to our happiness? Is it not, on the contrary, agreeable to our nature to think well of nature and of its author; to represent him to ourselves in the most amiable char-acters; and can we so paint him out to ourselves, without admiring and loving him, and feeling the strongest disposition to imitate his perfec-tions, and to gain thereby his favour and approbation? In fine, let us review all the affections implanted in us by nature; and tho' we will find that there is none of them that may not be sadly misguided and abused, yet they are all of them of excellent use, and the foundations upon which most noble virtues may be raised: none of them directly leadeth to evil, or seems implanted in us to make opposition to our progress in virtue, but rather to be rendered itself a virtue, and an assistant, or incentive to all other virtues. Anger and resentment may at first sight be thought contrary to benevolence. But when duly considered, they will be found to be very useful instincts, and to have an inseparable connexion with the sense of virtue. For what is sudden anger, as it is distinguished from resentment, but an instinct, that works as naturally and necessarily, as the disposition to close our eyes upon the apprehension of somewhat falling unto them; and no more implies any degree of reason than the latter. And the reason and end for which man was made thus liable to this passion, is, that he might be better qualified to resist and defeat sudden force, violence and opposition, considered merely as such. It is in reality the necessary operation <314> of self-defence. And it is very fit, that self-defence should thus operate, since there are many cases, especially where regular governments are not formed, in which there is no time for deliberation, and sudden resistance is the only security. This is the case with respect to momentary anger, which is raised without any appearance of injury, as distinct from hurt and pain. It is not the effect of reason, but is occasioned by meer sensation and feeling. But the only way in which our reason and understanding can raise anger or resentment, is by representing to our mind, injustice, or injury of some kind or other. Its object is not natural but moral evil: it is not suffering, but injury; it is not one who appears to the suffering person to have been only the innocent occasion of his pain or loss; but one who has been in a moral sense injurious either to ourselves or others. Resentment therefore in us is plainly connected with a sense of virtue and vice, of moral good and evil. The indignation raised by cruelty and injustice, and the desire of having it punished, which persons unconcerned feel, is by no means malice. No, it is resentment against vice and wickedness: it is one of the common bonds by which society is held together: a fellow-feeling which each individual has in behalf of the whole species, as well as of himself. It does not appear, that this, generally speaking, is at all too high amongst mankind. And this seems to be the whole of this passion, which is, properly speaking, natural to mankind: namely, a resentment against injury and wickedness in general; and in a higher degree when towards ourselves than for others; as must needs happen; for from the very constitution of our make we cannot but have a greater sensibility to what immediately touches or regards ourselves.

But the natural object or occasion of deliberate resentment being injury, as distinct from pain or loss, it is easy to see, that to prevent and to remedy such injury, and the miseries arising from it, is the reason <315> and end for which this passion was implanted in man. It is to be considered as a weapon put into our hands by nature against injury, injustice and cruelty, which may be not only innocently, but very usefully employed.[a]

Love of power, because, when it is misguided or wrong directed, it produces very great evils in society, may at first sight likewise be considered as repugnant to virtue. But we have shewn in the *principles of moral philosophy,* that it is necessary to all virtuous improvements; or that without it the greater virtues could not take place among mankind. Without it we would be utterly incapable of them, it being indeed as far as, properly speaking, it is natural to us, no more than a desire to improve or enlarge our powers, and extend our sphere of activity, our liberty, our dominion, our independence. Noble ambition and emulation could not take place without such a natural disposition toward power or love of it. And envy is but the misguidance of it; or more properly the product of sloth and indolence, in consequence of our want of the power we naturally desire, and yet are too much plunged in indolence to pursue with the vigour and perseverance necessary to obtain it. For this is the case with respect to envy, whether the objects of it be natural or moral qualities. The mind is fretted and galled to perceive itself surpassed. The soul, which steadily pursues its own improvement and true dominion or power, is quite a stranger to this idle, slothful, peevish passion, the bitterness of which consists in that mixture of self-dissatisfaction, which necessarily goes along with it, or makes the chief ingredient in it, and consequently renders it its own punishment.

To conclude, however much some philosophers have laboured to prove, that there is nothing social or generous in the human frame; yet the contrary is really the truth: there is nothing in it naturally, *i.e.* <316> uncontracted by vitious indulgence, which is not social and generous. If one can doubt of it, he needs only impartially consider, what strange explications certain philosophers are forced to give of compassion, nat-

---

a. Dr. *Butler's* Sermons. *Sermon on resentment.* [This long paraphrase, starting on p. 764, is from Joseph Butler (1692–1752), *Fifteen Sermons,* Sermon VIII: "Upon Resentment" §8, in *The Works of Joseph Butler,* ed. W. E. Gladstone, 2 vols. (Oxford: Clarendon Press, 1897), vol. 2.]

ural affection between parents and their offspring, and the other affections which carry us beyond ourselves, and directly to the good of others, in order to make out their system. Let me only observe, that to say, all must be resolved into self-love, because none can be pleased with what does not give him pleasure, is to say no more, than that whatever pleases us, ought to be called our pleasure. And so certainly it may. But when it is granted, that acts of benevolence could not please us without giving us pleasure; and therefore that the pursuit of the pleasures acts of benevolence afford us, is a pursuit of pleasures to ourselves, or a pursuit to which our love of our own happiness impells us; when this is granted, will it follow that such pursuits are not benevolent? When our nature is said to be social and benevolent, it is said to be so constituted, that its greatest pleasures consist in affections and actions which produce publick good, and have it as immediately for their object, as hunger, for instance, hath food for its object. And therefore, in order to prove, that there is nothing social in our nature, it must be proved, that the pursuit of publick good, in consequence of our constitution, affords us no pleasure. All our pleasures, whencesoever they come, are our own pleasures. And in that sense, if philosophers will, all our pursuits or gratifications are selfish, and none of them are disinterested. But what is such language but play with words? All the arguments brought to recommend benevolence from the pleasures, it, and it alone can give, acknowledge, that self-love, or the desire of happiness, is natural to all beings capable of reflexion; for they are addressed to this desire, in order to shew it how its end may <317> be best obtained: the result of them all is briefly this, that if one is rightly or wisely selfish; that is, if he duly consults his own interest, he will not oppose, but encourage and improve the affections in his nature, which lead him to the pursuit of the good of others; the affections which intend it, aim at it, and are gratified by it. And one may as philosophically, as consistently say, that none of our affections can tend towards an external object, if we have self-love; as say, we cannot have self-love, and at the same time have affections towards the good of our fellow-creatures. Yet that several of our affections tend towards, and rest in objects, without or beyond ourselves, will hardly be denied.

But that I may go on to another remark on christian morality, I shall just give one specimen of the manner in which some passages of scripture are wrested into the defence of a doctrine, that indeed subverts all religion and morality. "In the prophesy of *Jeremiah,*[a] it is thus writ, 'The heart of man is deceitful above all things, and desperately wicked, who can know it?' This passage, divided from the context, and considered as a general proposition, has been used to prove, that men are not acquainted with themselves, and cannot know their own views and intentions, and that all men are originally full of corruption and wickedness, desperately, incurably depraved. But if we consider the connexion and the general reasoning the prophet is pursuing, this will appear to be a very gross misinterpretation of what he asserts. In the fifth verse, God is introduced as denouncing a woe against all those who fix their ultimate dependence on human power and policy. And in the seventh and eighth verses, the wisdom and happiness of trusting in the Lord, and making him our strength, is described. Then follows the text we <318> are considering, which by all rules of good interpretation must be referred to the same argument, and contain another reason against making man our confidence. 'The heart is deceitful above all things, and desperately wicked, who can know it?' *i.e.* There may be infinite devices and subtleties in the hearts of men, which cannot be penetrated. While they promise fair, and make the warmest protestations of affection and zeal for your interest, their intentions may be directly contrary, and their views very selfish. Their resolutions are fickle, and many little circumstances may prevail with them to change their purposes, and so render their promises vain and delusory. Nay, 'tis possible they may arrive at such a pitch of premeditated and desperate wickedness, as to endeavour, even under friendly pretences, to undermine your interest. Place not therefore your supreme confidence in man, but repose in the unchangeable God, who, as by reason of the perfect and necessary rectitude of his nature he can't deceive thee, so, as he is absolute Lord of the universe, and the incontroulable disposer of all events, he must be able with ease to effect every thing that is necessary for thy security and happiness."

a. Chap. xvii. 9. See Mr. *Foster*'s Sermons. [James Foster, Sermon 10, in *Sermons* . . . , vol. 1, 4th ed. (London, 1745), 259–61.]

II. In order to shew, that christian morality no where sinks too low, let me but just suggest the true notion of that humility and poverty of mind recommended so earnestly to us by Christ and his apostles, which some are pleased to turn into ridicule, confounding it with pusilanimity, and total want of courage and ambition.[a] "Blessed are the poor in spirit, for theirs is the kingdom of heaven," says our Lord.

Now we can be at no loss to find out the true meaning of the virtue here recommended, as odd as the words may sound to some, if we but reflect, <319> that in the *Jewish* language, what we now call *literal* and *figurative,* were commonly denoted by the words *flesh* and *spirit.*

"The flesh, says our Saviour,[b] profiteth nothing; the words that I speak unto you, they are spirit, and they are life."

His meaning is, he intended not to be understood literally, but figuratively. To be therefore, or do any thing in spirit, signifies, being or doing that thing figuratively, in the spiritual or moral sense, in opposition to the gross and more literal meaning, in which the same words may at other times be understood. Thus, that moral holiness and purity of mind which is opposed to the ritual and ceremonious performance of the *Jewish* law, our Saviour calls *worshipping the Father in spirit and in truth.*[c]

And that absolute departing from all unrighteousness so effectually required in the gospel, of which the *Jewish* circumcision was but an emblem, is by the apostle most elegantly stiled,[d] *circumcision in the spirit.*

Answerable therefore to this figurative manner of expression in so many other places, the phrase, *poor in spirit,* in contradistinction to literal poverty of estate, signifies a temper of mind, disengaged from the covetous and ambitious desires of the present world; that moderate and good temper or disposition of mind, which enables those who have riches not to set their hearts upon them, not to trust in them, not to place any merit in having them, but to employ them virtuously to the

a. *Matthew* v. 3.
b. *John* vi. 63.
c. *John* iv. 23.
d. *Rom.* ii. 28.

good of mankind, and to be at all times willing rather to part with them, than betray the interests of truth and virtue: and which, for the same reason, enables those who have no riches to be contented, and not murmuring nor unthankful towards God, but willing rather to con-<320>tinue always in a mean and low estate, than to gain riches by wicked and unlawful methods. This is being poor in spirit. This is the temper of those, whom St. *James* calls the poor of this world, but rich in faith, and heirs of the kingdom: the temper of which St. *Paul* declares, that godliness with contentment is great gain; and which our Saviour describes in his character of the church of *Smyrna.*[a]

"I know thy works, and tribulation, and poverty; but thou art rich; rich in virtue, rich in good works, rich towards God, rich with respect to a future life; richly prepared for great happiness in it." According to this account of the virtue of being poor in spirit; an eminent instance thereof was the practice of *Moses,* when he refused to be called the son of *Pharaoh's* daughter, chusing rather to suffer affliction with the people of God, than to enjoy the pleasures of sin for a season. And the contrary spirit is that which our Saviour speaks of,[b] "So is he that layeth up treasures for himself, and is not rich towards God." This excellent temper of mind is what the poor are naturally led to by their very circumstances; being under the advantage of escaping many temptations, which others are continually subject to; and being perpetually called upon by the afflictions of this life, to turn their thoughts to the expectation of a better. And therefore the christian doctrine calls upon us to consider it as matter of just comfort; and support; nay, even of thankfulness under many kinds of temporal wants and afflictions, that such circumstances give men great advantages for obtaining this virtue of being poor in spirit. It is because our Saviour looked upon this virtue as so natural and easy to be practised by persons in that state, and so properly their vocation or the duty they are called to by their circumstances, that he sometimes <321> uses that general and seemingly unlimited expression, "Blessed be ye poor, for yours is the kingdom of God." And, "Blessed are they that

a. *Revel.* ii. 19.
b. *Luke* xii. 21.

mourn, for they shall be comforted." For the same reason, on the other side, to those who abound in riches and power, and the good things of this life, our Saviour suggests particular matter of caution, by annexing the heavenly reward to that temper and disposition of mind, which they in particular are surrounded with so many temptations to depart from; so that when he sometimes pronounces in words seemingly absolute, "Wo unto you that are rich, for ye have received your consolation," his design was to admonish and put us in mind, how dangerous a state great prosperity generally is; how full of temptation; how ready to puff men up with pride and arrogance; how apt to make them covetous, insolent, and vain-glorious; and to destroy in them that meek, that humble, that equitable, that moderate disposition of mind, which is the foundation of virtue, or rather the chief of the virtues.

In fine, if we keep in mind, that the scripture represents this life as a state of preparation and probation for another; and consequently all the various circumstances of the present state of mankind, prosperous or adverse, as means of trial; as calls to the study and exercise of certain particular virtues, each condition of life having virtues more properly belonging to it, it will be very easy to conceive what it is to be *poor in spirit*, and *rich towards God;* to lay up *treasures to ourselves, not in earth, but in heaven.* They only in the scripture language are rich, who are rich in virtue and good works; they who are not, however prosperous their state may be, are poor, blind, wretched, miserable; and why, but because this is our seed-time, the state which succeeds to it is our harvest. We are here to make provision for our after-state; to make ourselves meet for great <322> happiness in it; to enrich ourselves with those virtues, the fruits of which are immortal glory, honour, and felicity. We are here to make the best use of the circumstances in which we may be placed, whatever they are, in order to the building ourselves up in holiness; in order to qualify ourselves for high felicity of the spiritual or moral kind in another life. We are here, not to amass worldly riches, and to give ourselves up to sensual indulgences; but to mortify all the evil affections, which great possessions are apt to excite and foster in the mind; and thereby to prepare to ourselves a stock of good affections and virtuous habits, which being properly placed in another life, must yield an unspeakable harvest of truly rational happiness. This is evidently the temper of mind, which is recommended to us by the christian doctrine, under the notion of poverty of spirit, or spiritual poverty. Nor can disengagement from worldly views and carnal appetites be more properly expressed than by that appellation. But whatever may be thought of the phrase itself, the temper meant by it, as plainly appears from several other passages of scripture, and indeed from the general tenor of the christian doctrine, is a truly noble and sublime virtue: it is that contempt of carnal gross pleasure, without which it is impossible to be stedfast to virtue: It is true greatness of mind; for it consists in despising those things which it is greater to despise than to possess, as several heathen moralists have said of the pomp and pageantry of this world, and of all merely sensual gratifications. It is greatness of mind, because it is to cleave firmly to that which is truly great and noble in spight of all temptations from the side of pleasure or pain to forsake it. And to do this requires not only an enlarged understanding, and just judgments of things deeply fixed and rooted in the mind; but vigour and strength of soul sufficient to oppose the most impetuous appetites, and <323> to persevere in adherence to that which is good and right, whatever forfeiture of pleasures or painful sufferances it may cost. It is not a narrow, mean, timorous disposition to which we are called in scripture; but, on the contrary, a bold, undaunted, and truly noble courage; the most lofty and generous ambition; courage that fears nothing but vice, or the degradation of our nature into a state of slavery to impure, disorderly and ungenerous passions; courage that dreads sin, as the greatest calamity that can befal a reasonable being: ambition to shine in virtue; ambition to distinguish one's self by good works; ambition to deserve the approbation of God, and all good and wise beings; ambition to acquit ourselves in such a manner here, as to be fit for and worthy of being highly exalted in the life to come. In fine, poverty of spirit is the opposite to having our minds wholly set on the riches and honours which so dazzle and bewitch sensual and corrupt men. And without this poverty of spirit, that is, without sincere indifference to, or rather contempt of all enjoyments that may come into competition with a good conscience, and the pleasure arising from the merit of acting the best and worthiest part, neither fortitude, magnanimity, patience, nor benevolence, can have their perfect work in us. It is the very soul of all these virtues. And in this does the excellency of the christian morality consist, as the great *Verulam*ᵃ observes, "That there never was any philosophy, religion, law, or discipline found out in the world, which so far exalts regard to the publick good, and debases private interest, as the christian institution hath done." Without ambition; that is, without great and noble views, or without affections set upon truly noble and worthy objects, a man cannot do great and generous actions; he can neither *bear* nor *forbear* with firmness <324> and constancy of mind. But what are the views which ennoble the mind; or what are the affections which prompt to glorious deeds, and enable one to adhere to duty unmoveably, in despight of sensual gratification, or of violent suffering? Is it not the love of virtue, desire to approve ourselves to God, regard to the publick interest of society, and the contempt of all vice can give or procure? And where are these considerations more strongly recommended or enforced upon us, than by the christian religion? In what else does it place virtue and merit? Or to what else are the glorious rewards of another life it sets before us annexed? The constant language of christianity is, *"Set your affections on the things that are above, and not on things that are below,"* that is, on God, or virtue, on rational exercises and employments, and not upon the gross pleasures of unbridled, ungoverned sense, and the vain honours and possessions which tempt men, unmindful of their true dignity and happiness, to forsake virtue, and to do base and unworthy, mercenary actions. *For what,* saith our Saviour, *is a man profited, if he gain the whole world, and lose his soul? Or, what can a man have in exchange for his soul?* What can compensate the loss of virtue; the loss of a good conscience; the loss of inward probity and worth; the loss of that virtuous taste and disposition of mind, which alone can recommend to the divine favour here or hereafter; which alone can qualify one for the best and noblest enjoyments here; and alone can constitute capacity, or fitness for moral happiness in the

a. Advancement of learning, *Book* vii. *chap.* 1. [Bacon, *Advancement of Learning,* VII.1, in Francis Bacon, *The Advancement of Learning,* ed. Michael Kiernan (Oxford: Clarendon Press, 2000), 136.]

life that is to come, in which the natural harvest of virtue and vice must take place, and every one shall fully reap as he has sown. A regard to futurity is greatly insisted upon in the christian doctrine; but such a regard to futurity as is indeed the very perfection of virtue, and produces regard to publick good above all temporal interests. A regard to futurity that is utterly inconsistent with selfish and mercenary views <325> in this world, and begets and upholds publick spirit. We shall see afterwards, that it is impossible for any but a virtuous person, to set his affections upon the future rewards promised by christianity, because these rewards are nothing else but virtuous exercises. But he who sincerely believes the scripture doctrine concerning future rewards hath an idea of virtue, and of the constitution and government of the world, that must render the sincere and perseverant pursuit of publick good here, the sole end of all his thoughts and actions; an idea that must render a vitious life the greatest folly in his sight, in respect of interest, as well as exceeding base and shameful in its nature; and that must hold forth virtuous progress to his view, in a light that makes its cause truly triumphant. Virtue is in itself exceeding amiable. And so it is every where in scripture represented to be. But then alone is virtue beheld or contemplated in a view that gives it compleat force in the mind, when it is considered to be the chief or rather the sole object of the divine love and concern for ever and ever; when it is considered to be an immortal principle or source of happiness, in consequence of the frame and constitution of things; a progress towards perfection, that after its state of schooling and discipline is at an end, shall then fully appear to have been indeed contending for glory, honour, and immortality. This therefore being the representation christianity every where gives of virtue, providence, and the life to come, no system of morals can possibly excell it, or have greater force; because virtue cannot possibly be set forth in a more engaging, a more inviting and perswasive light. And, on the other hand, every scheme of morals which falls short of this view of virtue, must be, in respect of it, exceedingly deficient. Now if we keep this representation which chri-<326>stianity gives us of our duty and end before us, we can never be at a loss to find out the true meaning of any of the expressions, by which it recommends any particular virtue to us, or virtue in general. For in the case now under our consideration, is it to be wondered at, that an institution designed to refine and purify mens minds from all carnal desires and appetites, into the pure love of virtue, should recommend to us that love under the notion of moral or spiritual poverty; since, if we duly attend to the nature of things, we must perceive, that prosperous circumstances are in themselves of a contagious and corrupting nature; and that, as the poor are less liable to pride, vanity, sensuality, and many other vices than those who abound in wealth; so the sincere love of virtue will render a rich man as great a stranger to those vices, as moderate and temperate, as uncarnal and self-denied, as if he were quite destitute of the means of sensual indulgences, with which he is surrounded. The exhortation to poverty of spirit really means, being more effectually weaned from those sensual lusts, which riches tend to engender and nourish in the mind by right inward government, than the poor man is or can be by his real poverty; or attaining amidst affluence to the virtues which mean circumstances render easy to be acquired, and prosperous ones, on the contrary, make very difficult. Our Saviour's words may be thus paraphrased, "Blessed are those who are in the most pinching straits in this life, if they do really set their affections on spiritual objects, or God and virtue, and their minds are filled with those graces, to the study and practice of which their circumstances call them. For they are not bettered by distresses, or outward poverty, whose imaginations and affections are set on worldly riches; but they, who likewise are morally poor; or, whose minds are as far removed from the love of luxury and sensuality <327> as their outward circumstances are from the means of such indulgences, they only are really gainers by their poverty; and being fit for, they shall have a glorious share of true happiness in the kingdom of God; that kingdom in which nothing avails but true inward merit. And blessed are those, who in the midst of prosperity and temptation to worldly-mindedness and carnal living, are pure in their desires, humane, meek, and beneficent; and not placing any merit in their riches, but having their affections set upon qualities and enjoyments of a higher nature, are as great strangers to voluptuousness as the poorest can be. Such, though they be rich, are poor in a spiritual sense; they, in spight of all temptations, are as clean from the pollution, and contagion of wealth, as if they were outwardly poor. And they, by their virtuous use of their earthly treasures; by their temperance, their humility, and their charity, shall lay up for themselves much greater treasures in the kingdom of heaven." This, if we compare several ways of speaking about the same thing in scripture together, is the true meaning of that poverty of spirit, which some carp at as a very uncouth precept. And were it necessary, it might be shewn, that the best antient moralists have not only represented virtue as consisting in the contempt of wealth, in escaping its pollutions, and in placing our happiness in things so remote from and independent of outward circumstances, as to be able to be happy even in poverty; and in the midst of plenty, to live as abstemiously, in order to make a generous use of riches, as if one was really poor: the best ancient moralists, I say, have not only so defined virtue, but have likewise expressed the fruits of this temper in almost the same manner; that is, in such a way as that, at first sight, they seem to be really recommending poverty, or a voluntary renunciation of riches.[a] But it is sufficient for us <328> to observe, that according to the law of nature, as well as the gospel, it is our duty to employ riches to virtuous purposes; neither to seek after them, nor to use them as means of sensuality, but always to maintain in our minds that superiority and command over all our fleshly lusts, which, because it maketh the poor man happy, and the rich moderate, humble and spiritual, even amidst his plenty, may be justly called poverty of spirit. For this must be the duty of reasonable beings made for society, and the pursuit of publick good here, and for an immortal happiness hereafter, which is to result from a well-governed mind, highly improved rational powers, and their exercises about objects adequate to their vigour and perfection. It is the same excellent temper of mind which is thus represented to us in the epistle of St. *Paul* to *Timothy*.[b]

a. See the lives of *Pelopidas* and *Epaminondas* in antient authors. [For the story of Pelopidas and Epaminondas see *Plutarch's Lives,* ed. and trans. Bernadotte Perrin, 11 vols., Loeb Classical Library (London: Heinemann; New York: Putnam, 1914–26), 5:347ff.]
b. 1 *Tim.* vi. 5, *&c.*

"Withdraw thyself from those who count gain godliness." This is the doctrine of corrupt minds, destitute of the truth. But godliness with contentment is great gain. For we brought nothing into the world, and it is certain that we can carry nothing out. And having food and raiment, let us be therewith content. But they that will be rich, fall into temptation and a snare, and into many foolish and hurtful lusts, which drown men in destruction and perdition. For the love of money is the root of all evil: which, while some coveted after, they have erred from the faith, and pierced themselves through with many sorrows. But thou, O man of God, flee these things, and follow after righteousness, godliness, faith, love, patience, and meekness. Fight the good fight of faith, lay hold on eternal life. Charge them that are rich in this world, that they be not high-minded, nor trust in uncertain riches, but in the living God, who giveth us richly all things to enjoy. That they do good, that they be rich in good <329> works, ready to distribute, willing to communicate, laying up to themselves a good foundation against the time to come, and that they may lay hold on eternal life. [a]

III. Let us now enquire a little into the meaning of the exhortations in scripture, to guard against the deceitfulness of sin, and to watch over our own heart. 1. Sin is represented to be exceeding deceitful; the world is said to be full of snares and allurements to vice; and a life of virtue is held forth to us under the notion of guarding, watching, fighting, and wrestling against the wiles, the delusions, the artifices of evil passions. After what hath been said in another place of the scripture language, I need not stay here to prove, that by the snares, temptations, and wiles of the devil or evil one, is to be understood corrupt lusts and passions, and the various arts by which they seduce into sin; their tendency to blind, darken, and pervert the judgment; to obscure our sense of duty, and to hurry and transport us into unreasonable and wicked pursuits. "Whosoever is tempted, saith the apostle St. *James,* [36] is drawn away of his own lust and entic'd." Now, no person who is acquainted with hu-

a. Poverty of mind, is not to be disinterested; to despise riches; to be above the insolence of wealth.

36. James 1.14.

man nature, will wonder, that the scripture should insist so much upon the seducive artifices of evil passions. For their cunning and sophistry is indeed extreamly dangerous, extreamly difficult to see through and guard against. And vice, in a constitution like ours, must have a very strong party on its side, till virtue by long practice is arrived to great strength and firmness. If we look into ancient moralists, we shall find them discoursing in the same strain of the enchanting fancies or passions by which men are deceived into perverse paths, contrary to the dictates of their reason, and their natural abhorrence of vice. By these moralists the temptations to sin are very properly set forth to us as the delusive devices of false pleasure. And in holy writ, because <330> when corruption prevails universally, we are then not only continually sollicited to irregular indulgences by our sensitive appetites, and the objects which are ever assailing them; but evil example hath itself a very contageous, depraving influence, and is a very strong temptation; for these reasons the world is represented to us as the great seducer. Love not the world, neither the things that are in the world, says St. *John:* [a] if any man love the world, the love of the Father is not in him. Now what the apostle means by the world, and the things that are in it, he expresly declares in the following words. For all that is in the world, saith he, the lust of the flesh, and the lust of the eyes, and the pride of life, is not of the Father, but of the world. *The lusts of the flesh; i.e.* the desire of unlawful pleasures, all intemperance, lasciviousness, and impurity. These are called the lusts of the flesh, because men are hurried or seduced into them by passions and appetites, which the scripture stiles, *flesh,* in opposition to the dictates of reason or moral conscience, which is called in scripture, *being led by the spirit.* Now, though all the good things of life, which God hath created to be enjoyed with temperance, according to the ends and measures of nature, within the limits of reason and good order, and consistent with the more noble views and improvements of our rational and social part; though they be all the gifts of God, who *giveth us richly all things to enjoy;* yet when men, instead of bridling and governing their appetites by reason, do on the contrary suffer their reason to be over-

a. 1 *John* ii. 15.

ruled by passions and appetites, subverting the natural order of God's creation, and denying due authority to those superior faculties designed to distinguish men from mere sensitive creatures; their enjoyments in this case are not of God, but are condemned by him; they are of what the apostle here stiles, by <331> way of opposition, to the design and will of God, *the world.*

The lusts of the eye, the desire of riches by unlawful means, and to no valuable purposes. And these are here stiled, the lusts of the eyes; because the love of riches, as such, and as it stands here distinguished from other vitious affections, *the covetous desire of riches for riches sake,* without any regard to the true, and beneficial uses of them, is but feeding the eyes with a mere fruitless view of unprofitable treasure, with the empty shows of vanity and deceit. It is the vice described thus by the wise man, "There is one alone, and there is not a second, yea, he hath neither child nor brother, yet is there no end of all his labour, neither is his eye satisfied with riches; neither saith he, for whom do I labour, and bereave my soul of good?" This also is vanity. And from hence have been derived those particular manners of speaking in scripture, where liberality is styled, a bountiful eye, and a single or open eye; and covetousness, an evil or niggardly eye. Whenever riches are desired and employed as instruments of liberality, or of doing good service to society, they are then indeed real blessings of providence. Blessings to the possessors of them whom they enable to have great influence in promoting virtue, and every thing that is valuable in society, or adds to the happiness of mankind. And blessings to others who are partakers of those good influences. But when they are only, what the apostle here stiles, the lust of the eyes; the food either of covetousness merely without use, or of vanity and folly in an ill use of them, the desire of them in that case is not an appetite of God's creating. *'Tis not of the Father, but of the world.* 'Tis the creature merely of a perverted imagination, and of a corrupt will: 'tis a desire that will perpetually put men upon obtaining wealth by ill methods, and upon employing it contrary to the design of God, in creating mankind, and the means of outward enjoyment. <332>

The pride of life, i.e. ambition, or the unlawful desire of dominion and power. And this is here stiled the pride of life; because, both the desire of obtaining power by unrighteous methods, and the pleasure of increasing it in ways of insolence and oppression, have their whole foundation in pride; in a presumptuous imagination, that right reason and equity are things of no reality, and which may, at any time, give place to our will and pleasure. Desire of power, in order to increase it to the benefit of our fellow-creatures, is indeed a noble passion. But the desire of power for the purposes of ambition only, and for the pleasure of tyranizing over others, is with great propriety called here the pride of life, which *is not of the Father, but of the world*. 'Tis that pride, or that setting up of self-will, in opposition to reason and equity, which is the ground and foundation of almost every immorality. The intemperances and debaucheries men are guilty of for want of improvement of themselves, are most properly included under the first head, which is the *lust of the flesh*. The second head, which is the *lust of the eye,* or the covetous desire of riches, for riches sake, is also frequently the occasion of much corruption, of many and great particular acts of injustice and oppression towards others. But the most general and extensive cause of an habitually injurious and inhuman temper is this *pride of life;* this love of power, domination and self-will. From hence arise wars, desolations, tyrannies, and all the great, extensive and merciless oppressions which totally extinguish that universal benevolence towards mankind, which is the *charity* represented in scripture as the fulfilling of the whole law; because benevolence ought to preside in the mind, and while our appetites are ruled by it, they are regular and orderly, and answer the good ends for which they were implanted in us.[a]

Those evil appetites are the tempters by which we are misled into the ways of unrighteousness and filthi-<333>ness, contrary to our reason, and inward sense of virtue and duty. And they are not of God: *they are not of the Father;* because, tho' all our appetites after outward objects, all our sensitive affections and desires, as well as our rational powers be of God's creation; yet he hath given us a governing principle to direct them; he hath created them on purpose to be restrained and regulated

---

a. This paraphrase is chiefly taken from Dr. *Sam. Clarke*. See his Sermons. [Clarke, Sermon 154, in *Works*, 2:251–56.]

by the rules of virtue and sober reason; to be the subjects of our moral government, and thus to be to us the means, the occasions, the materials of various virtues. Separate them from us, and we have nothing to rule, nothing to curb or regulate. Take them away, there would be indeed no temptations to excesses and irregularities. But at the same time, what would become of self-government, of temperance, of fortitude, of benevolence, and in one word, of all that gives a man a title to the character of virtuous and good. Wherein the virtues of other created agents may consist, or what the objects of them may be, we cannot tell; but with respect to us, 'tis our sensitive part chiefly that is the object of our good or bad administration; of our reasonable or unreasonable deportment. And with regard to all beings capable of virtues analogous to ours, there must be similar means and objects of moral government. The moral perfection of the Deity consists in not exerting his power omnipotent, for the sake of triumphing in his power, but in exercising it for the greater good of his creation, according to the rules of justice, equity and truth.

Now, how our natural appetites sollicit us to place our happiness in giving full swing to them, and oppose themselves to the government of our reason, we may all feel, if we but attend to our minds: for do we not, on many occasions, experience *a law in our members warring against the law of our minds.* The real state of mankind, as corrupt as the world is, is this: men have naturally a strong sense of virtue and good or-<334>der in the government of their sensitive affections; so that it is not easy for them to despise the dictates of reason and conscience. And therefore, few men become highly corrupt all at once: few begin, in their first instances of unrighteousness, with acts of violent oppression; few run immediately into all excess and extravagancy of debauchery and riot; seemingly small immoral indulgences present themselves first, and gain admittance into their hearts, under the deceitful colours of very venial ones. But when a man has yielded to one sin because it is but small, he cannot resist the next, because it is not much greater; and so, by the same delusive argument, and by the same foolish repeated temptation, he is by degrees betrayed into the commission of the most enormous crimes; which, if any man at his first being tempted to transgress, had foretold that he should in process of time be induced to commit, he would have answered, as *Hazael* did to the prophet that foretold his cruelty, "Am I a dog that I should do this thing?" But at last, these very greatest of crimes make no more dreadful an appearance to his corrupted conscience, than at first the least sins did to his innocent and undebauched judgment. When men have once been guilty of some great enormity, having lost the guard of their innocence, the banks of modesty and good resolution being broken down, the customs of a wicked world, and the habits of debauchery prevail over them, and bear them down irresistibly like a torrent: men thus become gradually reconciled to vice; the second crime is committed with less reluctance than the first; and the habit of wickedness growing upon them by repeated acts, in process of time, besides the proper and immediate temptation to every act of sin, the very custom of having done it makes it difficult for them not to return to it. They at last become ashamed to retreat, and indeed have no other arguments to oppose to the enticements of sin, and to the importunities of vitious <335> company, than such as having been often baffled and overcome have little or no force. And thus their return to virtue becomes, in a manner, as difficult as that *the Ethiopian should change his colour, or the leopard his spots.* The temptations which one could not resist in the days of his greater strength and best advantages, are become much more powerful by being often complied with; and if ever he recovers from the slavery of sin, it must be by overcoming an enemy much stronger, when he at the same time is much weaker himself. The effect of this is, that the conscience at length becomes fear'd and insensible, and the heart entirely hardened; and the sinner has no desire left of recovering his liberty, any more than he has power to do it. The last and highest degree of this evil is, when a man having wholly laid aside the thoughts of reforming himself, makes it his business, on the contrary, to corrupt others, and to tempt them likewise into debauchery, intemperance, corruption and venality; when he makes a mock of virtue, of sobriety, and honesty, of publick spirit, religion and conscience, when he scoffs at piety and goodness, and *sets himself down* (as the Psalmist expresses it) *in the seat of the scornful.* [37] St. *Paul,* after a long catalogue of sins which

37. Ps. I.I.

the light of nature clearly discovers to every person to be highly abominable, gives this character of those who are arrived to the utmost heighth
of depravity; *"Who knowing the judgment of God (that they which commit
such things are worthy of death;* worthy of the punishments threatened
by God against sin, worthy of the direful effects a corrupted immoral
temper and life must produce in a good administration of moral beings;)
not only do the same, but have pleasure in them that do them."[38] No man
thinks it possible for him, at his first setting out in the world, ever to
arrive to such a monstrous degree of wickedness; but this is the natural
progress of vice, which nothing can prevent but firm resistance to every
temptation, to every im-<336>moral indulgence, however trifling it may
appear; or a strict guard against being betrayed into any sin, by the fairest,
the most specious solicitations of any of our appetites after outward
pleasure. It is for this reason that the scripture commands us to watch
over our hearts, to take heed to our ways, to commune often very seriously with our moral conscience, to examine ourselves, and to call ourselves frequently to a very strict account for all our actions. "Take heed,
brethren, says the author of the epistle to the *Hebrews,* lest there be in
any of you an evil heart of unbelief, in departing from the living God.
But exhort one another daily, while it is called to day, lest any of you be
hardened through the deceitfulness of sin."[a] To *be hardened,* or to *harden
a man's own heart,* signifies to have laid aside that natural abhorrence of
sin which usually, at first, restrains men from venturing upon great wickedness. It signifies to have lost or laid asleep that quick sense, that uneasy
judgment of the mind and conscience, which by continually representing to us the baseness and vileness, the danger and evil consequences of
sin, will not permit men (so long as they give attention to it) to become
abandoned sinners. It signifies, men's being at length reconciled to sin;
their chusing it with deliberate choice; their becoming shameless and
incorrigible, open and daring, not only in committing wickedness, but
in defending it; and denying all moral differences of actions. Men do
not fall into this wretched state on a sudden and at once; but they arrive

a. *Heb.* iii. 12–13.
38. Rom. 1.32.

at it by degrees, being seduced into it insensibly by the enticements, and drawn on gradually by the *deceitfulness of sin*. This is the natural tendency of our yielding to temptation, of our complying with the customs of a depraved world, and suffering ourselves to be overcome by any passion or appetite till we have first examined it at <337> the bar of reason and conscience. There is, nor can be no other way of preserving ourselves secure against this most fatal of all evils to which reasonable beings can be exposed, and which, for that reason, was the only thing that certain ancient moralists would call evil; (total depravation of the mind) but not to enter into the road which directly leads to it; or if we are betrayed into it, to recover ourselves by reflexion and resolution immediately, and to redouble our watchfulness over the language of our passions to us. This direful growth or progress of the vitious temper in consequence of our listening to false pleasure, or unexamin'd appetites and fancies, is frequently represented to us by ancient moralists in the most rousing and awakening manner. And indeed they must be utter strangers to the ballance of the affections, which constitutes soundness and integrity of mind, to the power of habits; and, in one word, to all the laws relative to our progress in virtue, and to all the effects of not maintaining our reason and moral conscience in full and uncontroulable power and authority, who do not see the necessity of our keeping a strict watch over our minds, and of giving heedful attention to the enticing shapes and forms in which our appetites after outward objects are apt to represent them to us, especially when we have in any degree accustomed them to rule and guide us. 'Tis by such moral discipline alone that men can retain their integrity, improve in virtue, nay, not degenerate gradually into absolute depravity. Several moralists have unfolded and laid open to our view the seductive promises with which different passions often tempt us. And there is not indeed any thing more necessary to mankind, than that they should be early apprised of the deceitful representations of things our appetites are apt to exhibit to us, and of the false assertions and judgments we cannot but be betrayed into by them, if we are not exceedingly upon our guard against being deluded; if <338> we are not severe self-examiners, severe chastisers of all our ideas or fancies; for according to them will our affections and pursuits be. It is impossible that one can preserve his dominion over his appetites any longer than he looks upon a right mind as the greatest of all treasures, and a corrupt one as the most horrible of all evils; any longer than he looks upon generous affection, and the calm and steady presidence of reason, as having more beauty and charm than all other things in the world besides, and a grain of honesty and native worth is of more value, in his apprehension, than all the adventitious ornaments, estates or preferments, for the sake of which so many turn knaves; forsaking their natural principles and sentiments, quit their true honour and freedom for a mean, timorous, shifting state of gaudy servitude; and for insipid wretched honours of a deceitful kind, exchange inward merit, honour, and a character of a sincere and lasting relish. But how can this just notion of worth be kept up in the mind, otherwise than by the habitual self-examination and watchfulness so earnestly recommended by the excellent moralist[a] whose words I have been now quoting, which is indeed the very same with that *keeping* of the heart with all diligence, that frequent *meditation* upon the excellence of virtue, the dignity to which human powers may be improved, the end of our being, and the will of our creator; and that continued, unintermitted *attention* that we be not deceived by the delusive appearances of sin, so often inculcated upon us in the sacred writings. 2. Let me only add to what hath been said, that the commands in scripture not to trust to our own hearts, and to take heed that we do not deceive ourselves, do not imply any other difficulty in knowing ourselves, or in judging truly of our advancements in virtue, besides what arises from self-love or self-flattery; of which he, who <339> is not aware, must be very unacquainted with human nature. It is certainly of moment to us, in order to our progress in virtue, not to be deceived with regard to our moral character, or not to imagine ourselves more perfect, or more proof against sollicitations to vice of any kind than we really are. With regard to other qualities, as beauty, strength, agility, learning, wit, &c. it cannot but be owned that very few are able to prevent very

---

a. See *Arrian, Marcus Antoninus,* and the Characteristicks. [The sentiment is well represented in Shaftesbury's "Miscellany" IV in *Characteristics,* ed. Klein; see especially 422–25. See also Marcus Aurelius Antoninus, *Meditations* VI.13.]

great partiality in their judgments about their share of them. For how apt are we to magnify all our accomplishments, and to extenuate all our imperfections to ourselves? How doth flattery work upon persons so as not only to perswade them that they may perhaps have good qualities in a higher degree than they imagined, but even so as to induce them to venture on undertakings far above their abilities.—How doth this happen but through our disposition to judge too favourably of ourselves? Were it not for this tendency to flatter ourselves, the flattery of others could never seduce us. The latter indeed can only hurt us in proportion to the power the other hath over our minds. Now surely, none will say that there is danger from our aptitude to partiality with regard to ourselves in every other respect, and no danger of our mistaking with regard to our moral character, or our improvements and advances in virtue. But if it be possible to deceive or flatter ourselves in that respect, it is certainly a self-deceit, a self-flattery which ought to be strictly guarded against; for no other branch of self-partiality can be of so dangerous consequence to us. Surely in this article, *if a man thinketh himself something when he is nothing, he deceiveth himself*.[a] But the only way to be certain we do not deceive or flatter ourselves in this important article, is not to suffer ourselves to relish praise from others which we are not very sure of our deserving, upon a close and <340> severe review of our heart, temper and life; not to take our idea of ourselves from others, but from our own inward conscience alone. "That no man may deceive himself, saith the Apostle St. *Paul,* let him prove his own work; and then shall he have rejoicing in himself alone, and not in another":[39] Then the flattery of others will not mislead him into a false opinion of himself; and then shall he, if he be injuriously calumniated, have rejoicing in himself from the testimony of a good conscience. The great danger with respect to mistaking our moral character lies in our not attending to the real difference between our being deeply affected with a sense of the excellence of virtue, as often as it is presented to us, and our being actually virtuous. Some men fancy themselves highly improved in virtue, and absolutely

a. *Gal.* vi. 3, *&c.*
39. Gal. 6.3–4.

secure, at least against every gross vice, whatever temptations to commit it they may happen to fall into; because at times they have very high notions of the beauty and amiableness of virtue, and of the deformity of every sinful passion and action. But they do not consider, that the worst of men must, on some occasions, feel the same sentiments excited in their minds; and that the sincerity and reality of virtue is to be measured by the good deeds it produces, by the general tenor of the life; for if sentiments of virtue and duty do not govern the life, they do not make one really good, because they do not render one really useful and beneficial to mankind. If a man have not good sentiments, he cannot be virtuous, but in order to deserve the character of a virtuous man, his good sentiments must be a principle of action in him; a living, a moving, an active principle. The soundest faith, the best notions about God and virtue are dead, saith St. *James,* unless they shew themselves to be active by the good fruits they bring forth. *Faith without works is dead.* As others can have no evidence of our good principles but by the advantages they reap from the good fruits of them in <341> our lives, so we are to prove our faith, our good principles and sentiments, our right notions of things to ourselves by our conduct and behaviour: Not to flatter ourselves on account of the truth and reasonableness of our opinions, or of the warmth with which we at times contemplate virtue, but to call ourselves to an account for the good we actually do in consequence of these good principles; and then only to pronounce ourselves good, when we are really useful to society. It signifies but little how virtuous the head be, if the heart be not equally so. Virtue means a virtuous temper, working habitually all the good it hath opportunity of doing; a generous benevolent disposition, that controuleth every sensual appetite, and delights to exert itself in promoting, with unwearied assiduity, the best interests of mankind. Now every man hath it in his power, almost every day of his life, to do some good to society. And he therefore hath just ground to suspect his virtue, who not being able to point out to himself what he does that is truly good, easily prevails upon himself to believe it was because he had no opportunity, or it was not in his power. For that is not the language of virtue, but of indolence or self-love. And this leads me to observe in the first place, that many placing virtue or religion in acts of pious meditation and worship, not only dispense with their not laying themselves out to be useful to society, but think themselves much better employed than if they minded temporal affairs, or concerned themselves about what they diminutively call *worldly business.* But christianity calls upon us to be diligent in some useful business, and to be rich in good works. And because *our righteousness,* as the scripture speaks, *cannot profit God,* then only is it profitable, or of real worth, when it is profitable to our fellow creatures. We are placed in this world not to retire from it; but to be active in it, and to exert our selves to promote publick happiness. And indeed to suppose, that the virtue required <342> of us is any thing besides such a temper of mind as prompts and excites to doing good in the world, is to suppose our excellence to consist in separating ourselves from our kind, and living independently of them. It is to place it in something that cannot make us like God, whose moral perfection consists in the continual exertion of his goodness; in something which absolutely centers in ourselves, and is therefore wholly selfish. If we have just apprehensions of God, religious meditation must be of excellent use to excite and strengthen the generous affections, and to subdue the narrow or impure appetites, which are the great obstacles to virtuous activity. But if what is called devotion, pious contemplation, or acts of religious worship, have not this effect, we may be as sure that we are deceived by some false opinion about God, and what is acceptable to him, as it is plain and evident "That he made us so to govern our appetites, and so to exert ourselves every one in his sphere as may best serve to advance publick happiness." Now, tho' christianity had not told us so, what can be more evident, than that nothing can be acceptable to God, or recommend to the divine favour, but our acting the best part as rational and social creatures, as creatures not made for ourselves, but for the general good? Some, in the second place, are easily perswaded that acts of religious worship are not sufficient to compleate the character of a good man, but that if to frequent exercises of devotion, almsgiving be joined, then is a man perfect. But St. *Paul*[a] distinguishes between charity, and giving to the poor. "Tho' I bestow all my goods on the poor,

a. 1 *Cor.* xiii. 3.

saith he, and have not charity, it profiteth me nothing." The charity which in scripture is called fulfilling of the law, and the bond of perfectness, is now too generally understood to mean no more than almsgiving, which is but a small part <343> of it. It means that universal love to mankind which not only disposes us to pity and compassionate our fellow creatures in distress, but excites us to employ our whole life busily in some way advantageous to society. Very great things are indeed spoken in scripture concerning this particular virtue of liberality to the poor. But it deserves to be particularly taken notice, that not only in the text just cited, but in all other places also, without exception, through the whole new testament, the word *charity* never once signifies the giving of alms, but always that sincere benevolence and good will towards all men, of which almsgiving to the poor is but one single branch, or one particular effect. It is very plain that almsgiving, if it springs not from a right principle, if it be accompanied with, and made subservient to designs of pride and ambition, of imperiousness and dominion, of party, faction and worldly power in matters of religion, it is of no esteem in the sight of God: it is not a virtue but when it proceeds from real love to mankind; and in order to its answering the end of the principle from which it ought to flow, in order to be called a virtue, it ought to be directed by wisdom in its choice of objects and means.

Pretences of love towards God, which do not produce benevolence towards our fellow-creatures, the apostle St. *John* tells us,[a] they are nothing more than mere enthusiasm, and a gross deceit. "If a man say, I love God, and hateth his brother, he is a liar." The reasons he gives for it are, He that loveth not mankind, knoweth not God, for he is love.—And, he that loveth not his brother whom he hath seen, how can he love God whom he hath not seen. The meaning of which reasoning is plainly to this effect. He who is not benevolently affected toward mankind cannot have a just notion of God, for God is love; he cannot love God, without considering him as infinitely be-<344>nevolent and good: But how can one love infinite benevolence, without having a benevolent disposition. Besides, it is only a benevolent disposition towards mankind that can

a. 1 *John* iv. 20, *&c.*

lead one to that delight in an universal father of mankind, and of the whole world of perceptive and rational beings, in which the love of God consists. We cannot rise to that sublime act of love, but gradually from acts of love and kindness towards beings which fall more immediately under our observation: if our love doth not operate towards our kind, there can be no such principle of benevolence in us, as is necessary to our being able to form to our selves an idea of God, and to delight in him.

Now, as for a principle of real benevolence, either toward God or mankind, tho' it be very true that, as the same apostle says,[a] that whosoever hath this world's goods, and seeth his brother have need, and shutteth up his bowels of compassion from him, it cannot be in him; for how dwelleth the love of God in such a breast, saith the apostle: Yet that principle doth not satisfy it self with frequent giving for the relief of the poor; but the person who is really influenced by it, will be led and determined by it to devote his whole life to the service of mankind. He will be diligent to find out ways of being really and constantly useful to society, and will think every moment lost in which he is not employed in doing something really good. Persons in the lower stations of life are very apt to censure those who have large estates for their idleness, and particularly for their doing so few deeds of generosity in proportion to their fortunes. And they are indeed highly culpable. But let no man deceive himself, by saying to himself he would do great and beneficial things, if he had a plentiful income, unless he dare say to himself, that he does all the good in his present power; that he lays himself out to be useful to society to the utmost of his ca-<345>pacity; and is in no respect less beneficial than he may be. Christianity exhorts in the strongest terms to charity, to benevolence, to active virtue. But tho' we had no such extraordinary calls from divine revelation to be assiduous in advancing the general good and perfection of mankind, every one of us, in some particular way best suited to our abilities, genius and circumstances, how can we answer it to our natural conscience; to that inward sense of duty to God, and of right and wrong, which the author of our nature hath

a. 1 *John* iii. 17.

implanted in all men, to point them to their proper employment, as active and social creatures, if we are mere cumberers of the earth, like the barren unprofitable tree, which only serves to draw away nourishment from the good and fruitful ones? Yet such are all men who do not exert themselves to be useful to others. They are barren unprofitable trees; for what fruits doth society, for whose good all men are born, reap from them? The greatest vice in the world is idleness. It is justly said by moralists to be the mother of irregular passions. But, independently of that consideration, an idle life is contrary to the first and fundamental law of nature, with regard to our improvement, and to the improvement of mankind and human happiness in general, by which all is the fruit or purchase of industry. To improve ourselves, is to fit ourselves for doing great good, for being more extensively useful to society; and therefore time wholly laid out in improving ourselves in knowledge, without ever exerting our abilities for the advantages of others, is laying out our time wholly upon having the means by which an end may be gained, and no part of it upon the end itself. But if to enrich our minds with knowledge, without employing ourselves to be serviceable to mankind by it, be but at best the most innocent sort of idleness, what must be said of those who are indeed mere drones, who live luxuriously upon the industry of the active and laborious? 'Tis a fatal mistake, to affix an idea <346> of meanness to any business or employment which is really beneficial to society. And it is an equally pernicious one for any to think, that they have a right by their lucky birth, to be exeemed from all concern about the advancement of publick happiness; and to imagine they do enough, if now and then they are prevailed upon to part with a little of their superfluity for the relief of the indigent and distressed. No man is born for himself; and therefore no man discharges the duty of his life, or lives answerably to the end of his creation, who doth not consider himself as obliged to be a useful member of society, in proportion to his power of doing good; and to increase his abilities and power, in order to increase his power of doing good. This is not the language of christianity only, which is thought by some, upon that account, to impose a grievous yoke upon the rich and great by birth. It is the language of natural religion also; and is accordingly set forth to us as our duty in the most urgent and emphatical, moving manner, by several heathen moralists. Nor is there indeed any possibility of evading the necessity of acknowledging the obligation of all men equally to active virtue, till it can be proved, that all men are not made for society; but that some have by birth-right, or may acquire by getting wealth, a dispensation from all obligation to society, and a right to live as they list, without any concern about the interests of mankind in general, or of their country in particular. In truth, one cannot be idle without being really hurtful. But supposing there were any kinds of innocent idleness to which one's life might be wholly devoted;—Is it the life of a man; the proper life of a creature endued with reason and active powers; the proper life of a social creature, blessed with so many faculties capable of such highly beneficial exercises? Is it a life that can be approved of by God; or merit happiness in another world? What merit hath such a life with regard to men; and how can it but be condemned by God and all good beings? To what rewards <347> or honours can it intitle hereafter? Their memory here must quickly be lost; and what can they flatter themselves to have deserved or prepared themselves for in another world? But the memory of the good man shall ever be *precious here as ointment poured forth;* and the good works he hath done in this world shall *follow him* into another, and obtain him a place suited to his worth, among those who have lived here, *not to themselves,* but to the *glory of God,* who created men to be co-workers with him for promoting universal good. I need not stay to prove that every man who from a sense of his duty to society, exerts himself with assiduous and cheerful application to some useful business, to do good to society, is an honourable member of society, and truly deserves the character of a virtuous man; nor that there is no man, especially in a well-governed society, who may not be useful. But I cannot choose but take notice of that affecting transition of the son of *Syrach* [a] from magnifying God in all his works of creation and providence to the praise of good men. "Let us now praise famous men. The Lord hath wrought great glory by them, through his great power from the beginning. Such as did bear rule in their kingdoms, men renowned for their power, giving counsel by their

a. *Ecclus.* xliv.

understanding, and declaring prophesies. Leaders of the people by their counsels, and by their knowledge of learning meet for the people, wise and eloquent in their institutions. Such as found out musical tunes, and recited verses in writing. Rich men furnished with ability, living peaceably in their habitations. All those were honoured in their generations, and were the glory of their times. There be of them that have left a name behind them, that their praises might be reported. And some there be which have no memorial, who are perished as though they had never been."[a] <348> The ways of being really useful to society are innumerable, and will be easily found out by those who have a principle of active virtue in their minds; that virtue or wisdom, which, as St. *James* expresses it, is pure, peaceable, gentle, and easy to be intreated, *full of mercy and good fruits.* And what a poor thing is it, said even a wise heathen sage, not to hurt him, whom you ought to benefit? It was a noble saying of *Plato,* which *Tully* hath beautifully enlarged upon in his offices. "We are not born for ourselves alone; our country, our parents, and our friends have all a share and an interest in our being." 'Tis a maxim with the Stoicks, saith *Tully,* that as the earth, and all the productions of it, were created for the use of men, so men themselves were brought into the world, that they might assist and benefit each other. In this we ought to follow the guidance of nature, to bring common goods together, and freely lay them in common, and by an intercourse of giving and receiving kind offices, by art and industry, and all our faculties, to cement the society of mankind. It is more agreeable to nature, saith the same author, for a man to undertake all sorts of labour and trouble for the service and advantage of society, than to live in solitude, not only free from cares, but in the midst of the greatest pleasures. We are all members of one great body. Nature produced us under mutual relation, from the same principles, and for the same designs. It is she that has inspired us with love one for another: it is she who has taught us the lessons of equity and justice. It is upon account of her constitutions that we ought to

a. It appears from hence, that in ancient times making honourable mention of great and good men, to excite noble emulation in the living, was a part of religious service.

esteem it a greater unhappiness to do hurt, than to receive it. It is by her orders that our hands move so readily to the assistance of an injured neighbour. Let that good saying therefore be ever in your mind, "I am a man, and I esteem nothing foreign to me which is of kin to humanity. Let us lay our natural powers in common. Human society is built like an arch of stones, which is <349> by this means only supported and upheld from ruin, that each part hinders the fall of the others." This is the constant language of the ancient moralists concerning benevolence and virtue. And it is indeed the language of nature, as well as of revelation, that he who thinketh himself virtuous because he hath pious or virtuous sentiments, contenting himself that he does no hurt, without laying himself out, to the utmost of his power, to be useful to society, mistakes the shadow for the substance. "For, as the apostle St. *James* reasons,[a] if a brother or sister be naked, and destitute of daily food, and one say unto them, Depart in peace, be you warmed and filled, but does not give to them those things which are needful, what doth it profit? Even so faith, if it hath not works, is dead being alone. Yea a man may say, Thou hast faith, and I have works: shew me thy faith without thy works, and I will shew thee my faith by my works." No opinions, no faith, no perswasion, no sentiments, can be of real use or value but in proportion to the good influence they have upon one's actions. If they produce a good temper and disposition of mind, that good temper will produce a conformably good life. And till principles influence the temper, they are but ideas floating in the head. It is not the head but the heart, said a good ancient, that makes the man of probity and worth. And in vain doth one pretend to a good heart, if he is not fruitful in good works. For it is not more true, that a good tree bringeth forth good fruit, than that a good heart is not barren, but active and fruitful in counsels, in words, and in deeds, which are of real utility to all within its reach or influence. I have insisted the longer upon these mistakes about virtue, because, as nothing more effectually supplants true science than false learning; so nothing more effectually prevents progress in real virtue, than the pursuit of something <350> that has a fair but false shew of it.

a. *James* ii. 15–18.

And in christian countries, placing religion intirely in contemplation and acts of religious worship, and in almsgiving, instead of placing it in benevolent assiduous industry to promote the good of society, seems to be a very prevailing mistake, tho' christianity expresly declares, that our duty consists in doing good, in being ready to distribute, willing to communicate, and in being *rich in good works;* and this is laying up to ourselves in store a good foundation against the time to come, in which every one shall reap as he has sown; and God the righteous judge and governor of the world will render to every one according to his works. And indeed, did it teach any other doctrine, or place religion in any thing else, it could not come from God. For reason plainly declares to us, that the good of society is the end of our creation; and that promoting it is our duty; and that nothing else can recommend us to the love and approbation of God, who is perfect goodness, but being steadily and uniformly actuated by a benign disposition: or, in other words, that in consequence of a constitution of things, framed and upheld by an infinitely perfect author, active benevolence must be the temper of soul from which alone eternal happiness can spring. To imagine the rewards in another life annexed to any other qualities but benignity and goodness of mind, is to imagine God to love, honour and reward something of inferior merit more than that which constitutes his own supreme excellence. It is to suppose him to delight in something inferior to virtue more than in virtue. And, on the other hand, to measure the goodness of mankind by any other rule or standard but the good fruits it produces, that is, the good it does in society, in proportion to our circumstances, or the extent of our power duly improved and exerted, is the same absurdity in morals, as it would be in physicks to say, that the cause is not proportional to the effect, and alternately the effect to the <351> cause. The rule must hold equally true in both, that as is the cause, such are its effects; as is the cause, such is the power or energy with which it operates. The only mark therefore by which thorough, unaffected, sincere benevolence may be known is this, that it will not be satisfied with itself, while it is conscious of its having neglected any opportunity of benefiting mankind it hath or could have had in his power, by duly exerting itself, while in the mean time it is very indulgent to others, and presumes very charitably of them, instead of rashly condemning or censuring them. Let us therefore judge favourably of others, and severely of ourselves; that is, call ourselves to a strict trial, and make our pretences to virtue and goodness give an account of their good effects, being perswaded that as nothing can assimulate us to God but goodness of heart; so goodness is and must be proportional to the energy with which it works, to its operativeness or fruitfulness. This may appear a severe test; and it is impossible to lay down rules about it, without entering into the examination of particular circumstances and cases. But if there be any such thing as religion or morality, it must consist in benevolence; that is, in the prevailing power of benevolence over all our other affections: benevolence must have the ascendant; or be the governing principle in our mind. And hence *love* is justly called in the scripture *the fulfilment of the law.* Whatever affection is not submitted to it, but baffles and overpowers it, whether it be revenge, pride, ambition, private interest, or sensual gratification, must be stronger than it. But when one regulates all his appetites and pursuits by a principle of benevolence, then are all his affections in due order; then is he with respect to himself, sober, temperate, chaste, nay, self-denied; and with respect to others, social, humane and generous; not merely just, but beneficent, merciful and affectionate. Nothing can be of consequence to mankind, or any creature but happiness. <352> And therefore, this is all which any person can, in strictness of speaking, be said to have a right to. We can *owe no man any thing,* but only to promote his happiness according to our abilities. "We therefore, as the apostle speaks,[a] can owe no man any thing but to love one another: for which reason, *he that loveth mankind hath fulfilled the law.* For this, thou shalt not commit adultery, thou shalt not kill, thou shalt not steal, thou shalt not bear false witness, thou shalt not covet; and if there be any other commandment, it is briefly comprehended in this saying, namely, thou shalt love thy neighbour as thy self." The phrase, *as thy self,* cannot be understood to mean an equal, much less can it mean a greater sensibility with regard to others than ourselves, for that is impossible, it is a contradiction. But the meaning

a. *Rom.* xiii. 8, *&c.*

of it is well explained by that most equitable rule,[a] "Whatsoever ye would that men should do unto you, do ye even so unto them," *i.e.* be willing to do, or do cheerfully and willingly that always to another which you can in reason expect another should do to you. Put your self in your neighbour's circumstances, and whatever you would think reasonable to expect from another, were you in these circumstances, let that be the rule of your dealing with him who is actually in these circumstances.

This, says our saviour,[b] *is the law and the prophets.* This is that great rule wherein is contained our whole duty to our neighbour. This is the sum of true religion, of righteousness and equity: This is what the nature and the reason of things teaches: This is a rule of easy application: And this is what all God's revelations to mankind tend ultimately to establish. He who loveth mankind will make the joys and sorrows, the interests of his fellow creatures his own. It is from self-love that we form the notion of private good; and love of our neighbour, where it prevails, will dis-<353>pose us to appropriate to ourselves his good and welfare; and thus it will not only prevent our being injurious to him, but will also put us upon promoting his good. As the private affection makes us in a peculiar manner sensible of justice or injustice, humanity, equity, tenderness and beneficence, when it is exercised towards our selves; love of our neighbour would give the same kind of sensibility in his behalf; teach us what we ought to do toward our neighbours, by making us feel what we would highly approve of, if done by a neighbour to us in the like circumstances. And we may certainly fix upon this general rule with regard to benevolence, that the more of our care and thought and labour we employ in doing good to our fellow creatures, the nearer we come up to this law of perfection, *"Thou shalt love thy neighbour as thy self."* The love of our neighbour, in proportion as it prevails, will be an advocate in our breasts to take care of the interests of our fellow creatures, in all the competitions and interferings, which cannot but be from the imperfection of our nature, and the state we are in; and which, as hath been often observed, are in a great measure designed for the trial and

a. *Matt.* vii. 12.
b. *Gal.* v. 14.

exercise of benevolence, in order to its being brought to perfection in our breasts. It will likewise, in a great degree, lessen that interfering, and hinder men from forming so strong a notion of private good, exclusive of the good of others, as we are apt to do. It will lead us naturally to examine the dictates of self-love, and to observe whether it gives us a just and fair representation of our true interest. For it is not commanded us, nor is the seed and principle of it implanted in us to exclude self-love, but to direct and guide it. And indeed, as a person who hath benevolence prevailing in him to any degree, if he takes a view of his frame and constitution, and of the natural connexions and tendencies of things in his state, must soon perceive, that the gratifications of benevolence, considered as a particular af-<354>fection, are far superior to the gratifications of any other particular affection; and that benevolence, considered as forming a general temper of mind, is itself the temper of satisfaction and enjoyment; so in reality, competition or interfering happens much oftner between pride, revenge, sensual gratifications and private interest, than between private interest and benevolence. For nothing is more common, as an excellent writer has observed on this head,[a] than to see men give themselves up to a passion or an affection, to their known prejudice and ruin, and in direct contradiction to manifest and real interest, and the loudest calls of self-love: whereas the seeming competitions and interfering between benevolence and private interest, relate much more to the materials and means of enjoyment, than to enjoyment itself. There is often an interfering in the former, when there is none in the latter.

As for the love of God, scripture as well as reason tells us, that it cannot take place but where benevolence is the reigning principle in the heart; and that as benevolence cannot rise to the love of God, unless it hath first operated towards our fellow creatures, so where it prevails towards our kind, the idea of an infinitely good being can no sooner be formed, than it must embrace such an object with the highest degree of com-

a. Dr. *Butler.* Bishop of *Bristol,* in his sermon on *Love to our neighbour,* whence this whole reasoning is taken. [Joseph Butler, Sermon XI: "Upon the Love of Our Neighbour," §18, in *Works,* vol. 2.]

placency, delight and love. And thus benevolence is the root of piety: and all virtue and piety at last necessarily runs up into one and the same point; and love is in all senses the *end of the commandment, the bond of perfectness.* Benevolence does really, in the nature of things, include in it all that is good and worthy; all that is good which we have any distinct particular notion of. We have no clear conception of any moral attribute in the supreme Being, but what may be resolved up into goodness or benevolence. And therefore, if we consider a reasonable or moral agent, abstractly or without <355> regard to the particular relations and circumstances in which he is placed, we cannot conceive any thing else to come in towards determining his merit, but the degree in which benevolence prevails in him, its largeness or comprehensiveness, and its force and power in his mind.

What stress christianity lays upon the prevalency or ascendency of benevolence in the mind, and its fruits, is very evident; for it commands us in the strongest terms, not only to be just and equitable in our dealings, and as much as in us lies to follow peace with all men, but to overcome evil by good; to forgive our enemies.[a] Ye have heard, says our Saviour, this law *Thou shalt love thy neighbour,* misinterpreted, as if it meant, Thou shalt love thy neighbour, and hate thine enemy. But I say unto you, "love your enemies, bless them that curse you, do good to them that hate you, and pray for them which despitefully use you and persecute you, that ye may be the children of your Father which is in heaven; for he maketh the sun to rise on the evil and on the good, and sendeth rain on the just and on the unjust: for if ye love them which love you, what reward have you? what merit have you, or what extraordinary reward do you deserve? do not even the publicans the same? It is no more than what is generally done by persons of the lowest character, persons of very little virtue. And if ye salute your brethren only, if ye be kind and friendly only to those who are the same to you, what do you more than others? Do not even the publicans do so? This is no more than what the worst of men think themselves bound to do in common gratitude. Be ye therefore perfect, even as your father which is in heaven is perfect:

a. *Matt.* v. 43.

be ye merciful even as your father which is in heaven is merciful: let your charity and well-doing extend itself universally, in imitation of the divine goodness, which is the greatest excellence and perfection of God." Now, however much this precept, and others having the <356> same meaning, have been carped at, yet if the obligation to benevolence be owned, then must these precepts likewise be confessed to be obligatory. Benevolence comprehends them. For surely, if benevolence be obligatory, all malice and revenge which are directly opposite to it, must be forbidden. But what is it, not to indulge malice and revenge, but to moderate our resentment, and to extend our good-will even to the unthankful, even to our enemies? When we consider ourselves as creatures liable to many defects and faults, we must certainly think it reasonable that others should consider themselves as the same, and shew compassion, indulgence and tenderness to us. When we have failed in our duty to our neighbour, do we not think it fit and equitable, or due to human nature, that we should be forgiven when we return to a sense of our fault, and are willing to make all the reparation or satisfaction in our power; and that forgiving instead of avenging is a noble and highly approveable part? In fine, do we not in general, look upon man as the proper object of good-will, whatever his faults be, when they respect others? But, as an excellent writer observes,[a] if all this be true, what can a man say who will dispute the reasonableness or the possibility of obeying the divine precept we are now considering. Let him speak out, and it must be thus he will speak. "Mankind, *i.e.* a creature defective and faulty, is the proper object of good-will, whatever his faults are, when they respect others, but not when they respect me myself." Now, that man should be affected in this manner, and act accordingly, is to be accounted for like other vices; but to assert that it ought, and must be thus, is self-partiality posses'd of the very understanding. Thus love to our enemies, and those who have been injurious to us, is so far from being *rant,* as it hath been profanely called, that it is in truth the law of our nature, and what every one must see and own, who is not quite blinded with <357> self-love.

a. Dr. *Butler*'s Sermons. [The question Turnbull ascribes to Butler is answered by Butler *in extenso* in Sermons XI and XII, "Upon the Love of Our Neighbour," in *Works,* vol. 2.]

The same author observes, that as God Almighty foresaw the irregularities and disorders, both natural and moral, which would happen in this state of things, he hath generously made some provision against them, by giving us several passions and affections, which arise from, or whose objects are those disorders. Of this sort are fear, resentment, compassion, and others, of which there could be no occasion or use in a perfect state: But in the present we should be exposed to greater inconveniencies without them, tho' there are very considerable ones which they themselves are the occasions of. They are necessary to us here, some of them as a guard against the violent assaults of others, and in our own defence; some in behalf of others; and all of them to put us upon, and to help to carry us through a course of behaviour suitable to our condition. Mankind naturally feel some emotion of the mind against injustice, whoever are the sufferers by it; and even tho' the injurious design be prevented from taking effect. This indignation is natural, and is generally moderate enough in mankind, in each particular man, when the injury which excites it doth not affect himself, or one whom he considers as himself. Therefore the precepts to forgiveness, and to the love of our enemies, do not relate to that general indignation against injury, and the authors of it, but to this feeling or resentment, when raised by private or personal injury. But no man could be thought in earnest who should assert, that tho' indignation against injury, when others are the sufferers, is innocent and just, yet the same indignation against it, when we ourselves are the sufferers, becomes blameable. These precepts therefore cannot be understood to forbid this feeling in the latter case, tho' raised to a higher degree than in the former; because, from the very constitution of our nature, we cannot but have a greater sensibility to what concerns our selves. Therefore these precepts must be understood to forbid only the excesses <358> and abuses of this natural feeling in cases of personal injury. And all these, excepting that of retaliation, do so plainly, in the very terms, express somewhat unreasonable, disproportionate and absurd, as to admit of no shadow of justification. But suppose retaliation innocent, and what would be the consequence? Malice or resentment towards any man hath plainly a tendency to beget the same passion in him who is the object of it, and this again increases it in the other. It is of the very nature of this vice to propagate itself, not only by way of example, which it does in common with other vices, but in a peculiar way of its own; for resentment itself, as well as what is done in consequence of it, is the object of resentment: Hence it comes to pass, that the first offence, when even so slight as presently to be forgotten, becomes the occasion of entering into a long intercourse of ill-offices: neither is it uncommon to see persons in this progress of strife and honour, change parts, and him who was at first the injured person, become more injurious and blameable than the aggressor. Put the case then, that the law of retaliation was universally received as an innocent rule of life; and the observance of it thought by many (and then it would soon come to be thought by all) a point of honour. This supposes every man in private cases, to pass sentence in his own cause; and likewise, that anger or resentment is to be the judge. Thus, from the numberless partialities which we all have for ourselves, every one would often think himself injured when he was not: and in most cases, would represent an injury as much greater than it really is: the imagined dignity of the person offended would scarce ever fail to magnify the offence. And if bare retaliation always begets resentment in the person whom we retaliate, what would that excess do? Add to this, that he likewise has his partiality.—There is no going on to represent this scene of madness: It is manifest there would be no bounds, nor any end. Further, that mankind is a community; that we are all one body; that there is a <359> publick interest of society, which each particular is obliged to promote, is the sum of morals. Consider then the passion of resentment as given to this one body, as given to society. Nothing can be more manifest, than that resentment is to be considered as a secondary passion, placed in us upon supposition, upon account of, and with regard to injury; not, to be sure, to promote and further, but to render it and the inconveniences and miseries arising from it, less and fewer than they would be without this passion. Thus then, the very notion or idea of this passion, as a remedy or prevention of evil, and as in itself a painful means, plainly shews that it ought never to be made use of, but only in order to produce some greater good. The gratification of resentment, if it be not conducive to publick good, must necessarily contradict not only the general obligation to benevolence, but likewise the particular end of that passion itself; because the end for which it was given is to prevent or remedy injury, *i.e.* the misery occasioned by injury, *i.e.* misery itself. And the gratification of it consists in producing misery, *i.e.* in contradicting the end for which it was implanted in our nature. This reasoning is built upon the difference there is between this principle, this passion, and all others. No other principle or passion hath for its end the misery of our fellow creatures. But malice and revenge meditates evil itself; and to do mischief, to be the author of misery, is the very thing which gratifies the passion: This is what it directly tends towards, as its proper design.

Thus therefore, it plainly appears that malice and revenge are contrary to the law of nature; and that it is naturally our duty to moderate our resentment, as benevolence, or regard to the publick good, directs and requires. And accordingly, loving our enemies, and overcoming evil by good, have always been acknowledged by the best ancient moralists[a] to be duties of the law <360> of nature. They are the natural fruits of benevolence, and have ever been recommended as such. After what hath been said, I need not here stay to prove, that the meaning of the christian precepts is not that christian magistrates are to neglect the punishing of malefactors; not that private christians are to forbear bringing publick offenders to justice; not that it is not lawful for men to recover their private just dues, by such methods of law and equity as are in well-regulated countries appointed for the administration of justice; nor that in common life we are, in such a sense, to forgive those who continue to wrong us, as that we needlesly and causelesly trust them, and as it were tempt them to wrong us more: but we are to forgive those who do repent. And those who do not repent, but persist in injuring us, we are to pray for, and be willing to do acts of charity and humanity to them, when need requires; and not to be sollicitous for revenge, but much rather to desire their amendment, and by all reasonable means promote reconciliation: And if at any time we are forced, by the necessity of things, to

a. See *Plato*'s Gorgias, Crito, Repub. 1. Xenophon Mem. Soc. l. 2. [Plato, *Gorgias* 478B–479E, *Crito* 49C–E, *Republic* bk. 1 passim; Xenophon, *Memorabilia*, "Socrates" I.2.]

have recourse to the magistrate to do us right, we are even then to desire only equity for ourselves, and not needless damage and vexation to our adversary. Now forgiveness of injuries, and love to our enemies in this sense, is of the law of nature; for it is equitable that men, conscious of their own weaknesses and passions, and of their aptness to be too soon and too often provoked, should be very ready to forgive, and be reconciled to others. It is dealing with others, as we would think reasonable they should deal with us. It is a desirable temper, for the inward peace and ease of mens own minds, that they should not be under the power of fretful passions, and the lasting resentments of a revengeful spirit; but that they be meek, gentle, peaceable, and easy to be reconciled. This meekness is in a peculiar manner a reward to itself. "The merciful man, saith *Solomon*,[40] doth good to his own soul, but he that is <361> cruel troubleth his own flesh." Nor is it less beneficial to the publick, being the greatest preservative against that beginning of strife which the same wise man elegantly compares to the *letting out of water*. It is also the most effectual way of doing ourselves right, as is implied in the expression, "Be not overcome of evil, but overcome evil with good"[a] for gentleness, meekness, and easiness to forgive, is the most probable way of working upon men, if they be at all capable of amendment. And how can we with any assurance ask or hope for pardon from God, if we are of an unforgiving temper? How can we presume to pray to God that he would graciously forgive our failures, but in the way our Saviour has taught us to pray. "Forgive us our trespasses, as we forgive them that trespass against us." The reasonableness of the condition is well expressed by the son of *Syrach* in a passage already quoted. "He that wrongeth shall find vengeance from the Lord, and he will surely keep his sins in remembrance. Forgive thy neighbour the hurt that he has done thee; so that thy sins also be forgiven when thou prayest. One man beareth hatred against another, and doth he seek pardon of the Lord? He sheweth no mercy to a man which is like himself, and doth he ask forgiveness of his

a. *Rom.* xii. 21.
40. Prov. 11.17.

own sins?"[41] In fine, he who hath not a forgiving temper cannot have benevolence, for benevolence is tender and compassionate, slow to wrath, ready to forbear and forgive; far less is he like to God, whose principal attribute is his mercifulness. Creatures sensible of pain must be offended, provoked, and roused to self-defence by hurt or pain. And creatures who have a sense of virtue and vice, justice and injustice, must feel indignation arise within them against injury or injustice. But God, who hath implanted these useful affections in us, hath likewise implanted in our nature a strong principle of pity and compassion to bridle <362> and restrain them from the excesses into which they would otherwise run. If therefore our resentment is excessive, or goes beyond the bounds necessary to publick good, or to prevent the mischievous consequences of injustice, where is our compassion.—But if our compassion does not work, is not an affection wanting in us, which as naturally hath place in the human constitution as any other? Thus therefore, setting aside all other considerations but the natural texture of the human mind, it is evident from the ballance intended to be preserved amongst our natural affections or passions, that malice and revenge are contrary to nature; or that resentment ought to be mixed with and tempered by compassion. And if we consider ourselves as formed for the imitation of God, and high attainments in virtue, what must our scope be? Must it not be to attain to that which includes in it all the divine perfections, and without which no other of his moral attributes can be conceived, even perfect benevolence? But what is benevolence, when we remove from the idea of it readiness to forgive; nay, goodness even to the obstinately unthankful? This alone is truly divine, or god-like bounty and generosity, to have bowels of pity and compassion towards those who cruelly hate and persecute us. Of this Christ set us a noble example: And who can reflect upon Christ expiring with this divine prayer, "Father forgive them, they know not what they do"; or St. *Stephen,* in imitation of his example, with these generous words, "O God lay not this sin to their charge?" Who can reflect upon these noble acts of benevolence without admiring them; without feeling how much more glorious it is

41. Ecclus. 28.1–4.

to forgive than to revenge? In truth, no man is so lost to humanity, and to all sense of the beauty of virtue, but he must admire and approve the forgiving, generous temper; hate the revengeful, cruel, unrelenting, unforgiving one, and esteem the conquest of passion and resentment as greater, more heroick, more noble and praise-<363>worthy, than the conquest of a kingdom. "He that ruleth or conquereth his own passions, says the wise man, is greater than he who taketh a city." Without love to mankind, and sincere ardent regard to publick good, there can be no such thing as true heroism: without benevolence and generosity, courage is cruelty. And therefore, in the opinion of all wise men even among the heathens, those who are vulgarly called heroes, were reputed ravagers and destroyers of mankind; savage, blood-thirsty monsters. The meekness, the gentleness, the forgiving spirit, the generous beneficence even to the ungrateful, recommended by christianity, is not a mean, submissive dastardly temper, but true goodness, nay, true greatness of mind, and it is so natural to mankind, that it is properly called humanity.

III. Let us proceed to consider whether the christian morality is deficient in any respect; leaves out, excludes or overlooks any virtue. Now, so particular are the precepts of the christian institution with regard to relative duties, that it seems needless to prove to any who are acquainted with it, that these cannot be more particularly or fully explained and enforced than they are by it: yet it hath been objected that those which are rank'd among the most heroic virtues among moralists, are no essential parts of christian charity; namely, private friendship, and the love of our country.

Now, in answer to this censure upon christianity, a most excellent writer[a] hath observed, 1. "Universal benevolence is the supreme law to all rational beings, a law of eternal and immutable obligation, the authority of which ought not to be superseded, limited, or in the least weakened, by any selfish or partial affections. For if there be any beauty and amiableness at all in doing good, the more extended our views are, it must be so much the more meritorious and honourable; and <364>

a. Mr. *Foster* in his admirable Sermons, whose reasoning I here abridge. [James Foster, Sermon 3, in *Sermons,* 1:51ff.]

consequently, to aim at the universal good must be the highest degree of virtue.—Nothing forms so great and worthy a character.—'Tis indeed the chief part of God's moral rectitude;—and must therefore be the supreme dignity and perfection of man. Again, the happiness of the whole species cannot be too intensely pursued, whereas all other affections are no longer innocent than as they are at least consistent with this; are only virtuous, so far as they directly promote it, but are base and detestable when they interfere with it. 2. To apply this to the case of private friendship. When my regard to my friend is inconsistent with the love I owe my country, and much more with the general good of mankind, to whom all my services are more immediately and strictly due, 'tis an unnatural passion, and ought to be rooted out of the mind; because, were it universally indulged, it would introduce the utmost confusion, and an intire subversion of all order and government. This being the great rule by which we are to determine in all cases concerning the expediency and fitness of private friendships, it follows, that they have nothing truly generous in them, but as they tend to cultivate and improve universal benevolence, and are a natural means to make the whole species happy. For if they are not chosen for this reason because they are best upon the whole, if they are only not contrary to the publick happiness, but have no direct influence to promote it, our views must be mean and selfish; and friendship will become a mere matter of private convenience, or else of humour and fancy; in either of which cases it must be uncertain and variable, as circumstances, opinions and interests alter: or finally, it will be the love of ourselves, *i.e.* of the resemblance of our own way of thinking, dispositions and manners in others; and consequently, nothing like the sublime and heroic virtue for which it has been recommended, and which indeed, it is in itself, so long as 'tis the *medium of universal benevolence.* Again, all <365> friendship, in order to its being truly rational and praise-worthy, must be founded in virtue. For this is the only ground of that esteem and steady confidence which are inseparable from a worthy and generous friendship. 'Tis in this way alone that it can be useful, or in any measure promote the end of every lesser alliance, *viz.* the welfare of the great community of mankind. 'Tis this distinguishes true friendship from the vile cabals of robbers and traitors, men of dark and mischievous designs, who may have all the other characters of it, such as 'similitude of tempers, passions, interests, secrecy, confidence, constancy; nay, a reciprocal tenderness and affection for each other.' And from hence it follows, that the love of a friend must be proportioned to his real merit, otherwise it is foolish and unreasonable partiality; and we ought to prefer every man before him that has really a more excellent and useful character. In our esteem we must necessarily do it, unless our private affection has blinded and perverted our judgments; and there are some cases supposable, in which, if we would not forfeit the glorious character of being the friends of mankind for a little fantastick name of friendship, we must do it in our services too. I may add, there is something in almost all accounts of private friendship, that is in a great measure mechanical. A high esteem of a wise, virtuous and useful character, an ardent zeal to serve our friends, and faithfulness to their interests, is what all may attain to; but the fervour and strength of passion that sometimes mixes with it, what we may call the enthusiasm of friendship, depends very much upon a particular constitution. 'Tis the more gross part.—And if we separate the mechanical part, and all extravagant transports from private friendship, and consider it as a thing that reason may approve and justify, we shall find it is nothing more than the reciprocal esteem and affection of virtuous minds, united by a harmony of inclinations, views and interests, all upright and ge-<366>nerous.—That it never exceeds in any instance the rules of justice, truth and honour,—is always subservient to the great law of universal benevolence;—and valuable, not as 'tis an attachment to private persons, but as a means of promoting the cause of virtue, and the happiness of the world. 3. The same may be said of the love of our country. That it is a rational and virtuous disposition, not merely as it is a regard for a particular part of the species, but as it has a tendency to advance the universal good. For their security against injury and violence, and to answer in the most effectual manner the great end of their benevolent and generous affections, mankind found it necessary to form particular societies. The reason of supporting these voluntary combinations is not only self-defence, but because such a method is for the general good. These two ideas ought never to be separated, because things can't continue in a regular and natural state, but while the good of every part is considered as subordinate to the whole. Now the good of the whole is unquestionably best promoted by every person's having a hearty affection for the society to which he belongs, and a strong zeal for its welfare. This is his immediate concern;—the station and sphere of usefulness that providence has assigned him. The undeniable consequence of which is, that love of one's country is only a rational principle, when it is intirely consistent with, and subservient to the supreme law of universal benevolence. Universal benevolence is infinitely the most exalted and heroic spring of action, because the universal good can't be pursued to an excess; but private friendship, and the love of our country, may be so perverted as to become mischievous and destructive principles. The former is intirely disinterested, and can proceed only from the love of goodness, and consequently is a most god-like disposition: the latter may both spring from little selfish motives, and terminate in a narrow private interest. The former contains every instance of restrain'd <367> and partial affection, and is therefore the whole sum of social virtue; whereas the latter, without more enlarged views than the mere pleasure of a friend, or the welfare of our country, forms a character so far from being eminently good, that it wants the very essentials of goodness.

"This alone, saith our author, is sufficient to vindicate our saviour's scheme of benevolence. But, 4. further, let it be considered, that the christian principle includes both these, so far as they are founded in reason, and have any thing virtuous and praise-worthy in them. Universal benevolence must, in the very nature of the thing, comprehend every species of real benevolence: and a command to promote the general good, necessarily implies all the proper means of doing it; and consequently, every instance of private friendship, and zeal for the interest of particular communities that appears to have this natural tendency. 'Tis no objection against moral discourses, that they lay down chiefly general rules for the right conduct of life; for these alone are eternal and unchangeable morality: and the true application of them to particular cases must be left to every man's own reason, because it depends on a variety of circumstances that alter the expediency of things. General benevolence is a fixed and immutable duty, but friendship is not a strict duty upon all, but, for the most part, a purely voluntary engagement.

"An esteem of good and virtuous characters is always rational, because it is necessarily connected with the love of virtue itself. But this is not the notion of friendship, which is a peculiar relation, form'd by a consent and harmony of minds, as well as founded in virtue; from whence it is an undeniable consequence, that it can't be every man's duty, since it evidently depends on circumstances that are quite out of our power. There are innumerable instances in which persons may find several among their acquaintance, and in the same <368> sphere of life, whom they highly esteem, but not one proper to be chosen for a close and intimate friend: so that the recommending private friendship in the general must have been very absurd, since it is only a rare and accidental obligation, and never falls in the way of a great part of mankind. And besides, it might have been attended with mischievous effects. For the bulk of mankind thinking it a duty of religion, and a necessary branch of sublime heroic virtue, would enter into rash, unconcerted and disagreeable alliances, which must naturally produce a great deal of disorder, and disturb the peace of societies: whereas, while they act upon the principles of universal benevolence, no ill consequences can ensue; and therefore the inculcating this principle only as an essential part of morality, and leaving private friendship to fall in as a branch of it, just as prudence, on a view of all circumstances, directs, is the wisest and best way of instructing mankind. Further, there has been very little need in any age, to put men upon cultivating private friendships, and the love of their country; but rather to give a check to these narrow limited affections, and correct the exorbitancies of them. The experience of our own times, and the history of all ages, is an ample justification of the truth of this remark. Friendships have always been frequent enough;—but of what kind are they? Do they not spring from humour and caprice, from a harmony of odd, whimsical and unaccountable tempers, from singularity and selfishness?—Or are they built upon the solid foundations of honour and virtue? In like manner, zeal for the interest of a particular country is it not universal?—But then, is it truly benevolent and publick-spirited? It is more commonly an absurd and childish prejudice that makes men so extravagantly fond of themselves as to treat all other nations with insolence and contempt. It is a zeal that makes an idol of our country, and is ready to sacrifice even the good of the whole species to it. <369>

"There was no reason then, that our saviour should particularly inculcate these things, to which mankind have so natural a turn, and are so apt to indulge to excess. His great work was to rectify all disorders, and in an especial manner the abuse of good principles, and the extravagancies that arise from it. And this he has effectually done in the case before us, by enforcing the obligations of universal goodness, which will regulate all inferior affections, without destroying them. For the observing this rule, will lead to every instance both of friendship and love of our country that is really amiable and beneficial, and discourage such only of either kind as are unmanly and mischievous. But besides, there was a particular reason, from the circumstances of the world at that time, why the christian religion should not directly recommend the love of our country; for then an affection for particular countries was a *general nusance,* and triumphed over justice and humanity: for it is well known that the *Jews* were so partially fond of their own nation, that they looked upon themselves as the only favourites of heaven; which made them severe and rigid in their censures, and morose and unsocial to all who were not of their religion.—And as for the *Romans,* whose noble lectures of benevolence and generosity are so much boasted of, and their love of their country represented as the very perfection of heroic virtue, they were the plagues and scourges of mankind, and had actually carried their arms and conquests, and together with them terror, slavery and ruin, through the greatest part of the then known world.—Was this now a time to recommend narrow views, and an attachment to particular societies, when the general interest had suffered so much by it? It was rather the way to have destroyed publick benevolence altogether.

"In the last place, he adds, that tho' the christian religion does not, for these weighty reasons, particularly enjoin private friendship, and the love of our country, <370> yet it is a false insinuation, that it has given no encouragement to them. For we have in the character of Christ himself an eminent example of each of these virtues, which is equally binding as an express law, upon all who acknowledge his authority. He chose but twelve persons to be his immediate and constant followers, and one of them he made his friend. Accordingly we read in the history of the New Testament, of the disciple whom *Jesus loved;* whom he always treated with confidence, and particular marks of tenderness and affection.

"And was not his weeping over *Jerusalem* from a sense of its impending ruin, a noble proof of his ardent concern for the publick welfare? Were not all his labours to make his people happy, by reforming their corruptions and vices? Was it not for this that he suffered so many abuses? Nay, did he not even die for the good of his country? I may add to this the example of St. *Paul,* who was so transported by his affection to his country, as to wish that the greatest of evils might befal himself, *even to be accursed from Christ,* if by that means he might be the instrument of preserving and establishing their prosperity.[a] These are instances, than which, if we take in all circumstances, none ever were, or can be more great and heroical: and had they been found among the old *Greeks* or *Romans,* they would have been celebrated with the most laboured and magnificent encomiums."

Thus, we have sufficiently vindicated the christian scheme of morality, by shewing its congruity with the affections and powers naturally belonging to man, and its tendency to raise him to a truly noble degree of perfection. And the following truths are either plainly included in the preceeding reasonings, or do directly follow from them. <371>

Corolary I

We are not merely commanded by christianity to do good, but to love goodness: not merely to do justice, and to act humanely and generously, but to love justice, mercy and bounty. We have implanted in our nature not only all the affections necessary to the private system, or to self-preservation; but all the affections necessary to lead us to right conduct with regard to our kind, or to make us social in our behaviour: and besides, the particular affections of this sort, as compassion, natural affection, resentment against injury, love of reputation, and others, we have likewise, as hath been often observed, a disposition to love and approve goodness. And as the christian precepts to love and approve whatever is praise-worthy and truly commendable, suppose this natural determination in our minds; so they are chiefly to be understood as calls upon

a. *Rom.* ix. 3.

us to cultivate and improve this excellent disposition to its highest perfection: as calls to cultivate and improve to its highest perfection, that
moral judgment, sense or conscience originally placed in us to be our
guide, by which we are necessarily determined to approve virtue, and to
disapprove and abominate vice. 'Tis this faculty that makes a being capable of virtue: other beings who want this sense may be good, because
their affections may stand right; or they may operate naturally in their
just tones and proportions towards the welfare of their species. But in
order to have virtue or merit, a being must have a reflecting capacity, by
which it can discern good and evil; and such a being is only virtuous in
proportion as this discernment is quick, lively, uncorrupted, uniform,
and steady in its influences over him. The foundation of virtue, therefore, lies in preserving this sense intire and unvitiated; that is, in daily
quickening, invigorating and enlarging it by proper exercises; for if it
does not improve, it must <372> degenerate. Such is its nature; nay, such
indeed is the nature of all moral qualities, affections or powers. And so
indeed is it universally throughout all nature; or with regard to natural,
as well as moral qualities. But this hath been often taken notice of.

Corolary II

From the preceeding reasonings, it is obvious that by virtue in the holy
scriptures is meant a continued progress toward moral perfection. That
neither reason nor revelation can require of us absolute and compleat
perfection, an absolute and complete freedom from all sin, is plain, since
scripture, in conjunction with experience, and with the reason of things,
clearly assures us, *that in many things we offend all;* and *that if we say we
have no sin, we deceive ourselves, and the truth is not in us.* Agreeably to
which, and to the known infirmity of the nature of man, holy *Job* declares of himself, "If I justify my self, my own mouth shall condemn
me: if I say I am perfect, it shall also prove me perverse."[a] But the plain
meaning of that degree of improvement in goodness to which the scripture gives the title of perfection, is, 1. An intire uprightness of the in-

a. *Job* ix. 20.

tention and endeavour: an integrity of the heart and affections. Hence uprightness, or integrity and perfection, are promiscuously used in the same sense. "Mark the perfect man, and behold the upright, for the end of that man is peace."[a] The signification is not being free from all frailties and imperfections, which in the present state is impossible, and there can be no obligation to natural impossibilities; but according to the best of our abilities, dedicating ourselves steddily and uniformly to the search of truth, and to the practice of righteousness and benevolence: not serving two masters, not dividing our affections <373> between *God and Mammon,* as the scripture speaks, *i.e.* between the love of sin, and the desire of obeying God's commands, which is the case of those who have but newly begun *to lay the foundation of repentance from dead works;* but sincerely setting ourselves to know and to do the will of God, and to add strength to our sense of duty, and our resolutions to adhere to it. 2. It signifies progress in virtue and goodness, till we have attained such a habit of doing righteousness, or of virtuous living, as that it is become easy and delightful, and in a manner natural to us, without any of that difficulty and reluctance which usually attend the first beginnings of reformation, especially when evil habits are deeply rooted and very inveterate. The progress of virtue is excellently described in the book of *Ecclesiasticus.*[b] "At the first, wisdom will walk with a man by crooked ways, and bring fear and dread upon him, and torment him with her discipline until she may trust his soul, and try him by her laws: then will she return the straight way to him, and comfort him, and he shall inherit her." When a man loves virtue, so as to be able to say with the Psalmist, that his delight is in the law of the Lord; and with our Saviour, that his meat and his drink is to do the will of him that sent him; then he begins to approach towards the angelic state: nay, he becomes partaker, says St. *Peter,* of the divine nature. Now, if we attend to the nature of habits, we will easily perceive how virtuous ones must be formed; or that progress in virtue is gradual advancement, by repeated acts of virtue, to a temper thoroughly virtuous and good. As progress in knowledge of any

a. *Psal.* xxxvii. 37.
b. Chap. iv. 18–20.

sort means daily advances to greater perfection in it, in consequence of continued application, so progress in virtue means daily adding new force to our love of virtue; and virtue in all its exercises, becoming daily by continued application more and more habitual to us. The man <374> who would arrive at virtue to such a degree, as to look upon no evil, no calamity, no distress, not death itself, as any evil, in comparison of the smallest vice, the least immoral indulgence, hath a noble and very high mark to aim at: and till this perfection of virtue is attained to, man is short of the scope he ought to set before him. He is only virtuous in proportion to his endeavours to attain to it; in proportion to his uninterrupted sincere diligence to become so thoroughly good. But what man hath arrived to such a degree of rational vigour in this respect, that he may be called perfect? And how can man attain to it, if he is not steady and indefatigable in his pursuit of it, and in that moral discipline, by perseverance in which it can only be attained? If we read ancient moralists[a] upon the perfection of virtue, and upon the necessity of constant attention to our actions, to our ideas and opinions, to the associations of ideas which naturally form themselves in our minds, and our judgments of things, to our affections and their government, we will not be surprized at what the sacred writings say of contending after virtue, of patient continuance in well-doing, of giving all diligence to add virtue to virtue, to mortify and subdue carnal affections, and to spiritualize our minds, to advance daily in purity, holiness and benevolence, in patience, fortitude, publick spirit, and the love of God. And indeed if we look into our own constitution, and the state of the world, we must perceive that the moral rectitude of which human nature is capable, is what cannot be attained to without close and unwearied application to strengthen every affection into the habitual turn and bent which is its perfection; and to work the mind into such a thorough love of goodness as is able to stand proof against all temptation to vice. It is therefore a sincere and vigilant, unintermitted pursuit of moral perfection, which in the scripture is called *perfection*. 3. Now, in the third place, he who is engaged in

a. *Marcus Antoninus* in particular. [Marcus Aurelius Antoninus, *Meditations*, III.11 §2.]

this pursuit, far from indulging himself in any known vice, <375> will never think himself sufficiently advanced, but gaining continually a more and more compleat victory over his frailties and infirmities, over the passions which are aptest to prevail over him, and betray him into sin; he will go from *strength to strength,* in the improvement of virtue here, till he appear before God in the perfection of holiness. "He will, with St. *Paul,* never think he has already attained, or is already perfect; but forgetting the things which are behind, and reaching forth unto those things which are before, he will press toward the mark, for the prize of the high calling of God in *Christ Jesus."* [42] And what is this mark and prize to which we are called by God in *Christ Jesus?* The call is, "Be ye perfect as God is perfect; for without holiness no man can see the Lord." He will give all diligence to cleanse himself from all filthiness of the flesh, perfecting holiness in the fear of God. And therefore the path of the just is said to be as the shining light, that shineth more and more unto the perfect day. From hence we may learn in what sense it is that the Scripture says, a good man does not sin, nay, cannot commit sin. "Whosoever is born of God doth not commit sin, says St. *John;* for his seed remaineth in him; and he cannot sin because he is born of God." [a] The whole design of this epistle is to inculcate that great truth upon us, that as God himself is light and love, that is, perfect and unmixed holiness and goodness; so no man who liveth in impurity and wickedness can have fellowship with him. That pretending to know God or love him, without setting one's self seriously to purify himself even as God is pure, is a mere deceit: that all other methods of recommending ourselves to God, besides that one of imitating his moral perfections, are gross impositions upon ourselves; in one word, that there is one only manifest and infallible mark to distinguish between the children of God <376> and the children of the Devil: "Whosoever doth not righteousness is not of God, neither he that loveth not his brother: whosoever is born of God doth not commit sin." *Whosoever is born of God.* This phrase, as we have elsewhere observed, by an easy figure signifies a heavenly disposition of mind, or a temper

a. 1 *John* iii. 9.
42. Phil. 3.12–14.

that assimulates us to God; it is the same as what is called in other places, being *born after the spirit.*[a] One born after the flesh, means a worldly and sensual person, who has wholly given himself up to gratify his bodily appetites, and pursue the sinful enjoyments of this life, instead of making due improvement of his mind by virtuous practice, in order to prepare himself for a better state hereafter. On the contrary, a good man who subdues the irregular appetites of sense, and keeps them in subjection and obedience to the laws of reason, and the spiritual doctrine of christianity, is said *to be born after the spirit, born of God.* The intention of both these phrases is to signify, that true religion, or a just and deep impression of the great truths of morality and religion, which are inculcated upon us by the christian doctrine, makes such an improvement of our nature, so great a change in the disposition and life of a man who has formerly been wicked, that it is not improperly expressed, comparatively speaking, by his being, as it were, born into a new state. Civility and government, learning and good manners, transform the nature of man from savage to humane; and true religion exalts it still higher from humane even to divine. Now, whosoever *is born of God* in this sense, it is said, doth *not commit sin, i.e.* a man who has a just sense of religion and virtue, a just sense and impression of the scripture doctrine concerning God, virtue, and a future state, never allows himself in the habit of any known sin; nor suffers himself to fall into any of those enormous crimes, which <377> being utterly repugnant to all sense of virtue, are expresly said to exclude men from the kingdom of heaven. Sin, in the new testament, most commonly signifies either the habit of vice, or at least (which are equivalent to it in guilt) the acts of some great and glaring crimes: as when our Saviour tells us, he will bid to depart from him all the workers of iniquity:[b] and that whosoever committeth sin is the servant of sin.[c] These phrases plainly denote the general custom or habit; and so likewise do those declarations of the apostles, that the wages of

a. *Gal.* iv. 29.
b. St. *Luke* xiii. 27.
c. St. *John* viii. 34.

sin is death,[a] and he that committeth sin is of the devil.[b] But we use the word vulgarly in a different signification, and so also does the scripture itself, when it says that all men are sinners, and none righteous. The meaning of which, and the like expressions in some places, is to signify the great corruption of the generality of men at some particular time or place. Thus, when we read,[c] "God saw the wickedness of man was great in the earth, and that every imagination of the thoughts of his heart was evil continually," 'tis plain this was not intended for a character of all mankind, at all times, and in all places, but of the generality of those who then lived. Thus, when St. *Paul* affirms, that the scripture has concluded all under sin,[d] and that all have sinned and come short of the glory of God; his intention is not to give a character of every individual person in particular, but to declare in general the prevailing corruption of the *Jews,* as well as the *Gentiles.* In other places, the like manner of expression signifies, that no man is free from failings and imperfections, from infirmities, surprizes and inadvertencies. In this sense it is, that St. *James* confesses that in many things we offend all;[e] and St. *John* declares, if we say we have no sin we deceive ourselves.[f] To commit sin, in the scripture sense, signifies to be know-<378>ingly and deliberately a worker of unrighteousness; to continue in the habitual practice of any vice whatever; or to commit any of the greater and more enormous crimes; such crimes as are evidently contrary to reason, and to the plain design of the sacred scriptures, and absolutely inconsistent with any sense of, or regard to virtue. Whosoever is born of God, or hath just notions and impressions of religion, of the religion of Jesus Christ in particular, doth not at all commit sin in that sense.

The reason is given. *For his seed remaineth in him.* The word of God in scripture is called the *seed,* the *good seed.* So our Saviour calls it in the

a. *Rom.* vi. 23.
b. 1 *John* iii. 8.
c. *Gen.* vi. 5.
d. *Gal.* iii. 22.
e. St. *James* iii. 2.
f. 1 *John* i. 8.

parable of the sower.[a] And those who are persuaded by the doctrine of the gospel to amend their lives, and to study holiness, are said to be born again, not of corruptible seed, but of incorruptible, even by the word of God, which liveth and abideth for ever.[b] The meaning is, whosoever is a true christian, the motives and arguments to the study of virtue are thoroughly embraced by him and fix'd in him; and, like good seed, is fruitful, bringing forth the fruits of the spirit, or all the moral virtues, righteousness, temperance, benevolence, fortitude, and perseverence in holiness.

It is said such cannot sin. Now *cannot* in scripture, as well as in common use, signifies most frequently not any absolute natural impossibility, but what morally speaking cannot happen, what cannot be done without great difficulty, what cannot be done without forfeiting a man's character, and ceasing to be what he was. So that when the apostle affirms whosoever is born of God cannot commit sin, his meaning is not that there is any impossibility of his turning, but that he cannot sin without ceasing to be what he was, without forfeiting his character of being born of God, without becoming corrupt, and losing his sense of duty, and <379> that vital principle of virtue which once actuated him; even as we say a just man cannot deceive. Our Saviour says, a good tree cannot bring forth bad fruit; and no more can one who hath a true sense of God, and the obligations to virtue remaining firm in him, live in the habitual practice of any known sin. If he does, he forfeits his character, and has no longer any title to the character of *a child of God*, unless he recovers himself again by a repentance, as exemplary as his fall, from so excellent a state was scandalous. As man cannot arrive at great strength in virtue but by degrees; so a man cannot degenerate from it but gradually. And while a sense of virtue is alive, it must operate; it must be continually improving, like the good seed, which being sown in a proper and well manured soil, bringeth forth its fruits, and ripens into mature harvest. In proportion as one grows in grace, in wisdom, in virtue, the seeds of virtue, wisdom and grace are lively in him. And in proportion

a. St. *Luke* viii. 5, 11.
b. 1 *Peter* i. 23.

as he degenerates into vice, or becomes fruitless or barren in good works, the seeds of piety and virtue are become dead in him. The connexion in morals is the same as in nature. Nor can the progress of virtue be more significantly illustrated to us than by that resemblance the scripture so often makes use of, taken from good seed. Principles of virtue are the moral seed, good affections and actions are its fruits, and perfected habits of virtue are its maturity, its harvest; and the culture of the mind, in order to attain to good habits, must be as constant and uninterrupted as the care of the husbandman about his vineyard or garden.

COROLARY III

From the preceding reasonings it plainly follows, that all positive and ritual observances must be subordinate to the practice of moral virtues. The latter is the end, and the former can be considered only as <380> the means to the latter, and therefore are only valuable in proportion to their conduciveness to that end. This is too evident to be insisted upon. And it is the express doctrine of christianity concerning the few positive duties commanded or recommended by it.[a] Certain duties of a moral nature, that is, resulting from certain relations of beings to one another, may be only discoverable by revelation. But such duties cannot be called positive in any other sense, but that the discovery of the relation upon which they are founded, or from which they naturally and necessarily arise, is owing intirely to revelation, and could not have been made without it. The relation being known, the duties resulting from it are deducible from it by reason, in the same way that other duties are inferred from relations known without revelation, or by experience and reasoning from experience. And therefore the relation being known, such duties are moral duties, which differ from other moral duties in no other respect, but that the relations whence they result are not known in the same way that the relations are known whence other moral duties are inferred, but are relations made known to us merely by revelation. But

a. See these few positive duties vindicated, in my *Enquiry concerning the connexion between the doctrines and works of Jesus Christ.*

it is sufficient to my purpose to have just suggested this observation; my design not being to enquire further into christianity, than to discover what it represents to us as the chief end of man; or in what it places the perfection of virtue and goodness. Now, our Saviour and his apostles often declare to us in the strongest terms, that they who place religion in any thing else but virtue deceive themselves: that nothing else can recommend us to the divine favour, or prepare us for eternal happiness in another life. Many passages to this effect have been already quoted, I shall therefore only add two more. "Lay apart, says St. *James*,[a] all filthiness and super-<381>fluity of naughtiness, and receive with meekness the engrafted word, which is able to save your souls; but be ye doers of the word, and not hearers only, deceiving your selves. For if any man be a hearer of the word and not a doer, he is like unto a man beholding his natural face in a glass. For he beholdeth himself and goeth away, and straightway forgetteth what manner of man he was; but whoso looketh into the perfect law of liberty, and continueth therein, not being a forgetful hearer but a doer of the word, that man shall be blessed in his deed. If any man amongst you seem to be religious, and bridleth not his tongue, this man's religion is vain. Pure religion and undefiled before God and the Father is this, to visit the fatherless and widows, and to keep himself unspotted from the world." And our Saviour himself expresly declares,[b] "The sabbath was made for man, and not man for the sabbath." The plain meaning of which assertion is, that all duties of a ritual nature and positive appointment are subordinate to moral duties, and only commanded for the present use of man, to be subservient and assisting to the more convenient practice of the duties of religion, of perpetual and indispensable obligation. That it must be so in the nature of things, is as evident as that the perfection of a reasonable creature must consist in the perfection of his moral powers; and that means to promote his perfection can only be of use or value in proportion as they contribute toward that end. And shall it be reckoned an absurdity in every case but

a. *James* i. 21, *&c.*
b. *Mark* ii. 27.

that alone, which is of the greatest importance, to rest in the means? <382>

Corolary IV

From the preceeding account of virtue, it is manifest, that it is represented in the sacred writings to be a progress towards a future state, in which virtue shall have its full reward. It is called, Laying up treasures to ourselves in heaven,—Laying a foundation for eternal happiness,—Being rich towards God,—Rich in the fruits of eternal, incorruptible life,—The fruits of immortality,—Pressing forward toward the perfection, to which suitable endeavours to improve in virtue shall attain in the life to come. And in the progress toward the perfection in holiness and virtue, which the scripture sets before us, as the scope man ought to set before him, and as the glorious end which all shall attain to, who, by patient continuance in well-doing, seek for glory, honour, and immortality; we are commanded to keep our eye always on that noble issue of our labours, and to comfort and animate ourselves with that cheerful blissful hope. Now, sure, none will pretend, that such a hope must not be a very strong incentive to diligent, unwearied, undaunted perseverance in virtue. And that none can be encouraged, animated, or excited by the scripture account of a future state, but those who sincerely love virtue, will appear when we come to consider the scripture account of a future state. Mean time, let us but consider which of these two is the most consistent idea of the present state of things; to suppose man furnished as he is for progress in virtue, and to receive happiness from virtuous exercises, to perish at death with his body; or to consider him as furnished for virtue, or virtuous happiness, as he is, in order to improve in virtue for ever, in proportion to his care to advance in it; and to receive greater happiness in another life from virtuous exercises, than the present circumstances of mankind admit of; which are, however, very proper for the education, trial, and improvement of virtue? One surely needs not ask which of these two is <383> the most comfortable opinion. And that the one gives us a consistent view of the whole of nature, and the other gives such a view of the moral world as we can neither reconcile with the notion of an infinitely good creator and governor, nor with the manifold instances we every where see of wisdom and goodness in his administration, is no less evident. Let us now proceed to compare the scripture account of a future state with reason and experience.

The scripture account of a future state compared with reason and experience.

We have of necessity anticipated, in a great measure, the scripture doctrine concerning a future state, in discoursing upon the former heads; so that it will be sufficient to add to what hath been said, some few illustrations on the following propositions, in order to shew, that as they are the doctrines of christianity, so they are exactly agreeable to what experience, analogy, and reason teach us with relation to an after-life.

Let it only be premised, that if the gospel of Jesus Christ does really pretend to be the doctrine of a future state, or to have brought life and immortality to light, it must be highly unreasonable not to give it a fair hearing and examination. If one is absolutely unconcerned about his interest and happiness, the end of his present situation, and what is to happen to him after this life; if one is heedless, and takes no thought about these momentous enquiries, does he deserve to be called a rational being? But how can one be concerned about his interest and happiness, and yet be indifferent with re-<384>spect to a doctrine which pretends to set not only his present, but his future, his eternal happiness in a satisfying light; or to give a clear and satisfactory account of his way not only to the present greatest felicity, but to immortal glory and blessedness? Now this is what the gospel of Jesus Christ pretends to do. It must therefore be worthy of our most serious attention and impartial scrutiny; or immortal happiness is an object of no moment, which surely no person can be so absurd as to assert. The christian religion doth not exact a blind, precipitant, implicit reception: it only requires, that we should give it such a fair trial, and diligent examination, as the importance of its pretentions evidently makes highly reasonable. Let those, therefore, who having opportunities of being instructed in the gospel of Christ, and the evidences of its truth, quite overlook, neglect, or despise it; let them consider what it is they despise, or refuse to give due attention to. They neglect and despise a doctrine, which, most certainly, merits their examination, if any thing can deserve it. They neglect and despise a doctrine which profers them instruction in matters of the last consequence to them; instruction in life and immortality: *i.e.* instruction in the way to eternal felicity. I am afterwards to consider the evidences, the plain and full, the truly philosophical evidences which *the christian doctrine* carries along with it of its truth *as such*. But in order to excite all thinking persons to enquire honestly and candidly into those evidences, I am now to shew that the gospel of Christ gives an account of a future immortal state that must be acknowledged to merit the attention of every one who desireth happiness, or who cannot approve to himself absolute indifference about his highest concerns, which no reasonable being can. For is it possible that any person who can reason, or think at all, should say, that a doctrine which pretends to make discoveries to us about our greatest interest, does not deserve an impartial attentive audience, an unbyassed and careful <385> examination? And yet, this is all that christianity requires of those to whom it is proffer'd: christianity, which pretends to have brought *life and immortality to light*.

Before we enter upon the grave and momentous enquiry now proposed, it is proper to make this preliminary observation.

A PRELIMINARY PROPOSITION

Nothing can be explained or made intelligible to any beings, which hath not some analogy or likeness to their present state: wherefore, so far only can our future state be laid open, or discovered to us by revelation, as it bears an analogy or likeness to our present condition and circumstances.

All our ideas or conceptions are and must be derived from experience, and analogy to experience. In other words, we cannot form or receive any notion, but either by immediate experience, or by analogy to such ideas as we have received by experience. As we could have no notion of colours and their various modifications, nor of any thing resembling them, had we never received these ideas from without; so is it, in like manner, with regard to all our other perceptions, into whatever classes they are distinguished: they are all of them ultimately owing to experience: and we can have no new ones till we have new experience. Were not we ourselves reflecting, rational beings, we could never have had any idea of rational powers, and their operations. And we cannot form to ourselves any notion of other rational beings, but by ascribing to them powers and operations of powers analogous to those we experience in ourselves. We can frame ideas of beings inferior to us, by imagining them possessed of some of the powers belonging to us, in an inferior degree. And as we can, in that manner, form to ourselves notions of very <386> various orders of beings inferior to man, rising, as it were by steps, nearer and nearer to the qualities and sphere of activity, which constitute us what we really are, or our rank and dignity in nature; so, on the other hand, we are able to form conceptions of various orders of beings ascending above mankind in a regular gradation, by supposing them endued with powers analogous to our rational faculties, in different degrees of perfection superior to us. We can thus by imagining powers like to our rational powers, rising one above another in various degrees of perfection, ascend to the idea of an infinitely perfect mind; the source of all created or derived power and perfection, in whom all excellencies meet and are united in their most perfect degree. But how is it we are able to do this, but by conceiving all the intelligent powers we are endued with, and all the perfections we are thereby enabled to acquire, belonging to the first author of all power and perfection, in a way absolutely removed from all imperfection and limitation. In fine, our ideas, the materials of all our knowledge or reasoning, cannot, as all philosophers agree, extend beyond our experience.

Now, from this obvious acknowledged truth, it is manifest, that no rational being, however superior to man, can make his own state known to us any farther than that state bears an analogy or likeness to our present state, and its laws and connexions. And for the same reason, the nature, circumstances, laws and connexions of our future state can no farther be declared, explained, or made intelligible to us at present by any being, however superior to us in the knowledge of nature and providence, than it is analogous or like to our present state. It can only be described to us so far as we are able to conceive or take ideas of it by the help of present experience; for our ideas cannot reach beyond the boundaries of our present experience: it can therefore only be so far described to us as it really hath any similitude to our present state; so far only as analo- <387>gy to present experience can furnish us with ideas or images of it.

This being certain, beyond all possibility of doubt, these two inferences plainly follow.

COROLARY I

Hence it is plain, that a future state, being a new one, or a very different one from the present, which can only be similar or like to it in a few general respects, it can only be positively revealed, *i.e.* discovered or made known to us here in the few general respects, in which it is analogous or like to the present state of mankind. If we are to have there new ideas, new materials of knowledge, a new sphere of activity; if we are to have new experience; or, in other words, if there are to be any absolute differences between our future and present state, these differences, or whatever is absolutely new in it, cannot now be discover'd to us in a positive manner; no more than the ideas of light and colours can be to a blind man.

COROLARY II

Hence it follows, in the second place, that in any account that can be given to us here of our future state, the greater number of truths discovered about it must run in a negative strain, or be merely negative propositions. A positive account of a state different from our present situation and circumstances can only be given us, so far as it is not different; so far as it is not absolutely new. The laws, the connexions, the circumstances, which are new, or different, can only be explained negatively. If, therefore, our future state be really a very new, a very different one, which is only analogous to our present condition in a few general respects, the positive account of it cannot reach beyond these few general respects in which it is analogous to our pre-<388>sent; and the account given of it must chiefly run in the negative way, by telling us, that it is not like to the present in such and such respects. I shall not stay to observe what all who are acquainted with the sciences will readily grant, *viz.* that a very considerable part of what is called science is but negative knowledge. It is sufficient to my present purpose to remark, that to object against a revelation, that most of the doctrines in it concerning our future state are but negative propositions, would be in reality to object against a revelation, because an account is not given by it of a future state, which cannot in the nature of things be given.

But having just suggested these general objections, I now proceed to shew, that the account given by the christian doctrine of a future state is very full, and very satisfactory, and comfortable. And as we advance in this discourse, it will plainly appear, that even the negative accounts which christianity gives us of a future state are of the highest moment, and do by themselves make up a very important discovery concerning it.

PROPOSITION I

The thinking part of man does not perish at death, but is immortal.

That the thinking part of man does not perish at death, but endures for ever, is plainly imply'd in what the scripture says of our entrance after death into a state of rewards and punishments. There are not, indeed, any formal reasonings in the books of revelation to prove the immortality of human souls; but it plainly asserts a future eternal state after death: and therefore assumes to itself the title of the doctrine of eternal life; the doctrine of immortality.[a] Our Saviour exhorts his disciples not to suffer themselves to <389> be terrified by powerful, violent men into that which is displeasing to God, because though they can kill the body,

a. 2 *Tim.* i. 10. 1 *John* v. 11.

they cannot *destroy the soul*.[a] And in the epistle to the *Hebrews*[b] we are
told, it is appointed unto men once to die, but *after this the judgment*.
And[c] the same apostle tells us, that though in this life we continue not,
yet after this life there is *a continuing city*, a continuing state. "We have
no continuing city here, but *we seek one to come*." And to cite no more
passages to prove a point which none, who are acquainted with the scriptures, can call into question, St. *Paul*,[d] in his epistle to the *Thessalonians*,
thus comforts them; "Christ died for us, that whether we wake or sleep
we should live together with him: Wherefore, comfort yourselves together, and edify one another, even as also ye do." It hath been disputed,
whether the doctrine of a future state made any part of the *Jewish* dispensation or revelation. But whatever be determined as to that point, it
is beyond all doubt, that a future state was known to the *Jews;* or, that
they generally believed the immortality of the soul, and an after-state of
rewards and punishments, immediately succeeding to this state of moral
trial and discipline. And, indeed, mankind, in all ages and countries,
have been universally persuaded of this truth. But having sufficiently
enlarged upon this important article in the *principles of moral philosophy*,
let me only observe, 1. That christianity is said to have brought life and
immortality to light, not as containing arguments from the attributes of
God, and the nature of moral agents, to prove it, but because it assures
us of the immortality of human souls and a future state, by another kind
of evidence, which shall afterwards be explained; and gives us a very
satisfactory view of a future life, as we shall immediately see. 2. In truth,
the hope of a fu-<390>ture life natural to all men, is itself a sufficient
proof that there is a future life. For whence could this universal hope,
which is so noble an incentive to great actions; which so exalts and ennobles, or greatens the human mind in proportion to its steady prevalence; *i.e.* in proportion as it is exercised and indulged,—whence could
it come?—or to what other origine can it be attributed, but to the kind

a. *Mat.* x. 28.
b. *Heb.* ix. 27.
c. *Heb.* xiii. 14.
d. 1 *Thess.* v. 10–11.

care of heaven to give us a presentiment of our being designed for a
greater, a nobler end than merely to exist a few years in this our present
sphere, and then to perish for ever? But if it really takes its rise from an
instinct or anticipation so implanted in us, it is a hope which cannot
deceive us;—on the contrary, it is a hope which was intended to excite
and animate us to live as becomes beings of celestial birth, and made to
acquire to ourselves immortal honour and happiness in a future state;
and to comfort and uphold us under all the discouragements or oppositions our adherence to virtue, truth, and goodness may now meet with
while it is in its probationary state. 3. And how can those, who believe
an infinitely wise and good providence, ever allow themselves to imagine,
that any being perishes, or is annihilated? The question about our immortality is commonly so stated, as if it meant to enquire by what special
marks or arguments we men can prove, that we are not to be annihilated,
after having been allowed to exist for some little time, since all other
beings within our ken cease to be, or are destroy'd:—It is stated, as if
the enquiry was concerning evidence for some peculiar grant, or charter,
to us of immortality. But in reality, a providence being admitted, the
only remaining question is in general, whether there be any reason to
apprehend that any beings perish, or are destroy'd. And a providence
being supposed, that question can hardly bear any dispute: for we not
only see no instances of a destroying disposition in nature, so far as we
are able to pry into its revolutions and changes; but if the words <391>
justice and goodness have any meaning in the mouths of men, we cannot
but conclude it to be not merely ungenerous, but unjust to destroy any
being, any perceptive being,—and *a fortiori,* to destroy beings of a moral
or rational kind. We can conceive a consistency between good government, and the gradual rise or progress of beings: we can likewise conceive
a consistency between good administration, and the gradual sinking of
beings, or their powers, according to certain laws of improvement and
degeneracy.—And of all this we see examples in nature. But we clearly
see an inconsistency between the wilful positive destruction of perceptive beings and benevolence: and we see no instances of such destruction
in nature. If the government of the world be good, (and what is it that
we fully know of nature which does not proclaim boundless, pure good-

ness?)—If the government of the world, I say, be good, no being can ever be destroyed; for that cannot be done, but because the greater good of the whole requires such destruction. But tho' the greater good of the whole may require gradual rising and sinking of moral powers, according to certain laws, yet it can never require the destruction of any being, unless to annihilate a certain quantity of capacity for happiness can be necessary to make a greater quantity of happiness, or greater good in the whole, which is a downright contradiction. For the quantity or sum total of capacity for happiness being lessened, the quantity of attainable happiness must of necessity be lessened. 4. If we consider man in particular, the only thing that can create any suspicion with regard to his subsistence, after what appears to us so terrible a shock, death, is this, that in this state our thinking powers have a very great dependence upon the laws of matter and motion, insomuch that certain bodily accidents make very dismal changes upon them. But there is ground to presume, that were the phenomena of that kind carefully collected and ranged, there <392> would remain no foundation for doubting about our immortality on that score; because, there are many instances of dying by diseases which gradually consume the body, while at the same time moral faculties remain intire, untouched, unviolated, nay, wax stronger and more vigorous; and there are many instances of emerging out of diseases, by which moral powers had been sadly depressed, to former vigour of understanding and virtue: And as we know that there can be no communication with a corporeal world, without subjection to its laws to some certain degree and extent; (because, being variously affected by the operations of the laws of a corporeal world, *i.e.* well by some, and ill by others, is implied in the very notion of union or communion with it;) so we likewise find, that the further we are able to carry our researches into the laws of our present corporeal state, or our present union with bodies, and by that means with a sensible world, the more and clearer evidences we perceive of the wisdom, fitness and goodness of these laws in various respects. Further, since it is evident, and is indeed acknowledged by all philosophers, that the connexions between different sensible qualities are arbitrary, or must be ultimately resolved into the will of the creating mind appointing them for wise and good ends; that it is mind alone that can properly be said to exist; and that all the ideas a mind receives from without, are conveyed into it by laws of arbitrary institution, or according to an order of positive establishment for good ends; since all this is so evident, that it is not disputed by any philosopher, it plainly follows, that whatever connexions may now take place between mind and body, or however the former may be affected by the latter, yet all these connexions and influences are arbitrary, and consequently may cease to take place, and yet mind or moral powers may continue in full vigour, fit for exercise independent of such connexions, or to be influenced and affected by connexions of a quite different nature. <393> Wherefore, all the arguments taken from the consideration of our moral powers, together with the moral attributes of the Creator and Governor of the world, to prove the immortality of our moral powers, have the same force as if no such connexions between our bodies and minds, as now take place, did subsist. That is, whatever probability or certainty, whatever degree of evidence results from the consideration of the manifold tokens we every where perceive of the wisdom and goodness of providence, that no beings capable of happiness, and much less moral beings, capable of moral, the highest happiness in kind that can be conceived, shall be destroyed; all such evidence remains the same as if there were none of those appearances of that strict intimate connexion with, and close dependence upon the laws of matter and motion in our present state, whence all doubts about our immortality are derived. In fine, the phenomena relating to our moral powers, and their dependence on matter and motion, what do they amount to but an arbitrary dependence, which produces many very good effects while it lasts, and which cannot last always: And therefore it is so far from being repugnant to the idea of good administration, when it is not considered as the only state the moral powers thus subjected, are to be placed in, that it is itself considered as but the first state of those moral powers, exceedingly agreeable to such an idea: whereas, on the other hand, what can be more opposite to all the signs of wisdom and good government we every where meet with in the world, and to all notions of divine benevolence, nay, of ordinary goodness, than to suppose any perceptive beings to be wilfully destroyed, any degree of capacity for happiness to be annihilated? Either we understand what wisdom and goodness mean, and may reason about these ideas, or they are words without any signification, and we cannot reason at all about any such ideas as these words seem to import. But if we can reason with any certainty at all about these ideas, we may rest satisfied, <394> that the rising or progress of perceptive beings to higher capacities; and the advancement of moral agents in moral perfection, in proportion to their care to cultivate and improve their rational faculties, the necessary opposite to which is sinking in consequence of neglect and abuse, are essentially involved, in the very idea of a good whole, or of perfect administration. We cannot otherwise give any coherent account or explication to ourselves of what would deserve to be called good administration, or of that government of the universe which we are led to apprehend, by whatever appearances we perceive to be tokens of wisdom and benevolence, and naturally rejoice in as such. But when we thus represent nature, or the universe to ourselves, all is agreeable, pleasant, consistent, harmonious; we comprehend it clearly to deserve the character of perfectly wise, kindly, generous: The worst appearances admit a solution on this supposition: And upon the contrary hypothesis, appearances in nature are the more unaccountable, in proportion to their seeming wisdom and goodness; because they evidently point out wisdom and goodness, which, were they what they have all the appearance of being, any instances of good and wise management can suggest to those who see not the whole of things, would certainly operate in a way directly opposite to what is supposed, when beings are imagined to be wilfully destroyed. This reasoning does not barely mean, that it is impossible for a benevolent mind to discover instances of wise and good administration, as far as it can carry its enquiries; especially in those things, which at first sight, or till they were more fully canvassed and understood, appeared very irregular and exceptionable, without being disposed to believe the government of the universe thoroughly perfect; but this reasoning means further, that as there is no reason to infer any thing but the most perfect administration, from samples of wisdom and goodness in the government of the world; so he who <395> hath, from whatever arguments, once inferred a divine providence over-ruling all things, must, of necessity, acknowledge the immortality of all perceptive beings;

it being impossible to frame a clear consistent idea of good government, without so conceiving of all beings. But having elsewhere insisted at full length upon the arguments for our future existence, I shall now pass to another proposition. Let me only add, that the christian revelation sets our immortality beyond all doubt, the chief intent of it being to excite to the practice of virtue here, as laying a foundation for our perfection and happiness in an immortal state, to which death is the transition or entrance; and to give us a just idea of the rewards and punishments, the laws and connexions in a future life, so far as is requisite to that excellent end. Now that it does so, will appear when we have considered the ensuing propositions.

PROPOSITION II

Our future state, which immediately succeeds to this life, is a state of rewards and punishments, in which it shall be rendered to every one according to the deeds he hath done in the body, whether they be good or evil.

Not only is a future state asserted in the christian revelation, but this future state is affirmed to be a state of rewards and punishments, *i.e.* as the scripture explains it, a state in which it shall be rendered to every one "according to the deeds he hath done in the body"; according to the deeds done in this present life: a state in which every one shall reap the fruit of his doings, whether good or evil: a state in which he who hath in this life sown to the flesh shall reap corruption, and he who hath sown to the spirit shall reap the fruits of the spirit, the fruits of virtue, the fruits of righteousness, and a well formed mind; the fruits of joy and peace, <396> which virtue alone can give. Thus it is the sacred writings speak in innumerable places.[a] "Be not deceived, says St. *Paul,* God is not mocked": the rule of his government, resulting from his immutable moral rectitude, which cannot therefore be changed nor frustrated is, "That whatever a man soweth in this life, that shall he reap in the life to come. God will then render unto every one according to his doings."

a. See the texts quoted in the introduction to this discourse.

Now, what do these and such like equivalent phrases amount to, but that this present state is our state of education, trial and discipline, to which our succeeding state shall be exactly proportioned and correspondent: Or that as this is the state in which we have opportunity of forming our minds to knowledge and love of virtue, or moral perfection, so our future state shall be correspondent to the state of mind formed and acquired in this our present school of discipline and improvement. The state of our rational powers and affections formed in this state, shall be the rule and measure, the foundation and source of our condition in our succeeding state: our *after-harvest,* as the apostle speaks, shall be answerable to this our *seed-time;* to this our present state of culture. "As we sow, so shall we reap." Harvest cannot precede seed-time. The effect cannot take place before or without the cause. The end cannot prevent the means. The effect of education and culture cannot go before education and culture, or take place without it. The happiness which is the result of a good temper and disposition of soul, of a well-improved mind, of moral perfection, or virtue arrived by proper diligence in improving it to a certain degree of excellence, cannot take place till the mind is well-improved; or is by due exercise and discipline arrived at that degree of moral perfection. But, saith the holy scripture, whatever may be the outward situation of the virtuous mind in this state of education <397> and discipline, yet in a future state, duly improved, virtues shall have their natural and compleat effect, and produce unspeakable happiness, by being then placed in circumstances suited to such perfection, and proper to give it due happiness, by affording it suitable means, occasions, and subjects of exercise. In order to compleat happiness, there must be powers and objects adjusted to one another. Powers cannot make happy, unless there are objects suited to them. Nor can objects make happy, unless there are powers congruous or suitable to them. But virtuous powers, or more properly speaking, powers which render capable of virtuous qualities, and their proper exercises and employments, must be formed and advanced to a perfect state by gradual culture, and the exercises which such gradual improvement require. And therefore, in the nature of things, they cannot receive happiness from objects suited to their perfect state, till they are brought to that state. But when they are arrived, by due culture, to an improved state, which they cannot be brought to previously to culture or probation and discipline, then, saith the scripture, God the righteous judge and governor of the world, will render to virtue according to its perfection; that is, place it in circumstances suited to its improvement. The harvest, in this part of God's government, shall be congruous to the seed-time, correspondent to the husbandry and good culture. Now, what idea can we form of a future state, more agreeable to the perfections of a just, a wise, a benevolent ruler of the world, and more agreeable to the nature of rational creatures, and their powers, than such a future state as hath been described, in which a well-improved mind shall reap the full and compleat harvest of its good sowing, its good culture, its good labours, its noble and glorious acquisitions: a state in which, as the scripture speaks, glory, honour and immortal life shall be rendered to those who by[a] patient <398> continuance in well-doing have sought after, contended for, and rendered themselves capable of the happiness which can only result from highly improved rational faculties; the happiness which can only flow from a pure and sanctified mind; or the empire of reason over all the passions. But if the reward, the recompence, the fruit, the harvest of a well-formed mind, and a well spent life, be joy, peace and happiness; what must be the reward, the fruit, the harvest of an impure corrupted mind, a defiled conscience, a life spent in degrading, abusing and prostituting the powers which constitute the dignity of mankind, and his capacity of moral happiness, instead of refining and exalting ourselves to a capacity and fitness for rational felicity! Must not opposite causes have opposite or contrary effects in the moral as well as the natural world? Can good and evil, happiness and misery spring from the same root? Can virtue, which is the improvement and right use of moral powers, and vice, which is the abuse and corruption of those powers, have the same effect, the same result? Can they produce or terminate in the same harvest? If of two things diametrically contrary one to another, as improvement and degeneracy, virtue and corruption certainly are, the natural fruit, or the just reward of the one, be eternal happiness resulting from moral perfection suitably placed; must not the

a. *Rom.* ii. 7, 8, *&c.*

fruit, the wages, the punishment of the other, be proportionable misery, resulting from deformity, guilt and pollution? The fruit of good seed and good husbandry (to keep to the apostle's excellent similitude) cannot be more different from the fruit and product of corrupt seed and bad husbandry in the natural world, than the ultimate result or harvest of virtue and improved reason must be from that of abused reason and confirmed vice, inveterate corruption. These truths are of great importance, and therefore it is proper to enlarge yet more <399> fully upon them, and for that reason to separate them into several distinct propositions.

Proposition III

The scripture assures us, that in the future state of rewards and punishments, distributive justice is strictly observed.

This is the express doctrine of the holy scriptures in almost innumerable places.

"He cometh to judge the earth: and he shall judge the world with righteousness, and the people with his truth."[a] "If thou sayest, Behold we[b] knew it not: doth not he that pondereth the heart consider it? And he that keepeth thy soul doth not he know it? And shall not he render to every man according to his works?" "God shall bring every secret wish into judgment, with every secret thing, whether it be good, or whether it be evil."[c] "The eyes of God[d] are upon all the ways of the sons of men, to give every one according to his ways, and according to the fruit of his doings." "But we know, says St. *Paul*,[e] that the judgment of God is according to truth. And thinkest thou this, O man, that judgest them which do such things, and dost the same, that thou shalt escape the judg-

---

a. *Ps.* xcvi. 13. xcviii. 9.
b. *Prov.* xxiv. 12.
c. *Eccl.* iii. 17. xii. 14.
d. *Jerem.* xxxii. 19. *Ezek.* xxxiii. 8, 9.
e. *Rom.* ii. 2–6.

ment of God? Or despisest thou the riches of his goodness and forbearance and long suffering, not knowing that the goodness of God leadeth thee to repentance? But after thy hardness and impenitent heart,
treasurest up unto thy self wrath against the day of wrath, *and revelation
of the righteous judgment of God,* who will render to every man according
to his deeds"—For there is no respect of persons with God. So likewise
St. *Peter,*[a] "It is written, Be ye <400> holy for I am holy. And if ye call
on the Father, who without respect of persons judgeth according to every
man's work, pass the time of your sojourning here in fear."

These declarations are very clear and full, and naturally lead every
thinking person to the following reflexions.

I. That as, if the reality of virtue be not owned, justice and righteous
judgment are words without a meaning; so the reality of virtue cannot
be conceived, without concluding, that if the governor of the world be
just, true, righteous, such must the constitution, the frame, and administration of things be, that every moral being shall reap the fruit of his
doings, the proper consequences of his behaviour and conduct: or, in
other words, the frame and government of things must be agreeable to
the essential immutable differences of things, and consequently in favour of virtue; which it cannot be if virtue and vice have the same or
equivalent effects, with regard to happiness and misery in the sum of
things; or if virtue and vice is not distinguished according to its excellence and merit. Justice involves in its idea a regard to a rule in the distribution of things, or in appointing and adjusting their consequences.
If there be no essential difference between virtue and vice, there can be
no rule with regard to the distribution and connexion of things; but if
there be any rule, a just governor must adhere to it in his government.
And what other can that rule be, but regard to virtue, love of it, and
concern about it; care to provide for it, and to honour and reward it
suitably to its excellence? Now this being supposed to be the rule with
regard to virtue, it necessarily follows, that with regard to the opposite
to virtue, opposite conduct must take place. If the constitution of things
be in favour of virtue, it cannot be in favour of vice. If virtue is to be

a. 1 *Pet.* i. 16, 17.

treated according to its excellence, and suitably di-<401>stinguished, vice cannot but be treated in the contrary manner, or suitably to its contrary demerit; that is, it cannot but be the road to misery: it cannot but be attended with consequences correspondent to its natural repugnancy to virtue and good desert. We are too apt to consider the rule of justice only on one side. But we cannot take a full view of it without perceiving, that we cannot affirm positively there is justice in the administration of the world, with respect to virtue, without, at the same time, affirming as positively, that such is the government of the world, that vice must have as bad consequences in it, on the whole, as virtue has good consequences. It cannot be the general law in the government of moral beings, that virtue shall make happy, without being the general law, that vice shall make miserable. These are, in reality but two different views, or rather expressions of the same general law. 2. With regard to punishment in particular, our natural notions of justice necessarily lead us to conceive, that in the government of the world, the consequences designed to be the punishments of vice, are exactly proportioned to the ends of good government, not appointed or inflicted in an arbitrary way, that can only serve to produce pain and misery; but so regulated and adjusted, as the greater good of moral beings in the whole absolutely requires. We reason in this manner concerning vindicative or punishing justice in human society. And if we do not reason in the same manner with regard to vindicative or punishing justice in the government of the world, we quit our sole idea of justice, and utter words without any meaning. But if we thus conceive of justice in the government of the world, we in other words assert, that there will be no punishments in the government of the world, merely for the sake of producing pain or suffering; none but what the great and good end of that government requires; none but what are necessary to virtuous administration; or to a constitution of things, in favour of <402> virtue, and in opposition to vice. 3. Now, if we keep this idea of justice before us, we can never be at a loss to understand any ways of speaking in scripture concerning the punishments of the vitious in a future state, either with respect to intenseness or duration. Because such phrases must be consistent with what is necessarily implied in the justice and righteousness attributed to

God as a governor and judge, in the strongest and clearest terms. But to clear up some difficulties with regard to the scripture doctrine of punishments, it is not amiss to suggest the few following remarks. 1. The punishments threatened to the wicked in scripture, when they are represented under the idea of punishments (I say, under the idea of punishments, because the evils which are to befal the vitious in another state, are often represented to us in scripture under another view, as we shall see afterwards) they are represented to be strictly just, strictly approportioned to ill desert; to be punishments which wise and just government make necessary. God is no where represented as delighting in exercising his power to inflict evil: punishing is on the contrary represented to be his *strange work;* or what he is obliged to by his regard to virtue, and to the great ends of moral government. He is not willing that any should perish, but on the contrary, he wills that all men would act so as that they may have eternal happiness: and the evils sinners draw upon themselves are commensurate to their desert; such as they themselves shall see to be just and equal; the effects of laws and rules necessary to perfect government. Governors of human societies may be tyrants, and delight in cruelty; or may err in their judgments, as well with regard to the general laws of punishment, as with regard to the particular applications of the general laws, without any evil intention, merely through imperfection of knowledge.—But God cannot err in any of these respects,—far less can he act arbitrarily. And what is the consequence of this, but that his judgments, <403> his punishments, must be according to right and truth, agreeable to justice, exactly fitted to serve the great purpose of his administration, which can be nothing else but the greater good of moral beings? Wherefore, nothing can be meant by the phrases expressing the duration, or the kind of future punishments, which is contrary to justice, nothing which is arbitrary or tyrannical. But he who ventures on a sinful life, because he thinks the punishments to be inflicted upon sinners after this life can neither be so intense, nor of such long continuance, as some ways of speaking about them in scripture seem to import,—how must such a person reason with himself, if he believes the reality of virtue, and consequently the reality of God's adherence to the interests of virtue in the government of the world: how must he reason with himself: let him but speak out his meaning clearly to himself, and he will soon cease to be any longer influenced by such unaccountable reasoning. For however he may disguise his reasonings upon this subject, this must ultimately be the meaning of it. "The constitution of things, if it be just, if it be good, it must be in favour of virtue; but surely regard to virtue and its interests cannot make the consequences of vice so extremely fatal as the scripture speaks: 'tis true, the scripture says all the direful consequences of vice are just, are necessary to perfect government; but surely, as odious as vice is, it cannot have so very unhappy effects; and therefore I may venture upon sinful indulgences: I am sure, in a just government, virtue must be fully distinguished from vice; virtue alone can recommend to the divine favour; and vice must have very miserable consequences: I am sure, on the one hand, that there can be no consequences of vice which are not agreeable to justice, to perfect government; but I am as sure, on the other, that under a good administration, virtue only can be the road to rewards, to happiness,—yet I can't think a vicious life will render so intensely and lastingly miserable as the <404> scripture speaks; and therefore, I need not be quite so afraid of continuing in a sinful course as these scripture phrases would make me, did I take them in their severest sense." This, I say, must be the reasoning that passes in his mind who believes the reality of virtue, and of a divine infinitely perfect administration, when he would diminish his fears with respect to his continuance in an irregular, dissolute, vitious course of life.—And what thinking man can approve of such reasoning, or draw any encouragement to sin from it? Can any way of diminishing fears, or solacing one's self, be more weak and unreasonable? And yet this is indeed all it amounts to. If persons do not believe the moral differences of actions, and a divine providence, I am not now reasoning with them. But if they do, how can they possibly draw any consolation to themselves, from an imagination, that tho' the consequences of a vitious life must be very fatal, yet they cannot be such very intense or durable evils as the scripture threatens? Is it a way of arguing with themselves, that they can possibly vindicate? 3. Let it be observed on this head farther, that in whatever phrases the intenseness, the kind, or the duration of punishments in another life are expressed, it is the wicked, the hardened, the impenitent, which are said to suffer them. It is no where said, that moral agents lose their liberty; their moral agency, and cease to be intelligent free beings.—It is no where said, that moral agents are tied to vice by any other setters but those which arise from the power of evil habits, with which wicked men are held so fast entangled, as we see by experience, that they become not merely impotent, but really averse with respect to virtue. But, on the other hand, the scripture, as well as reason assures us, that without virtuous habits there can be no happiness, no reconciliation with God, no attaining to his favour and love. And what is the conclusion from all this, but that the scripture represents to us in the strongest terms, the necessity of <405> virtue in order to happiness, in order to avoid extreme misery, in consequence of the justice and perfection of the divine government, in consequence of the divine moral rectitude, or of his strict regard to the unalterable relations of things; the essential differences between virtue and vice, in consequence of the divine benevolence, or his disposition to promote the moral perfection, and moral happiness of intelligent beings, capable of moral improvements and enjoyments; all these ways of considering providence being, according to the scripture account of God's government or providence, necessarily connected together, if not essentially involved in one another. 4. Let me add, that some of the best ancient moralists, in their representations of, or reasonings about the punishments of a future state, have considered some diseases, *i.e.* some vitious states of the mind, as incurable. *Socrates* says, "The design of wise and just punishments must be, not only to better others, but to better the immediate sufferers: But in cases when the disease being incurable, the latter end cannot be gained, still the former end may make punishments necessary, and will sufficiently justify them."[a] And that excellent philosopher often speaks of the havock vice long continued in makes upon the mind; upon our mental powers, in the most awakening manner. He says oftner than once, "That voluptuousness so dissolves the force of the mind, so putrifies it, that it at last renders it quite incapable of moral exercises." And indeed when we seriously reflect upon the fatal tendency of vitious indulgences in that re-

a. *Plato*'s Gorgias. [Plato, *Gorgias,* 525c.]

spect, we have good reason to tremble at the thoughts of losing the empire of our reason, and suffering evil passions to prevail over it, till it is as it were extinguished by them. I am apt to think the ancient doctrine of the Metempsychosis, was designed as an allegory to express the different direful changes va-<406>rious vices make upon intellectual powers and capacities, and the temper or bent of the mind. But whether that doctrine was so intended or not, it is visible, that if the mind is not daily improving in rational perfection, it is daily sinking; if it is not cultivated, it corrupts.—And some do in this state, through vicious indulgencies of their passions, degenerate into such an utter disrelish of and incapacity for all rational exercises, into such a corrupt vitious disposition, that it seems morally impossible they can ever return to a condition or temperature of mind necessary to moral happiness and perfection, necessary to the gradual improvement such happiness presupposes.—Some indeed become so low, so mean, so sensual, so polluted and others so savage, so bloody, so cruel, so insolent, so ferocious, so malignant, that their degraded condition of mind, or vitiated disposition, cannot be expressed but by likening them to certain brute animals, according to the language of the Metempsychosis system. But not to insist longer on this melancholly subject, I shall conclude this article with observing, that according to reason, as well as scripture, there can be no happiness in a future state without virtuous habits; and the contrary to happiness is misery; and to object against christianity upon account of the strongest declarations of this truth (which is all it can be said to do) is to object against it for inculcating the advantages of virtue, and the danger of vice upon us, in terms that cannot lead us into any mistake about our happiness here or hereafter, while it remains true, "That virtue, and virtue only, can be acceptable to God, recommend to his favour, merit his esteem and love, or produce rational happiness."

III. I proceed to another observation upon the scripture doctrine of a future state of rewards and punishments, which is, that God is said to dispense them *without respect of persons.* Now this expression, so often repeated in scripture, ought to lead us to these <407> following reflexions. 1. That in the dispensation of future rewards and punishments, God the righteous judge, cannot fall into the error human judges may;

which is to be biassed in their sentences or determinations by any partial
regards, by prejudices of any kind, either in favour of persons, or contrariwise. This is a truth too evident to be insisted upon. It is however
worth while to remark, that there was good reason to insist much upon
it to the *Jews,* whose prevailing error it was, that they were in a particular
manner the only favourites of heaven; the only people for whom God
had any regard or love. Nor can we wonder that people should ever have
entertained so gross, so absurd a notion of God, if we reflect, that even
among christians, not a few seem to conceive of God, as having chosen
from among mankind arbitrarily, or without any reason, a particular determinate number of favourites, of elect persons to whom all his bounty
is confined. The *Jews* were distinguished from the other nations of the
earth in so extraordinary a manner, in order to carry on God's scheme,
not of partial, but of universal benevolence, that it may be easily conceived how they came to be puffed up with a very high conceit of themselves above all other nations of mankind, which it was extremely difficult, not only for their own prophets, but for our Saviour and his
apostles to correct. But after christianity hath declared to us in the strongest terms, *that no man, no nation of men, is common or unclean,* i.e. to
be deemed or called such: But that *of a truth,* God is *no respecter of
persons: But in every nation, he that feareth him and worketh righteousness,
is accepted of him:* [a] after this plain declaration, that the favour of God
extended to all men equally; and that his giving a particular revelation,
with other distinguishing privileges, to the *Jews,* was not done out of
any partial regard to them, <408> as earthly kings may distinguish particular favourites to the prejudice of their states in general; but with a
benevolent purpose towards all mankind in general; after this declaration, to imagine contrary to the clear voice of reason, that God hath any
other purpose, or will judge according to any other rule, in the dispensation of future rewards and punishments, besides regard to good and
ill desert, is certainly something extremely unaccountable. 2. But it is
sufficient to have just mentioned that absurdity; and far less need I stay
long to prove, that in the dispensation of future rewards, God will not

a. *Acts* x. 28, 34, 35.

pay any regard to the distinctions of rich and poor, high and ignoble birth, &c. which now take place among mankind. This is so manifest, that it does not stand in need of any illustration. But how happy would it be for the world in general, and for persons of distinction, as they are called, themselves in particular, if they would frequently reflect upon this plain truth. The more obvious it is, the more unaccountable certainly is every sentiment, every behaviour which is not strictly agreeable and correspondent to it. And yet surely pride and insolence, in whatever degree, on the account of temporary external distinctions, are by no means reconcilable with that truth. Thinking men will not find it an easy matter to conciliate certain distinctions which are the sources of most insufferable vanity and arrogance, and by consequence, of great depression and misery in society, with the law of nature; or what must, according to it, be the sole legitimate end of magistracy and government, *viz.* to diffuse happiness, as universally as may be, among mankind. But whatever be as to that, surely it is fit for the distinguished, for the great, as they are called, frequently to reflect, that in the life to come, God the righteous judge cannot pay regard to persons in any other sense but that of personal or real merit; and consequently, those who have had great power, large means in their hands in this life for doing good, <409> have a proportionably large stock to account for. 3. What hath been said of merely external advantages, such as birth and riches, and their concomitants in this life, is equally true of intellectual endowments and acquisitions; that is, God in the dispensation of future rewards and punishments, will not pay regard to the understanding, the imagination, the reasoning faculties and their improvements, as constituting a kind of merit by themselves. For without virtue, *i.e.* without a benevolent disposition reigning in the heart, and submitting every appetite and passion in the soul habitually to the publick order and good of society, there is no merit in the finest imagination, nay, nor the most extensive reach of understanding. Great abilities, without a good heart, must render one in the sight of God exceedingly contemptible; for do they not appear so in the eyes of all good men? And in what community must they not, in the nature of things, be pernicious! What makes it chiefly necessary to dwell a little on this head is this. Men are too apt to place a great deal

of merit in cultivating their imaginations into a fine taste, and in re-
plenishing their understandings with great variety of knowledge; and no
doubt, this is a very worthy employment, and every man's duty in proportion to his circumstances, as we have already had occasion to prove:
But all this we know may be often done to a very high degree, while yet
the heart remains very vitious in many respects; very sensual, very ambitious, nay, very inhuman. For how many men of vast learning, and of
exquisite taste, are yet quite slaves, some to one and some to another very
wicked and unruly appetite? And yet certain it must be, that if the temper be not virtuous, if there is not perfect inward liberty, or self-
command, and an exact government of the passions; *i.e.* if to attain to
virtuous habitudes be not the chief study, such a man is really not a good
man, however many other qualifications he may possess; he is not in the
way to be a partaker of the divine na-<410>ture or temper; he is not in
the way to be like God; or to have that real worth and excellence which
alone can merit his favour and approbation, and the want of which is
indeed highly aggravated in his sight by other mental accomplishments.
This is a plain consequence from what hath been said of the nature of
virtue or moral perfection. And it well deserves our attention, that we
may not lay too great stress upon our care to improve our understandings, as if such care comprehended in it the whole of human duty and
perfection, and could not but qualify for and entitle to great rewards in
another life. All improvements of our intellectual faculties are certainly
very valuable acquisitions, and do fit for high exercises and enjoyments,
when united with virtue, or a well governed mind; but when real merit
and demerit is to be judged in order to be rewarded or punished, they
cannot enter into the consideration in any other view before God, than
as aggravations of guilt, if virtue be wanting; for such just judges
amongst men must account them. 4. God is no respecter of persons, but
will render to every one according to his real desert; according to his
works, whether they be good or bad; according to the character of his
mind: that is, it is virtue and vice that shall then only make the distinction or difference among men: then shall they be fully perceived to make
the only difference among men in the sight of God. Where there is a
right disposition of soul; diligence to improve our understanding in the

knowledge of God and his works, and of moral relations and obligations, and in all useful science, in proportion to its moment or usefulness,
to the utmost of his power, will not be wanting; that will evidently be
perceived to be duty; and it will be constantly and seriously in one's view
as such; but the circumstances of mankind being very different with
respect to the acquisitions of knowledge, as well as the actual exercise of
several virtues, it would be unjust, according to all our notions of justice
and <411> injustice, according to which we must reason, to reward or
punish men in another life according to any other rule, but the virtue
that prevails in the temper of their minds, and their serious disposition
to have improved themselves, and bettered society here, as far as they
could by all their diligence to enlarge their powers and exert them. This
would be unjust; for nothing else depends upon us, or is at our disposal:
all other things are independent of us, and no man can be justly punished or rewarded for what it neither depended upon him to do, nor not
to do. This would be to respect persons in the same sense that we say,
judges on earth respect the persons and not the merits of men. Accordingly the scripture doctrine is, that God will require of men according
to what they have received; according to the stock put into their hands
for improvement and doing good in the world. a"For the kingdom of
heaven, saith our Saviour, the method of God's dispensations and dealings with mankind, which I am come to declare unto you, may be fitly
represented by this similitude: A certain man being to take a long journey
into a far country, divided a stock amongst his servants. Now, to one he
gave five talents, to another two, to another one, according to each one's
prudence and ability: and then took his journey, expecting that every
one should make an improvement proportionable to what had been
committed to him." Thus the gifts, talents and abilities wherewith God
entrusts men, are many and various, and God will require of each one
proportionable to his power and opportunities of doing good. "Then
he that had five talents traded and gained five others: likewise he that
had two talents traded and gained two more." Thus some men improve
according to their proportion, those gifts and faculties wherewith God

a. *Matt.* xxv. Dr. *Sam. Clarke*'s Paraphrase. [Clarke, *Works,* 3:110–12.]

<412> has endued them to the increase of virtue and religion, and the good of the world. "But he that had received one talent, traded not with it, but hid it, and it became useless." Thus other men make no improvements of those gifts wherewith God has blessed them, but they live idly, and are useless in the world. "After a long time the lord of these servants returned home, and called them all to an account." Thus God will call all men after their state of probation to judgment. "Then he that had five talents gave in his account, that he had traded with them and had gained five talents more: and his lord commended him for having been faithful in a small trust, and advanced him to a place of greater honour, and gave him a very great reward. In like manner, he that had two talents gave in his account, that he had traded with them, and gained two talents more: and his lord commended him also for having been faithful in a smaller trust, and gave him likewise a great reward." Thus those who have less or fewer abilities and opportunities than others, if they do but diligently improve and suitably use them they are endued with in their several proportions, shall be suitably or proportionably honoured and rewarded with higher trusts, with greater abilities and opportunities. "But he that had received one talent, and made no use of it, began to excuse his own negligence, by accusing his lord's severity in exacting more of him than had been committed to him. But his lord answered and said; you are an idle and slothful person: if you knew that I expected an improvement of what I left you, why did not you trade with it and improve it, that when I came home I might receive my own encrease." Thus wicked men, who make no use of those abilities and opportunities which God has put in their hands, think it a hardship that God should require them to take pains and improve his gifts, and employ and use them for the good of the world. But when God calls them to an account, <413> they shall be silenced and condemned, because though they know that God expected they should employ and improve his gifts to his honour, and to their own and others advantage, yet they were slothful and did it not. "Take away therefore, saith the lord of the servants, from this slothful servant his one talent, and give it to him that has ten, that he may increase more and more, and cast the unprofitable servant out of doors, into darkness and misery." Thus God, to those who improve his

gifts and graces here, will add more in the world to come, that they may
yet farther encrease, and be more fully blessed by so doing: but from
those who improve not his gifts, and the advantages he affords them, he
withdraws what he had already given, and finally punishes them with
misery proportionable to their negligence, sloth, or misuse. This is an
excellent account of the method of God's dealing with mankind. It is
exactly agreeable to the best notions of equality, and justice, and good
moral government. For the plain purport of it is, that it is according to
the diligent use we have made of our trust for the good of mankind that
we are to be rewarded, and in proportion to our neglect or misuse of
our trust that we are to be punished. Men are not to suffer for not having
done or acquired what it was not in their power to do or acquire, but
for their not improving to the best advantage the faculties and opportunities put into their hands by providence. Now, as it hath been shewn,
to acquire a right temper of mind, command over the passions, and
contempt of sensual enjoyments, in comparison of the exercises of
moral powers, the exercises of a benevolent disposition, more particularly is in every man's power, whatever his outward situation may be: and
our outward situation ought to be looked upon by us, whether it be
prosperous or adverse, as a situation we are to make the best use of for
attaining to self-command, inward liberty, and mastership of the mind,
love to God and mankind, and every virtue it <414> gives us opportunity
of exerting and strengthening. And it is therefore for improvement in
virtue, and actual exercises of it, suitable to one's circumstances, for
which every man is to be called to account, and according to which he
is to be accepted or condemned by God, the judge and governor of all
moral beings, the end of whose government must as certainly be the
promotion of moral perfection and moral happiness, as he is holy, pure,
just, and good. Various differences among mankind, as it hath been often
observed in this essay, are necessary to make them one community, having a common interest to be effected by common rightly conjoined force.
And in so constituting one kind or community, whatever share of the
differences requisite to that effect be ascribed to original formation; or
to the external circumstances in which beings are placed, *i.e.* to the
operations of external laws, by which various circumstances are occa-

sioned: however, I say, the differences necessary to community be divided between these two sources, to one or the other of which they must all be owing; there is in so constituting a community no act of arbitrary sovereignty, no arbitrary predeliction, if the good of the whole be the reason of that constitution; that is, of the differences which compose it. In truth, variety of parts being once acknowledged necessary to a constitution or whole, to ask why such a one is such a part, and not another, is to ask why the parts necessary to a whole are themselves the parts necessary to that whole. It is the same absurdity *as to ask why the eye is not the ear* in the natural body. If God, the creator of mankind, pursues the general good in framing and placing mankind, he is no respecter of persons, in originally constituting that community, whether we consider him as originally framing various genius's; or, if we may so speak, casting minds in different moulds; or appointing general laws, which by their operation shall produce different influences, or give different turns to the same powers and affections, unless to regard the good of the whole, <415> in framing the parts, and in appointing all the general laws, according to which the members composing the whole shall be influenced, be to respect persons, to respect parts or members, and not the whole. Now that there cannot be a whole, moral or natural, without parts, is self-evident. And there is no reason to imagine, that the independent creator of a whole world could have any end in view besides the good of the whole. But which is yet more satisfactory, the further, the more narrowly we enquire into any of the parts of the system, of which mankind is a part, and into the frame, constitution, and situation of mankind in particular, the better reason we perceive to conclude, that our author intends the universal good. Wherefore it is highly reasonable to infer, that the greater good of the whole is the scope intended, and that will be effected by God in his creation and government. He is therefore no respecter of persons in the formation of mankind; and he will not be a respecter of persons in judging mankind, and allotting them their several situations in another life. If he be not a respecter of persons in the former, there is no ground to apprehend he will be so in the latter. But if he be not a respecter of persons in the latter, but intends and pursues the general good of the whole, then it must be true not only; first, that mankind will be judged and called to account, in order to be rewarded or punished only for the right use they have made of their abilities and opportunities for doing good, and not for what was not committed or entrusted to them: because to treat moral beings otherwise would evidently be contrary to justice, truth, and benevolence; diametrically repugnant to that advancement and promotion of moral perfection and happiness, which must necessarily be the greater good of a moral system. 2. But it must likewise be true, in the second place, that mankind will be called to a strict account for their imployment of their trust, and be re-<416>warded or punished accordingly: because not to distinguish beings in this manner after their state of probation, would not be to respect persons according to their merits and demerits: such government could not be called moral government, for promoting virtue and virtuous happiness; it would be quite the reverse. The idea the scripture gives us of God's moral government, (and that idea alone can be stiled just moral government) is not respecting persons, but pursuing the general good of moral systems, *viz.* that he will dignify and reward, degrade and punish moral beings in a future state according to their behaviour in their state of trial and discipline. Thus, and thus alone, can virtue be promoted, or moral government answer any of the ends that can be supposed to be pursued by it, when we conceive it to be just or good. And there is no reason, from the present constitution of things, to apprehend that the government we are under is not such a government. There is, therefore, no reason to apprehend, that the scripture account of God's government, and of a future state, is not true. And to whom, indeed, can this idea of God's government be disagreeable; nay, not highly comfortable, but to such as absolutely hate virtue, if any such creature there can be. Every man hath it in his power to be good. And therefore there is no man to whose interest this scheme of government is repugnant. Can it possibly be made an objection against it, that if this be the case the vicious must be great losers? And yet no other objection can be made against it: for according to it virtue is great, unspeakable gain. But that such is the scheme of divine providence, that in the whole of things virtue shall be the gainer beyond all expression, and vice the only loser or sufferer, in proportion to its guilt and demerit—that this is the scheme of providence, as the scripture declares to us in the strongest terms, who can doubt; since, even in this life, such is the constitution and situation of mankind; such are all the powers, laws, <417> and circumstances of powers belonging to our present state and rank, that in reality it is owing to the want of virtue, and to the prevalence of vice, that men are not exceeding happy—even in our present state of probation, such is the natural tendency; such is the natural influence of all causes, that mankind are more or less happy, more or less miserable, in proportion as virtue or vice prevails—in proportion as men unite and confederate to promote virtue, in proportion as society is well constituted and regulated, and wisdom and virtue have the ascendant. For this being the case, as it evidently is, what else can we imagine the ultimate result of things must be, but the depression of vice and the prevalency of virtue, or the triumph of virtue over vice, and the full effect of its natural influence and tendency, which is happiness? If we consider what a happy effect a well ballanced civil constitution, *whose orders,* to use the words of a very great man,[a] *would constrain the members to operate towards the best interests of the whole,* must necessarily have—how can we either doubt of the real excellency of virtue—its necessary connexion with private and publick happiness—of the wisdom and goodness of our author—or of the excellent final tendency of the powers and laws of powers which constitute our present condition—the excellent final tendency of virtuous dispositions and improvements? How great, how glorious a happiness hath that excellent author shewn to be within the present reach of mankind, because it would be the natural and necessary result of good government? And is the author of our nature to be blamed for only putting it in our power to attain to such happiness in that way? Or hath he by so doing given us such a convincing proof of his generous, beneficent intention towards us; and shall we doubt of the justice, the goodness, the full perfection of that scheme which he is carrying on to-<418>wards its completion? Virtue is the basis of private and publick happiness here; and vice is the source of all the greatest evils or miseries we complain of

---

a. Mr. *Harrington* in the *Oceana.* [This appears to be a paraphrase, rather than an exact quote, from Harrington's *Oceana;* see *Political Works,* ed. Pocock, 171–73.]

in this life. Ought we not therefore to conclude, that virtue and vice must be in another life, the former the compleat source of happiness, and the latter the proportionable source of misery? Is it reasonable to judge of the whole government of the moral world, contrary to what we perceive of it? But what else does what we perceive indicate, but a natural tendency in virtue of itself to produce publick and private happiness, and a natural tendency of vice to produce publick and private misery; and what does this point out to us, but that the government of the Author of our nature, and of all things, is as much in favour of virtue as it can be in a state for forming and improving virtuous habits; and that our Maker and Judge will finally render unto virtue and vice, according to their natural or essential desert, without respect of persons? This reasoning deserves to be more fully developed. Let me therefore enlarge a little upon it. The scripture doctrine, that God will finally reward and punish men in another life according to this rule, namely, as they act virtuously or vitiously here, certainly falls in much better with our natural apprehensions of just and good government, than not rewarding or punishing; or doing so by any other rule whatever. That method of government necessarily appears more natural than any other, to minds formed as the author of nature has framed ours. Our frame and disposition to approve distributive justice in the government of the world, to look out for it and to expect it, is a natural presage or warning to us, that it actually obtains: it is, upon any other supposition, a most unaccountable make and formation. We can easily satisfy ourselves how it comes about, that till the scheme of providence be further advanced, we should not be able to see such a perfect distributive justice in the administration of the world, as our natural deter-<419>mination to apprehend and approve it, as a right rule, unavoidably disposes us to conclude, must obtain in the whole. But upon supposition, that there is not in the whole perfect distributive justice, we cannot possibly account for the frame of our mind, by which we are unavoidably led to the conception and approbation of it, as the only right rule. There is, therefore, at least a very strong presumption from the abstract consideration of our moral nature, independently of all other arguments, that the distributive justice, which revelation assures us of, does actually obtain in the government of the world. But the conviction arising from this single consideration is mightily enforced, when we look attentively into the connexions of things with regard to virtue and vice, even in this present state: for there we plainly discover, first, several clear and striking evidences of that distributive justice, of which revelation assures us, and which our own moral frame naturally leads us to apprehend: such clear evidences of distributive justice, that we can then reason with ourselves in this manner; "The distributive justice, which revelation assures us shall be compleated in a future state; and which our natural apprehensions and sense of things determine us to think must prevail in the whole of the divine government, is actually begun here, it prevails in a very great degree: there are plain traces of its being begun: and therefore there is no reason to doubt but it will be carried on to its completion." Secondly, we may learn from our moral frame, and the connexions of things, several reasons why distributive justice does not perfectly appear here; why it cannot, in the nature of things, fully take place in this state; and if this likewise be the plain language of nature to us, then the full language of the present constitution of things concurs with revelation, and manifestly declares to us, "That according to the established frame and order of things the distributive justice, which our natural disposition of mind leads us to <420> look out for the observance of, in the government of the world, as the only approveable rule of government, is begun and carried on here as far as the present state of things permits, and will be compleated when the scheme of providence is farther advanced."

Our great business here is, to attend to our own make and frame, its situation, and the connexions of things relative to us; relative to our moral powers in particular; to observe what is the natural language of these connexions; what kind of government they point out to us; and to consider how our behaviour ought to be directed in consequence of the language they speak to us; or the rules they indicate to us. Now, if we attend to the connexions of things, and their natural language, we shall clearly perceive the beginnings of distributive justice, such a tendency as plainly points out the same distributive justice here in kind, which revelation says, is to be perfected in degree hereafter. For are not all the good and bad effects of virtue and vice here, whether upon mens own minds, in consequence of our moral determination to approve the one and disapprove the other, or in consequence of the course of human affairs, turning chiefly upon the same moral make; the same approbation and disapprobation unavoidably influencing mankind to favour and reward virtue, and to discountenance and punish vice—are not all these effects plain evidences of an administration in favour of virtue, and in opposition to vice; or, in other words, of distributive justice actually begun? It is to no purpose to say, that it is not the author of nature who rewards and punishes when effects are brought about by the instrumentality of men. For that course of nature in which the instrumentality of men bears a part, whatever that part be, is still the course of nature; it is still a course approved, established, and upheld by the supream Author of nature: it is still his government; and therefore, whatever distributive justice is in it, is distributive justice in God's government, or <421> in consequence of the order settled and established by him. That in the present order of the world, the instrumentality of men makes a part, is no ground of objection against the wisdom of the course of nature, unless it can be thought a good ground of objection against it, that there should be created moral agency in the course of nature; that is, moral creatures: for where there are created moral agents, there created moral agency, or the instrumentality of moral agents, must be a part of the course of nature: or, unless it can be thought a good ground of objection against providence, that there is such a particular kind of moral agents as mankind in the world: for if men exist, the instrumentality of men must be a part of the course of nature. But the instrumentality of men being admitted to be a part in the course of nature, against which there is no ground of objection, the distributive justice in the course of nature that is so brought about, can be no ground of objection against nature: that is, 1. Deficiencies in distributive justice necessarily or unavoidably arising from the dependence of distributive justice upon the instrumentality of men, are no ground of objection against the course of nature; because that from which they arise is no ground of objection against the course of nature. 2. Whatever distributive justice takes place in the course of nature by the instrumentality of men, since it takes place in

consequence of the moral nature God has given to man, and the condition in which God has placed our moral nature in order to its operation, it is distributive justice intended by God, carried on by his government, or in consequence of the connexions of things established by
him, and therefore plainly bespeaks to us his regard to virtue and dis-
regard to vice. I mention the former of these two conclusions, because
punishing and rewarding mean making happy or miserable in some degree; and the instrumentality of men in the course of nature, means our
dependence upon one another in respect of happiness <422> and misery; whence it follows, that deficiencies in the present state of the world,
with respect to rewarding the virtuous and punishing the vitious, *i.e.*
deficiencies in distributive justice in the course of nature, which are resolvable into the instrumentality of men, *i.e.* into our mutual dependence upon one another in respect of happiness and misery, can be no
objection against the present course of nature, unless it be a reasonable
ground of objection against the course of nature, that we men are dependent one on another; we men, who are made to attain to comprehensive views and virtuous habits by observation and exercise, or, in one
word, gradual culture: *And yet,* it is evident to every one who will reflect
upon the order and connexions of things, and the events happening in
consequence of them, that the greater part of what is called deficiency
or imperfection with respect to distributive justice in this world, is to be
resolved into the dependence of it upon men; that is, into the dependence of human happiness and misery upon the instrumentality of men,
who cannot be perfect but by perfecting themselves. Distributive justice
must depend upon the instrumentality of men, as far as the mutual dependence of men upon one another in respect of happiness and misery
reaches. As far therefore as the imperfection of men reaches, must there
be deficiencies or imperfections in it, which can only amend as men
amend, *i.e.* as men become wiser and better. And therefore ultimately,
all deficiencies in distributive justice resolvable into the imperfections
of men, are accountable in the way that the imperfection of men is accountable: they do not make a separate objection, though they be often
stated as if they did; but being a necessary consequence from the imperfection of men, they stand or fall with it. But as it hath been often

said in this discourse, when we consider the natural furniture of mankind for advancement to great moral perfection, to bring an objection from the imperfection of men against the wisdom of providence, <423> is to accuse providence for having made a species of beings which has in its power to attain to a very great degree of moral perfection, by due culture and diligence to improve; which is ultimately to object against providence for creating a certain capacity of virtue and merit; for furnishing creatures with powers and means of improving, is all that can be done to produce virtuous creatures, or beings capable of merit. To demand more is to demand something that cannot be specified.

The other conclusion, *viz*. That whatever degree of distributive justice takes place by the instrumentality of men, naturally points out the regard of God, the maker and governor of the world, to distributive justice, is no less manifest: For whence comes it about that virtue is rewarded or vice punished by the instrumentality of men in any degree? Does it not arise from the moral nature of man, and the circumstances influencing that moral nature to act, determining men to approve virtue and disapprove vice; to esteem, countenance and honour beneficent intention, and to despise, abominate and resent injurious intention? Were there no such disposition prevailing in men, virtue would never be esteemed, rewarded or honoured as such; nor vice hated and punished as such. And therefore, whatever honour, esteem and reward virtue meets with in the world as such; and, on the other hand, whatever hatred and punishment vice meets with in the world, as such, must be ascribed to our disposition to approve virtue and disapprove vice. And for that reason, such a disposition in our minds must be considered as a provision the author of nature hath made for distributive justice among mankind. The more perfect men are, and the more perfect society is, the more prevalent will this moral disposition be; the more steady and uniform, as well as more discerning will its operations be; and consequently, the more perfect will distributive justice be. Were society perfect, there would be but small ground <424> of complaint against the course of distributive justice: righteousness would flow through as a river, and there would be no complaining of iniquity or oppression heard in the streets. Consequently, whatever provision the author of nature hath made for the perfection of mankind, the perfection of human society; such provision hath he made for the perfection of distributive justice. So that the fact with regard to distributive justice here, as far as it depends upon the instrumentality of men, stands thus: "It is proportionable to the perfection of men; to the perfection of human society: it increases and decreases with it. And therefore all the provision made by the author of nature for the perfection of mankind, of human society, whether in respect of affections, powers, means, occasions, or in whatever respects, is really provision for a proportionably perfect course of distributive justice."

I have said all along distributive justice, as far as it depends upon the instrumentality of men; or, in other words, upon our dependence on one another, because there are rewards of virtue and punishments of vice, which are the effects of the course of nature, independently of the instrumentality of men; and are therefore called natural by way of distinction from those which accrue to virtue and vice through the instrumentality of men; not as if the latter were not as natural, or as much the effects of settled connexions of things as the former; but to denote the more direct and immediate manner in which they are produced. Of this kind are the immediate effects of virtue and vice upon the mind and temper; the different inward feelings with which they are naturally, and in a considerable degree necessarily attended, which have been often mentioned in this discourse. Now, these being immediate effects of the frame of our minds and the constitution of things, by compensating the deficiencies in distributive justice, arising from its dependence on the instrumentality of men, which, by a careful observation of <425> mankind, they will be found to do in a greater measure than is commonly apprehended, they sufficiently shew on which side the administration of the world is, and whither it tends: namely, in favour of virtue, and against vice. But having sufficiently, on several occasions, shewn what these natural rewards of virtue and punishments of vice are; I shall conclude all this reasoning with the few following queries, to such as may happen to doubt of the fundamental point I have been endeavouring to prove: queries, which I think studiers of nature will own to be proposed in the proper way of stating questions about the government of the world; questions about fact, as all questions about the government of the world, natural and moral, are in the nature of things; and ever ought to be considered to be.

QUERY I

Whether the constitution of mankind, and of all things relating to mankind, or of the world in general, does not, so soon as we reflect upon it, clearly point out to us the necessity of conducting ourselves prudently; the necessity of studying the connexions which obtain in nature; the necessity of acting agreeably to the connexions of nature, in order to judge of or execute ends; the necessity of improving as much as we can in the knowledge of the connexions that obtain in the world; the necessity of directing our conduct by this knowledge; and consequently, the necessity of having the knowledge of the connexions in the world constantly present to us; and the necessity of self-command, or an established deliberative habit of thinking well before we act. But is not the whole language of such a state of things, a language that inculcates prudence, deliberation and self-command? Is it not wholly a state of discipline? And if such a state of discipline has once its due effect upon us, are we far from a state of virtue? <426>

QUERY II

Can we conceive to ourselves, that is, does the analogy of nature lead us to conceive any other first state (in kind) of created moral agents? I say in kind, because the question I now propose is not, whether we cannot conceive moral creatures gathering their knowledge faster, retaining it more easily, and so attaining prudence sooner than men; but whether we can conceive to ourselves any state of moral agents differing in kind from our state, or in which knowledge of their sphere of activity, however large it be, and of the connexions of nature, by which they are to regulate to themselves, and the habit of judging readily of connexions, and acting with promptitude and alacrity, in conformity to them, are not acquired by observation and exercise? It might justly be questioned in general, whether knowledge can be got but by observation; or habit but by exercise. And it might as justly be asked, whether there be any merit, any foundation for self-approbation, or for praise from others, but in acquired knowledge, and acquired virtuous habits. But it is sufficient to carry the question so far as we have done; because it is evident, that however much strangers to the connexions of things men must have been at their first setting out; it is plain that a great deal of knowledge must soon be acquired, by giving attendance to the connexions in nature; and men having once acquired knowledge, they have it in their power easily to communicate it to others; so that, after a few men had subsisted for some time in the world, if they did not acquire a good deal of knowledge, it must have been owing to their not attending to nature, to which attention all their interests conspired to excite them; and if they who had acquired knowledge themselves, did not take care to communicate it, it must be owing to their not acting according to impulses in their nature, to as-<427>sist others in that and every respect, than which better in kind, or better for the purpose, cannot be conceived. Perhaps what has been now said will be better understood by the following query.

QUERY III

Whether we can conceive a better provision in kind for exciting men to acquire the knowledge of nature, and to preserve and communicate it; or a better provision in kind, for directing and exciting men to act rightly, previous to their knowledge of nature, than the instincts or determinations with which men are originally furnished, such as the love of knowledge, curiosity, love of power, or inclination to extend our capacity and sphere of activity; compassion, benevolence, and a moral sense of beauty in veracity, gratitude, and every action which by experience will be found to be really conducive to publick good? But if better provision for that effect in kind cannot be imagined, let us consider.

QUERY IV

Whether the augmentation of all our affections, appetites and powers by exercise, be not one of the best laws that can be imagined with respect to improvement? Whether any other method of augmentation would have such good or agreeable effects? Now these questions being premised about our constitution in general, let me ask in the next place,

Query V

Whether the social affections and moral sense with which our minds are endued; and the feelings which virtuous and vitious actions produce in us in consequence of them, be not a rich provision for qualifying < 428 > and exciting us to be virtuous, to be social and benevolent; and be not an argument, that the author of nature designed us for virtue, for virtuous improvements and enjoyments: whether it be not an argument for such intention, of the same kind with all arguments from final causes; as for example, that we are not made to live either in fire or water, &c. Natural connexions, as they are called commonly, in contradistinction to moral connexions, or those which relate more immediately to our moral powers, are allowed to be a language of nature, that tells us what we ought to do, and what we ought to forbear. But are not the moral connexions just mentioned also a language with respect to our conduct and the intention of our maker. If the former, and not the latter are a practical language in the sense mentioned, what makes the difference? And if the latter, as well as the former, speak a language with regard to our conduct,—what else is that language but a call to us to be virtuous, in order to have the best enjoyments,—the full meaning of which, when our dependence on one another is considered, than which nothing can be more evident, since every thing suggests it to us, amounts to this exhortation to us, "Enter into a right form of society or union for the promotion of general happiness; of the general best happiness of beings, endued with the affections, appetites and powers, that is, with the capacities of happiness you are as men naturally possessed of, in order to be happy by right social union." If this be not the language of our frame to us, final causes, a language of nature, rules of imitation or practice deducible from natural connexions, are words without a meaning. But,

Query VI

If mankind should enter into a right society, such as perhaps never wholly obtained, but such however as < 429 > nature fully points out to us, and prompts us to establish; would they not be extremely happy? Would not knowledge, virtue, and all the goods of the mind, as well as all outward goods, be very largely and very universally shared? Are not societies happy in proportion as their social union approaches to the best model of it; and are they not miserable, in proportion as their manner of union or confederacy is distant from it? Is there not in nature a really practicable union, which would make men very virtuous and proportionably very happy? And is[a] not such an union being practicable, the intention of nature? Is any thing that nature could do to establish it wanting, that can be specified? And if so, is nature, the author of nature to be blamed, that it is not established?

QUERY VII

But as the world goes on still, and ever did, if we abstract from what a good model of government, to which nature sufficiently directs, alone can produce, what goods or evils in the world flow from blameable causes or laws. Those which proceed from the law of industry, by which goods internal and external must be acquired by application to acquire them, certainly do not proceed from a bad law. Those which proceed from the law of habits, do not flow from a bad one. And those which proceed from perversions of passions, which are in themselves of great use, or rather necessity, are not the effects of bad laws or causes. What effects then, in the course of nature, are with respect to their causes bad? None certainly can be named: for all the goods and evils in human life are reducible into something comprehended in one or other of these causes. The evils flowing from the sources mentioned, are not <430> evil in respect of their sources, for their sources even where the greatest confusion prevails in consequence of want of right civil government, or of bad civil government, are the sources of great goods; and they are not only necessary to qualify men for a social union, from which unspeakable

---

a. If any one can doubt of this, let him consider Mr. *Harrington*'s scheme of government, and his reasonings upon it. [Harrington's "scheme of government and his reasonings upon it" are developed *in extenso* in his *A Commonwealth of Oceana* and *A System of Politics*, in *Political Works*, ed. Pocock.]

happiness and perfection would as naturally arise as good fruit from a good well cultivated tree; but they are incentives, prompters, nay directors and guides, to finding out and executing such a model.

Query VIII

Now, all these things being considered, is not the present establishment or order of nature as much in favour of virtue and against vice, *i.e.* is there not as much provision made for distributive justice, in the course of human affairs, as can be supposed to take place in consequence of natural constitutions, in a first state of mankind, formed to acquire knowledge and virtuous habits by culture, and to arrive to happiness by right social union? Especially, if we add to all that hath been said one other consideration, which is the fitness or rather necessity of various temptations to vice, and of various trials of virtue, in order to the formation of virtuous habits; or in a state where they are not yet acquired, but to be acquired. I add this consideration, which hath been often already mentioned, because it well deserves the serious reflection of those who believe the reality of virtue, and yet are perplexed with doubts about the government of the world (for with such only am I now reasoning) whether the result of all that disorder and confusion in the world, which right human government would in a great measure diminish, if not put an end to, can be said to amount to, more than such trials of virtue and temptations to vice, as make a very proper theatre for forming the virtues, for making mens characters known, and for improv-<431>ing in moral prudence and every great and noble accomplishment of the mind those who set themselves to do it; which cannot be called a bad constitution, since, while it serves that excellent purpose, it is in a great degree but the effect of the want of that right social union man is excellently fitted for, and strongly incited to by nature; and to which therefore, as hath been already said, we must be understood to be called by the author of nature, by natural connexions, in the same sense any other connexions are said to speak or point out a rule of action to us. Here then is evidently great good arising by the constitution and government of things, out of an evil against which there is, by the same constitution, all conceivable remedies, *i.e.* all the remedies consistent with leaving it to men to improve themselves, and to work their own happiness, *i.e.* all the remedies consistent with the first state of beings capable of exercising reason, acquiring knowledge, and gratifying either self-approbation or benevolence. And therefore, last of all let me ask,

QUERY IX

What seems to be the natural tendency of such a state, whether total extinction at death, or continued existence and a transition into a new state. And if the latter, whether is it more probable that it shall be a state in which virtuous habits being formed, virtue shall have its excellent natural tendency fully accomplished; or a state in which vitious habits shall be the gainer by the exchange of conditions, and triumph over virtue; a state in which men having attained to characters, to formed tempers and dispositions, distributive justice, the same we perceive here in our first state, while our characters and tempers are but forming in kind but to a higher degree, *i.e.* in a proportion and manner suitable to formed tempers and characters: or a state in which virtuous dispositions and habits shall meet with disappointment, find no objects <432> correspondent to them; and vice shall exult over virtue, in the vile employments, exercises and enjoyments belonging to its corrupt nature. The former revelation assures us shall be the case. And is it not likewise the language of the present state of things that it shall be so? What else does it presage, to what else does it tend? But shall not the end be as the beginnings prognosticate? Shall not the completion be answerable to the present tendency? And when we consider the nature of an infinitely perfect author and governor of the universe, must we not reason with ourselves in this manner: "It becomes the father of rational beings, it is agreeable to his wisdom and goodness to pursue the best methods of promoting virtue: for of all his works rational beings are the most excellent: and the highest excellency of rational beings is well-improved reason, a virtuous temper and right action. It therefore highly becomes the universal Father and governor, to make every thing contribute to the increase, the promotion, the honour and advantage of virtue. It must be the noblest exercise of his wisdom and goodness, and the greatest benefit to the universe, to execute a scheme for forming, exercising, exhibiting, illustrating and rewarding the virtue of all beings, according to their several ranks and degrees; and if that be the scheme God intends and pursues, he will certainly make the promotion of virtue the measure and rule by which he acts, in conferring benefits and favours, in distributing happiness and misery; and consequently virtue must be sufficiently taken care of in all its stages; and vice cannot in the ultimate result of things be the gainer, the triumpher; but must, on the contrary, be made fully to feel its odiousness to God, on account of its intrinsick deformity and guilt, its contrariety to the rational nature, and its repugnancy to all the noblest exercises of moral powers."

Thus then, whatever view we take of things, the scripture doctrine of a state succeeding after death to <433> the present, in which distributive justice shall have its compleat accomplishment, is the most natural, consistent and probable opinion. This sure is saying the least of it. But let it be but granted to be the most probable opinion, what its influence ought to be upon our conduct in life, is too evident to be insisted upon.

Proposition IV

The Scripture represents the future state of the virtuous as a state in which they are separated from the vitious.

The virtuous are said to enter into a "kingdom, the kingdom of their father, a kingdom prepared for them, into which no wicked or unclean person can enter, a kingdom of the just, a society of the pure in heart, and of the spirits of just men made perfect: And the wicked are said to be refused admittance into this kingdom or state; to be cast out from it into a state of darkness and misery; it is said they cannot inherit it; they cannot enter into it; their state is represented to be a state of fallen, degenerated, corrupted, impure beings."ª Now we may easily conceive

a. *Matt.* viii. 11. xiii. 43. xxv. 34. *Luke* xii. 31. *James* ii. 5. *John* xvii. 22. 2 *Cor.* v. 1. 1 *Thess.* iv. 17. 2 *Tim.* ii. 10. iv. 8. *Heb.* xi. 10. xiii. 14, *&c.*

how the distributive justice begun and carried on here, as far as the nature
of a first probationary state of mankind permits, may have its full effect,
according to this representation, if we but reflect what would be the
natural result, even in this world, of a state in which virtue reigned; or
how very happy such a state would be; and, on the other hand, how
miserable a state consisting intirely of vitious beings, or in which there
was little or no virtue, must be. If we figure to ourselves such states, we
will immediately perceive the natural tendency of virtue and <434> vice;
that it is the mixture of virtue that is in the world, in any society, which
makes it tolerably happy; and how virtue and vice would, in consequence
of a separation of the just from the unjust, naturally and necessarily
display their opposite natures and tendencies; naturally and necessarily
produce happiness and misery; naturally and necessarily produce good
and bad effects, exactly corresponding to merit and demerit, *i.e.* how
distributive justice would have its full completion. This is a mixed state,
in consequence of its being a state of formation and discipline, in which
characters are to be formed and displayed; and in such a state virtue being
mixed with vice, the effects of the one must be mixed with those of the
other; nor can a separation be made of characters, till they are formed
and have been exhibited; but characters being formed, if we suppose the
separation the scripture teaches to take place, we can be at no loss to
conceive what the effects must be. For then, on the one hand, the effects
of virtue will not be mixed with those of vice; the tendencies of virtue
will not be thwarted by those of vice: there will be no other mixture but
what arises from differences of genius's, abilities, and turns, consistent
with virtuous temper, and a rightly disposed and modelled heart: And,
on the other side, the effects of vice will not be mixed with those of
virtue; the tendencies of vice will not be thwarted by those of virtue;
and there will be no other mixture but such as arises from differences
which may obtain even among the vitious; from variety of talents and
abilities, consistent with a vitious temper, or an impure corrupted malignant heart. This present state of mankind (and every first state of
moral creatures must be such in kind, in some proportion) is a state in
which men are placed to form themselves, to improve their rational powers; and accordingly in it they are provided not only with the powers to

be formed and improved into virtues, but with all proper means and occasions for so doing. Now such a state must be mixed: in it, to use our Saviour's excellent similitude, the tares must <435> grow up with the wheat;[a] nor can the wicked be separated from the good without violent interpositions, which would make this state a most irregular one, no more than the tares can be plucked up or destroyed before harvest, without destroying the wheat also: but as at the natural harvest the tares are separated from the wheat; so at the moral harvest, the end of this state of our probation and discipline, shall the sincere and good be separated from the wicked and hypocrites. And this separation being made, there are no expressions in the scripture representing the happiness of the one state, or the opposite misery of the other, of which the significant propriety may not be understood. That of the wicked must be a state of great misery and horror, violent remorse, anguish, disappointment: a state in which vitious tempers, impure appetites, tumultuous passions, evil-consciousness, deformity, corruption, guilt, must have their effects, unmixed with, and therefore unallayed by virtue. And that of the virtuous must be a state of great virtue, great glory and perfection; a state, in one word, wherein dwelleth righteousness, and all its happy effects, unallayed by the evil consequences and fruits of vice.

All this will be yet more evident, if we call to mind that,

Proposition V

The Scripture represents the future state of the virtuous as a state free from all pains and uneasinesses; and the state of the vitious, as one in which none of their sensual appetites and passions can have any gratifications.

I. It represents the future state of the virtuous as a state far removed from all the pains and uneasinesses which disturb the present state. It must be free from <436> all those which are occasioned by vice, in consequence of the separation just mentioned. It must likewise be free from all pains and uneasinesses of the sensitive kind, or which arise from our present

a. *Matt.* xiii. 24, 40, &c.

union with bodies, and a material world; and that not only in a state of
separation from our present bodies, but even in that state of re-union
with bodies, of which christianity speaks; because, as we shall see afterwards, the bodies with which our souls are to be united at the resurrection, are not animal, mortal, corruptible bodies, like to our present bodies; but spiritual, incorruptible, immortal ones. Now to these two classes
are all the pains and uneasinesses of the present state of the virtuous
reducible. And the sacred writings declare, that in the future happy state
of just men, or of the souls of just men made perfect, there shall be no
more any pain or sorrow, but that God shall wipe away all tears from
their eyes. [a] We have often had occasion in this discourse to observe, that
all the laws in this state whence pains and uneasinesses arise are excellent
general laws; and that pains and uneasinesses are necessary to the formation of virtue, of patience, magnanimity and resignation to the will
of God; and to give opportunity for exerting compassion, benevolence,
and every generous and social virtue. This is one of their chief present
uses; that is, it is the use that ought to be made of them, and which the
Author of our reasonable nature intends we should make of them. But
the virtuous habits being once formed; a good temper of mind being
once acquired and fully established, the mixture of evils, *i.e.* of uneasinesses and pains requisite to the formation and establishment of good
habits and dispositions, is no longer requisite on that account; and therefore, consistently with the ends of moral government, that is, the formation and promotion of virtue, they may then cease, <437> as the
scripture assures us all pains and uneasinesses do in the future state of
the virtuous. It cannot, certainly, be asked here why the means should
take place in this state, by which patience, fortitude and magnanimity
must be formed, since there being no evils in a future state, those virtues
can be of no use in it. For though there can be no scope for patience,
when sorrow shall be no more, there may be need for a temper of mind
which shall have been formed by patience: And there must always be
need for that habitual resignation to, and approbation of the divine will,
which is a temper that cannot be attained but, like other habits, by ex-

a. *Revel.* iii. 4, *&c.* vii. 9, *&c.* xxi. 22. *Isa.* xxv. 8. 2 *Pet.* iii. 13, *&c.*

ercising ourselves in exerting it: a temper, for forming which trials by affliction make a proper discipline.

The general doctrine of the scripture is, that we are here in this state to acquire, by various exercise, the several virtuous habits which constitute the temper of mind requisite to happiness in a future state, as making in itself the most perfect character of a rational mind: that this state is excellently fitted for that end, excellently fitted to be a state of discipline for our improvement in piety and every virtue: not, to be sure, whether persons will or will not fit themselves to improve their minds; but if persons will set themselves to make a proper use of this state, to form and improve in their minds the habits of virtue; in like manner, as the fittest school for being improved in any science is a proper school for those only who will give attention: and lastly, that the virtuous temper being formed, or man being advanced to the perfection which belongs to his nature, and which he is intended to acquire, in the circumstances peculiarly fitted to be a state of discipline to him for his improvement in virtue, the state of discipline shall then cease, and be succeeded by a state for which the virtuous temper prepares or renders meet. This is the scripture doctrine; and as we know that habits of virtue are improvement in moral perfection, which must be made in circumstances fitted to their <438> formation; so we know, that improvement in virtue must be advancement in happiness, if the government of the universe be morally good, that is, if its end be the formation, illustration and promotion of virtue. Wherefore, supposing revelation gave us no particular account of the objects and exercises constituting the future happiness of virtue; but merely declared in general, that it is a happiness for which virtue only can prepare and qualify; that would be sufficient for our direction, and for our comfort. For what more is necessary for our direction and comfort, but to be assured, that the habits which a proper use of our present circumstances will form in our minds, are necessary to qualify for happiness in a future state; and that there is a future happiness, which as they qualify for, so they shall certainly be put in possession of? This consideration is not only sufficient to satisfy us with regard to the fitness, in respect of a future state, of a present state of discipline for the formation of patience, fortitude, magnanimity and resignation to the will of God; or, more properly speaking, for the formation of that temper of mind which these acquired virtuous habits constitute: It is not only sufficient to take off any difficulty with respect to such virtues; but it serves to give us satisfaction with respect to another question, which may naturally come across the reader's mind, in consequence of what hath been said of virtuous improvements, and their future result: namely, "How there will be scope in a state of spirits of just men made perfect, where there are no sorrows, no evils, for the exercises of veracity, justice and benevolence?" It is sufficient to satisfy any reasonable person even as to that point likewise. For though we could not imagine to ourselves any particular exercises of these virtues in a perfect state, yet it will not follow from hence, that there can be, or will be no sphere of exercise for those virtues: much less will it follow, that because we are not able to figure to ourselves in our imaginations the particular exercises of those virtues in a future state, that there <439> will be no occasion for that frame of mind or character, which is formed by the daily practice of those particular virtues here, or which results from it: or, in other words, that there may not be a future happiness for which, the temper arising from the virtuous habits formed by the repeated exercises of justice, sincerity and charity here, qualifies, and alone can qualify. It is certain, that if the government of the world be virtuous, or morally wise and good, the temper and character formed by the repeated exercises of virtue must in some way or other be the condition of our happiness, or the qualification for it. And revelation assures us, that it is so. But it hath been already observed, that revelation cannot make a future state positively known to us, farther than its analogy to the present reaches. And yet after all this, when we come to consider the scripture account of the happiness of a future state more particularly, we shall see that in consequence of it, or consistently with it, by means of analogy, we can form to our selves some idea of large, proper scope for all the active virtues in a perfect state. In the mean time, 2. We are to consider, that the scripture represents the future state of the vitious, as absolutely removed from all objects and means of gratification to their wicked appetites, lusts and passions. Beings divested of their bodies, and quite separated from a material world must be so. And how miserable must they then be, whose affections and appetites are wholly carnal; whose passions are wholly fixed upon sensual pleasure, and who are utter strangers to all rational exercises and enjoyments? What can then be the effect of their impure desires, their corrupt passions, and gross vitious habits, but utter misery? If we but suppose added to this, a sense of guilt; a sense of neglected opportunities for improvement in rational and virtuous qualities; conciousness of inward worthlesness and deformity in the sight of God and all wise beings; self-dissatisfaction, and conviction of the justice of their suffer-<440>ing; a full view of their own obstinacy in not listening to the dictates of their reason, and the plain language of nature to them while they were in this world what condition can be conceived more intolerable? The state of corrupted impure minds, when far removed from all the objects of their desires, what else can it be but a state of anguish and despair; a state of the most bitter suffering and torment? Burning lusts that cannot be satisfied, are indeed a scorching, a tormenting, a consuming fire; and the gnawing of a worm, of a gangrene, or of any pain of the most vexatious fretful kind, are but faint expressions to mark out all the tortures of a guilty conscience, when it sees the beauty of abandoned virtue, the excellence of all its enjoyments; and it can find no relief from the vile gratifications which were once preferred before them, in opposition to the strongest calls from reason and a moral sense; in opposition to the clear language of nature, as well as to revelation.

But let us turn our minds to a more pleasing subject.

PROPOSITION VI

The Scripture represents virtue or holiness not only as the condition of, and the qualification for the happiness of a future state; but it represents the happiness of a future state as consisting in, or resulting from virtuous exercises and enjoyments: and it represents a future state of happiness, as immortal, as enduring for ever.

The scripture, as we have seen, represents God's government as a moral government for the promotion of virtue, and for advancing happiness in proportion to improvement in virtue. Such a government is a government in which distributive justice, in the proper just sense of it, prevails; and such does the scripture represent the moral government of God to be. According to revelation, this our present state is but our first probationary state. All this we <441> have already seen. And consequently there can be little or no difficulty in apprehending why sometimes the future happiness of virtue, and the future misery of vice should be set forth under the notion of rewards and punishments, and sometimes be represented as effects or consequences resulting from the nature, the constitution and order of things. For it is plainly the same to all intents and purposes, whether it is said that such is the constitution of things and the conduct of providence, that virtue in a future state shall be happy, and vice miserable; or that by the administration of things, virtue shall be rewarded, and vice punished in a future state. There cannot be so much as any seeming inconsistency between these two different expressions to those who know and reflect that the course of nature can mean nothing else but the order of things established by the author of all things; that the tendency and result of things can mean nothing but the tendency and result of connexions established and upheld by God; and that whatever happiness, or whatever misery, is the final result of God's government, is the effect of his will, by which all things are appointed and effected. When things are said to happen, either in this world or in a future state, or at any period in consequence of general laws, the meaning is not, that certain rules or laws operate independently of a governing mind; for that is a direct contradiction or absurdity: But the meaning is, that the Author or Governor of the world hath appointed such and such effects to happen, according to such and such general laws or rules. Now, the advantages that are, in consequence of the will of the author of the world, the Father of all rational beings appointing a certain order and constitution of things, to happen to virtue in a future state, and the disadvantages that are to happen by the same will, and in consequence of the same constitution and order of things, to vice, because they are to happen by that cause, and in that manner, are as properly the natural results of things, as any ef-<442>fects of the material kind are natural effects: but then the constitution appointed by the governor of the world being a good moral constitution, or a constitution intended for and adjusted to the promotion of virtue, and for that reason to the advancement of happiness with improvement in virtue; that being the end of the constitution appointed by the Author and Governor of the world, the high happiness to which virtue is to be advanced in a future state, after it hath been formed and established here by a course of discipline, may very properly be called its reward, being the honour and happiness to which it shall then be advanced, and to advance it to which, by fitting it for it, is the scope of its present state of discipline; and the future misery which is to be the fate of a vitious life in a future state, may very properly be called its punishment, being the depression and misery into which the abuse of moral powers in a state fitted to be a state of discipline for improvement in virtue, shall, according to the moral constitution and order of things, sink and degrade minds indued with rational affections and powers. For in this sense is the perfection one attains to in science, the reward of study; and is ignorance, on the other hand, the punishment of unattention and thoughtlessness, or wilful neglect of instruction: In this sense likewise, the honour and preferment bestowed on one, because he is qualified for it, and deserves it, is a reward to merit; and, on the other hand, the refusing favours to one who does not deserve them, is not qualified to use them well, or disposed to make an ill use of them, is a punishment to demerit. In this sense do we use the words *rewards* and *punishments:* it is the proper application of them. But to clear up a little the nature of future rewards and punishments, as well as to shew that there is no inconsistency in representing the same effects at the same time as rewards or punishments, and as the natural result of certain qualities; let it be observed, that 'tis not powers alone that can make happy, but in order to hap-<443>piness there must be powers, and objects suited to powers. Wherefore, when the happiness of the virtuous in a future state is said to be the effect of virtue, the effect of sowing to the spirit, reaping the fruits of one's doings, or reaping as one had sown; the meaning must be, that it is a happiness resulting from moral powers improved into virtues, as exercised about objects proper or suited to them. There are, by consequence, two things which must concur to make the virtuous happy in another world, The improved state of their minds, and objects

suited to that state of their minds. Now 'tis only the improved state of
the mind that can properly be said to be the effect of virtuous exercises
here: the objects which in a future state are the means of employment
and gratification to the virtuous are not the effect of virtuous habits acquired here, but their existence or their taking place is the effect of the
will of the governor of all things, in order that improved minds may
have due happiness in a future state. The former properly comes under
the denomination of the effect of a general law with regard to improvement in virtue in a state of discipline established by the Author of nature,
the Father of spirits. The other comes properly under the denomination
of an appointment of the same universal Father of all rational beings,
for rewarding virtue after it is formed and acquired in a state of discipline; an appointment for making it happy, or for suitably employing
and promoting it; and may therefore be very properly called positive
reward. So that to speak properly and distinctly of a future state, as well
as consistently with the scripture account of it, we ought to say, "there
is a future happiness, a future glory, for which virtue alone can render
fit, actually prepared for the virtuous, in order to reward their diligence
to attain to moral perfection, by the right use of their moral powers in
their first state of education and discipline." This is the scripture doctrine concerning this present life, and our future state. And it highly
<444> concerns us frequently to call to mind all these important truths,
that we may be habitually influenced by them in our conduct.

I. *Virtue or holiness is the condition of eternal happiness; without it we
cannot have a right to it, or be made sharers of it.*

It is expressly said, that nothing that defileth, no unclean or wicked
person can enter into the kingdom of God, or heaven. The wicked cannot inherit that kingdom. It is the inheritance of the sanctified. Without
holiness none can see the Lord, or dwell with him. In order to partake
of the felicity of the blessed, one must partake of the divine nature; be
holy and pure, as God is holy and pure. And therefore the constant language of holy writ to us, is, "having therefore these promises, this hope,
let us sanctify ourselves, let us cleanse ourselves from all filthiness of the

flesh and spirit, perfecting holiness in the fear of God."ᵃ And indeed we must first be persuaded that the government of the world is immoral, or that there is no difference between moral good and evil, before we can imagine that the happiness, the rewards of a future state can be given to any but the pure in heart, the virtuous, those who have given all diligence to perfect their rational nature. This is not a principle merely of revealed religion; it is the basis, or rather the whole of natural religion. It stands upon the same bottom with the reality of virtue and of a divine providence. But further,

II. *Holiness or virtue is absolutely necessary to qualify for future happiness.*

The happiness of the virtuous in a future state is represented to us under all the pleasant, grateful images that can raise our admiration, excite our desires, or rouse our ambition, to contend diligently for it: and <445> it is said to excel all that we can now be made to conceive, all description. "Eye hath not seen, ear hath not heard, neither hath it entered into the heart of man to conceive the good things God hath prepared for, and will bestow upon those who loving him, give all diligence to imitate his holiness, and to become like to him." But, at the same time, we are assured, that it is a happiness resulting from virtue, or for which a virtuous mind only is qualified. "It is reaping the fruits of a well-improved mind; the fruits of having sown to the spirit, the fruits of righteousness, and holiness, and charity." It is a happiness of a pure and rational kind; a happiness suited to rational powers duly refined and improved by culture in a state of discipline. It is declared negatively to be a happiness which the vitious, the carnal, the impure and corrupt cannot relish, or are utterly incapable of. And it is declared positively to be a felicity resulting from, of a kind with, and proportioned to the rational nature; a happiness of which the pure, the holy only are susceptible, and which to them shall give light, liberty, joy, and felicity unspeakable. The meaning of all which is, briefly, that it is happiness

---

a. *Mat.* v. 8. xiii. 43. xxv. 34. *Rom.* ii. 7. 10. 1 *John* iii. 2. iii. 7. 2 *Cor.* vii. 1. *Ep.* i. 4. iv. 1, 17, 20, *&c.* 1 *Thess.* ii. 12. 1 *Tim.* ii. 2, 4, 7, 8. *Titus* ii. 11, 12.

unspeakable, arising from the exercise of a virtuous mind, about objects suited to its excellent disposition, suited to its noble affections, and highly improved powers.

The scripture represents the happiness of all beings superior to man, as consisting in virtuous dispositions suitably exercised. Nay, the happiness of God himself, the Father of spirits, is represented as resulting from the purity, the holiness of his nature, or his absolute moral perfection. And whence else can the chief happiness of any moral being arise, but from its moral powers improved into a capacity for being exercised about objects adequate to improved moral powers? If such happiness be not superior in kind to all other enjoyment, then are not moral powers superior in kind to merely animal faculties, which is an absurdity too gross to be <446> asserted, as hath already been often shewn in this discourse. But if moral powers, and the happiness they are capable of receiving by means of their natural exercises about proper objects, be superior in kind to all other faculties and their gratifications, then to imagine any other rewards for virtue, for moral perfection, besides the happiness resulting from the exercises of improved moral powers about objects commensurate or adapted to them, is to suppose them rewarded by a happiness in its nature inferior to those exercises, which is likewise absurd.

III. *Further, the scripture specifies to us the exercises from which the future happiness of the virtuous flow.*

I. It represents that future happiness as resulting from knowledge, that is, from the exercises of the understanding about objects fitted to give it high delight, fitted to give it noble employment and full satisfaction. We are told in the passages already quoted, that we shall see God, and rejoice in the light of his countenance. The meaning of which must be, that we shall see far into the works of God, far into the scheme of providence, and all that wonderful order and beauty which must prevail throughout the government of an infinitely wise and good ruler. To see or know any mind is to have a clear and satisfying view of its character from its productions, its plans, its thoughts, its sentiments and affections, its conduct: and therefore to know God, in whatever degree of perfection, must mean, to have, to a certain degree, a clear and satisfactory view of his temper and character, from the knowledge of his works, his productions, his scheme of government. And how delightful is the contemplation of the order and harmony that appears in God's works, to those who search them out, even now that we are able to see so small a part of them? How unspeakable therefore must our satisfaction be when we <447> shall have a fuller view of them; when all that is now involved in darkness shall be light to us? We now see but a very small part, we have now but a very narrow confined view; and yet what we see sufficiently manifests to us the infinite perfections of the great Creator and Governor of the universe; his eternal power, wisdom and goodness; and therefore highly ravishes and transports the mind. But then we shall have a much larger prospect of God's government; then we shall be daily advancing in a more perfect knowledge of his administration? The knowledge we shall then be capable of receiving shall be so great, in comparison of what our present situation or point of view can afford us, that in respect of the former the latter is called, *knowing as children know*—Nay, so far superior shall it be to our present knowledge, in clearness, comprehensiveness, and satisfaction, that in respect of it our present knowledge is called, *seeing but darkly, as thro' a glass;* and it is said to be, *seeing God face to face, and knowing him even as we are known of him.* The scripture, 'tis plain, here labours to give us a very high conception of our delight, arising from the perfection of our knowledge in a future state; and the expressions must not be understood as meaning that our knowledge shall ever bear any proportion to the fullness, the infinite perfection of the divine knowledge. What they are designed to signify to us, is the vast superiority in respect of extent and delight by which our future knowledge shall surpass the most perfect insight we can now acquire into the works of God. It shall be, in comparison of our present knowledge, what seeing and conversing with one, is in respect to knowing him only by report. It is seeing God, not darkly through a glass, but face to face. It is seeing him in his works, so as not to mistake him, but to have a clear and just apprehension of their beauty and excellency, and his perfections. It is seeing his divine excellencies fully display'd, as we see the character of one fully manifested <448> to us by his actions and

conversation, with whom we are in intimate acquaintance and correspondence. 'Tis no wonder that some men, endeavouring to comprehend the full adequate meaning of such expressions about the perfection
of our future knowledge of God, have over-strained or over-heated their
imaginations, and quite lost themselves: their full import is too big for
our present comprehension: and it is dangerous for us to indulge our
imaginations upon so raptorous a subject, without keeping a strict guard
over ourselves. For the command and ballance of the mind may be lost
by admiration, even when the subject is truly noble and pure, as well as
by too great indulgence to other affections. And it is sufficient for our
present comfort to know, that there is a state prepared for well improved
minds, in which their joy resulting from the intelligent admiration of
God's works, or of God in his works, in his administration, shall far
exceed what revelation can now describe or paint out to us by the strongest images. Those who are acquainted with the pleasures of knowledge,
the divine satisfaction which the discovery of beauty and order in the
works of God now affords to an enlarged understanding, united with a
sound, a well disposed heart, cannot be at a loss to conceive what is
meant, when the happiness which is to arise from larger and clearer, yet
ever growing knowledge of God, and the pious affections such knowledge must excite and maintain in the mind, is said to be unutterably,
inconceivably great.

II. But our future happiness is not represented in scripture, as wholly
consisting in the pleasures accruing from the contemplation of God in
his works, from knowledge of the divine perfections and administration,
and the devout affections towards God, which the knowledge of him
must kindle and keep alive in the mind. It is represented, as, in a great
measure, the fruit of active, social exercises and employments. If we
<449> judge at all from the analogy of nature, we must suppose that
our hereafter state will be a community; nothing which we at present
see can lead us to the thought of a solitary, unactive, unsocial, disunited
state in another life. Nothing here leads us to imagine, that men do not
continue to be in another life one kind, mutually dependent one on
another: much less does any thing here lead us to suppose, that men cease
to be agents; or to have active powers and faculties. Nor can we, indeed,

in our thoughts, imagine men to become so many unactive, solitary individuals, without sinking and degrading mankind, instead of exalting them in our imagination. And in scripture, a future life is not represented as a solitary, disunited, unactive state; but, on the contrary, as a community, and an united, active state. We are not represented as merely contemplative beings, wholly engaged, each particular by himself in contemplation, admiration, and worship, without any correspondence, without any sympathy, connexion, dependence, or commerce. No: a future state of happiness is represented as a kingdom, a city under the supreme direction of God, of which the blessed inhabitants are fellow-citizens, contributing to one another's happiness, mutually serving and served. It is called a glorious kingdom, the glorious kingdom of God, a glorious city, a new Jerusalem, a heavenly state, or community; a kingdom wherein dwelleth righteousness; a city whose builder and maker is God, and which abideth for ever; and the rewards constituting the happiness of that state are expressed by receiving a kingdom, a trust, a rule. "Thou hast been faithful, saith our Saviour to the righteous and profitable servant, over a few things, and therefore I will make thee ruler over many."[43] The blessed are said to reign with God, and to rejoice in doing his will, in executing his commands, and to receive a crown from him, a crown of righteousness. <450>

Let it be observed on this head, that the scripture no where represents to us any state of unactive happiness. The happiness of God himself is set forth to us as consisting in the continual communication of his goodness; in the uninterrupted exercise of his power and wisdom, for the best and noblest purposes, in order to promote the greatest general good. This is the idea the scripture gives us of the divine felicity: it consists in his unbounded, uninterrupted, active benevolence. Now, in order to be happy in another life, we are told in scripture, we must be like to God in love, *i.e.* benevolence; and that must certainly mean active benevolence; but not surely in order to have no occasion for an active principle of benevolence. The idea of the happiness of angels and archangels, and of all the choirs of celestial beings superior to man, is represented as

43. Matt. 25.21.

consisting in their being ministring spirits to God; or beings employed
in great and important offices to promote the glorious scheme of divine
providence, and who are extreamly happy in this their instrumentality;
or in their thus co-operating with God, or for God.[a]

Again, Jesus Christ in scripture is represented as delighting to do the
will of God; as rejoicing in executing his commands; as having a high
charge committed to him, and as having fulfilled it in part, and going
on to fulfil it thoroughly. Two things are very evidently asserted in scripture concerning Jesus Christ, his visiting mankind, and his return to the
Father after his resurrection, when he ascended into heaven. "That what
he did for mankind was undertaken and performed by him from a noble
principle of benevolence and virtue, in obedience to the will of God,
with great delight and complacency; and that the commission <451>
with which he was trusted was given him because of his worthiness; that
he undertook and executed it with high satisfaction; and that he was to
receive, and has received, for what he did on earth, a glorious recompence
of reward. Lo, I come, I delight to do thy will, O my God, yea, thy law
is within my heart. He loved righteousness and hated iniquity; therefore
God, even his God, anointed him with the oil of gladness above his
fellows. He was made flesh, took upon him the form of a servant, and
was made in the likeness of man: and being found in fashion as a man,
was in all things tempted as we are. He became obedient to the death,
even the death of the cross—and God raised him from the dead, and
set him at his own right hand in heavenly places, far above all princi-
palities and powers, might and dominion, and every name which is
named, not only in this world, but also in that which is to come, and
hath put all things under his feet, and gave him to be the head over all
things in the church—Thou art worthy to take the book, and to open
the seals thereof—for worthy is the lamb which was slain to receive
power, and riches, and wisdom, and strength, and honour, and glory,
and blessing—The kingdoms of this world are become the kingdoms
of our Lord, and of his Christ, and he shall reign—Blessing, honour,

a. *Heb.* i. 7. 14. *Ephes.* i. 20, 21, &c. *Philip.* ii. 5, &c. *Heb.* i. 2, 3, &c. *Rev.* v. 5, &c.
Rev. vi. 15, &c. *Heb.* xii. 2, 3.

and glory, and power be unto him who sitteth upon the throne, and
unto the lamb for ever—" And we are thus exhorted by the author of
the epistle to the *Hebrews:* "Let us run with patience the race that is set
before us; looking unto Jesus, the author and finisher of our faith; who,
for the joy that was set before him, endured the cross, despising the
shame, and is set down at the right hand of the throne of God. For
consider him that endured such contradiction of sinners against himself,
lest ye be wearied and faint in your minds."[44]

Now, from all these ways of speaking laid together, without enquiring
at present into the commission given <452> to Christ, with regard to
mankind; or what that part is which he is employed in carrying on in
God's universal government; it is very manifest, 1. That his commission
was given to him on account of his worthiness, his consummate virtue.
The plain language of the scripture, of all that is said in the holy writings,
about Jesus Christ, his commission, the power, the authority given to
him of the Father, is, that true virtue is the only valuable consideration
that prevails with God, the only power or quality, in heaven or in earth,
that can be honoured and rewarded by him. 2. That as in this world, or
God's visible government, all is carried on chiefly by the instrumentality
of men; so the invisible government of God is carried on by the instrumentality of agents superior to man. And, indeed, we must suppose the
happiness of other rational agents to arise in a manner analogous to the
happiness of good men, though in a superior degree, from their instrumentality in doing good; from their virtuous employments in promoting
universal happiness. 3. It is no less evident from what is said of Jesus
Christ, and his glorious commission and charge from the Father, and of
the angels being ministring spirits to the heirs of salvation, and to execute
other great purposes of God's universal benevolence, that beings of the
noblest and most perfect orders may have occasion for fortitude, for
magnanimity and resignation to the divine will, in order to their noble
employments, in the execution of which they are happy beyond all expression. The patience, the magnanimity, the resignation to God, and
the benevolence to mankind, with which Jesus Christ bore the contra-

44. Heb. 12.1–3.

diction, the raillery, the persecution of sinners, is set before us in scripture, at once as an example of, and a strong motive to our sedulous study
of those virtues. And they shew, that there may be occasion for these
virtues in the most perfect state. But my design being merely to shew
the consistency of the principles of religion discoverable by reason, with
the fundamental < 453 > doctrines of revelation concerning God, providence, virtue, and a future state, and not to enter into any enquiry concerning any doctrine peculiar to christianity; 'tis sufficient to have observed, that according to the accounts given us in scripture of the divine
felicity, and of the happiness of all moral beings, there is no ground to
imagine, that the happiness of any moral being in any state, however
perfect, is an inactive happiness. And therefore though we are not able
to see here into the employments of our future state; nor indeed to receive any account of them from revelation, except a very general one, as
hath been observed, we have reason to conclude, that our happiness in
a future state is not an inactive but an active one, to which all the habits
of virtue formed in this present state of discipline are necessary prepar-
atives, or qualifications. Nor can we indeed conceive ourselves changed
into a passive state without being sunk and degraded. Though the scripture had not expressly said, that our future state shall be a society, a regular social state, we must, we cannot chuse but imagine it to be such;
for analogy inevitably leads us to conceive every state of moral beings
of whatever rank or dignity, as such. And considering what variety there
must be in respect of genius, temper, and abilities among men, as they
enter into a future state upon their leaving this world, partly owing to
original differences, and partly the effect of various situations and circumstances in this life; all which diversity is very consistent with virtuous
tempers—what immense variety of happy employments may we fancy
to ourselves in consequence of perfect union and harmony—perfect
government to promote universal good, universal advancement in
knowledge, and higher moral perfection? For though the habits of virtue
be necessary to qualify us for the heavenly state, let us not imagine, that
there is no farther progress to be made, after our entrance into it, in moral
perfection. This is equally contrary to scripture, and to all our ideas of
< 454 > moral beings. Their capacity of progress knoweth no stop, no

bounds; but their perfection will ever be advancing in proportion to culture, which, the first habits of virtue being well established in the mind,
will never afterwards be wanting. In order to help our imaginations in
this pleasing attempt to form some faint idea of future happiness in the
active way, let us first figure to ourselves the vast happiness that mankind
would enjoy even here in consequence of perfect government; such government, as the best writers on politicks have demonstrated human nature to be capable of, and consequently not to be impracticable—and
then let us raise our minds to a celestial state of beings, compleatly virtuous, and unanimously conspiring to the promotion of their best common interests, in a social well-regulated state, the orders of which secure
the constant advancement of the greatest publick good such beings are
capable of—*i.e.* the souls of good men are capable of in a state where
they can take in larger views of God's providence; and are redeemed from
the necessity of attending to low animal cares. For let it be remembered,
that though christianity tells us we are again at the general resurrection
to be embodied; yet, according to the account christianity gives of that
re-union with bodies, it is to be with bodies capable of affording our
minds higher and nobler means of enjoyment and exercises than our
present bodies are. Our present bodies are admirably adjusted to the
present state of our minds. And the bodies with which the spirits of just
men made perfect are to be cloathed at the resurrection, shall be equally
well adapted to that state of our souls.ᵃ "All bodies, saith St. *Paul,* are
not the same. There are terrestial and celestial bodies. And the glory of
the celestial is one, and the glory of the terrestial is another. There is one
glory of the sun, and another glory of the moon, and another glory of
the stars; for one star differeth from another in glory. So also is the resurrection of the dead. It is sown in corruption; it is raised <455> in incorruption. It is sown in weakness; it is raised in power: It is sown in
dishonour; it is raised in glory: It is sown a natural body, it is raised a
spiritual body. Flesh and blood cannot inherit the kingdom of God.
Neither doth corruption inherit incorruption. This corruptible shall
therefore put on incorruption; and this mortal shall put on immortality."

a. I Cor. xv. 39–44, 50, 53.

And these bodies are to qualify us for inheriting a new heaven and a new earth, wherein dwelleth righteousness.ª "Then shall the tabernacle of God be with men, and he will dwell with them, and they shall be his people, and God himself shall be with them, and be their God." By these and many parallel passages is evidently pointed out to us a happiness to the virtuous, to commence at that period, resulting from righteousness, the universal prevalency of righteousness, from perfect government and society; from a government so perfect as to deserve, in a peculiar manner, the name of a Theocracy, or God's immediate government. The revelation of these future things cannot extend beyond certain bounds; because nothing can be discovered to us concerning future felicity, but what is analogous to our present experience. And there may be wise and good reasons for its not being so extensive and full as analogy admits, though we cannot possibly determine whether it is so or not. It is sufficient for us, that revelation concurs with reason to assure us of a future state, in which every man shall reap as he has sown here. The holy scripture represents the future state of the virtuous, as a social active state. And reason and analogy oblige us to conceive of it as such; to conceive of every state, of every class of moral beings as such; *i.e.* as a state in which their power encreases with their knowledge of the connexions of things; a state in which all goods, all enjoyments are the purchase of industry, and in which there is a common interest to <456> be promoted. Here in our present state, to use the expression of a very great man, "nature sells all to industry: it is the treasure which purchases all of God." And there is good reason to imagine, that this law of industy is universal. It seems, indeed, necessarily to belong to the very character of created agents. We cannot suppose this law altered, with regard to the exercise of power, and the acquisitions of industry, without sinking created agents into a lower class of merely passive beings. Agency includes in it a capacity of extending power by knowledge, and of acquiring by the exercises of intelligent power. Beings who have no power can acquire nothing; they cannot act. And as it is acting, and acquiring by acting, which alone distinguishes an agent from a merely perceptive being; so it is difference

a. 2 *Peter* iii. 13. *Isa.* lxv. 17, *&c. Rev.* xxi. 3, *&c.*

with regard to spheres of power, that constitutes higher and lower, superior and inferior agents in nature. Wherefore, if beings in a future state have no more any sphere of activity, they are no more agents. But where there is a sphere of activity, there industry or exercise of power is the purchaser of all goods. Further, where there is no activity, no sphere of power, and where the law of industry does not take place, there can be no virtue or merit. For what is virtue or merit, but greatness of mind, or a disposition to extend and enlarge one's power, guided and directed by benevolence: a disposition to promote publick good by our power; and to extend our capacity to promote it. We can form no other notion of virtue or merit: it can be nothing else in any state. It cannot therefore belong to any state of beings, where there is no sphere of activity, and where the law of industry does not take place. Again, where the law of industry takes place, and beings are capable of virtue and merit, there must be a publick interest to promote, as well as a private one. Virtue and merit, as they suppose a sphere of activity or power, so they include in their notion the dependence of a publick interest upon the use <457> particulars make of their power, a mutual relation and connexion, regular society and the instrumentality of particulars in promoting the general interests. What entertainment, in fine, what employment can we imagine to belong to beings who have no sphere of power, and no common good to promote? Such beings must be lower than men are in their present state. And, on the other hand, what a variety of excellent, noble entertainments and employments may belong to men, in whose minds benevolence predomines when their sphere of activity being enlarged, *i.e.* their capacity of encreasing in knowledge, and of encreasing in power proportionably to encrease in knowledge being enlarged, they have a great common good to pursue, even the common advancement of the whole society, or state of good men from greater to greater moral perfection; in a state where no differences inconsistent with virtue remaining, every particular will be continually laying himself out with full complacency and delight to promote the publick interest; in a state where the habits of virtue being fully established in every mind, the diversity which then takes place shall be no other than what is necessary to lay a foundation for mutual union, for mutual giving and receiving;

and thus every one shall mutually give and receive; and all shall be equally happy in giving and receiving: what a vast variety of very noble employments may, must take place in such a perfect state? And towards such a state is the natural tendency of reason, of virtue, of a moral constitution. Whatever happiness would be the effect of general virtue here, in our first state, while our powers are but in embrio, as it were, and while our sphere of power, though not contemptible, but rather great, is yet narrow in respect of what it may be in another situation; that happiness must, however, be but inconsiderable in comparison of the happiness general virtue must produce, when our powers are formed to great perfection by culture, and our sphere <458> of activity, is greatly enlarged, and continually enlarging. And yet, who can express all the happiness which the prevalence of virtue, according to its natural tendency, would produce even in our present state? It is almost above description. Our present sphere of activity is very well adapted to our powers in their first state to be perfected by culture; very well adapted to make a proper school of exercise for perfectionating them; for perfectionating virtuous habits in us in particular; and our present happiness depends upon the prevalence of virtue, and rightly constituted society, in order to make men good, or promote virtue: it is the effect of the natural tendency of virtue; and holds proportion to its prevalence. And therefore as it is reasonable to think, that enlargement of our sphere of activity will be the reward of virtue; so the general prevalence of virtue in a state where our sphere of activity is enlarged, and continually enlarging, must, in consequence of the natural tendency of virtue, produce the most perfect happiness—happiness too big for the mind at present to comprehend—the prospect of which ought powerfully to animate us to give all diligence now to add virtue to virtue; to grow and advance in spiritual strength, in vigour and perfection of mind, and not to faint or weary; forasmuch as we know that our labour shall not be in vain; that our acquisitions shall not be destroyed; but that in a future state we shall continue to go on from strength to strength, from glory to glory, rejoicing in God the rewarder of virtue. This delightful hope ought ever to be present with us, that we may look upon every circumstance in our present life, as an opportunity for perfecting ourselves in some virtue, for which there is a glorious recompence in store; for some virtue which shall add to our crown of glory in the life to come, where the righteous shall shine in proportion to their righteousness; and those who by their counsel, joined with a noble example, have turned many to righteousness, shall rule with God. <459> These strong expressions are authorised by the scripture. And it is no small satisfaction to a virtuous mind to find all good and wise men in all ages of the world representing the future state of the virtuous in like expressions: for as an excellent ancient philosopher observes, "the greater, the nobler the mind is, the more it becomes in love with virtue and virtuous exercises; the more it delights itself in the hopes of future happiness in the society of the virtuous, resulting from greater power and greater perfection in virtue proportioned one to another, or keeping pace one with another." It only now remains to observe in the last place,

IV. *That according to the scripture account of the state of the virtuous in the life to come, it is a state of unchangeable, immortal glory and happiness.*

Now it is absurd to imagine this security to arise from an impossibility of falling from virtue; for a possibility of falling from virtue is included in the very nature of moral or free agency. This security arises from the perfection of virtue acquired in a state of discipline; from the strength and power of virtuous habits gradually formed. Some men arrive in this state to such a perfection of virtue, that we say, without any hesitation, it is impossible for them to degenerate. *i.e.* It is morally impossible they should, on account of their strong sense of the excellency of virtue, and of the firmness of their virtuous habits, settled and fixed in them by long practice; by habitual self-government uniformly and vigorously persisted in, till now virtue is become the very temper and bent of their soul. And in this sense is it, that the virtuous, in a future state, are secure from degeneracy. It is, 1. Because their virtue is become habitual, become temper, or is firmly established. It is a state of discipline that must form this perfect virtue; but the habits of virtue being formed in a state of discipline by <460> habitual self-government unto perfection, they will then be in no danger of being over-power'd, but will bind to virtue by the cords of love, by that close union and coherence which confirm'd love of virtue, and continued practice in it, necessarily produces, in consequence of the very nature of habit. There is no reason to imagine that there will be no particular affections then belonging to us, or that many of our present particular affections shall not then remain with us: self-love must remain while sensibility remains: and the desire of extending our power, together with delight in the happiness of others, and desire of their esteem, and all other social affections, will doubtless remain. But benevolence being settled into a firm principle, our sense of the excellency of virtue, and our satisfaction with virtuous exercises, as the best, the noblest, and pleasantest exercises of the mind, being deeply rooted in us by long practice, by various trial and discipline, reason and virtue will govern us uniformly and irresistibly; order and harmony will prevail uninterruptedly in our souls. It will be impossible to fall away from virtue, because it will be impossible to lose sight of its excellence, to lose the relish of its uncloying delights; and to become vitious would cost the violentest, the most painful struggle. 2. No doubt, the remembrance of our state of discipline, and a larger view of the fatal consequences of vice to rational minds, in consequence of the moral rectitude of the divine government, together with a more comprehensive knowledge of the wise ends of all the trials alloted to the virtuous in this state, will add mightily to the strength of virtue in a future state, and by consequence, to the security of the virtuous; as well as make a considerable part of the happiness of that state. For how doth a just view of the excellence of virtue, and of its agreeableness to God the Father of spirits, and the hope of eternal happiness in consequence of the perfection of the divine government, strengthen and <461> embolden here, even amidst prevailing corruption, and when virtue is most violently persecuted? 3. And when virtue is general, then must virtuous ambition and emulation be universally prevalent: then virtue will animate virtue: it will be continually whetted and invigorated by noble examples. Evil example is indeed a powerful corrupter, but good example is a no less powerful incentive to virtue: and how can virtue decline, while the sense of its excellence, the unspeakable blessings it daily rewards with, and glorious patterns of it are incessantly stimulating to make further advances in what we shall then feel not to have been fruitless labour in our first state of discipline;

but to have been indeed contending towards glory and fulness of joy, far beyond what we could then conceive, that shall daily augment as we advance in moral perfection, which, in the nature of things, knows no bounds or limits? How can virtue degenerate in such a state? It is impossible. Before virtue is perfected into habit, it may decline, even after great advances have been made in it; but after it is fully established by discipline, and hath tasted the fruits of its perfection, it must then be natural to the mind; it must then be, so to speak, the very complexion, the very temperament and constitution of the soul, which cannot be changed. The happiness of the virtuous endureth for ever, because their righteousness endureth for ever; and righteousness, or virtue thoroughly formed, is in its nature a living principle, a never dying, immortal, unchangeable principle.[a] Righteousness, says the wise man, is immortal; "wisdom is glorious, and never fadeth away." The very true beginning of her is the desire of discipline, and the care of discipline is love, and love is the keeping of her laws, and the keeping of her laws is the assurance of incorruption, and incorruption makes us near to God: therefore the desire of wisdom bringeth to a kingdom, a kingdom immortal. <462> The righteous live for evermore, their reward also is with the Lord, and the care of them with the most high: therefore they shall receive a glorious kingdom, and a beautiful crown from the Lord's hand; but as for the wicked, they shall say, "this was he whom we had sometimes in derision, and a proverb of reproach; we fools accounted his life madness, and his end to be without honour: but now is he numbered among the children of God, and his lot is among the saints! therefore have we erred from the way of truth, and the light of righteousness hath not shined upon us, and the sun of righteousness arose not upon us; we wearied ourselves in the way of wickedness and destruction; yea, we have gone through desarts, where there lay no way: but as for the way of the Lord we have not known it. What hath pride profited us? or what good hath riches with our vaunting brought us? all those things are passed away like a shadow,—and we are consumed in our wickedness."

To conclude, why may we not suppose the security of the virtuous

a. *Wisdom* i. 15. vi. 10, 18, &c.

in a future state to arise in a great degree from the perfect government of that state; from its excellent orders conspiring to preserve and promote virtue. In this our first state, while virtue is but in the very initial steps of its progress, "good orders in a government make good men; virtue is promoted and prevails in proportion to the aptitude of the orders constituting government to promote, spread, and advance it." And if we suppose any public union or government in a state of *just men made perfect,* as we cannot chuse but suppose there must be, that government will be perfect; it will be immortal; it will be a government so constituted, that virtue shall never perish, but be ever advancing, and by its perpetual advancement be perpetually adding to the glory and felicity of the citizens of that heavenly state. Thus analogy leads, nay, in a manner necessitates us to paint out a future state to ourselves; and revelation, by re-<463>presenting a future state to us as a community, sufficiently authorises our figuring it to ourselves under the notion of perfect happiness, resulting from perfect government, in consequence of the natural tendency of the universal prevalence of virtue and virtuous union. In this sense it is properly called the harvest of virtue; its ripeness; its completion: and this life is as properly represented to be our seed time. In such a state as hath been described, every one shall reap the fruit of the seed he hath sown here; the fruit of his doings. To improve in virtue is to lay up treasures in heaven; or to lay a foundation for eternal happiness: and if the government of the moral world be moral, *i.e.* wise and good, this must be the rule; "that whatsoever a man soweth, that shall he also reap." All we have said of providence, of virtue, or of a future state, is concluded in the meaning of this comprehensive, emphatical doctrine of St. *Paul,* which it was proposed to illustrate: "Be not deceived, God is not mocked: for whatsoever a man soweth, that shall he also reap; for he that soweth to his flesh, shall of his flesh reap corruption; but he that soweth to the spirit, shall of the spirit reap life everlasting. Let us not therefore be weary in well-doing, for in due season we shall reap, if we faint not."[45] As certain as it is that the government of the world is under the direction of an infinitely wise and good God, so certain is it that

45. Gal. 6.7–9.

there is a future state succeeding to this life, in which virtue shall be fully rewarded; and that the serious study and practice of virtue here must finally terminate in perfect happiness, arising from perfect habits of virtue suitably placed, in order to have proper exercise, and high enjoyment by such exercise: for if there be a God, he must delight in virtue; and what he delights in, he will make happy: but improved virtue can only be made happy by being placed in circumstances for larger exercise of virtue, and higher advancements in it. If there be a God, and that there is all <464> nature cries aloud, his government must be equal, wise, and good, exceeding good; but if the government of moral beings be such, moral improvements and acquisitions will not be destroyed or annihilated by him; but virtue shall at last have the full effect and completion of its natural tendency, which is to make a society of the just perfectly happy. Virtue, or care to improve moral powers, is the delight of God, and it shall have success; it shall have its wishes and desires accomplished, which is to arrive at perfection and great felicity, in consequence of that perfection suitably situated or circumstantiated. Finally, if there be a God. He who soweth to the spirit, and not to the flesh; he who by patient and unwearied diligence in well-doing seeketh for glory, honour, and eternal happiness, shall obtain it, and not be disappointed: He shall reap the glorious fruits of his labours, the fruits of righteousness, joy, and peace; all the happy fruits which highly improved virtue is able to afford to the mind, if it be placed suitably to its merit and tendency. But if the natural harvest of moral improvements be happiness; if, by the constitution of things, virtue be the road to eternal happiness, what must the natural harvest, the natural effect, the ultimate result of sowing to the flesh and corruption, or of abused reason, impure affections, and a vitious life, be? All this is included in the apostle's account of the divine government, and of the final issue of things, after our state of probation, our seed-time is at an end. And all these important truths have been illustrated and confirmed in this discourse from various considerations. The following general corolaries do therefore manifestly result from what hath been proved to be the joint doctrine of reason and of revelation concerning God, providence, virtue, and a future state. <465>

Corolary I

That there is a God, and a future state, and that to grow and improve in virtue, is the duty of mankind, is a doctrine which reason clearly teaches: it is a doctrine deducible from the natural relations and connexions of things; it is therefore a doctrine which may be known to be true without revelation.

Corolary II

And by consequence it is a doctrine which divine revelation cannot contradict. There can be no doctrine in a divine revelation inconsistent with this immutable truth. Nay, revelation must place the whole of religion in living agreeably to this doctrine. It may add a particular kind of evidence to this truth, distinct from what it intrinsically carries with it, very proper to engage men to attend to its intrinsick evidence. But it cannot substitute any thing in the room of natural religion; for natural religion must remain the same, while the nature of things remains unchanged; while moral creatures are moral creatures; or a moral constitution is a moral constitution. The practice of virtue is therefore the whole of human duty, and the sure road to eternal happiness, whether there be any such thing as a divine revelation or not. And they are led into a fatal mistake by revelation; *i.e.* they sadly pervert divine revelation, who understand it as commuting the practice of virtue for any thing else; or as substituting any other thing in its room: for revelation cannot misrepresent the nature of things; it cannot contradict the very principles upon which its own evidence must depend. But it is plain from the nature of things, that there is a God, and that virtue alone is acceptable to him: <466> and this principle being removed, divine revelation is a term without any meaning.

Corolary III

If God hath at any time given to mankind a revelation of his will concerning their duty and interest; or if any being hath at any time by divine authority interposed to give mankind a call to the study of virtue, by giving them an account of God's government of rational beings, and the final issue of things with regard to mankind; such an event must be considered as making a part of the general scheme of God's just, righteous, and merciful government; and not as an accidental event, not originally comprehended in the design or plan of providence, but extraneous to it, and quite separate from it: as a part therefore of God's universal plan for promoting general good, by promoting moral perfection among his moral creatures. This plainly follows from what hath been said of God's government by general laws. But a revelation from God to take mens minds off from the study of virtue, to place their duty, to place religion and piety in any thing else is a downright contradiction: to suppose such a revelation coming from God, is to suppose God become an immoral agent, or a promoter of vice. This follows from the nature of virtue and the perfections of God; or from the very nature of moral powers, as hath been shewn.

COROLARY IV

It must therefore be a perversion or gross misunderstanding of revelation, to derive any hopes from it of eternal happiness without virtue; without true and sincere goodness of heart and mind. One must be an utter stranger to the course of nature or providence to object against revelation, because the pro-<467>motion of virtue and happiness among mankind is there ascribed to the instrumentality of Jesus Christ. But without entering into an enquiry which belongs not to our present design, we may most certainly conclude that it is mistaking revelation fundamentally, because it is destroying the very fundamentals of natural religion to hope for salvation, favour with God, and eternal felicity, without virtue. If there be no natural religion, there can be no such thing as revealed religion. But what is the very essence of natural religion? Is it not that the sincere study and practice of virtue is the sole way to the divine favour and approbation; and that as it is the only way, so it is a sure and certain way to it? In what indeed doth the belief of a God and a providence, of the reality of virtue and a future state ultimately ter-

minate, but in this momentous truth, "That according to the constitution and government of things it being morally good, virtue is the only
road to eternal happiness; nothing else can give a right to it; nothing else
can qualify for it." If this be not true, natural religion is a mere sound;
and consequently it is absurd to enquire about a divine revelation. But,
on the other hand, if it be true, we must carry that truth along with us
in our enquiries, as the test by which we are to try pretences to revelation,
and as the key for interpreting a divine revelation. And in reality it is
ignorance of natural religion, or losing sight of its very first principles,
which hath misled men, or suffered them to be misled into mistakes
about christianity, and given rise to interpretations of scripture, which
encourage vice, and subvert the very foundations of morality. For whatever may be thought obscure in it, this is its plain and uniform language,
"That without holiness no man can see the Lord." But the truth I chiefly
proposed by this discourse to establish, is, <468>

Corolary V

That whatever motive may induce one to treat christianity as an im-
posture, he who imagines that, christianity being removed, the obligations to the practice of virtue become less strict and rigid, is an utter
stranger to the extent of natural religion and moral obligations. It would
be a breach of that charity which christianity so strongly recommends,
to suppose that all who doubt of christianity are seduced into that scepticism by inclination to give themselves up to corrupt affections, without
fear of hereafter. But it is of great importance to us to fix this truth firmly
upon our minds, "That virtue, firm adherence to virtue, is a moral obligation arising necessarily from the nature of a moral creature; and that
every immoral indulgence is as repugnant to the law of nature as it is to
christianity." And it is to prove and enforce that important truth that I
have been comparing the doctrine of the christian revelation concerning
God, virtue, and a future state, with the doctrines of reason; with what
may be plainly deduced from the nature of things; or may be clearly
perceived to be true by all who will but give any attention to the frame
and constitution of the human mind, and the connexion of things about
us. It is not because it is a difficult, but because it is an important truth,

that I have insisted so long upon all the more considerable branches and consequences of it; and because as he who does not often meditate upon it, passes his life in a most irrational manner; so he who daily reflects upon it with due attention will thereby be daily excited to more and more diligence to improve in virtue, in purity of mind, in true goodness; and he will never want true joy; joy which nothing can take from him, and in comparison of which all other delights are mere vanity.—Joy which may be <469> justly called *joy in the Lord,* because it is joy arising from the belief of his moral rectitude and all-perfect administration; from the sense of his esteem, approbation and love, and from the assurance of eternal happiness in consequence of his good-will toward virtue, his love of it, and delight in it. "Having therefore this hope, let us act agreeably to it, and comfort ourselves with it: having this glorious hope, let us cleanse ourselves from all pollution of the flesh, and of the spirit, and perfect holiness in the filial fear of God, for as much as we know that our labour shall not be in vain in the Lord: for unto every one who by patient continuance in well-doing seeketh for glory, honour, and immortality, God will render glory, honour, peace, and eternal life, whether he be *Jew* or *Gentile;* for there is no respect of persons with God; but in every nation he that feareth him, and worketh righteousness, is accepted of him; and we know that under his infinitely wise and good government all things shall work together for the eternal good of them who love him, and loving him imitate his moral excellencies."[46] This is the doctrine of reason, and it is likewise confirmed to us by revelation, by an evidence of another kind.

I shall conclude by shewing what kind of evidence divine revelation gives to that important, joyful truth.

CONCLUSION

And here I shall endeavour to prove that the christian revelation gives a very proper, full, and truly philosophical evidence for the truth of that doctrine concerning God, providence, virtue, and a future state, we have

---

46. The quoted passage starts with a paraphrase of Rom. 2.7, 10, followed by Acts 10.35.

found to be the joint doctrine of reason and the christian revelation; and evidence, which however leaves full room and scope for all rational in-<470>quiries, or does not incroach upon the province of reason, which is to gather knowledge from nature by analogy, induction from experience, and the comparison of our ideas. Now in order to shew that the evidence with which the teaching of Christ and his apostles was accompanied, is a natural, proper, adequate and truly philosophical evidence of the truth of the christian doctrine concerning God, providence, virtue, and a future state, of the whole of the christian institution, we have only to consider how Christ and his apostles reasoned upon the subject; *i.e.* what evidence they profered and appealed to for the truth of their doctrine; and then to examine the nature of such reasoning, such evidence. In the first place, it is obvious from the history of Christ and his apostles, that they appealed to the miraculous works they did as proper proofs of the truth of their doctrines, and of their divine authority or mission to teach them: they appealed to the works they wrought, to the samples they gave of their power to foretell future events; their power to cure instantaneously all diseases of the body; their power to cure in the same extraordinary manner all diseases of the mind, or to convert bad into good dispositions; their power to bestow gifts and blessings of all sorts bodily and spiritual; and their power of raising the dead. I think all the works Christ and his apostles appealed to as proper proofs of their doctrines, and of their divine mission to teach them, are reducible into one or other of these abovementioned classes. 2. So that when Christ appealed to his works, to the works he did himself of these kinds just mentioned, and to the works of the same kinds he gave his apostles power to do, for the truth of his doctrine, his reasoning amounts briefly to this plain invincible argument, "The works I do, and enable others to do, shew such an extensive knowledge of nature, such an extensive knowledge of the government of the natural and moral world, and such a large command in nature, that you can <471> have no reason to doubt of my qualification to instruct or inform you concerning the government of the world; and you have no ground to doubt of my good will toward you, my benevolence, candor, and sincerity: you have therefore sufficient reason to give full credit to what I assure you to be fact or truth, with relation to the Governor of the world, and his government; with regard to your duty and interest in consequence of his character and government."

This is the plain meaning of what our Saviour asserted when he said, "The works that I do testify of me. Believe me for my work's sake." And this reasoning is, as was said in the beginning of this discourse,[a] truly satisfactory, truly philosophical. For it proceeds upon the following principles, none of which can be refused.

I. That one who hath a larger insight into or knowledge of nature and the connexions of things, *i.e.* of the government of the world, is qualified to instruct those who have not so large an insight into, or knowledge of the government of the world.

II. That samples of knowledge are proper proofs of knowledge, and samples of power are proper proofs of power; and consequently samples of large knowledge of nature, and of a large sphere of activity, or of extensive power and command in nature, are proper proofs of large knowledge of nature, and of a large extensive power and command in nature.

III. That there can be no reason to doubt the truth of the assertions of one concerning certain truths or facts with relation to the government of the world, who gives samples of very large and extensive knowledge of nature, and very large and extensive command in nature, if there be no contradiction or absurdity in such assertions; and if there be no reason <472> to doubt of the sincerity and integrity of the asserter or informer; but, on the contrary, all the reason that can be required to believe his honesty and candor.

If these propositions be true, the evidence which Christ gave for the truth of his doctrine concerning the Governor and government of the world, must be a full and proper evidence of its truth; or it must be said, either that he did not give sufficient samples of his benevolence to mankind, his regard to truth, honesty, and sincerity, which was never asserted, such an uninterrupted series of generosity, benevolence, and sincerity was his life: or that the many works he wrought of the kinds above

a. Sect. I.

mentioned, were not samples of a very large insight into, and power in nature; which will be to affirm that samples of power to see into men's minds, and foretell their future actions; power to change mens minds; power to deliver from evils of all sorts, corporeal and mental; power to confer gifts of all sorts, bodily and spiritual; power to raise the dead; power to transfer to others this same extensive power he himself was possessed of, did not shew a very large and extensive knowledge of nature, and power in nature. One or other of these two must be asserted, or the evidence Christ gave of the truth of his doctrine must be admitted to have been a proper and full evidence of its truth; for we have already shewn that there is no absurdity in his doctrine concerning God and the government of the world, virtue or human duty, and a future state. But the first never was and hardly will ever be asserted: and the other cannot be affirmed without denying that samples of power and knowledge are a proper evidence of power and knowledge; *i.e.* without absurdly demanding some other proof of power and knowledge besides samples or specimens of them. For what larger power or knowledge can we conceive, (creating power excepted) than universal knowledge of, and command over mens minds, and bodies, earth, sea, air, every element, <473> and even death itself, of which Christ's works were specimens, in the same sense that samples of skill among men to build, paint, cure diseases, move the passions, &c. are samples of skill to do these things? Surely it will not be said that specimens of knowledge are not specimens of knowledge: and as little can it be said that the works of Christ were not specimens of such a vast insight into, and command in nature, as shewed him to have a very comprehensive view of nature. But to say that having sufficient evidence of one's honesty, we may not trust his account of nature upon his giving us specimens of his large acquaintance with nature, is in fact to say that testimony is never to be depended upon or credited: it is to say, for instance, that those who are not able to cure their own diseases, or do not thoroughly understand the medicinal art, can never have good reason to trust to a physician, whatever evidences he may give of his skill: it is to say, one has or can have no reason to believe a mathematician, or natural philosopher, whatever evidences he may have given of his knowledge, when he asserts any truth, unless we are

able ourselves to investigate it, or at least to comprehend his demonstration of it: it is, in one word, to say that testimony, with whatever
circumstances of credibility it may be attended, ought never to create
trust. In fine, when instruction is offered to us in the government of the
world, our first business is to compare that instruction with what we
know of nature; and if it be agreeable to what we know, if there be no
absurdity in it, the reason to credit it must be in proportion to the assurance we have of our instructor's integrity and knowledge, our instructor's sincerity, and his capacity or qualification to instruct us. If therefore
the instructor gives sufficient samples of his sincerity, and sufficient samples of his knowledge, or his capacity to instruct us, we have sufficient
reason to credit him, or there can never be sufficient reason to credit
testi-<474>mony. But in order to see the full force of this argument, it
is not improper to put two cases.

I. First therefore, let us suppose instruction in the nature of God, in
human duty, and in a future state, of the kind that hath been delineated
in this discourse, to be offered to a people plunged in ignorance and
superstition, quite strangers to true natural religion; or, which is worse,
having very false and perverted notions of it: now if such instruction
were given to a people in this situation, attended with works of the kinds
abovemention'd, no doubt the works would, if any thing could, rouse
their attention.—What, therefore, would be the evidence to such a people of the truth of such instruction, previously to their being able by
reason to find out an intrinsick evidence in the doctrines thus taught
them, as truths or facts to which they ought to attend in the conduct of
their lives?—What would be the evidence in this case? would it not be
precisely this? "We have no reason to doubt of the good-will and sincerity of this instructor, and his works plainly shew his large acquaintance with the frame, constitution, and government of the world, natural and moral; we have therefore as good reason to trust his testimony,
as we can have to trust any testimony; but trust testimony we must in
innumerable cases: we have as good reason to trust this testimony, as we
have to trust testimony upon which we venture our greatest interests,
and therefore it would be highly unreasonable not to trust such testimony."

Now let us see how the evidence will stand, when any among such a people so instructed, being excited to exercise their reason, have compared the instruction so received with what they are able to learn from the language of nature, or the connexions of things: if they find that the further they carry on their enquiries into nature and the government of the world by reason, the clearer evidence they perceive by reason for the truth of their teacher's doctrines concerning <475> God, human duty, &c. what will, in that case, be the state of the evidence? will they not thus find a new evidence for the truth of their teacher's doctrines, which will confirm them in their reliance on his testimony? a new evidence, which, if it do not augment the former, at least leaves it as it was. For surely, one who had admitted the truth of a proposition in geometry, or of an experiment in natural philosophy, upon the testimony of one skill'd in these arts, in whom he had reason to confide, has no ground to doubt of such testimony, when having made further advances in geometry or experimental philosophy, he comes to see the truths he had formerly received upon testimony, as it were with his own eyes. And must not the same hold true with respect to moral truths?

II. Let us now put the case therefore, that the people, or at least many among them to whom such instructions as hath been described was offered, had by their acquaintance with nature, or by reasoning about morals, a very clear knowledge, and full conviction of the greater, the more essential part of such instruction (for the truths of natural religion, as hath been observed, must necessarily be the greater, the more essential, the fundamental part of a revelation) what will be the evidence for such instruction in that case? Will it follow that there is no reason to rely upon or trust to such testimony, because there is another evidence for the greater the more essential doctrines it asserts or teaches? Surely it cannot be said, that because one kind of evidence for a truth is good, that therefore another kind of evidence is not good. And therefore the evidence in such a case must stand thus. "Here there is a double evidence for certain truths; an evidence from the nature of things; an intrinsick evidence; and likewise an extrinsick evidence, or an evidence from testimony, upon which there is a sufficient reason to rely independently of all other considerations." If there are no other doctrines taught by such

<476> instruction, but doctrines which are capable of proof from the nature of things, the only fair conclusion is, that there is so much the better reason to believe such instruction, that there is nothing in it but what may be perceived by accurate enquirers into the nature of things to be true. For it cannot be said, that a testimony attended with evidences of credibility is not credible, because there is other evidence for the truth of the facts it asserts. One kind of evidence may be inferior to another kind of evidence, but every evidence is what it is in itself, independently of any other evidence. And to assert, that in such a case evidence by testimony is superfluous, and that therefore it is absurd to suppose any such evidence to be offered to us in a wise government, is certainly to take too much upon us to assert. Grant it to be superfluous evidence, and it will not follow from thence, that it is not good evidence: but to assert any instruction of the kind mention'd to be unworthy of good and wise administration, or to be instruction that can serve no useful purpose in the divine government, is to assume to ourselves a right of dictating to the Governor of the world: it is to claim such full knowledge of all that is necessary to the general good of moral beings, or fit for God to do in carrying on the great purposes of his government, as we certainly have no title to pretend to. If we should grant that thinking men have no occasion for such instruction, no occasion for such a call to virtue and piety,—will it follow from hence, that such a call to virtue, such instruction in the character of the Governor of the world, and in the final issue of things, is absolutely useless?—Are all men philosophers?— have all men sufficient capacity or leisure for accurate enquiries into nature?—are all thinking men sufficiently virtuous?—or if they are, and being wise and good, perfectly whole, they have no need of such instruction, such discipline, such a wholesome monitor and physician, does it follow that the igno-<477>rant, the blind, the unthinking have no need of such information, such admonishment? Supposing such instruction in the nature of God, human duty, and a future state, offer'd to the world in the manner mentioned; if any, thinking themselves wise and virtuous enough, should have said, "We know all this you pretend to teach us sufficiently; we knew it long ago, and have no need of your teaching," would it not have been a very proper answer, "Well, if you

are wise and righteous; if you know all these things, and knowing them walk answerably to such principles, you have indeed no need of me; I come not to you; the whole have not need of the physician; the righteous have no need of repentance; I come to the ignorant, to the sick, to sinners; and as the sick have need of the physician, so have sinners of repentance, and the ignorant of instruction."

Again, if together with the greater and more essential part of such instruction in religion (for the truths of natural religion, as it hath been often said, must be the greater, the essential part of revealed religion) some other doctrines are taught, how will the evidence for them stand? If they are contradictory to the other greater and more essential part, or to any principles of reason, then the testimony must be rejected, whatever evidences the teacher may give of his power and knowledge. But that not being the case, or when no doctrine taught by an instructor giving sufficient samples of his extensive knowledge of nature and command in nature, can be proved to be inconsistent with any principles of reason, then the more evidence is found by enquiring into the nature of things, of the truth of the principal or fundamental doctrines in such instruction, the more ground there is to rely on the testimony for the truth of all it asserts: because no doctrines contained in it being contrary to reason, there is either good reason to credit that testimony, or no testimony whatsoever can be sufficient to create trust; no samples of honesty are suf-<478>ficient evidences of honesty; no samples of insight into nature, and the government of the world, are samples of it; and no being, however superior to others in knowledge, is qualified by his superior knowledge to instruct those who have not so large a view of nature. In such a case the evidence must necessarily stand thus. There being no contradictory or absurd assertion in the doctrine of this teacher, the evidence for his testimony is in proportion to the samples he gives of his honesty, piety and virtue, his candor and good-will to mankind, and his regard to the supreme Being, and to the samples he gives of his comprehensive knowledge of nature and the government of the world. This we may lay down as a general theorem concerning instruction by a being of large and comprehensive knowledge. And therefore the evidence Christ gave of the truth of his testimony, there being no contradiction or absurdity in any of his doctrines, must be in proportion to the evidences he gave of his sincerity, piety and virtue, and to the evidences he gave of his comprehensive knowledge of nature, and extensive command in it. If the general truth concerning extraordinary instruction be true, the evidence Christ gave for the truth of his testimony cannot be invalidated but by shewing that there was no reason to trust his honesty; or, that the samples he gave of his knowledge and power, by the works of the kinds abovementioned, bear no proportion to the knowledge necessary to qualify him for instructing us in the truths he asserted; neither of which hath ever yet been attempted by any of the disputers against christianity.

It is ridiculous to say, in general, that facts and doctrines have no relation one to another; and, therefore, that no works of whatever kind can prove the truth of doctrines. For all true doctrines or assertions concerning the state and government of the world are facts: every assertion concerning the nature or connexion of things is an assertion of a fact; it is saying such or such a thing is fact. In one word, all truths <479> are facts; and all facts are truths. What is any mathematical proposition concerning a circle, for instance, but a proposition affirming, that if there be in nature a circle it must have such property, or such a property in fact belongs to it? What is any doctrine or proposition in natural philosophy, but an assertion of a certain fact; as for example, that the air is elastic? And what is any moral truth, doctrine, or proposition, but an assertion of a fact in the moral world; as for instance, that the law of habits works so and so in certain circumstances. All this is very obvious; and I only mention it in order to shew how unphilosophical that assertion is, which hath been so often repeated in disputing against christianity, and upon which so great stress seems to be laid by a late writer:[47] "That doctrines and works can have no relation, no connexion, and therefore the truth of doctrines can never be inferred from any works." For how absurd is this affirmation, when we consider that all doctrines

---

47. Benedictus de Spinoza (1632–77), *Tractatus theologico-politicus,* ch. 6. See his *Tractatus theologico-politicus* (Gebhardt edition, 1925), trans. Samuel Shirley (Leiden: Brill, 1989).

are facts: it is saying, that facts and works, *i.e.* facts and facts have no
relation, but are *disparata;* which, I think, none will assert in direct
terms. But the absurdity of a certain general, vague, but very dogmatical
way of throwing aside miracles, as things that can have no relation to
the truth of doctrines, which hath been very often repeated since *Spinoza*
first suggested it, as something so evident that it needs no proof; the
absurdity of a heterogeneousness between works and doctrines, which
is supposed by certain objectors against the evidence of christianity to
be manifest and quite indisputable, will appear, if we consider how we
reason in natural philosophy, or how we reason in the affairs of life. How
do we reason in natural philosophy? Does not the whole of that science
consist in inferring doctrines or facts from experiments, that is, from
works? How does the philosopher prove the air, for instance, to be elastic
and ponderous; or gravity to be an universal law of nature? Does he not
prove it to be so by induction from expe-<480>riments, from facts or
works which are samples of that property or law? And how do we reason
in life? How are we determined to act in cases of the greatest moment
and concern to us in matters of health, of property, in every affair; is it
not from samples, from experiments, from facts or works, that we draw
our conclusions? How, in fine, do we reason to prove the doctrine of the
divine existence, *i.e.* how do we reason to prove, that in fact there is a
God and a providence? Is it not from the facts in nature, which are samples of power, wisdom, and goodness, that we infer this truth? In all
these cases, therefore, doctrines are inferred from facts, *i.e.* facts are inferred from facts. Facts in all these cases are the medium of proof: they
make the premises from which the conclusion is inferred. And therefore
facts and doctrines are not heterogeneous: but facts and doctrines have
the nearest relation; the same relation that any medium of proof has to
the conclusion deduced from it.

Now to apply this to the present case. When instruction in the government of the world, or in certain facts relating to the Governor and
government of the world, and human duty and interest in consequence
of that government, is offered in the manner above-mentioned; doctrines are taught, but what are these doctrines? They are doctrines asserting certain facts. And what is the medium of proof offered? Certain

works. How then are these works a medium of proof for the truth of the doctrines they are wrought to confirm? They are evidences of their truth in the same way that experiments in natural philosophy, or in moral reasonings, are proofs of the conclusions or doctrines inferred from them. They are proofs of their truth, in the same manner that samples of knowledge or power are samples of knowledge and power. They have the same relation to the instruction they are brought to confirm, that other experiments, specimens, or samples have to the fact, the law, the property, or, in gene-<481>ral, the truth of which they are samples, specimens, or experiments. They are brought to prove a large and comprehensive knowledge of nature, and they are samples of it: they are brought to prove a large and extensive command in nature, and they are samples of it. They therefore make a proper proof of it, a truly philosophical evidence of it, because they make the same proof of it that experiments make of the conclusions deduced from them in natural philosophy. The only enquiry that remains with regard to such evidence, if there be no absurdity or inconsistency in the doctrines, is whether the samples given are analogous in kind, and bear a suitable proportion in quantity or moment to the knowledge or power claimed. And therefore the evidence Christ gave of his qualification to teach us was a proper, a full, a truly philosophical proof of his qualification to teach, as being a proper adequate proof of the power and knowledge he claimed; unless it can be shewn that the works he did were neither analogous in kind nor proportioned in moment or quantity to the power and knowledge he claimed. Because such signs of power and knowledge as are analogous and commensurate to a claim, are a proper proof of it: the only proof of it the nature of the thing admits; and to demand any other is an absurd demand. It is true, signs of power are only signs of power. But we have already observed, that signs of goodness are proper proofs of goodness. And with relation to Jesus Christ, the works he did to prove his knowledge and power were at the same time samples of his benevolence and goodness. For it is observable, that he delighted not in shewing his power to inflict miseries; he delighted not in cursing, but in blessing. It was not unnecessary to give some examples of his power to curse as well as bless; to inflict pains, as well as to deliver from evils and bestow benefits, because a few instances of power to hurt make a deeper impression on some minds than a thousand examples of communicating blessings. But he chose to shew his power to in-<482>flict pains and miseries, to curse, blast, or make miserable, but in a few instances; and those of such a kind as could do but little mischief, as in cursing the fig-tree, and sending the devils into the swine. All his other works were works of mercy and goodness. He went about continually doing good.

Thus, therefore, we see how, in general, works may prove doctrines, by proving the capacity or qualification of the teacher to instruct us in them. And with relation to Christ in particular, we see that his works were a full and proper evidence of the power and knowledge he claimed, a full and proper evidence of large and comprehensive knowledge and power, sufficient to qualify him for instructing us in the facts relating to the government of the world he asserted or taught. The works he did were not only proper to rouse and awaken a people plunged in superstition to attend to the great and important truths, of which they had lost, as it were, all sense and feeling; but they were sufficient to shew, that he was an instructor every way qualified to assure us of the reality of the important doctrines or facts he averred to be true.

But the propriety, the aptitude, the adequate fitness of the evidence Christ gave by his works of the truth of his doctrines, will appear yet in a stronger light if we compare his principal doctrines each of them singly with the works he did to prove their truth. They may be reduced to these few general heads, the doctrine of a future state of happiness to the virtuous, and misery to the wicked, and a resurrection from the dead, the doctrine of forgiveness of sins, or assurance that the sincere penitent who reforms and becomes virtuous shall find favour with God, and the doctrine of assistance to the sincere penitent in conquering his bad habits, and in making progress in holiness, especially in times of difficulty and trial. Now all his works were proper specimens or samples of each of these doctrines. He delivered the penitent from grievous evils; bestowed <483> great blessings upon them, external and internal; and he, in order to prove a future state, died and rose again from the dead, raised the dead; and gave power of raising the dead to his apostles, as well as of working other extraordinary works. While he was upon earth, he was continually giving instances of the most extensive knowledge and power in nature over every element, every disease, over body and mind, over death itself. And before he left earth, and ascended into heaven, he promised to send upon his apostles, who were to be employed in propagating his doctrines, the extraordinary gifts necessary to them for that effect, which accordingly he did; thus giving an indisputable proof of his power and good-will to fulfill all he had promised. So that of what yet remains to be accomplished by him we have just reason to say, "He who did the greater, can he not, will he not do the lesser?" But having fully consider'd the doctrines of Jesus Christ in this light, *i.e.* as exemplified by his works in my *philosophical enquiry concerning the connexion between the miracles and doctrines of Jesus Christ,* I shall not now insist farther upon it.

The truth of the history of Jesus Christ and his apostles stands upon an evidence which must be admitted while moral or historical evidence is admitted. And therefore the enemies of christianity in no age have ever attacked that evidence. But the truth of the history being yielded, the evidence of christianity must be indisputable, if samples of power or knowledge are proper evidences of power or knowledge; which, I think, cannot possibly be denied. For that general proposition being allowed, it cannot be said that the works of Christ were not analogous in kind to his general pretension to be a well qualified instructor; or, that they were not analogous in kind to each particular doctrine he taught. That hath never yet been asserted: nor hath it been said, or can it be said, that the samples he gave of various power in the natural and moral world were not <484> proportioned to the moment of his claim as a divine instructor. That is, no objection hath ever hitherto been made against christianity, which hath any tendency to invalidate it. For it is self-evident, that, admitting the truth of the history, there is no way of invalidating the claim of Christ to be a sufficiently qualified instructor in the doctrines he taught, but by shewing either that his works were not samples of his claim in kind, or not proportioned samples of it; there being no way of proving that a claim to knowledge or power is not sufficiently proved by samples, but by shewing that the samples are not analogous or not proportioned in moment to that claim: A general truth, so evident, that I should not have insisted so long upon it, had I not observed, that it is not attending to it that makes numbers swallow down, so readily, objections against christianity, which due attention to it would quickly shew to make nothing at all against christianity; or to have no force but what lies in sophistically misrepresenting the state of the question. Let me only add, 1. that there being intermixed with the history of our Saviour and his apostles, and their other writings, together with the doctrines taught by Christ, and an account of the miraculous works wrought by him, and by his apostles in consequence of power delegated to them by him, to qualify them for propagating his doctrine, certain prophecies of future events, the gradual fulfilment of these prophecies makes a growing evidence for the truth of the history and the doctrines of Christ. This is a consideration of great importance; for it shews that the christian doctrine is not left by its great teacher to depend merely upon an evidence of past facts; but is built upon an evidence to which gradual fulfilment of prophecies was gradually to give new force and strength. But this argument is so fully, so accurately handled in an excellent late treatise[a] upon the *connexion of natural and* <485> *revealed religion,* that it would be arrogance in me to attempt to add any thing to what is there said. 2. An instructor in the nature of God, and in several important facts relating to the government of the moral world, and to human duty in consequence of that government, who confirmed his instruction in the manner above-mentioned, might justly argue in this manner: My doctrine is so comfortable, so beneficial to mankind, and hath so direct a tendency to promote true piety and virtue, that nothing can be more unreasonable than to suppose, that I have an ill design, or am assisted in the works I do by any malicious spirit, endued with extraordinary knowledge and power. It is to suppose an evil spirit acting contrary to its natural disposition. It is to suppose a wicked being employing all its power and skill to promote virtue, piety, and goodness. And thus our Saviour reasoned in answer to those who said, he worked

a. By *A. A. Sykes,* D.D. [Arthur Ashley Sykes (1684?–1756), *The Principles and Connexion of Natural and Revealed Religion Distinctly Considered* (London, 1740), ch. 8.]

miracles by the assistance of the devil. "The pharisees said *in their hearts,*[a] this fellow doth not cast out devils but by Beelzebub the prince of the devils. And Jesus knew their thoughts, and said unto them, Every kingdom divided against itself is brought to desolation; and every city divided against itself shall not stand. And if Satan cast out Satan, he is divided against himself: how shall then his kingdom stand? And if I by Beelzebub cast out devils, by whom do your children pretend to cast them out?[b] Therefore they shall be your judges. But if I cast out devils by the spirit of God, then the kingdom of God is come unto you. Or else how can one enter into a strong man's house and spoil his goods, except he first bind the strong man, and then he will spoil his house."

3. But if it be said, the question is about Christ's pretension to a commission from God to instruct; to this the answer is obvious. For if one gives by his works <486> such sufficient samples of the power and knowledge he pretends to, that there is reason to trust to his instruction, independently of all consideration of his pretension to a divine commission to instruct; his pretension to such a commission cannot render his works insufficient evidences of his capacity to instruct. And therefore, such an instructor might reason with those to whom he offered instruction in this manner. I have given you sufficient evidence of my capacity to instruct you in certain truths, and of my integrity, you have therefore good reason to believe my word, and receive my instruction, tho' I had pretended to no divine commission, but to come to you of my self purely and solely out of my own good-will towards you. Since therefore I tell you, that I am commissioned by God to instruct you, and do not claim the honour to myself, but ascribe it to him who sent me, what reason have you not to believe me? Is my testimony less credible, or are the works I do less proper evidences of my qualification to instruct you, because I do not take the glory to myself, but give it wholly to him to whom truly it is due, even unto God, who sent me to instruct you, and gave me all the power in heaven and earth my works shew me to

---

a. *Matt.* xii. 24, *&c.* [Clarke, *Works,* 3:47–48; see also Clarke's comments in his Sermon 86, in *Works,* 1:539–40.]

b. See Dr. *Clarke*'s Paraphrase.

have for that effect; even to satisfy you that I am sent by him well qualified to instruct you in the doctrines I teach. And in this manner do we
find our Saviour actually reasoning: "My doctrine is not mine,[a] but his
that sent me. If any man will do his will, he shall know of the doctrine
whether it be of God, or whether I speak of my self. He that speaketh
of himself seeketh his own glory; but he that seeketh his glory that sent
him, the same is true, and no unrighteousness is in him." "Jesus answered,[b] I have not a devil, but I honour my Father, and ye dishonour
me. And I seek not mine own glory: there is one that seeketh and judgeth.
If I honour myself, <487> my honour is nothing: it is my Father that
honoureth me, of whom you say, that he is your God." Christ pretended
to a divine commission; and 'tis evident, that if his qualification to instruct, and the particular doctrines he taught, were sufficiently justified
and proved by proper samples, the truth of the divine commission to
which he pretended must necessarily be admitted. For what reason can
there possibly be to doubt of the mission, when the particular knowledge
or power the missionary claims as missionary, is sufficiently ascertained
by proper samples? But besides, the whole series of the miracles of Jesus
Christ were appealed to by him as one continued proof of his pretension
to a divine mission: as one continued proof that he was qualified by God
to be our instructor; and that his power was given to him for that end.
His works were therefore at the same time proper samples of his divine
mission, and of his capacity to instruct. What indeed can a divine mission mean, but a certain sphere of knowledge and power bestowed by
God, and employed by his authority, to instruct in certain truths? But
this being the meaning of a divine mission, samples or experiments of
power and knowledge, analogous and proportional to the power and
knowledge claimed, and analogous to the particular doctrines taught,
are a proper proof of a divine mission: the only proof that can be demanded or imagined, if samples or experiments of knowledge and
power be proper evidences of knowledge and power. And sure there can

a. *John* vii. 16, *&c.*
b. *John* viii. 48, *&c.*

be no other way of shewing knowledge and power, but by giving certain specimens of it. But this argument is fully illustrated in my *enquiry into the connexion between the miracles and doctrines of Jesus Christ*. I shall therefore only add, in the last place, that as the evidence Christ gave of the truth of his doctrines, and his divine mission to teach them, is a proper, full, and truly philosophical evidence of his pretensions; so christianity leaves full room for all rational enquiries into < 488 > the government of the world, and does not in the least encroach upon the province of reason. The christian doctrine is an account of certain important facts relating to the government of the world, virtue, piety, and a future state, confirmed by testimony attended, as we have seen, with all the proper, all necessary tokens or signs of credibility: but such an account is not intended to hinder, prevent, or cut off our enquiries into the natures and connexions of things. It discovers to us several truths, to the knowledge of which we cannot attain by our enquiries into nature, or by reasoning from any truths so discovered. It also discovers to us several truths, which may be known to be true, by attending to the nature and connexions of things, or by reasoning from truths so discovered. But it leaves room for us to search as deeply as we can into the government of the world, in order to have intrinsick evidence for those truths, distinct from that extrinsick evidence which it gives for their truth, by well qualified testimony. It is therefore absurd to say that it is not consistent with divine wisdom to give us any instruction in truths discoverable by reason, besides what we may have from reason, to which kind of instruction none can be superior. For supposing, which is not the case, that there were no truths in the christian revelation, but such as are discoverable by reason, or capable of scientific proof, it would not follow that it would be inconsistent with wisdom and goodness to give us a testimony concerning their truth, upon which we might depend; since such testimony might be of use to such as are not capable, or have not time to make rational enquiries into nature, and thus to get scientific conviction of their truth; of great use to comfort and direct such in the practice of virtue: and since as it leaves rational enquiries upon the same footing as if there were no such instruction by testimony, so it may be, it cannot but be of great use to rouze men, capable of being rouzed, to due diligence in carrying on rational <489> enquiries, in proportion as they have time and opportunity for such useful and laudable employment.

Surely none who is acquainted with the history of the world at the time when Christ appeared, will say, that instruction in true religion was not very seasonable at that time: and how it can be proved to be inconsistent with divine wisdom to give men calls to virtue and instructions in important truths, relative to virtue and piety, when they are sadly corrupt and ignorant, by a teacher duly qualified to gain attention and give satisfaction by proper samples of power and knowledge, I am at a loss to imagine: and yet the greater part of the arguments against revelation seem to turn upon a supposition that such calls to virtue are evidently repugnant to divine administration. To say there never was or could be any such call, any such instruction, because it does not happen every where, in every age, or very often, and very universally, is a way of reasoning, which, if adhered to, would lead into numberless absurdities too evident to be mentioned. And to say it is not worth while to examine a pretension to divine authority to instruct in certain doctrines, because God cannot, consistently with his wisdom, at any period of time, give a people any instruction by the testimony of an extraordinary teacher, is certainly to take upon us to dictate to the Governor of the world. Sure I may say, that before one is thus hindered from examining a pretended revelation, he ought to have very clear evidence for the inconsistency with divine wisdom, by which he justifies his neglect or contempt of the pretension. It is manifestly unjustifiable, unless that inconsistency be proved: and when was it proved, or who ever yet attempted to prove it? To prove such an inconsistency, one must indeed first know all that is proper or requisite to promote the general good of moral beings, God's end of creation and government, which none certainly will, in direct terms at least, pretend to. Finally, to ask why, if christianity be a di-<490>vine revelation, it is not more universal, is to ask why the Governor of the world gave it to mankind in such a manner as to leave the propagation of it to be carried on by the instrumentality of christian believers, according to the common course of human affairs, *i.e.* it is to ask why God so orders the world, as to give christians an excellent opportunity of exercising their benevolence towards the rest of mankind, involved in ignorance and superstition, by taking proper methods to bring them to the knowledge of the most salutary and comfortable truths.

Christianity is therefore a most excellent doctrine, and is attended with sufficient evidence of its truth.

Finis.

BIBLIOGRAPHY OF WORKS CITED

Bacon, Francis. *The Advancement of Learning.* Edited by Michael Kiernan. Oxford: Clarendon Press, 2000.

———. *The Essayes or Counsels, Civill and Morall.* Edited by Michael Kiernan. Oxford: Clarendon Press, 1985.

———. *The New Organum.* Edited by Lisa Jardine and Michael Silverthorne. Cambridge: Cambridge University Press, 2000.

Berkeley, George. *An Essay Towards a New Theory of Vision.* London, 1709.

———. *A Treatise Concerning the Principles of Human Knowledge.* London, 1710.

Bond, Donald F., ed. *The Spectator.* 5 vols. Oxford: Clarendon Press, 1965.

Broadie, Alexander. *The Scottish Enlightenment: The Historical Age of the Historical Nation.* Edinburgh: Birlinn, 2001.

Broadie, Alexander, ed. *The Cambridge Companion to the Scottish Enlightenment.* Cambridge: Cambridge University Press, 2003.

Broughton, Thomas. *The Mottoes of the Spectators, Tatlers and Guardians, translated into English.* London, 1735.

Butler, Joseph. *The Works of Joseph Butler.* Edited by W. E. Gladstone. 2 vols. Oxford: Clarendon Press, 1897.

Cicero. *Opera omnia.* Edited by Cornelis Schrevel. 4 vols. Amsterdam, 1661.

Clarke, John. *An Enquiry into the Cause and Origin of Evil.* London, 1720.

———. *An Enquiry into the Cause and Origin of Moral Evil.* London, 1721.

Clarke, Samuel. *The Works of Samuel Clarke, D.D.* 4 vols. London, 1738.

Cooper, Anthony Ashley, third earl of Shaftesbury. *Characteristicks of Men, Manners, Opinions, Times.* Edited by Philip Ayres. 2 vols. Oxford: Clarendon Press, 1999.

———. *Characteristicks of Men, Manners, Opinions, Times.* 1732. Edited and with a foreword by Douglas Den Uyl. Indianapolis: Liberty Fund, 2001.

———. *Characteristics of Men, Manners, Opinions, Times.* Edited by Lawrence E. Klein. Cambridge: Cambridge University Press, 1999.

Fénelon, François de Salignac de la Mothe. *Dialogues sur l'éloquence en général, et sur la chaire en particulier.* Amsterdam, 1718.

Foster, James. *Sermons.* Vol. 1. 4th ed. London, 1745.

Gale, Thomas, ed. *Opuscula mythologica, physica et ethica. Graece et Latine* . . . . Amsterdam, 1688.

Harrington, James. *The Political Works of James Harrington.* Edited and with an introduction by J. G. A. Pocock. Cambridge: Cambridge University Press, 1977.

Hobbes, Thomas. *Leviathan.* Edited by Richard Tuck. Cambridge: Cambridge University Press, 1991.

Homer. *The Odyssey of Homer.* Translated from the Greek by Alexander Pope. London: Richards, 1903.

Hutcheson, Francis. *An Essay on the Nature and Conduct of the Passions and Affections, with Illustrations on the Moral Sense.* 1728. Edited and with an introduction by Aaron Garrett. Indianapolis: Liberty Fund, 2002.

———. *An Inquiry into the Original of Our Ideas of Beauty and Virtue.* 4th ed. London, 1738.

———. *An Inquiry into the Original of Our Ideas of Beauty and Virtue.* 1726. Edited and with an introduction by Wolfgang Leidhold. Indianapolis: Liberty Fund, 2004.

Lactantius. *Opera quae extant.* Edited by Thomas Spark. Oxford, 1684.

Leibniz, Gottfried Wilhelm. *The Monadology and Other Philosophical Writings.* Translated by Robert Latta. Oxford: Clarendon Press, 1898.

Locke, John. *An Essay Concerning Human Understanding.* Edited by Peter H. Nidditch. Oxford: Oxford University Press, 1975.

———. *Some Thoughts Concerning Education; and, Of the Conduct of the Understanding.* Edited and with an introduction by Ruth W. Grant and Nathan Tarcov. Indianapolis and Cambridge: Hackett, 1996.

Mandeville, Bernard. *The Fable of the Bees.* 4th ed. London, 1725.

———. *The Fable of the Bees.* Edited by F. B. Kaye. Indianapolis: Liberty Fund, 1988.

More, Henry. *Divine Dialogues.* Glasgow: Foulis Press, 1743.

Newton, Isaac. *Isaac Newton's Philosophiae naturalis principia mathematica: The Third Edition (1726) with Variant Readings.* Edited by Alexandre Koyré and I. Bernard Cohen. 2 vols. Cambridge: Cambridge University Press, 1972.

———. *Opticks: Or, a Treatise on the Reflections, Inflections and Colours of*

Light. 4th ed., 1730. Reprint, with a preface by I. Bernard Cohen, New York: Dover Publications, 1952.

———. *The Principia: Mathematical Principles of Natural Philosophy: A New Translation.* Edited by I. Bernard Cohen and Anne Whitman. Berkeley and London: University of California Press, 1999.

Plutarch. *Omnia quae extant opera.* 2 vols. Paris, 1624.

Pope, Alexander. *Pope: Poetical Works.* Edited by Herbert Davis. London: Oxford University Press, 1966.

Sallust. *Sallvstii philosophi de diis et mundo.* Edited by Gabriel Naudaeus. Rome, 1638.

Stephens, John Calhoun, ed. *The Guardian.* Lexington: University Press of Kentucky, 1982.

Stewart, M. A. "George Turnbull and Educational Reform." In *Aberdeen and the Enlightenment,* edited by J. J. Carter and Joan M. Pittock. Aberdeen: Aberdeen University Press, 1987.

Sykes, Arthur Ashley. *The Principles and Connexion of Natural and Revealed Religion Distinctly Considered.* London, 1740.

Thomson, James. *Liberty, the Castle of Indolence, and Other Poems.* Edited by James Sambrook. Oxford: Clarendon Press, 1986.

Turnbull, George. *Observations upon Liberal Education, In All Its Branches.* 1742. Edited and with an introduction by Terrence O. Moore. Indianapolis: Liberty Fund, 2003.

———. *A Philosophical Enquiry Concerning the Connexion Betwixt the Doctrines and Miracles of Jesus Christ.* London, 1731.

———. *Theses academicae de pulcherrima mundi cum materialis tum rationalis constitutione.* Aberdeen, 1726.

———. *Theses philosophicae de scientiae naturalis cum philosophia morali conjunctione.* Aberdeen, 1723.

———. *A Treatise on Ancient Painting.* London, 1740.

Wollaston, William. *The Religion of Nature Delineated.* London, 1724.

Wood, Paul. "George Turnbull." In *Oxford Dictionary of National Biography.* Oxford: Oxford: University Press, 2004.

Loeb Classical Library Texts

Augustine. *The City of God Against the Pagans.* Vol. 1. Translated by George E. McCracken. London: Heinemann; Cambridge: Harvard University Press, 1957.

Cicero. *Brutus.* Translated by G. L. Hendrickson; *Orator.* Translated by
     H. M. Hubbell. London: Heinemann; Cambridge: Harvard University
     Press, 1939.

—————. *De finibus bonorum et malorum.* Translated by H. Rackham. Lon-
     don: Heinemann; New York: Putnam, 1931.

—————. *De inventione, De optima genere oratorum, Topica.* Translated by
     H. M. Hubbell. London: Heinemann; Cambridge: Harvard University
     Press, 1949.

—————. *De natura Deorum, Academia.* Translated by H. Rackham. London:
     Heinemann; New York: Putnam, 1933.

—————. *De officiis.* Translated by Walter Miller. London: Heinemann; Cam-
     bridge: Harvard University Press, 1938.

—————. *De oratore, Books I and II.* Translated by E. W. Sutton. Completed,
     with an introduction by H. Rackham. Cambridge: Harvard University
     Press; London: Heinemann, 1942.

—————. *De oratore, Book III, De fato, Paradoxa Stoicorum, De partitione or-
     atoria.* Translated by H. Rackham. London: Heinemann; Cambridge:
     Harvard University Press, 1942.

—————. *De re publica, De legibus.* Translated by Clinton Walker Keyes. Lon-
     don: Heinemann; New York: Putnam, 1928.

—————. *De senectute, De amicitia, De divinatione.* Translated by William
     Armstead Falconer. Cambridge: Harvard University Press; London:
     Heinemann, 1923.

—————. *Letters to Atticus.* Translated by E. O. Winstedt. 3 vols. London:
     Heinemann; New York: Macmillan, 1912–18.

—————. *Letters to Friends.* Edited and translated by D. R. Shackleton Bailey.
     3 vols. Cambridge and London: Harvard University Press, 2001.

—————. *The Speeches: Pro Archia poeta,* . . . Translated by N. H. Watts. Lon-
     don: Heinemann; New York: Putnam, 1923.

—————. *The Speeches: Pro publio Quinctio,* . . . *De lege agraria I, II, III.* Trans-
     lated by John Henry Freese. London: Heinemann; New York: Putnam,
     1930.

—————. *Tusculan Disputations.* Translated by J. E. King. London: Heine-
     mann; New York: Putnam, 1927.

Columella. *On Agriculture.* X–XII: *On Trees.* Edited and translated by E. S.
     Forster and Edward H. Heffner. Cambridge and London: Harvard Uni-
     versity Press, 1968.

Horace. *Odes and Epodes.* Translated by C. E. Bennett. Cambridge and London: Harvard University Press, 1968.

———. *Satires, Epistles and Ars poetica.* Translated by H. Rushton Fairclough. Cambridge: Harvard University Press; London: Heinemann, 1929.

Juvenal. *Juvenal and Persius.* Translated by G. G. Ramsay. Rev. ed. London: Heinemann; Cambridge: Harvard University Press, 1940.

Lucretius. *De rerum natura.* Translated by W. H. D. Rouse. Revised by Martin Ferguson Smith. Cambridge: Harvard University Press; London: Heinemann, 1975.

Nepos. *Cornelius Nepos.* Translated by John C. Rolfe. Cambridge: Harvard University Press; London: Heinemann, 1984.

Plutarch. *Plutarch's Lives.* Edited and translated by Bernadotte Perrin. London: Heinemann; New York: Putnam, 1914–26.

Quintilian. *The Orator's Education. Books I–III.* Edited and translated by Donald A. Russell. Cambridge and London: Harvard University Press, 2001.

Seneca the Elder. *Declamations.* 2 vols. Translated by M. Winterbottom. Cambridge: Harvard University Press; London: Heinemann, 1974.

Seneca the Younger. *Ad Lucilium epistulae morales.* Vol. 1. Translated by Richard Gummere. Cambridge: Harvard University Press; London: Heinemann, 1917.

———. *Moral Essays.* Vol. 1. Translated by John W. Basore. London: Heinemann; New York: Putnam, 1928.

Tacitus. *The Histories.* 2 vols. Translated by Clifford M. Moore. London: Heinemann; New York: Putnam, 1925.

This book is set in Adobe Garamond, a modern adaptation by Robert Slimbach of the typeface originally cut around 1540 by the French typographer and printer Claude Garamond. The Garamond face, with its small lowercase height and restrained contrast between thick and thin strokes, is a classic "old-style" face and has long been one of the most influential and widely used typefaces.

Printed on paper that is acid-free and meets the requirements of the American National Standard for Permanence of Paper for Printed Library Materials, z39.48-1992 ∞

Book design by Louise OFarrell
Gainesville, Florida
Typography by Apex Publishing, LLC
Madison, Wisconsin
Printed and bound by Edwards Brothers, Inc.
Ann Arbor, Michigan